The
Pennant Races of 1916

Best Wishes to everyone
at St. Benedict's.

John Zumi   Paul Z

The Major League Pennant Races of 1916

"The Most Maddening Baseball Melee in History"

PAUL G. ZINN *and*
JOHN G. ZINN

McFarland & Company, Inc., Publishers
Jefferson, North Carolina, and London

John G. Zinn is also the author of
*The Mutinous Regiment: The Thirty-Third
New Jersey in the Civil War* (McFarland, 2005)

LIBRARY OF CONGRESS CATALOGUING-IN-PUBLICATION DATA

Zinn, Paul G.
The major league pennant races of 1916 : the most maddening
baseball melee in history / Paul G. Zinn and John G. Zinn.
p.   cm.
Includes bibliographical references and index.

ISBN 978-0-7864-3630-9

softcover : 50# alkaline paper ∞

1. Baseball — History — 20th century.   2. Major League
Baseball (Organization) — History — 20th century.
I. Zinn, John G., 1946–   II. Title.
GV863.A1Z56   2009
796.357'640973 — dc22   2008053465

British Library cataloguing data are available

©2009 Paul G. Zinn and John G. Zinn. All rights reserved

*No part of this book may be reproduced or transmitted in any form
or by any means, electronic or mechanical, including photocopying
or recording, or by any information storage and retrieval system,
without permission in writing from the publisher.*

On the cover: Hy Myers, Wilbert Robinson and the team mascot of the 1916
Brooklyn Robins (George Grantham Bain Collection, Library of Congress)

Manufactured in the United States of America

*McFarland & Company, Inc., Publishers
Box 611, Jefferson, North Carolina 28640
www.mcfarlandpub.com*

To

Elizabeth Lutz Zinn (1892–1983) and John G. Zinn (1892–1955)

Ann Winder Zinn (1916–1995) and Henry G. Zinn (1914–2002)

Sarah Kaufman and Carol Zinn

and
in memory of

Edith J. Ewing
1955–2008

1916

"The most hectic pennant chase in years is still in it [*sic*] infancy, as far as a logical or probable winner is concerned."

— Detroit *News*, August 6

"The greatest race the American League has known."

— George Robbins, *The Sporting News*, September 7

"The most frenzied six months in the history of the national sport."

— Lester Rice, Brooklyn *Citizen*, September 11

"The most maddening baseball melee in history."

— Nick Flatley, Boston *Herald*, September 14

"The players acted as if the future of the universe were at stake."

— New York *Times,* September 29

"The apoplexy-breeding National League Pennant Race."

— New York *Times*, October 1

"All the way it has been a bitter battle for all concerned. At times it was possible for a team to climb from sixth place to first within the short space of ten days or less. Always there has not been one challenger but several right on the heels of the leader. Every slip has been costly and much has depended on almost every ball pitched for the loss of one game sometimes has meant a drop of two or three places in the standings."

— I.E. Sanborn, Chicago *Daily Tribune*, October 2

"The nerve shattering strife for the baseball supremacy of the National League continued unabated."

— Jim Nasium, Philadelphia *Inquirer*, October 3

Table of Contents

Preface and Acknowledgments

In many ways this book began about 50 years ago with another book about baseball. When I was growing up in Wayne, New Jersey, in the 1950s, I had two passions — baseball and books. As my interest in baseball grew, I tried to read every book I could find about the sport. One in particular, John Carmichael's *My Greatest Day in Baseball,* stood out. Written well before Lawrence Ritter's classic, *The Glory of Their Times,* Carmichael's book is comprised of brief accounts of the memorable moments of legendary players. Although not the in-depth interviews that Ritter compiled, Carmichael had the advantage of being able to include the stories of such baseball immortals as Ty Cobb, Connie Mack and Three Finger Brown. These stories, particularly accounts of the famous 1908 Giants-Cubs Merkle replay game, gave a young boy an appreciation of baseball in the Deadball Era.

Over the past half-century, that appreciation has never lessened. Therefore, after finishing my first book, *The Mutinous Regiment* (McFarland, 2005), a Civil War history, my attention naturally turned to the Deadball Era. As was fairly typical in the 1950s, I adopted as my own my parents' favorite team, the Brooklyn Dodgers (regrettably, I never made it to Ebbets Field). So it was only logical that the initial search for a Deadball Era topic focused on the Dodgers. In looking through the 1901–1919 period, it was somewhat surprising to find that in the National League there were only two close pennant races — the almost mythical 1908 season and the far less well-known 1916 season. The competitiveness of that pennant race and the Dodgers' prominent role led to this book.

Any such book, of course, is a work of history, and history is always best told through the accounts of eyewitnesses, especially those written close to the event and unimproved by the passage of time. Unlike Civil War soldiers, Deadball Era ballplayers left behind little or nothing in the way of personal correspondence and journals. Accounts like those compiled by Carmichael and Ritter provide some personal testimony, but have the disadvantage of looking backward, in some cases more than 50 years. There are, however, multiple surviving eyewitness accounts of every 1916 game in the newspapers of the day. Looking backward from a world of radio and television, not to mention the Internet, it's difficult to appreciate the role newspapers played at the time and the number available to the baseball fan of the day. Today newspapers serve an audience, most of whom have probably already seen or listened to the game. In 1916, newspaper accounts were the primary source of information for fans since only a small percentage had actually seen the game. The breadth of coverage is illustrated by the number of papers covering baseball in each city. For example, four Brooklyn newspapers covered the Dodgers, Philadelphia had at least five papers covering the two local teams, while New York City had close to twenty covering three teams.

As I began looking at Dodger game accounts in the Brooklyn *Daily Eagle*, I quickly realized the overwhelming amount of information would make it impossible for one person to cover both leagues adequately. I then invited my son, Paul, to join me on the project by taking on the American League. Paul's background as a Bates College English major and a sportswriter for three different newspapers made this a natural fit. His residence is in the Boston area, which gave him easier access to information on the Red Sox. We quickly agreed to focus on the seven contending teams (four in the National League and three in the American League), picking a primary local newspaper for each team. We then read and researched the story of each contending team's 154 games. In addition, we read an account of each game from a local newspaper covering the opposition. Finally, we identified key games and obtained as many newspaper accounts for those contests as possible. In some cases, such as the crucial Phillies-Dodgers series during the last weekend of the season, this meant finding and reading more than 20 accounts of the same events. The multiple stories provided detailed information on the crucial days of the pennant race in addition to fascinating insights, such as the atmosphere in the rival clubhouses between games of the Phillies-Dodgers September 30 doubleheader. Among the outstanding writers whose accounts we came to rely on were Tom Rice of the Brooklyn *Daily Eagle*, Jim Nasium of the Philadelphia *Inquirer*, and Nick Flately of the Boston *Herald*, as well as that of Tim Murnane of the Boston *Daily Globe*, E.A. Batchelor of the Detroit *Free Press* and I.E. Sanborn of the Chicago *Daily Tribune*. The game accounts were supplemented by columns, including those of legendary writers like Damon Runyan, Grantland Rice, Sid Mercer and Sam Crane. Appendix B provides background information on many of the writers.

Our goal then is to tell the story of the 1916 baseball season. Most histories of individual seasons seem to take one of three approaches. One is to argue the season in question was the greatest or most exciting season in baseball history; at least two books have made this claim for the 1908 season. The stories of other seasons have been told in support of the idea that a certain team is the greatest of all-time — the 1927 Yankees being an example. Finally, other books take in-depth looks at seasons that saw a major change in the game, social or otherwise, such as Jackie Robinson's first season.

In this book we take a different approach. The 1916 season was simply baseball at its best. In the American League, Detroit, Boston and Chicago waged a season-long struggle; the race was so competitive that six of the eight teams spent time in first place. The National League season had an eastern flavor, featuring Brooklyn, Philadelphia and Boston fighting for the flag with some periodic interventions by the New York Giants. There was also no shortage of record-setting performances, especially some pitching marks that will never be threatened under today's philosophy of pitching. The season was bracketed by controversy; its opening marked the largest financial sale of a player in the history of the game, and its ending was marred by an event that threatened the game's integrity. Harder to quantify, but no less important, is the never-say-die approach that permeated 1916 teams, teams that continued to play hard no matter how many times they were counted out, in some cases even after their own pennant hopes died.

One example of how these elements come together helps set the stage. Seven times in 1916 pitchers took the mound attempting to start and win both ends of a doubleheader. Four of them were successful, a major league record that belongs in the will-never-be-threatened category. Five of these efforts took place in the National League, in September, illustrating both the closeness of the race and the fighting spirit of the teams and players in question. But even this wasn't without controversy, as in at least one case the manager (John McGraw) was accused of doing so to help the opposing Brooklyn Dodgers.

Our thesis is based upon what we found in our sources, and we had a great deal of help in finding them. The literally hundreds of pages of newspaper articles from more than 40 newspapers that we photocopied, read and analyzed came from a number of libraries. The list includes the New York Public Library, the Boston Public Library, the Cincinnati Public Library, the Arlington Public Library and the Cambridge Public Library. Thanks to those institutions and their staffs for their assistance and the ability to spend countless hours at microfilm readers. Inter-library loans made it easier to access material without significant travel; in that regard we wish to thank the Bloomfield College Library, the Verona Public Library and the Montclair Public Library. We made multiple trips to the A. Bartlett Giamatti Research Center at the National Baseball Hall of Fame in Cooperstown, New York. Special thanks to Freddy Berowski and the many research staff members who assisted us on those visits. We also want to voice a special word of thanks to the

Alexander Library at my alma mater, Rutgers University. Within its microfilm collections, the Alexander Library has full runs of at least six major daily newspapers from the Deadball Era. The convenient and easy access to this material was a major help in getting this project started while providing ample content to move ahead.

Although much of the work on this book was two people interacting with ninety-plus-year-old newspaper accounts, no book is written without help from other individuals. Members of the Deadball Era Committee of the Society for American Baseball Research responded to questions with helpful suggestions and advice. Bill Burgess' work on compiling biographical information on sportswriters (www.baseballfever.com) was also extremely helpful. Special thanks also to Mark Fimoff, who as this book moved into late innings helped us find some important photos of ballparks in Brooklyn, Detroit and Chicago.

As with any book about baseball, numbers and statistics are an integral part of the story. When writing about the Deadball Era, this has its own challenges. Some statistics were determined differently, while many that are common today weren't even kept in 1916. The criteria for deciding the winning pitcher is an excellent example of the former, as official scorers were given significant latitude in determining who they thought most deserved the win. On the other hand, records of RBIs were not kept during that time. The statistics in this book come from three different sources, all of which are documented either here or in the footnotes. One important source was Retrosheet (www.retrosheet.org), which proved especially useful for year-end records and historical data. The work of Dave Smith and his many associates made our work easier and is gratefully acknowledged.

The other two sources are the contemporary newspaper articles and the authors' compilation of data from those articles. This includes almost all in-season pitching and hitting records. It's important for the reader to understand these numbers may not match-up exactly with year-end data taken from Retrosheet and other sources. They are not intended to be the definitive final word, providing instead an indication of how players were performing at certain points during the season.

Family and friends were also very supportive of our efforts. We thank Janet Rassweiler for her ongoing support and friendship, but especially for a conversation that helped refocus our efforts and start us on the road to our thesis (she is in no way responsible for that thesis). Always supportive in many different ways, especially with badly needed humor (and unfortunately sometimes just bad humor), was my 5:30 A.M. running group, including Vince Dahmen, Margo DiStefano, James J. McDonald and Mark Zablow. What could have been innumerable bad days began better because of their good spirits. Finally, there are the numerous friends and acquaintances who showed ongoing support simply by asking, "How's the book coming?" Among them is a large contingent of Bates College alumni too numerous to name, although they know who they are.

In thanking family, we look at both the past and present. From the first perspective, this book is dedicated to Ann and Hank Zinn (my parents and Paul's grandparents) and Elizabeth and John Zinn (my grandparents and Paul's great-grandparents) because of their love of baseball, which they passed on to us. It's especially serendipitous to note that Ann Zinn was born on April 11, 1916, literally the eve of Opening Day. Paul, at this point, represents the fourth generation of Zinns who claim baseball as their favorite sport. The Zinns have lived in New Jersey since roughly 1850, and with this book complete, a future research project is to look for evidence of a family connection to baseball back into the nineteenth century. In the present generation, we want to thank our "professional" baseball fan cousins, Peggy and Paul Shubnell, for reading an early outline of this book, their hospitality on baseball trips to Michigan and Florida, and for introducing us to the concept of the baseball marathon. Thanks also to Paul's in-laws, Judy R. Kaufman and Steve J. Kaufman, for their ongoing interest in this project. As this book was being finalized, my long time and close friend Edie Ewing died after a 14-year struggle with metastic breast cancer. Although not a baseball fan, Edie was very supportive of all my endeavors including this one. I miss her greatly and always will.

We have intentionally reserved our final thanks for Sarah Kaufman and Carol Zinn, as we are indeed fortunate to be their husbands. They have supported this project in so many different ways, including trips to research libraries, accepting piles of files throughout our respective homes and tolerating our vacant looks when our minds were on a baseball season some 90 years in the past. The Boston Red Sox had not won a World Series since 1918 when Sarah and Paul moved to Boston in 2002, and Sarah became a Red Sox fan. Since then, they have won two, and since baseball fans are nothing if not superstitious, we can't believe this is a coincidence.

We also want to be clear that the content of this book is our sole responsibility. We hope all who read it enjoy the story of this long-ago baseball season. Nineteen-sixteen may not have been the greatest season, featured the greatest teams or marked a transition between eras, but in our view, it was baseball at its best. As such, it is a story that we believe is both worth telling and worth reading.

— John G. Zinn

CHAPTER I

"Carrigan's news was unbelievable, but it was true."

As an unusually warm October afternoon moved toward sunset, the Boston Red Sox faced the extremely unappealing prospect of a second consecutive overnight train ride. Hours earlier, the Red Sox and the National League champion Philadelphia Phillies had completed a 15-hour trip on the "rattlers" from Massachusetts. That trip began soon after Boston had taken a seemingly insurmountable three games to one lead in the 1915 World Series. Clearly the Red Sox players wanted to end the Series by winning this game at Philadelphia's Baker Bowl. But after seven innings the Phillies led, 4–2, which meant Boston faced a long night's journey into Game Six, where most likely they would face Philadelphia ace Grover Cleveland Alexander.[1]

In the eighth, though, things started to look up for Boston when Del Gainer led off with an infield single. The next batter, George "Duffy" Lewis, smashed an Eppa Rixey pitch over the fence, and just like that the Phillies' lead was gone. The game remained tied at 4–4 in the ninth, but Harry Hooper hit another Rixey pitch for a home run. It proved to be the game-winner, earning Boston its third world's championship and turning a potential grueling all-night train ride into an all-night celebration.[2]

The game marked the official end of the 1915 season and the unofficial beginning of the 1916 season. In 1916, the pennant races would be among the most competitive in baseball history. For the American League, this was largely the result of what happened during the 1914-15 offseason. Philadelphia's five-year dominance of the American League ended after the 1914 season with the equivalent of a modern-day salary dump. The net result simultaneously weakened the A's and strengthened the other American League teams, bringing more parity to the circuit. In 1915, the American League pennant race had been a three-team race won by the Red Sox, which held off stiff challenges from Detroit and Chicago. The Tigers and White Sox's respective second-

and third-place finishes marked the beginning of the end of a period that saw eastern teams dominate the American League. The further improvement of Chicago and Detroit in the 1915-16 offseason combined with a major personnel loss for the defending champion Red Sox would make 1916 even more competitive. Moreover, the death of the Federal League, a rival upstart circuit, broadened the available pool of talent.

Over in the National League, the regular season seemed to confirm that parity was the new norm. Until 1914, the Giants, Pirates or Cubs had won every National League pennant since 1901. Now the surprise triumph of the 1914 "Miracle Braves" had been followed by the Philadelphia Phillies' first pennant. While more competitive pennant races had helped baseball on the field in 1915, greater competition off the field had a negative impact on the bottom line.[3] However, the Federal League, one such source of competition, ceased to be a problem in 1916.

The Federal League was established in 1913. Initially, the situation was peaceful, for the Feds didn't seek American or National league players. By 1914, things changed as competition emerged between the new circuit and the existing leagues. Before long the likes of Joe Tinker and Three Finger Brown had signed with the Feds. Although the Federal League offered higher salaries and contracts with a less restrictive "reserve" clause, many players were hesitant to join, fearing potential retribution. If nothing else, the rival league was a bargaining chip for major league players. Many, among them Tris Speaker, used the new league for leverage, which helped salaries increase dramatically.[4]

The Federal League tried to force the issue in January 1915 by filing an anti-trust suit against Major League Baseball that threatened the very foundations of the sport. The case was brought before Judge Kenesaw Mountain Landis, a devoted baseball fan who had a reputation of trust busting. Apparently, Landis' feelings as a baseball fan won out as he took no action on the case. Ultimately, perhaps as Landis had intended, the fate of the Federal League was determined at the box office. Attendance dropped in 1915, and a peace settlement was reached on December 22, including the dismissal of the lawsuit. The price of peace was effectively a buyout by Major League Baseball, which cost the latter $600,000.[5]

As the Federal League was in its death throes, the potential 1916 pennant contenders in both leagues tried to improve their teams. At the time, trading for and purchasing new players were important methods of acquiring talent, but free agency or promotion from within an organization was not an option. Indeed, the structure of the minor leagues in 1916 bore little resemblance to today's farm systems. Although there were more minor league teams in the Deadball Era, they were independent operations, not under the control of major league teams. As a result, the standard progression to the majors was for a player to sign with a minor league team that would at some future date sell him to a major league team.[6]

In the case of the Phillies, management took the more conservative approach by staying with what worked in 1915. The Phillies had basically built their everyday lineup through acquisitions from other major league teams. The pitching staff, including ace Grover Cleveland Alexander, was much more homegrown. The only significant change during the 1915-16 off-season was the addition of long-time A's star Charles Bender. One of the key changes the prior year had been naming Pat Moran as manager in place of Charles "Red" Dooin. Other key moves included the signing of future Hall of Fame shortstop Dave Bancroft and trades that brought pitcher Al Demaree, left fielder George Whitted and third baseman Milt Stock to Philadelphia. The acquisitions of Stock and Bancroft and the 1914-15 off-season trade for second baseman Bert Niehoff improved the Phils' defense from worst to first in one year. The rest of the lineup consisted of George "Dode" Paskert in center field, flanked by Gavy Cravath, 1915's top hitter, in right and Bill Killefer behind the plate. With a combination of dominant pitching, strong defense and Cravath's power-hitting, it was hard to question management's decision to stand pat.[7]

Unlike the Phillies, the 1916 Boston Braves had changed dramatically from the team that shocked the baseball world in 1914. Less than two years later, five regulars had been replaced. Going into the 1915-16 offseason, the major on-field issues centered on the outfield and first base. However, as 1916 began, there was also an off-the-field change, as the team was sold to a group of investors, including Harvard football coach Percy Haughton. With ownership set and George Stallings back as manager, the Braves' leadership found a first baseman, an outfielder and some pitching help. After some hard negotiating they acquired a first baseman in Ed Konetchy and two Federal League pitchers, Frank Allen and Elmer Knetzer. With the addition of Konetchy, Boston had a strong infield with future Hall of Famers John Evers and Walter "Rabbit" Maranville at second and short, respectively, and veteran James Carlisle "Red" Smith at third. The outfield need had been filled by acquiring Joe Wilhoit from the Pacific Coast League. He joined former Giant Fred Snodgrass and former Phillie Sherry Magee as the mainstays of the Braves' outfield. Dick Rudolph continued to be the ace of a pitching staff that included Don Carlos Ragan, Tom Hughes and Art Nehf. Hughes led the National League in appearances in 1915 and would be one of Boston's most important players in 1916.[8]

The roster of the third-place Dodgers (or Superbas) had been formed differently than the Phillies and Braves, with most of the regulars beginning their major league careers in Brooklyn, most likely because owner Charles

Ebbets had hired Larry Sutton as one of the game's first full-time scouts. The Brooklyn pitching staff, however, was another matter. Apparently not satisfied with the pitchers he inherited when he became manager in 1913, Wilbert Robinson had been rebuilding the staff. In 1915, Robinson acquired Jack Coombs, Richard "Rube" Marquard and Larry Cheney, who joined incumbents Jeff Pfeffer, Sherrod Smith and William "Wheezer" Dell. With three starting pitchers and four regulars more than 30 years of age, Brooklyn was clearly built to win now. Another area of weakness was the outfield, where no one hit over .258 in 1915. Fortunately, Ebbets acquired Jimmy Johnston, a right-handed hitter, to complement the left-handed bats of Wheat and

Stengel. The Dodgers also added depth at third base and catcher. Mike Mowrey, a Federal League alumnus, would be the regular third baseman for Brooklyn in 1916, while at catcher, Robinson was reunited with another former Giant, John Tortes Meyers. Unfortunately, the potential big move that never happened was the acquisition of Charles "Buck" Herzog to play shortstop. Instead, Brooklyn began 1916 with a platoon system of Ollie O'Mara and Ivy Olson at that position.[9]

While the Phils, Dodgers, and Braves focused on small changes that might win the 1916 pennant, the New York Giants' goal was simply to become competitive. Nineteen-fifteen had seen John McGraw's team finish last, the only time that occurred when he managed a full season. One advantage the

Benny Kauff, the colorful New York Giants acquisition from the Federal League, in the team's distinctive 1916 uniform (National Baseball Hall of Fame Library, Cooperstown, N.Y.).

Giants had was ownership's willingness to spend money. The timing was fortuitous since the Federal League peace agreement put some talented players on the market. McGraw first combed the Federal League for pitchers, and like Robinson, he almost completely rebuilt his staff. Three hurlers from the Feds — William "Pol" Perritt (1915), John "Rube" Benton (1915) and Fred Anderson (1916) — joined veterans Jeff Tesreau and Christy Mathewson. McGraw also looked to Federal League alumni to significantly upgrade his regular lineup with the purchase of center fielder Bennie Kauff (the Federal League's best hitter) and catcher Bill Rariden. Kauff was a colorful character who claimed he would become the Ty Cobb of the Federal League. McGraw now had a team to take to spring training; how long he would be satisfied with that team remained to be seen.[10]

Over in the American League, the White Sox and Tigers faced the same predicament as the Dodgers and Braves, namely deciding what move or moves would put them over the top. Unlike Detroit, Chicago had little pennant-winning experience since owner Charlie Comiskey was still rebuilding his team. Comiskey began with prospects who were unproven or thought not to be of Major League caliber, such as catcher Ray Schalk and infielder George "Buck" Weaver. He had also added pitchers Eddie Cicotte, Ewell "Reb" Russell and Urban "Red" Faber before moving on to bigger names. Like the Giants, the White Sox had money, and the financial limitations of other teams worked in Comiskey's favor. Chicago was a major beneficiary of Connie Mack's salary dump when the White Sox purchased future Hall of Fame second baseman Eddie Collins for the enormous sum of $50,000. Later in 1915, Comiskey pulled off another blockbuster move, acquiring outfielder "Shoeless" Joe Jackson from the Cleveland Indians for $31,500 and three players.[11]

The key man behind the construction of the Tigers was Frank Navin, who brought both Ty Cobb and Hughie Jennings to Detroit, thereby finishing the foundation of a team that immediately won three straight American League pennants (1907–09). The two signings were Navin's most important steps in building the Tigers. Especially significant was the hiring of manager Hughie Jennings late in the 1906 season. Hughie, or "Eeyah" (due to his distinctive battle cry), was an aggressive and fiery leader whose style of baseball reflected his personality. In fact, it was Jennings' ability to get the most out of the brilliant but controversial Cobb that helped keep the Tigers competitive during much of the Deadball Era.[12]

Cobb remained the Tigers' leader in 1916, but fellow outfielder Sam Crawford was at the end of his career and would face a challenge for playing time. Bobby Veach, an excellent fielder and hitter who was purchased in 1912, rounded out the Detroit outfield. The Tigers' infield, including George Burns, Ralph Young, Donie Bush and Oscar Vitt, were primarily homegrown. It was a relatively young group, as only Donie Bush had more than four years of major league experience. The pitching staff was anchored by Harry Coveleski, George "Hooks" Dauss, Bill James and Jean Dubuc. Handling this staff was catcher Oscar Stanage, who had been with the team since 1909.[13]

If the Tigers' and White Sox's situations were similar to those of the Dodgers and Braves, the Red Sox's position mirrored that of the Phillies, but even more so. Owner Joseph Lannin and manager Bill Carrigan saw little reason to make significant changes. As a whole, the team was young but experienced, and built upon exceptional pitching. Still, of the three A.L. contenders, Boston's spring would be the most eventful.

The Red Sox roster had come together in two phases. The first occurred under prior ownership during the 1910 season when Lewis, Hooper and Tris Speaker first played the outfield together. Third baseman Larry Gardner was also part of that first group, signing straight out of the University of Vermont in 1908. After growing up in Enosburg Falls, Vermont (16 miles from the Canadian border), Gardner signed with the Red Sox and blossomed into an extraordinary clutch-hitting third baseman. His production at the most crucial times of the 1912 World Series was one of the main reasons Boston won that championship. The Red Sox broke the A's monopoly on the American League pennant in 1912, but they struggled in 1913. When things came apart, manager Jake Stahl was fired and catcher Bill Carrigan took over.[14]

Boston's 1912 world championship and the solid foundation of baseball talent appealed to Joseph Lannin when he purchased the Red Sox prior to the 1914 season. Originally from Canada, Lannin immigrated to Boston where he made his fortune in real estate. Undoubtedly, none of Lannin's key moves in the second phase of building the Red Sox loomed larger than the purchase of pitchers Babe Ruth and Ernie Shore and catcher Ben Egan for approximately $25,000 from Baltimore of the International League. The acquisitions occurred in the middle of the 1914 season, and while Shore pitched twice in the 1915 World Series, Ruth didn't become a standout hurler until 1916. Around the same time, first baseman Dick Hoblitzell was claimed off waivers from the Cincinnati Reds. The Athletics' fire-sale also paid dividends when Boston purchased second baseman Jack Barry during the 1915 season. Additionally, Lannin acquired shortstop Everett Scott (1914) and pitcher Carl Mays (1915). All in all, Boston was an exceptionally balanced team. The average age of the key members of the Red Sox was just under 27 years, even though the players had an average of 4½ years of experience in the major leagues.[15]

In preparing to sign his players for 1916, Lannin expected to have significantly more negotiating power since there was no competition from the Federal League. He wanted to stick with his 1915 championship team and would resort to signing Federal Leaguers only if he failed to reach agreement with the current squad. Despite his strong negotiating position, Lannin, unlike many other owners, didn't look to reduce all salaries, and kept many similar to 1915 levels. While trying to finalize his roster, there were rumors Lannin was considering selling the Red Sox. In the February 5, 1916, Boston *Daily Globe*, writer J.C. O'Leary reported that the Boston owner was in negotiations with Louis Coues Page to sell the team for a price in the $600,000 range. In spite of these rumors, Lannin continued to own the Red Sox until the fateful sale to Harry Frazee.[16]

Eventually, the only major unresolved personnel issues were the status of center fielder Tris Speaker and pitcher "Smokey" Joe Wood. Rumors circulated in late February that Speaker had been signed to a $10,000 contract, but these reports could not have been further from the truth. In fact, there was more involved here than the standard disagreement over salary. While the Red Sox were thought to be perfectly aligned for a title defense, there was evidence to the contrary regarding team chemistry. Though not the only culprit, the player at the heart of the problem was none other than Tris Speaker. Part of the issue went beyond baseball; like the city of Boston, the Red Sox were split along "sectarian lines." Speaker and Wood were at the head of a Protestant faction, while manager Bill Carrigan led the Roman Catholic contingent. Of greater concern was the issue raised years later by Fred Lieb that Speaker, a Texan, belonged to the Ku Klux Klan. Supposedly, Tris admitted this to "a prominent writer in the early 1910s." Speaker reportedly only wanted to play with "white Anglo-Saxon Protestants from below the Mason-Dixon line."[17]

Whether the Grey Eagle was a Klansman or not, he had been at odds with manager Bill Carrigan for some time. There were claims of a serious fight in the clubhouse earlier in their careers, and the two supposedly didn't speak much after 1911. There was also no love lost between Speaker and some of his other teammates, even his comrades in that exceptional outfield. In 1910, a spring training batting cage incident between left fielder Duffy Lewis and Speaker developed into an "instant enmity that lasted much of the rest of their careers." Lewis was another character on the Red Sox roster. His brash attitude fit right in with the likes of Speaker and Wood, as his early arrogance annoyed veterans. Duffy, who like Gardner consistently produced clutch hits, came to be known best for his fielding. After hours of practice, he mastered a 10-foot embankment in front of the left field wall that became known as "Duffy's cliff." In later years, Speaker mocked Lewis by knocking off his hat to reveal a receding hair line. Duffy retaliated by hurling a bat so hard at Tris that Speaker had to be helped off the field. Although right fielder Harry Hooper and Speaker developed a cordial and even friendly relationship, some members of Hooper's family didn't share those feelings. Hooper's wife, for example, found some of Speaker's antics to be arrogant, while Hooper's son, John, claimed that Speaker sometimes intentionally swung at bad pitches to hamper his father's base-stealing efforts.[18]

Although team chemistry was a real concern, money was also an issue. During the Federal League war, competitive pressures forced Lannin to double Speaker's 1914 salary to an extravagant $18,000. Speaker's holdout in 1916 was his second in four years, and both ownership and his teammates were none too pleased. In fact, a number of his teammates were reportedly "openly rooting" for the Red Sox to get rid of their star. Negotiations got off to a bad start and went downhill from there. Lannin, arguing that Spoke's batting average had dropped, made an initial offer of $9,000. This would have been a 50 percent pay cut, and the center fielder fought back, citing his runs scored and defense. Speaker was looking for $15,000 but lowered his demand to $12,000. As the Red Sox made their way to spring training, a volatile situation had developed.[19]

Spring training in the Deadball Era was dramatically different from today, where every major league team has an extensive training complex in Florida or Arizona. In 1916, with smaller rosters and a training period consisting of no longer than six weeks, there was no need for such facilities. Finances were also an issue since the only major source of revenue was gate receipts, of which there were precious few in spring training. Even the venues were very different in 1916, with Texas hosting more teams than Florida, while no teams trained in Arizona. Finding a site was also no easy matter, as smaller towns seldom had adequate facilities while larger towns hosted spring training for their own minor league teams.[20]

The Boston Red Sox headed for Hot Springs, Arkansas, considered to be a lavish vacation site in 1916. In fact, a number of major leaguers favored Hot Springs as a place to recover from the rigors of the offseason before spring training. The Red Sox practiced at Majestic Park, which was enclosed between ostrich and alligator farms as well as a zoo. The town itself had a carnival atmosphere, featuring both innocent diversions, such as hot-air balloon rides and concerts, as well as more lethal ones in brothels and race tracks. Once the players arrived at spring training, the first weeks consisted of practice and inter-squad games. Practice had some odd twists, such as hikes in the woods. Teams would then make their way back north, stopping on the way to play numerous exhibition games against semi-pro, minor league and major league clubs.[21]

Before the Red Sox left for Hot Springs, Joe Wood's situation heated up. The *Globe* claimed the reports regarding his being placed on waivers were true. While not directly denying the rumors, Lannin and Carrigan both stated they expected the pitcher to be at Hot Springs for spring training. Every team in both leagues had reportedly passed on the opportunity to claim Wood due to his arm problems. Lannin now had the option to send him to the minors or sign him to a contract, hopefully at a reduced salary. Ultimately, however, Wood didn't play Major League Baseball in 1916.

While Carrigan was unsure what to expect from Wood, the Red Sox pitching staff looked to be rounding into shape. After battling a knee injury for much of 1915, right-hander Carl Mays was healthy again. He would be part of a rotation that included Ruth, Hubert "Dutch" Leonard, Ernie Shore and George "Rube" Foster. Leonard was an extremely talented southpaw and would play a particularly critical role when the team struggled early in 1916. Unfortunately, he also presented another attitude problem for Lannin. Dutch came to Boston in 1912 but didn't make the team, instead going to Worcester of the New England League. After being annihilated in a start there, he showed up at Boston's team headquarters and complained about a lack of support. Once with the Red Sox, he had an exceptional 1914 season, in which he registered one of the lowest ERAs (0.96) in the history of the game. Leonard, however, would be part of chronic contract disputes, suspensions and complaints regarding ownership.[22]

On March 14, the *Globe* reported that an overweight Speaker had been sighted at the New York Giants' camp in Marlin, Texas. Perhaps speaking with more hope than knowledge, the writer implied he would be with the Red Sox on March 19. There was significant relief in Hot Springs on March 23 when it was reported that the Grey Eagle would arrive in the next day or so and start training without a contract. Reports suggested that last "minor" detail would be ironed out not with Lannin, but instead with the manager, Carrigan. Speaker arrived on March 24; the same day, Lewis was hit on the wrist by a pitched ball. Prior to that, Duffy "ran out of the car" that would take him to practice to welcome Speaker, who had just arrived. The injury forced Tris, who was reportedly overweight, into the lineup immediately.[23]

As Boston's time at Hot Springs came to a close, Tim Murnane wrote in the Boston *Daily Globe*, "Carrigan and Speaker seemed to be good natured and Speaker took hold as if he figured that the Red Sox would be his meal ticket for one more year, at least." Murnane felt that all was well between manager and star center fielder, especially when "Rough" said "the matter would be settled in New York." The Grey Eagle even spent an afternoon at the racetrack with numerous teammates, selecting many winners in the process. Based on 20–20 hindsight, the statement regarding the matter being settled in New York is more ambiguous than it first appeared. While the public statements made it sound as if Carrigan and the Red Sox wanted Speaker back, privately the sentiments could have been different. Perhaps limiting management's options was Lewis' wrist, which wasn't healing as expected.

Fortunately, an X-ray on March 29 revealed nothing more than a bad bruise on his thumb. With everyone seemingly on board, the Red Sox departed Hot Springs on March 31 in excellent shape. There was, however, a potentially significant off-the-field move, when on April 6 Lannin purchased outfielder Clarence Walker from the Browns.[24]

With Lewis' status for Opening Day still in question, the Speaker situation was indeed "settled in New York." Although there had been rumors in February that Lannin was negotiating with the Yankees on a Speaker trade, they had died down until an April 7 Washington *Post* headline screamed, "Tris Speaker to Yankees if Magnates Agree as to Terms." The deal reportedly centered on Fritz Maisel and cash from the Yankees. Lannin called these reports "all bosh" the same day. The center fielder had been with the team on good faith without a contract for the past two weeks, but the *Globe* and Carrigan claimed an agreement on a contract was imminent. Speaker apparently had the same impression, partially based on private conversations with the Boston owner. To say April 9 was an odd day in Red Sox history would be an extreme understatement. After hitting a two-run homer against Brooklyn the previous day, Speaker added a game-winning home run on April 9. In the clubhouse following the game, Lannin hugged Tris while shouting, "Great stuff, Spoke! You win. We'll sign when we get to Boston tomorrow."[25]

However, later that same day, former Red Sox treasurer and current Indians vice president and general manager Robert McRoy met with Speaker. He asked Tris if the latter would like to play in Cleveland, and the center fielder responded in the negative. McRoy then dropped the bombshell. Spoke had been sold to the Indians for $55,000 and two players to be named later shortly after the Red Sox-Dodgers game had ended. Speaker was outraged and begged McRoy not to release the news. Other reports said Tris and McRoy had multiple conversations that day, and Carrigan had been the one to actually tell Speaker. Regardless, moments later afternoon papers rushed to print the news, and the deal sent shockwaves through Boston. In the *Globe's* evening edition, Melville Emerson Webb, Jr. wrote, "No aeroplane bomb could have startled the little coterie of world's champions more than Manager Carrigan's announcement. Bill, President Lannin and even Speaker himself, only the night before, had told us that everything was fine — all except signing the contract." Not surprisingly, the universal reaction was one of shock. "Carrigan's news was unbelievable — but it was true. The proverbial pin could have dropped a million times in the hotel corridor and it would have made a noise like the sudden bursting of an automobile. Everyone was speechless."[26]

One possible explanation for the deal centered on a change in the ownership of the Indians. American League president Ban Johnson helped Chicago contractor James Dunn finance the purchase of the team after Charles Somers

The force behind the American League, Ben Johnson — standing (right) with J.E. Bruce, secretary of the National Commission — was a larger-than-life baseball man who may have helped orchestrate the biggest sale in baseball history (National Baseball Hall of Fame Library, Cooperstown, N.Y.).

had "cash-flow difficulties." There has been speculation that Johnson helped manipulate the trade to repay Dunn for his investment. The Boston *Post* believed Johnson was involved, suggesting Cleveland would turn around and deal Speaker to the Yankees since the A.L. president wanted a strong team in that city. That publication also claimed Tris had the opportunity to sign with Boston but rejected a $10,000 offer by Carrigan, prompting the sale. "Rough" denied this, noting the cash offered by Cleveland was so great that Speaker may have been sold regardless of whether he accepted Lannin's terms. The public behavior of the Boston owner was also very inconsistent. Following the exhibition game against the Dodgers, Lannin spoke publicly as if Speaker would be with the Red Sox in 1916, but McRoy told Speaker the deal was completed just after the end of the game. Especially suspicious is the fact that the afternoon newspapers had time to include the story, and the editions were reportedly on the street just moments after Boston's star player was told. It certainly seems that Lannin was being duplicitous, perhaps abetting Johnson's efforts to manipulate the deal.

The dollar amount paid was claimed to be the largest ever in baseball. Lannin said it was a business decision, which added to speculation he was planning on selling the team. Additionally, Carrigan, during an interview, suggested perhaps "Lannin's hotel operations needed a quick infusion of cash," and that was the reason. Speaker claimed the two had agreed on a figure just a few days before, but unfortunately for the Grey Eagle, nothing had been put in writing. Seeming to publicly distance himself from the decision, "Rough" also said, "It was never any secret that Speaker wasn't one of my favorite persons, and neither was I one of his. But I recognized his talent and was delighted to have him on our side. I hated to lose him." The deal came at the same time it was becoming clear Joe Wood wouldn't be back, and one can't help but speculate whether privately Lannin and Carrigan were trying to rid the best team in baseball of troublemakers.[27]

What actually happened will never be known, but what was certain was the risk Lannin was taking in parting with Speaker. He had been a regular since 1909 and was a critical part of the 1912 and 1915 world championship teams. During the first title run, Speaker led the team with a .383 batting average (third in the AL) and 10 home runs (tied for the league lead) and finished second on his squad with 90 RBIs. "Spoke" also led the league in on-base percentage and doubles on his way to the Chalmers Award, the MVP of the day. He also led the team offensively in 1915 with a .322 batting average. Just as significant was Speaker's defensive prowess, where the Grey Eagle led A.L. center fielders in putouts five times and double plays on four occasions. Twice Speaker had recorded 35 assists, still an American League record. In exchange, Boston essentially received only money, as pitcher Sam Jones would appear in only 13 games in 1916 and third baseman Fred Thomas wouldn't play at all. The Red Sox were breaking up one of the best outfields in the game's history for little in return.[28]

The public reaction was one of sadness on both sides. After a private conversation with Lannin, Speaker said all the right things, telling the Boston *Globe* he was sorry to exchange a winning team and his many Boston friends for a losing team where he was a stranger. Another aspect of the deal Tris denied was the rumor he would become the manager of the Indians as well. Speaker signed with Cleveland on April 12, also Opening Day in the major leagues, but even this was not without controversy. There were questions about whether Speaker would sign, and then when he finally did, whether or not he received part of the purchase price, and if so, how much and who paid it. In addition, Cleveland was also supposedly looking for Lannin to pay Speaker's so-called "signing bonus." The animosity between the two continued years later, when a 1950 Cleveland *Plain-Dealer* article said Tris refused to sign until Ban Johnson guaranteed Lannin would pay $10,000 of the purchase price. The Boston owner said at the time he hadn't paid a bonus to the Grey Eagle at all. While Speaker may have been sad about leaving, it wasn't at all clear those feelings were shared in the Red Sox clubhouse. Dick Casey, a close friend of Duffy Lewis, said that Lewis "was glad Speaker was traded. So was Hooper. They used to hate each other. Hate each other! That's why they had to get rid of Speaker. On the field he was terrible to them fellows."[29]

By comparison, the White Sox and Tigers' training camps were dull. Like Bill Carrigan, Chicago field general Clarence Rowland held a short but intense camp. This was probably due to a concern that longer, more strenuous camps in the past may have caused the Sox to weaken by mid-season after fast starts. In 1916, the White Sox started spring training three weeks later than usual with an exhibition schedule that was cut in half. While the costs of spring training were a burden for some owners, this was clearly not the case for Comiskey. The trip to Texas had almost a party atmosphere, as the White Sox owner brought 60-plus people, including friends and a moving picture man hired to film the journey.[30]

The only players not with the main guard were Faber, who was delayed by illness, and Joe Jackson, who arrived a few days later. Hailing from Iowa, Urban "Red" Faber didn't appear to be going far in baseball until he joined Minneapolis of the American Association in 1911. There he learned and began to perfect a spitball. His improved performance ultimately led to his being signed by White Sox owner Charles Comiskey in October of 1913 for a world exhibition tour. Faber had his breakout performance in 1915, by this time also relying on a curve and fastball. It was the ability to throw three pitches that made Red so successful.[31]

The biggest question of camp was third base, where Lena Blackburne (.216–0–25) headed a committee that struggled through 1915. Comiskey and Rowland had been unable to fill the voids through a trade and were now looking at other options, including youngsters Fred McMullin and Zeb Terry. Improvement at the hot corner would be the one position where Chicago could make up ground on Boston. One option was moving Buck Weaver to third and placing Terry at shortstop, which would be the ideal solution if the latter could measure up. That may have been expecting a lot, however, since Weaver had committed a team-leading 49 errors at shortstop in 1915.[32]

The theory held up at least during spring training, especially after Terry put to rest some of the concern regarding his offense on March 27, when he went 4-for-5 with a three-run homer. Chicago left Mineral Wells on April 1, and *Tribune* reporter I.E. Sanborn was excited about the lineup and the new combination on the left side of the infield. With the biggest question of the offseason answered, at least for the moment, there were few remaining issues. While the Opening Day starter had not been named, Faber, Claude "Lefty"

Williams, Reb Russell and Ed Cicotte would be key members of the pitching staff.[33]

Unlike Chicago, pitching seemed to be Detroit's biggest area for potential improvement in 1916. The Tigers' ERA of 2.86 (Chicago's was 2.43 and Boston's 2.39) was fourth in the American League, but the team's offense certainly made the pitching look weak by comparison. Detroit easily led the American League in batting average (.268), slugging percentage (.358) and runs (778). Much like the White Sox, Detroit's pitching staff was top-heavy, with Harry Coveleski (22–13, 2.45 ERA) and Hooks Dauss (24–13, 2.50 ERA) leading the way. However, Jean Dubuc and Bernie Boland were the only two other hurlers with double figures in victories. Each had ERAs in the threes, fairly high for the Deadball Era. The staff wasn't nearly as deep as Boston's, and there had to be improvement if the Tigers were to overtake the Red Sox.[34]

Detroit had a new spring training site in 1916 at Jungle Park in Waxahachie, Texas. On hand was Billy Sullivan, a former White Sox catcher and manager who was charged with improving the performance of the Tiger hurlers. Specifically, one of his tasks was identifying some promising youngsters, such as Grover Lowdermilk and George Boehler. Another tactic Tiger manager Hughie Jennings used was to play more exhibition games, including a series against the Giants. Most veterans were at camp on or around March 9, with the exception of Ty Cobb, who by the middle of the month still hadn't reported, which was no small concern. Not only did Jennings have to worry about Cobb's absence, he was also concerned the Tigers as a whole weren't rounding into form. It was apparently a team effort, or failure, as Henry George Salsinger wrote, "The work of the pitchers is terrible to behold, as one would expect; the fielders are doing poor work and the batsmen, except one or two, are not hitting the ball. The worst part about the team's showing in practice is stupidity." Such comments were not likely to make Tiger fans back in Michigan all that optimistic about the upcoming season.[35]

The continued absence of Cobb didn't concern Salsinger, however, as the center fielder was apparently already in good condition. Cobb finally arrived during the first week in April after being held up by fires in Augusta, Georgia, that threatened his real estate business investments. With the season fast approaching, some position battles emerged. Third baseman Ossie Vitt had struggled with a bad arm but was more experienced than youngster George Maisel, who was making a strong argument for the job. Still, it seemed Vitt would win the spot in the end. Additionally, first baseman George Burns had struggled at the plate for much of the spring, and it now seemed likely that future Hall of Famer Harry Heilmann would start the season there. It was a testament to the loyalty of Tigers owner Frank Navin and manager

Hughie Jennings that the franchise stuck with Heilmann. He was selected by Detroit in the 1913 Rule 5 draft but hit only .225 in 1914. After being sent down to the Pacific Coast League in 1915, Harry warded off a series of dizzy spells to have a successful season. That led to his 1916 spring training opportunity.[36]

The pitching staff, which was the primary concern, was depleted by injuries. Dauss and Coveleski were the only two reliable starters. The journey of Harry Coveleski to ace of the Tigers staff is a fascinating one. He had a brief span of astonishing success in 1908. While pitching for the Phillies, Harry defeated the Giants three times in five September days, in large part costing New York the pennant. Coveleski then stumbled into oblivion and out of the major leagues before resurfacing with the Tigers for the 1914 season. Out of nowhere, he won 22 games in each of the next two seasons. Following the duo of Harry and Hooks were such question marks as Jean Dubuc, Bill James (who wouldn't be paid a salary until he worked himself back into shape) and newcomer George Cunningham. Detroit hoped Lowdermilk and Boehler, two recruits, could provide contributions. The latter struck out 14 in an exhibition game on April 5, but inconsistency was Boehler's trademark. Oddly, the Tigers went south to decide on a pitching staff, but came back north with only more questions. With Opening Day just around the corner, it was time for Jennings to make some decisions regarding his lineup and hope his depleted pitching held.[37]

Another challenge to spring training as well as the entire season was travel. If the overnight World Series trips between Boston and Philadelphia were a nightmare, round trips by rail to places like Arkansas, Texas and even Florida were far worse. Teams training in Florida at least had the option of going part of the way by boat, thereby avoiding the multiple nights on the rails required for Texas and Arkansas. Given the remoteness of their spring training site, the Giants headed south before the other National League contenders. This early start, however, was also due to John McGraw's belief that pitchers became more out of shape during the offseason and needed additional preparation time. Marlin, some 100 miles south of Dallas, had been the spring training home of the Giants since 1908 and would continue to be so through 1918. McGraw favored Marlin because it combined a small-town atmosphere with fewer distractions and manageable train rides to larger Texas cities.[38]

In Marlin, the Arlington hotel served as a residence and locker room, including a common shower, since the hotel had no private bathrooms. Workouts began on February 28, and after a week of practice and inter-squad games, McGraw took his club to Dallas for two weekend exhibition games. The pattern of weekday workouts in Marlin and exhibition games in various Texas locales continued through the end of March. Almost ten days into spring training, Bennie Kauff finally came to terms with the Giants and was on his way to Marlin, accompanied by 52 bats and his considerable ego. Finally, on March 24 the Giants' time in Marlin ended when the Tigers came to town for an exhibition game.[39]

Spring training, however, still had a long way to go. Today major league teams stay in Florida or Arizona nearly until Opening Day and then fly to their destinations. The return home in 1916 meant numerous days and nights on the railroad, usually playing exhibition games along the way. For the Giants, spring training had been a time to get in shape, with little competition for starting positions. The infield was set, featuring Fred Merkle at first, a double-play combination of Larry Doyle and Art Fletcher, and Hans Lobert at third. As expected, former Federal Leaguers Kauff and Rariden started in center field and at catcher, respectively. With George Burns set in left, the only open position was right field, where Dave Robertson would ultimately prevail. One of the stops was an exhibition game in Chattanooga, Tennessee. After what was reported to be the worst loss of the spring, one reporter noted, "It was one of those days when everything went wrong for the Giants, and on those days, they can rival the rankest minor league team." Those were prophetic words for New York's up-and-down 1916 season. The next morning the Giants left for New York City, where they played two exhibition games before getting back on the rails for Philadelphia and Opening Day.[40]

Unlike the Giants, the Braves, Dodgers and Phillies all trained in Florida, significantly reducing the necessary journey, including making at least part of the trip by boat. However, after an ocean voyage that included a blizzard and a Nor'easter that left most players seasick, the Boston Braves may have had doubts about their supposed good fortune. After everyone arrived in Miami, Stallings held only one morning practice before playing the first inter-squad game. Never hesitating to promote his team, Stallings told reporters, "Take it all and all you have seen this afternoon what comes pretty near being a great ball team." Although there were some hopes that Bill James, one of Boston's 1914 pitching stars, might have recovered from arm trouble, he would never pitch effectively again. Forced to face reality, Boston signed former Cubs star and Federal League alumnus Ed Reulbach.[41]

After almost three weeks of spring training, the Braves saw what was reputed to be their first major league opposition, the Philadelphia Athletics, now a shell of their former selves. In one of the most overly optimistic claims in baseball history, sportswriters covering the A's said they "will have a pretty fair team this season." After a "lively" morning workout on March 30, the Braves packed their belongings, took a last swim at the beach and caught the train for the first leg of the trip north. On their way to Brooklyn to start the season, the Braves played exhibition games in Jacksonville, Florida; Rocky

Mount, North Carolina; Richmond, Virginia; Washington, D.C.; and Baltimore, Maryland. One exhibition game in Baltimore was snowed out, causing J. C. O'Leary to comment that they left for spring training in a blizzard and now returned in one. The Braves then headed for New York City to prepare for the opener with Brooklyn at Ebbets Field.[42]

Although their spring training facilities were also in Florida, the Phillies' contingent traveling from Philadelphia initially headed north to New York City to board the steamer *Lenape,* which would take them to Jacksonville on the way to St. Petersburg. Several other players traveled by train, which Jim Nasium of the Philadelphia *Inquirer* attributed to their preference for the rails over boats. They certainly made the right choice on this occasion, as the *Lenape* apparently hit the same storm the Braves' ship encountered. The Philadelphia party rendezvoused in Jacksonville, and after lunch the whole group was on the train for St. Petersburg, with the first workout planned for the next day.[43]

Workouts began at Coffee Pot Park under sunny skies and 80-degree temperatures. Unlike the Braves, who began inter-squad games almost immediately, the Phils devoted most of the first week to the order of the day, otherwise known as "batting practice and more batting practice with a little batting practice in between." Nasium claimed that far more time had been spent on batting practice in an effort to improve the previous year's weakness. In noting the team's strength, Nasium referred to the "oft repeated statement that 'pitching is ninety per cent of baseball.'" As 1916 would prove, Nasium may have been guilty of an understatement when he said that Alexander was "a whole pitching staff by himself."[44]

Grover Cleveland Alexander was described as "a whole pitching staff by himself" (National Baseball Hall of Fame Library, Cooperstown, N.Y.).

A new phase of camp began on March 18 when the Phillies began a series of exhibition games against a National League rival, the Chicago Cubs. Since the Cubs roster was a combination of last year's team and the Federal League champion Chicago Whales, manager Joe Tinker felt the consolidated club would be more competitive. However, a Philadelphia sweep of the seven games gave a more realistic indication of the Cubs' prospects. When spring training ended on April 3, the defending National League champions boarded "the famous southern rattlers" for an overnight trip to Jacksonville. Unlike the other contenders, the Phils did little barnstorming, with their only exhibition game stops coming in Richmond and Washington, D.C.[45]

Philadelphia split two games in the former Confederate capital, suffering their first loss of the preseason when surprisingly the Richmond team defeated Alexander. The second exhibition game in Washington was snowed out, leaving the Phils with two days to kill in the nation's capital. Only about 400 to 500 spectators "braved death from pneumonia to witness" the final exhibition game, which included a brief duel between arguably the two best right-handers in the game — the Nationals' Walter Johnson and Alexander. Afterwards, Pat Moran and his men caught a 7:05 train that took them to Philadelphia to begin the defense of their National League flag.[46]

While the Giants, Braves and Phillies entered spring training with hopes of recapturing recent glory, the Brooklyn Dodgers' expectations focused on something relatively new. The Dodgers' last National League pennant in 1900 had predated the American League and the World Series. Naturally, none of the players from that team remained, and on the current roster only John Meyers, Rube Marquard and Jack Coombs had any significant pennant-winning experience. Before gathering the full squad in Florida, Wilbert Robinson decided to send all of the veteran pitchers to Hot Springs, Arkansas, under the leadership of Jack Coombs for two weeks of preliminary training. Even though it was February, there was still some uncertainty about the spring training site. In what would be an unthinkable step today, National League umpire Charles Rigler went to Daytona for the Dodgers to evaluate the condition of the field. Although Rigler's initial report was negative, leading Brooklyn management to consider alternatives, Daytona, Florida, was the final choice.[47]

By March 3 the rookies and some veterans were arriving in Daytona and began taking part in two daily workouts with inter-squad games starting almost right away. One veteran already in camp was Charles Stengel, who was trying to recover from an off year. *Eagle* writer Thomas Rice mentioned how ill and weak Stengel had been in spring training the previous year. This was the "famous" illness that Fred Lieb claimed Stengel told George Underwood of the New York *Press* was "clap," but others believed was more likely typhoid fever.[48]

On March 10 the Hot Springs contingent arrived, all appearing to be in good shape, thereby allowing the team to move into a more regular routine. Unlike Moran, McGraw and Stallings, Wilbert Robinson had some real decisions to make about his starting lineup. The right side of the infield was set, with George Cutshaw and Jake Daubert at second and first, respectively, but the left side was unsettled. At third base, there was competition between Gus Getz and Mike Mowrey, while Olson and O'Mara were fighting it out at shortstop. With no clear winners in spring training, Robinson decided to keep all four on the roster. Robinson also chose to hold onto eight pitchers and three catchers, which limited him to four outfielders. With the inter-squad games behind them, the Dodgers played four exhibition games against the Athletics before leaving Florida. From there, they headed for Washington, D.C., where Rice wrote with his typical double entendre, they "would brave the windstorms of Capitol Hill." As might have been expected, Brooklyn ran roughshod over the A's, sweeping all four games. Rice, for one, recognized that "queer collection of human oddities which Connie Mack is directing is not a ball team and should not be counted as such."[49]

The Superbas' brief stay in Washington and Baltimore saw them win three games, with one rained out. Optimism continued to run high in the Brooklyn camp, due both to the quality of play and the lack of injuries, a remarkable improvement over the prior campaign. Rice felt the team entered the season in the best condition in ten years. Upon returning to Brooklyn, the Dodgers played exhibition games against the Yankees and Boston Red Sox, some of which were wiped out by bad weather. On April 11, the final exhibition game marked Jack Coombs' first and only appearance of the spring. Understandably, Wilbert Robinson was being careful with 34-year-old "Colby Jack." A graduate of Colby College in Maine, Coombs had been an ace pitcher on Connie Mack's great Philadelphia A's teams. In 1910, Jack won 31 games, including a record 13 shutouts. He topped that off with three complete-game wins in the World Series in just six days. Tragically, the star right-hander developed typhoid fever in 1913 that settled near his spine, nearly killing him. After a lengthy recovery, Coombs rejoined the A's in 1914, only to be released when Mack broke up his team. Signed by Wilbert Robinson in 1915, "Colby Jack" pitched almost 200 innings that year while winning 15 games for the Superbas. Even without the illness, at 34, Coombs' arm only had so many quality pitches left. One of Robby primary 1916 challenges was to use those pitches wisely. In any event, Opening Day and the start of the 1916 Major League season were at hand.[50]

Predicting the 1916 National League pennant race was not easy. The league had had three different champions in each of the past three years. In addition, the Dodgers' 1915 performance meant they could not be ignored as a contender. Furthermore, the poor showing of the Giants in 1915 made it hard to handicap their chances, especially since they were so dependent on Federal League players with little or no track record in the major leagues. Local writers such as Jim Nasium and Thomas Rice were optimistic to the point of over-confident about the home team's chances. *The Sporting News* predicted that the Phillies would repeat, with Brooklyn and Boston exchanging the second and third places. Nationally syndicated columnist Hugh Fullerton, who was credited as being "that genius for exact doping baseball by a system all his own," was certainly not afraid to take a chance with his 1916 predictions. His pick of the Braves to finish first was understandable, but he saw the Reds finishing second, followed by the Cubs, with Brooklyn filling out the first division. Fullerton was not a believer in the Phillies, as he had them coming in seventh. Little, of course, makes people more objective than a financial interest, which may have been what Grantland Rice had in mind when he provided the betting odds supplied by John Doyle, "Sporting Impresario." Doyle saw the Braves as an 11 to 5 favorite due to Manager Stallings, the pitching staff and the infield. Not far behind were the Phils and Dodgers, both at 3 to 1, while Doyle apparently believed in the rebuilt Giants, who he felt had a 4 to 1 chance. While some, like Fullerton, had hopes for the "western clubs," the clear consensus was the eastern clubs would be the major contenders in 1916.[51]

Over in the American league, the prevailing opinion among "dopesters" or analysts indicated the three toughest teams would be the Red Sox, White Sox and Tigers. Entering spring training, the Red Sox were a clear-cut favorite to defend their title; prognosticators now had to take into account the Speaker deal, which threatened to drastically change the balance of power in the American League. In the Boston *Daily Globe* "dopesheet," the Red Sox were still given the edge, putting Boston's pennant odds at 8 to 5, with Detroit (2½ to 1) and Chicago (3 to 1) close behind. Most agreed with the prognosis that the Red Sox, even without Speaker, had more than enough pitching to win the pennant in 1916.[52]

Boston was balanced, finishing second in the American League in batting average (.260) and ERA (2.39) and tied for third in fielding percentage (.964) in 1915. However, the Red Sox banked on pitching, having five players (Rube Foster, Ernie Shore, Babe Ruth, Dutch Leonard and Smokey Joe Wood) with 15 wins or more. Promising youngster Carl Mays, who had struggled with injuries in 1915, would add further strength to the staff.[53]

The White Sox were also well balanced, having no obvious weakness. Finishing second in fielding percentage (.965) and third in ERA (.243) and batting average (.258), Chicago appeared nearly as strong as the Red Sox. They had five pitchers with 10 or more victories and a pair of 24-game winners (Red

Tris Speaker (third ballplayer from left) with teammates (from left) Duffy Lewis, Larry Gardner and Heinie Wagner, not all of whom he got along with (George Bain Collection, Library of Congress).

Faber and Jim Scott) that not even the Red Sox could match. The difference as most "dopesters" saw it was Boston's extraordinary experience and chemistry. Nearly every Red Sox position player was entering at least his fifth Major League season, and while not as tenured, the pitching staff was by no means inexperienced. On the other hand, Chicago would need significant contributions from rookie Zeb Terry and second-year players Oscar "Happy" Felsch, Jack Ness and Fred McMullin. Even more important was Boston's pennant-winning experience. Such Red Sox regulars as Larry Gardner, Harry Hooper and Duffy Lewis had been part of two world championship teams. Of the White Sox regulars, as well as the pitching staff, only two players had significant postseason experience.[54]

The Tigers were certainly more experienced than Chicago, with some important carryover from the 1907–09 pennant-winning teams. Detroit's experience, however, still did not come close to matching that of the Red Sox. Boston also had a major advantage over the Tigers in pitching, which was where the latter had to improve. With Opening Day finally here, many probably hoped the picture would be clarified early in the season. But while the 1916 season would have many things, clarity would not be one of them.

CHAPTER II

"He couldn't hit an elephant with a banjo."

While baseball has changed a great deal since 1916, one thing that hasn't changed is the anticipation of Opening Day. During the Deadball Era, with no competition from other professional sports, this excitement may have been even greater than today. With the arrival of Opening Day 1916 and the beginning of the National and American league pennant races, the winners would be determined by a 154-game schedule, shaped by the realities of travel. Although Major League Baseball didn't extend past the Mississippi River, the distance between cities was a major issue since the railroad was the only means of inter-city travel.

The schedules in both leagues continued the pattern used throughout the Deadball Era. The season opened with all-eastern and all-western series. Then, east and west alternated visits to their counterparts. Additional eastern- and western-only match-ups were played in between these trips, and the two regions finished the season as they began, with all-eastern and western series. Since in 1915 the western teams traveled east first, the opposite occurred in 1916. This system led to road trips and homestands that are unthinkable today. Brooklyn for example, visited every city in the National League during a 28-game road trip, which lasted from mid–August to mid–September. Once back in Brooklyn, however, the Superbas would play their last 26 games at home.[1] For now, though, the eastern teams in the National League and their fans focused on Opening Day games in Brooklyn and Philadelphia.

In Brooklyn, it rained overnight, but the sun was out on the morning of April 12 as fans journeyed to Ebbets Field. The vast majority of National League ballparks in 1916 were either new or recently renovated, and Ebbets Field was no exception. Opened in 1913, the shape of the field (like most ballparks of the era) mirrored the shape of the land, a site so small it "wouldn't make a decent major league parking lot" today. Ebbets Field had the era's typ-

1916 Brooklyn Superbas team picture. *From left, top—* Casey Stengel, George Cutshaw, "Duster" Mails, Rube Marquard, Sherry Smith, Arthur Dede, "Wheezer" Dell; *middle—* Ed Appleton, John Tortes Meyers, Jeff Pfeffer, Larry Cheney, Nap Rucker, Ivan Olson, Gus Getz, Zack Wheat; *front—* Jack Coombs, Ollie O'Mara, Hi Myers, Wilbert Robinson, Jake Daubert, Jim Johnston, Otto Miller, Mike Mowery (National Baseball Hall of Fame Library, Cooperstown, N.Y.).

ical long foul lines and big outfield except in right, where the "urban grid" limited the distance to the foul pole to less than 300 feet. In left and center, however, the distance was a more typical 419 feet and 450 feet respectively. The more familiar, intimate version of Ebbets Field came after renovations in 1931.[2]

Once inside the ballpark, the excited fans found their seats among the 18,000 located in either a two-level grandstand or concrete bleachers, all in foul territory. The grandstand began just inside the right field line and continued around the infield to third base, and from there bleachers extended to the left field foul line. The left field wall housed a manually operated score board, containing lineups as well as scores of other National League games. Players did not wear numbers on their uniforms, so the numbers on the scoreboard matched those listed next to each name on scorecards sold at the ballpark.[3]

Although it rained the night before, the typically late-afternoon start time allowed the field to dry. However, there was a strong breeze, and as the game wore on and the sunlight wore out, it became much cooler. At about 3:00

P.M., Shaman's brass band led a procession of umpires and players to the flag pole. The parade was followed by the playing of "The Star-Spangled Banner," a meeting between captains Johnny Evers and Jake Daubert, and umpire Bill Klem's announcement of the starting batteries. With this, Brooklyn took the field, Rabbit Maranville hit Larry Cheney's first pitch foul, and "the 1916 season was on" before an estimated crowd of "15,000 fans and fannettes." The game was scoreless until the Braves broke through in the second when Sherry Magee tripled and scored on J. Carlisle "Red" Smith's sacrifice fly. Boston found the scoring column again in the top of the fourth on Magee's second hit, which drove in Evers. Brooklyn scored its first 1916 run in the bottom of the fourth, but unfortunately it was the only Dodger run of the day. The Braves added three more runs, partially due to poor Brooklyn defense, winning 5–1 behind Dick Rudolph.[4]

Not surprisingly, Tom Rice's optimism had taken a hit, and he complained the Superbas "played as if they were in a trance." There was little good to say from the Brooklyn perspective, especially in the pitching department. Although Cheney went the distance, he was wild, allowing five walks and throwing three wild pitches. Rice consoled himself by saying if the old adage that "a bad beginning makes a good ending" is true, "the Brooklyn Superbas should have the National League pennant clinched by July 4th." If he believed in omens, Rice could have taken comfort from knowing the same adage was used by an unnamed predecessor early in 1889, the year Brooklyn won its first pennant.[5]

Understandably, the Braves were well satisfied with the first day's results. Magee earned praise for his three hits, while outfielder Joe Wilhoit in his major league debut made two nice catches that even the Brooklyn fans applauded. On defense, Nick Flatley said the infield played "with the precision of machines." Special praise was also given to Dick Rudolph, the "bald pated marvel" who "slow balled and fast balled and spit balled and in general balled the Dodgers up." Rudolph's lack of hair would be noted on a regular basis throughout the 1916 campaign; given his performance, he probably deserved better treatment.[6]

About 100 miles south, the 1916 season began amidst even windier and chillier conditions. Unlike the Superbas' "fans and fannettes," the Phillies' faithful went to one of the oldest ballparks in the National League. First built in 1887, Baker Bowl's original wooden structure had burned down in 1894, a fairly common occurrence in the game's early days. A new double-decked ballpark, built of less flammable steel, brick and concrete, reopened in 1895. Located in north Philadelphia, about three miles north of Independence Hall, the facility was known as Baker Bowl, named after Phillies president William Baker. The ballpark did not lack for quirky features, starting with a Philadelphia and Reading railroad tunnel that ran under the ballpark, producing a hump in center field. Like the Polo Grounds in New York, the clubhouse at Baker Bowl was located on the second floor of a structure in left-center field. Similar to its more modern counterpart in Brooklyn, the ballpark had asymmetrical dimensions, ranging from 390 feet in left field and 388 feet in center, to a very short right field fence, only 273 down the line. Somewhat offsetting that tempting right-field target was a 40-foot-high brick fence covered with tin that produced more than its share of interesting caroms. The double-decked grandstand extended from the right-field foul line, around the infield, to about halfway down the left-field line. A single deck continued the grandstand to the clubhouse in left-center field for a total seating capacity of 18,000.[7]

The Giants took the field first, and many in the crowd "gasped" at the New Yorkers who were dressed in an "odd shade of gray uniforms, striped with black lines, making blocks about two inches square." Jim Nasium thought they resembled prison garb. Outside the park, the streets were "black with fans," as a capacity crowd filed into the ballpark. Also present were "all the city's celebrities," including the political leaders; seating for the latter was done "with as much care as the diplomatic hostess who entertained divorced couples." Unlike Opening Day, in Brooklyn there was no flag raising or parade of the players since such rituals, for some unspoken reason, were considered to be "out of fashion." Instead, the Phillies were presented with gold watches commemorating the 1915 National League pennant, as the Giants looked on, supposedly "with envious eyes."[8]

Given the chilly temperatures, everyone must have been glad when the ceremonies ended, and Grover Cleveland Alexander threw the season's first pitch. If Alexander's appearance was true to form, his uniform seemed "a little too big," while his cap would be on the small size and worn "a little crooked." Since it was Opening Day, his spikes would probably have looked as good as they would all season, as the Phillies ace tried to make one pair of shoes last the full season. Alexander used a sidearm delivery that made his pitches "seem as if they were coming out of a slingshot." The net effect was that both right- and left-hand batters felt the ball was coming toward them at an angle. Since he used the same motion for his fastball and curve and the latter broke late, one can only imagine the plight of batters trying to adjust at the last minute. Combining this with pinpoint control and working so quickly that games seldom lasted more than 90 minutes, it is little wonder Alexander dominated opposing batters.[9]

Grover Cleveland had indeed dominated the National League in 1915 and would be even more overwhelming in 1916. However, the season nor even the first inning did not begin that way, as two hits, a wild pitch and a Bancroft

1916 Philadelphia Phillies team picture. *From left, top*— Billy Maharg (asst. trainer), Dave Bancroft, Billy Killifer, Stan Baumgartner, Fred Luderus, Bobby Byrne, Ben Tincup, Bob Gandy, George McQuillan, Ed Kantlehner, Joe Oeschger, Wilbur Good, Jack Adams, Mike Dee (trainer); *middle*— Gavy Cravath, Ed Burns, Al Demaree, Oscar Dugey, Pat Moran, George "Possum" Whitted, Milt Stock, Claude Cooper, George Chalmers; *front*— Erskine Mayer, Grover Alexander, Eddie Naughton (mascot), Eppa Rixey, Dode Paskert, Gary Fortune (National Baseball Hall of Fame Library, Cooperstown, N.Y.).

error led to two Giant runs. Still, the Phillies rallied quickly, scoring one in the first and two in the second. In what was clearly not going to be a typically low-scoring Deadball Era game, New York tied it in the fifth and took the lead in the sixth on a home run by Fred Merkle. The Giants received good relief pitching from Ralph Stroud, but in the bottom of the sixth, a Rariden throwing error allowed the Phillies to tie the game. Matters remained knotted up in the bottom of the ninth and with two out, it looked like Opening Day was headed toward extra innings. However, the game had not exactly been a defensive classic, and it would not end that way, either. Stock walked and stole second as Giants catcher Bill Rariden dropped the ball. Rariden's problems got worse on the next pitch when the ball bounded past him to the grandstand, sending Stock to third. Probably unnerved to some degree by his catcher's struggles, Stroud promptly unleashed a pitch "four feet over Rariden's onion," bringing Stock across the plate and the Philadelphia fans home happy.[10]

Day Two of the National League season saw a rainout in Brooklyn, but down in Philadelphia, the precipitation held off, allowing the Giants and Phillies to play the second game of their series. The pitching match-up of Erskine Mayer for the Phils and Jeff Tesreau for New York kept things score-less until the ninth, when poor Philadelphia defense allowed the Giants to score twice. Bad baserunning in the bottom of the inning killed a potential Phillies rally, giving New York its first victory and Philadelphia its first loss. After a rainout on April 14, the Giants suffered another ninth-inning loss the next day. With the bases loaded in a tie game, the Phils' Dode Paskert took "one horrendous swing" before laying down a successful suicide bunt. The day was no doubt doubly frustrating for McGraw, as New York not only beat themselves with bad defense, but Milt Stock and Al Demaree starred for the Phils. The Giant skipper had traded the two to Philadelphia for Hans Lobert, who was injured and unable to play.[11]

Defeats of any kind were frustrating to McGraw, who requires the least introduction among the four contending managers. Connie Mack character-ized John best when he said, "There has only been one manager and his name is McGraw." A member of the "old Orioles," McGraw was part of the cre-ation of "inside baseball." Somewhat less admirably, the Giants skipper was a big proponent and practitioner of "judicious kicking" at umpires, which he claimed was worth 50 runs a season. McGraw emphasized pitching, defense and aggressive baserunning, preferring the hit-and-run to the sacrifice. Per-haps the best tribute to John's managerial skills in the Deadball Era is that while his teams won five pennants, only two Giant position players from the period are in the Baseball Hall of Fame. By 1916, four of those pennants had been won, but the Giants were now trying to recover from an ignominious last-place finish in 1915.[12]

McGraw's counterpart on the Phillies, Pat Moran, was not nearly as well known, but he had also learned the game from one of the nineteenth cen-tury's leading managers. While McGraw and Robinson were taught by Ned Hanlon of the old Orioles, Moran served under Frank Selee, the field leader of the Boston Beaneaters, another prominent nineteenth century National League franchise. By 1914, Pat was a backup catcher for the Phillies, then managed by Red Dooin. When Dooin was fired after the 1914 season, Phils owner William Baker allegedly planned to replace him with another Phils player. Fortunately for Pat, and ultimately for the Phillies, the players revolted at this prospect, saying Moran was the only current team member they would accept as manager.[13] Pat's immediate success in 1915 resulted in Baker sign-ing him to a multi-year contract.

Moran's contributions to the Phillies may have started long before he became manager. Supposedly, Dooin was ready to cut Grover Cleveland Alexander during spring training of 1911, but Moran, seeing Alexander's potential, talked him out of it.[14] If true, that alone would have established Pat's reputation as a judge of talent, but the Phillies manager also reportedly played a major role in the acquisitions of Whitted, Stock, Bancroft and Niehoff.[15] Moran especially excelled in recognizing and developing young pitching talent. There is no better evidence for this than the credit Moran received for the development of Eppa Rixey and Alexander (both future Hall of Famers). However, Moran's focus on the field was not limited to the pitching staff, as he stressed mental preparation and offensive and defensive fundamentals. Unlike McGraw and George Stallings, Pat did not yell at his players, believing and proving that it was possible to win while treating players fairly and like adults.[16]

While the Giants and Phils completed their series in Philadelphia, the resumption of play in Brooklyn indicated the time off was of little benefit to the Superbas. Boston went ahead 2–0 primarily through poor Dodger defense, but Brooklyn tied the game in the sixth. Things remained stalemated until the top of the eighth, when the Braves scored twice to win 4–2. Boston stroked only four hits to Brooklyn's nine, giving the Dodgers defense much to answer for. Asking the questions was Rice, who noted the first two Boston runs "were so tainted that a veteran health inspector would have feared to handle them with a pair of tongs." Feelings obviously were more positive on the Braves' side, as Flatley praised Tom Hughes' pitching along with the "team baseball," which allowed Stallings' squad to overcome its hitting deficiencies. Hughes led the National League in appearances in 1915 and would be a workhorse again in 1916.[17]

Like Phillies manager Pat Moran, George Stallings is not as well known as either Wilbert Robinson or John McGraw. This is somewhat understandable since Stallings' career record in 13 years of managing was below .500, including winning only one pennant. That pennant, however, earned him the title "Miracle Man." In 1914, he led the Braves from last place on July 4 to win the flag and sweep the heavily favored Philadelphia Athletics in the World Series. After following up with a second-place finish in 1915, Stallings' reputation as a manager was at its peak. Fiery managers have always been part of baseball, but in George's case, this was only one half of his personality. At the time of Stallings' death, Westbrook Pegler wrote that no one else in baseball had "the high gloss of gentility off the field" but "fretted so hotly during a game." George was equally creative with or without profanity. He cursed with "an aesthetic sense of rhythm, tone and power," but also used creative images without profanity, such as "he couldn't hit an elephant with a banjo." No less an expert on hot-tempered managers than Christy Mathewson said Stallings' chewing out of his players was worse than that of John McGraw.[18]

In spite of this highly combative management style, off the field Stallings was supposedly the image of a Southern gentleman. Like his 1914 World Series counterpart, Connie Mack, Stallings eschewed wearing a baseball uniform, preferring a business suit instead. Unlike Mack, however, George was hyperactive, sliding back and forth on the bench to the point that he wore right through the seat of his pants during the second game of the 1914 World Series. Mathewson, for one, felt Stallings' intense behavior was a plus, suggesting the key to his success was his "ability to keep his team at full speed continually." But there was more to George's managing than his temper; Johnny Evers (who knew something about intensity) said the Braves manager knew "more baseball than any man whom I have ever come in contact during my connection with the game."[19]

Even though the season was only two games old, one wonders how Stallings would have reacted had his team's performance been as bad as Wilbert Robinson's. Robinson, who seldom receives sufficient credit for his managerial ability, already faced his first challenge of the young season. The historical attitude toward Robbie is perhaps best summarized by John Meyers' comment in an interview with Lawrence Ritter. Meyers claimed that Casey Stengel won one more pennant than is credited in the record book, saying, "Of course, Robbie was the manager. But Robbie was just a good old soul and everything. It was Casey who kept us on our toes."[20] Meyers certainly had first-hand experience with Robinson as a manager, but the value of these comments many years later is somewhat questionable. Stengel was only 26 years old in 1916 and beginning his fourth full major league season. Regardless of Casey's contributions as a player, it is hard to believe that veteran players like Zack Wheat, Jake Daubert, Jack Coombs and Rube Marquard took direction or inspiration from Stengel, who wasn't even an everyday player.

A more balanced picture of Robinson requires going back to his playing career. One of Robbie's first managers, W.F. Prince, claimed he was a "born leader" and always "a great help to his pitcher." Ned Hanlon of the Orioles clearly recognized Robinson's leadership abilities by naming him captain in 1892. Before their celebrated breakup following the 1913 World Series, McGraw certainly depended on his rotund former teammate, especially with regard to pitching. Indeed, Robinson's ability to handle pitchers was seldom questioned, but he was unable to explain his success. This inability to provide a basis for his expertise may have something to do with the lack of respect Robbie received as a manager. Robinson's Falstaffian girth did little to help matters. When Wilbert took over the Dodgers in 1914, pitching was one of his greatest priorities, and by 1916, Robinson had both quality and quantity. This allowed the Brooklyn skipper to use a "loose rotation," pitching certain hurlers every fourth day while picking certain spots for others. At this point, Robinson also had quantity, if not quality in his everyday lineup, giving Brooklyn significant overall depth.[21]

The Saturday games marked the end of the opening series, with Boston moving to Philadelphia and the Giants to Ebbets Field. Before these series could begin, however, the first Sunday of the season intervened with its mandatory cessation of baseball hostilities. The eastern prohibition of baseball games as well as other amusements on Sunday was part of the Sabbitarian belief that sports could distract people from religious moral values. While these views had long been dominant in the United States, by 1870 a more permissive view allowing amusements, but not work, had become the norm west of the Allegheny Mountains. However, in the East, the Sabbitarian view still dominated. Although baseball owners tried unsuccessfully to maneuver around these restrictions, it took legislative action in New York (1919), then Massachusetts (1929) and finally Pennsylvania (1934) to end the ban on Sunday baseball.[22]

Unfortunately, a legislatively mandated day off was followed by another mandated by the weather. When the rain finally ceased on Tuesday, April 18, cold weather kept the Dodgers and Giants out of action. Although not much warmer in Philadelphia, the Phils and Braves began their now-abbreviated two-game series. Boston was brought down to earth as Philadelphia swept both games, beginning with a 4–0 win on April 18. This contest was a match-up between aces Grover Cleveland Alexander and Dick Rudolph, now referred to by Flatley as "the bald headed farmer of West Nyack." While Alexander's performance may have been off on Opening Day, he was now in mid-season form. He shut out the Braves, which as Nasium noted in a not very appealing metaphor, was "the best system yet invented for preventing a club from beating you to the prunes." The Phils' dominant performance in the first game was followed by a dramatic 6–5 win the next day. It was a back-and-forth affair before Philadelphia took a 6–5 lead in the bottom of the eighth, which Charles Bender made stand up in his first appearance of 1916. Afterward, the Braves left Philadelphia for an all-night train journey back to Boston and the home opener against the Dodgers.[23]

Meanwhile back in Brooklyn, the Superbas managed to finally get in the win column with a 7–3 victory against the already-faltering Giants. After poor performances against Boston, Robinson used his depth, putting Mike Mowrey and Ivan Olson at third and short, respectively. Olson was a major contributor, driving in three runs with two hits, including a bases-loaded single to break a 3–3 tie. Then Brooklyn was off to Boston to face its chief nemesis, the Boston Braves, on their home turf.[24]

The Braves faithful who welcomed home their heroes on April 20 did so at a ballpark that had not been used for a full year. Braves Field hosted its

1916 Boston Braves team picture. *From left, top*—Red Smith, Art Rico, Walt Tragesser, Hank Gowdy ("9"), Ed Reulbach ("12"); *middle*—Art Nehf, Jessee Barnes, Frank Allen, Dick Egan, Lefty Tyler, Joe Wilhoit ("10"), Zip Collins, Pete Compton, Tom Hughes; *bottom*—Sherry Magee, Pat Ragan, Fred Snodgrass, Johnny Evers, George Stallings (manager), Rabbit Maranville, Joe Connolly, Davis (*Spalding Official Baseball Guide—1917*, Library of Congress).

first game on August 18, 1915, before a crowd of more than 40,000, reported to be the largest ever to see a baseball game. Interestingly, the ballpark was only one mile from Fenway Park, the relatively new home of the Red Sox. Braves Field was intended to be "conducive to inside the park homeruns," and so it was since it took 10 years for a ball to be hit over the fence. From foul lines 402 feet away in left and 375 feet in right, the field expanded to 461 feet at the flag pole in center field and even beyond that to 542 feet to right center. In typical Deadball Era fashion, seating consisted of a covered grandstand extending past third and first base, supplemented by two bleacher sections that ended at the foul lines.[25]

Anyone who hoped a change in scenery would end Boston's dominance of Brooklyn was quickly disabused of this notion by the Braves' 8–0 victory in their April 20 home opener. Before a crowd of 8,000, the Superbas committed five errors, including three by second baseman George Cutshaw on three consecutive plays. The latter was an indication of a middle infield weakness that would be a problem for Brooklyn all season. The combination of poor defense and poor pitching by Jack Coombs put Boston ahead 7–0 after only two innings on the way to an easy win behind Jess Barnes.[26] After three straight relatively easy wins over the Dodgers, the Braves' attitude toward the Superbas seemed to become one of arrogance. The next day, in the first inning, on a bad field in bad weather in front of a bad crowd of only a few hundred, Boston's Rabbit Maranville got caught in a rundown between third and home. Instead of sliding into third, Maranville "jumped straight into Olson's breakfast" in an attempt to make him drop the ball.

This was clearly more than Olson and the Dodgers could stomach, both literally and figuratively. The ensuing fight was such that noted pacifist William Jennings Bryan reportedly would have "cried aloud with horror." Apparently no pacifist himself, umpire Charles Rigler chose an interesting method to break up the festivities when he "grabbed the excited Mr. Olson around the neck" and used him as a human "flail" to clear the "mob of angry athletes." Rigler then ejected both Olson and Maranville. Whether the incident jump-started the Superbas or not, Brooklyn pounded out two triples and a double to score five times in the sixth inning en route to a 10–3 win.[27]

While the Superbas helped the Braves open their home season, the Phillies did the same for the Giants at the Polo Grounds. The passage of time and the lack of nostalgia for the New York Giants make it difficult to remember that the Giants were the "tiffany franchise" of New York baseball during the Deadball Era. The Yankees had never enjoyed much success, while Brook-

1916 New York Giants team picture. *From left, top—* Jose Rodriguez, Duke Kelleher, Heinie Stafford, Brad Kocher, Way, Bill Ritter, Mickey Doolin, Slim Sallee, George Kelly, George Smith; *middle (staggered)—* Heinie Zimmerman, Walter Holke, Hans Lobert, Fred Anderson, Lew McCarty, Schepner, Ferdie Schupp, Pol Perritt, Buck Herzog, Jeff Tesreau, Art Fletcher, John McGraw (manager), George Burns; *seated on ground—* trainer, mascot; *front—* Dave Robertson, Rube Benton, Bill Rariden, Benny Kauff (*Spalding Official Baseball Guide—1917*, Library of Congress).

lyn's last pennant was in 1900. As the New York *Times* proclaimed in early April, "The Giants opening has always been the banner event in New York's baseball season and it promises to be the same this spring." As always, the opening would take place at the Polo Grounds, which had been newly renovated after a 1911 fire. Located in the north Harlem section of Manhattan, west of Eighth Avenue between 157th and 159th streets, the new concrete and steel structure could hold 34,000 fans. Built to "fit between Coogan's Bluff and Manhattan Field," the Giants' home ballpark had a rectangular or horseshoe shape with short foul lines and a vast center field.[28]

Although historically the Giants' home opener may have been a special day, in 1916 it was more symbolic of the frustration New York and their fans would experience all season long. After threatening to play extra innings three times in Philadelphia, the two teams did so at the Polo Grounds, going 12 innings before the Phils won, 7–6. Through six innings, it was a high-scoring game tied at six when relief pitchers George McQuillan of the Phillies and Emilio Palmero of the Giants turned the contest into a pitcher's duel that lasted until the 12th. At that point, a Gavy Cravath single drove in Dode Paskert, who then made a tremendous catch to preserve the win for Philadelphia in the bottom half of the inning. While New York fans may have felt good about their team's competitive play, they still had only one win, and another loss to the Phillies the next day confirmed the Giants' problems were real. For the second time in less than a week, Al Demaree came back to haunt his former team, and especially his former boss, allowing only two runs on three hits.[29]

After the games of April 21 the rains returned, preventing the Dodgers and Phillies from playing again until April 26, while the Giants and Braves were able to get a game in on the 25th. Unfortunately for New York, they went up against another former teammate and McGraw reject, Dick Rudolph. Although the Giants got to him for three hits and one run in the top of the first, Rudolph allowed only one hit thereafter. Pol Perritt pitched well for New York, but the three runs Boston scored were more than enough. All of the losing was clearly getting to McGraw (no doubt magnified by being reminded that he was wrong about Rudolph), who was ejected by umpire Bill Klem in the seventh inning.[30]

After another day of rain to mull over their problems, things got no better for the Giants on April 27. Jeff Tesreau, New York's only winning pitcher thus far in 1916, pitched well, but like Perritt two days earlier, was undone by a lack of offensive support in a 3–2 loss. McGraw's frustration now had infected the players as Bill Klem cleared the Giants bench in the fifth, sending nearly 15 ejectees marching off "like a pack of trained beagles." An inning later, the Giants manager earned his second ejection in as many days. Even this did not completely settle matters as Klem and McGraw, in a scene unimaginable today, reportedly continued the argument after the game and had to be restrained from fighting. No doubt the Braves enjoyed every minute of the affair as they used good defense, aggressive baserunning and the pitching of "Lefty" Tyler to sweep the short series.[31]

While the Braves and Giants had been able to play one game, the Dodgers and Phillies were rained out three straight times in Philadelphia. This meant Brooklyn would face Alexander when play resumed on April 26. Larry Cheney started for the Superbas and acquitted himself admirably over the first six innings in a game tied at one, with both scores surprisingly coming on home runs by Dode Paskert and Ivy Olson. In the top of the seventh, catcher Otto Miller's squeeze bunt scored Mowrey, opening the flood gates as Brooklyn scored five times. When the Phils rallied against Cheney in the bottom of the seventh, Robinson brought in Marquard to retire the last batter. In the bottom of the ninth, Marquard, whose problems were attributed to a lack of self-confidence, faced Paskert and Gavy Cravath with two on and only one out. Although it was not without some drama, the Brooklyn left-hander struck out both, regaining some confidence in closing out a 6–3 victory. Probably no one was surprised, but everyone was disappointed when it rained again the next day, meaning, Brooklyn would finish the road trip playing only four of eight games. In fact, the teams were lucky to complete the last game on April 28, as it rained "incessantly after the fifth inning." Brooklyn ultimately prevailed, 5–3, as Jack Coombs bested his former A's teammate, Charles Bender.[32] While beating the defending champions twice was obviously important, solid performances by Marquard and Coombs were also good signs for the Superbas.

At the conclusion of these rain-shortened series, Brooklyn returned to New York City to visit the Polo Grounds on April 29, while the Phillies traveled to Boston. The Dodgers continued to play well as they took three of four from the Giants. Although it was little solace to John McGraw and company, they at least won their second game. The opener lasted 12 innings and three hours as Brooklyn came from behind to take the lead in the top of the ninth, only to see the Giants tie it again in the bottom half. The Superbas finally prevailed, 5–4. When the series resumed on Monday, the first of May, the Dodgers won their fifth straight, 8–4, thereby moving into first place. Having been successful with Coombs' recent spot start, Robby tried to do the same with Nap Rucker, but the aging left-hander lasted only three innings. Fortunately, Coombs showed his versatility by coming back on two days rest to pitch the last six innings. For New York, it represented the Giants' eighth straight loss, putting them even deeper into the cellar. Both streaks ended the next day, however, as Jeff Tesreau stopped Brooklyn, 2–1, on three hits in only the Giants' second victory of 1916. Unfortunately, Tesreau could not pitch every day, and New York dropped the series finale, 6–4, in ten innings, after rallying from a 4–0 deficit. The heroes for Brooklyn were George Cutshaw, who drove in the winning run in the 10th, and outfielder Jim Johnston, who earlier in the ninth threw out the potential winning run at the plate.[33]

While the Dodgers and the Giants headed in different directions, the Braves and Phillies split a four-game series in Boston. Pat Moran opened the set on April 29 with his ace, Grover Cleveland Alexander, while Stallings countered with Tom Hughes. The Phils hit Hughes early and often, scoring five runs on 12 hits, more than enough for Alexander. Boston had lost three straight to Philadelphia, but the Braves bounced back to win the next two games by scores of 5–2 and 4–2. Stallings' decision not to match Rudolph against Alexander proved wise, as the Boston ace held the Phillies to only four hits in winning the second game. In the third contest on May 2, the Phils actually led 2–0 heading to the bottom of the eighth before the Braves rallied for the win, 4–2. In what was to become a pattern, Tom Hughes closed the game for the Braves, striking out Bancroft, Paskert and Cravath in the ninth. Unfortunately for Boston, the off-day prior to the last game on May 3 meant another start for Alexander. He shut the Braves out, 3–0, on six hits, driving in two of the three runs himself in his third win over Boston in the season's first month. With that, both teams were off to New York, Philadelphia to Brooklyn while the Braves visited the Polo Grounds and the rapidly sinking Giants.[34]

Since the Phils played in Boston and then visited Brooklyn before heading west, they would play 21 straight road games before returning home. The two series in New York followed the early-season patterns as the Dodgers continued to dominate Philadelphia, while the Giants continued to lose. Perhaps thinking as much with his heart as his head, John McGraw turned to Christy Mathewson to open the series against the Braves on May 4. It was Mathewson's first start of his 17th season in the majors, but the old magic was gone as Boston scored four times in the first inning. No one could accuse the Giants of quitting, however, since they battled back to tie the game on Fred Merkle's ninth-inning home run. But much like New York's other efforts to date, it was all for naught as Hank Gowdy singled in the winning run in the 10th. Once again, Tom Hughes excelled in relief for the Braves. Things got no better on May 6, as New York took a 5–2 lead against Rudolph, only to lose, 7–6. After these two difficult losses and a Sunday off, the Giants went quietly on May 8, losing the last game of the series, 6–2. With a 2–13 record as the Giants began their first western trip, it was hard to imagine a worse start for a team trying to recover from last year's last-place finish. Facing New York now were 13 games in the West, followed by eight in Boston and Philadelphia, against whom they were a combined 1–9. The Braves, on the other hand, left for Chicago in a much better frame of mind with a 10–5 record, leaving them only ½ game behind the league-leading Dodgers.[35]

Like Boston, Brooklyn left for the West in good spirits, coming off a three-game, rain-shortened sweep of the Phils. The series opened and closed the same way, with "Wheezer" Dell, who would win only eight games all season, pitching a shutout. First, Dell blanked Philadelphia, 1–0, on three hits in the May 4 opener. After a rainout on Friday, a big Saturday crowd, estimated at 22,000, saw the Superbas win, 3–2, in eleven innings. George Cutshaw sent Brooklyn fans home happy with "the freakest home run ever seen at Ebbets Field." Leading off the 11th, Cutshaw hit a line drive down the right-field line that had all the earmarks of bouncing off the wall. Instead, it hit a hard spot near the foul line and bounced over the wall for a home run. (In 1916, a ball hit into the stands on a bounce was a home run.) Supposedly, Cutshaw "crossed the plate amid a storm of laughter," including that of umpire "Lord" Byron, but understandably not the Phillies.[36]

Any Brooklyn fan who thought they had now seen everything was in for a surprise on Monday when "Wheezer" Dell pitched his second straight shutout, this time besting Alexander, 2–0, allowing just four singles. All told, the Phils wasted some good pitching, scoring only two runs in three games on just 15 hits.[37] The three-game sweep left Philadelphia at 8–8 and in fifth place, three games behind the first-place Dodgers. Brooklyn, on the other hand, after a 1–3 start, left home having won nine of its last ten, including a 5–0 record against the defending champions. Wilbert Robinson's shakeup of his lineup and effective use of his pitching staff had paid dividends.

So far in 1916, the eastern teams had traveled only between Boston and Philadelphia, but now they headed halfway or more across the country by means that were neither pleasant nor quick. Today, it is hard to visualize the virtual monopoly the railroad had on domestic travel during the Deadball Era. Before World War I, some 98 percent of all inter-city travel in the United States was by railroad, a dominance never exceeded, not even by the automobile.[38] Interestingly, the railroad system hit its maximum capacity in 1916, with more than 254,000 of route miles. Some 66 years later, in 1982, the Amtrak system consisted of only 23,500 miles.[39] Whether by design or not, all four teams began their first western journey from New York City, which gave them a choice between the New York Central and the Pennsylvania Railroad. Taking the New York Central meant riding the Twentieth Century on what was called the "water-level route," first heading north to Albany, and then west through New York state on the way to Chicago. The Pennsylvania Railroad's Broadway Limited, on the other hand, traveled from Newark to Philadelphia and then west through Pennsylvania, Ohio and Indiana on the way to the Windy City.[40] Although the "water-level route" was somewhat longer (978 miles to 909), both took between 18 to 20 hours.[41]

Although both alternatives were no doubt state of the art, it was far from a perfect means of transportation. Expressions such as "sway and bounce" and "clatter and roar" in an atmosphere of "dust, cinders, and wind" probably gives some sense of the experience. Air quality, or the lack thereof, was a major problem since the only source of ventilation was the windows, but opening them led not only to dust and cinders, but also smoke and partially condensed steam from the engine.[42] Unlike the average passenger who sat upright all night, at least the players rode on Pullman cars with heat, hot water, lights and toilets, along with sleeping facilities. Pullman cars typically accommodated 24 sleepers in a combination of upper and lower berths that folded into the wall and ceiling and converted into seats during the day. Bed time resulted in "minor pandemonium," as passengers had to avoid the porters making up the beds while making their own nocturnal preparations. Even after the berths were prepared, there was the challenge of getting in or out of an upper berth while wearing nothing but a nightshirt. The mind boggles at the thought of Wilbert Robinson attempting such a maneuver, but his seniority, if not his girth, doubtlessly entitled him to a lower berth. The difference between upper and lower berths was not limited to comfort or privacy. In one trip in 1924, Wild Bill Donovan graciously allowed George Weiss to take the lower berth. Tragically, Donovan was killed in the ensuing train wreck.[43]

Of the four eastern teams, the Phillies had the longest trip, journeying to baseball's western-most outpost in St. Louis. Pat Moran had multiple reasons to be unhappy. His team's 8–8 record, losing five of its last six and a 0–5 mark against Brooklyn, were chief among them. In St. Louis, the Phils played one of the Deadball Era's worst teams in one of the period's worst ballparks. Only four years from being abandoned, Robison Field was Major League Baseball's last wooden ball park, home to the only National League franchise that failed to win a pennant in the Deadball Era.[44] Although the Cards must have seemed like the perfect cure for the Phillies' woes, it certainly didn't start out that way as St. Louis won the first two games, 9–4 and 4–3, on May 10 and 11. Having lost five straight, not to mention seven of the last eight, Pat Moran shook up his batting order. Davy Bancroft moved from second to leadoff, while Milt Stock dropped to third and George Whitted moved to the fifth hole. Finally Fred Luderus, who was hitting only .206, was demoted to the seventh spot, replacing Bert Niehoff, who moved up to the second position. Also helpful was the return of catcher Bill Killefer to the starting lineup. The moves paid immediate dividends as the Phils won the series finale in 10 innings, even though Alexander had to come in to finish the game.[45]

Leaving St. Louis behind, Philadelphia moved east to Cincinnati for a four-game series that began on May 13, with Alexander shutting out the Reds on three hits. Clearly now moving in the right direction, the Phils proceeded to sweep the remaining three games. Back on the "rattlers," Moran's men headed further east to Pittsburgh for a series shortened to three games on account of cold weather. Alexander again opened the proceedings on May 18 with a shutout, this time a four-hitter. Although Philadelphia lost the next day to end its six-game winning streak, the Phils took the final game on May 20 behind Al Demaree's five-hitter before moving on to Chicago. After an 0–2 start, the Phillies were now 7–3 on the trip, and the team did not let up in Chicago, taking three out of four, coming from behind in each of its wins.[46]

Having completed a highly successful 10–4 western swing, the Phils had to be in a much more positive frame of mind as they boarded the train on May 24 for the long ride back home for a rematch with their early-season nemesis, the Dodgers. The Phillies had found their offense on the trip. After batting .245 as a team beforehand, they improved their overall average by more than 30 points away from Baker Bowl and its friendly right-field wall. Especially noteworthy was the clutch hitting of Niehoff as well as that of Paskert and Cravath, who both hit over .400. This more than offset the struggles of Bancroft, Whitted and Luderus, all of whom averaged below .200 while away from home. The pitching, of course, featured Alexander, who had three victories, including two of his signature shutouts.[47]

Unlike the Phillies, the Dodgers headed west playing well and in first place. The first stop was Cincinnati, where Wilbert Robinson and his crew competed at Redland Field, a ballpark built in 1912 on a site that had housed playing fields since 1884.[48] Like the Cardinals, the Reds were consistently a second-division ball club. In a pattern that would prevail throughout the western swing, the Superbas played .500 ball in Cincinnati, splitting the first two games on May 10 and 11 before the finale on May 12 was rained out. Tom Rice had apparently been promoting the Dodgers in the press box, since one Cincinnati writer noted "the well known authority of the Brooklyn *Eagle*" no longer had to use his long list of excuses, which "extend from Boston to St. Louis and back again."[49]

As the Dodgers moved on to St. Louis, injuries began to mount up as catchers Lew McCarty and John Meyers were on the sidelines, soon followed by Ivy Olson, who badly sprained his ankle in the May 13, 2–1 loss to the Cards. In spite of a depleted lineup, Brooklyn won two of the next three to earn its second straight series split. The second loss on May 16 was especially frustrating since it included a bad call by umpire Bill Klem and a poor performance by Rube Marquard. Having split the first six games of the trip, the Dodgers left St. Louis for Chicago, where they lost the first two to the Cubs on May 17 and 18. According to Rice, the problem was offense, since Brooklyn hadn't scored more than four runs in any of the last eleven games. However, the 1916 Dodgers were a resilient group, and rebounded to win the last two games of the series. After playing eight straight games, the Superbas split into two groups on Sunday, May 21, in order to play two exhibition games in different places while en route to Pittsburgh. Fortunately for the fatigued players (but not so fortunately for the owners), Monday's game against the Pirates became an unscheduled day of rest thanks to Mother Nature. In Pittsburgh, the Dodgers won the first two of the now three-game series, 6–0 and 3–2. Although Rice felt the 5–0 defeat in the May 25 series finale was a bad loss, everyone had to be happy Brooklyn had finished the first western trip with a winning record (7–6). Before arriving home, however, the Superbas had a date, or more specifically, four dates in Philadelphia with the red-hot Phillies.[50]

Like the Dodgers, George Stallings and his Boston Braves left the East in a good frame of mind for their trip west. Having won three in a row and five of their last six, the Braves headed for Chicago in second place, just a half game behind Brooklyn. Unlike their eastern counterparts, however, Boston didn't enjoy a successful trip. The first stop was Chicago for a three-game series in Weeghman Park (today's Wrigley Field), at the time hosting its first year of National League baseball. A "furious west wind" that blew throughout the May 10 contest, an 11–10 Braves win, may explain the uncharacteristic Deadball Era game that saw 26 hits. Tom Hughes came on in relief of Art Nehf in the fifth, and though he was hit hard, preserved the Boston lead. The two teams split the last two contests, the Cubs beating Rudolph behind their ace, "Hippo" Vaughn, while the Braves won the finale behind the pitching and hitting of Lefty Tyler.[51]

Having made the long trip to Chicago, the Braves headed back east to Pittsburgh. Although the series was slated for three games, cold weather wiped out the last one, which may have been a good thing since the Pirates won the games of May 13 and 15, 5–3 and 8–7. Now 2–3 on the trip, Boston made the relatively short journey to Cincinnati to meet the Reds, who had just been swept by the Phillies. The Braves easily won the May 17 opener behind Tom Hughes' four-hitter, as he made a nice comeback from a rare poor outing against Pittsburgh. However, the Reds swept the remainder of the four-game series, including a defeat of Rudolph in the last game, leaving Boston at 3–6 since leaving the East. The poor performance against lowly Cincinnati was a bad omen for future match-ups with the Reds. With that sour taste in their mouths, the Braves moved on to St. Louis, where they could do no better than a split after winning the first two. The series featured another strong performance by Tom Hughes and Dick Rudolph's second straight loss.[52]

Even members of the Braves with personalities less volatile than Stallings and Evers had to be frustrated as they settled down for the long train ride back to Boston. Of special concern were the hitters, who weren't producing. When the Braves won five of six before leaving the East, they hit .277 as a team. For the entire western trip, this norm had dropped to .261, but in losing five of the last seven, it had fallen even further, to .215. Stallings had to be concerned about Evers, who hit only .216 on the trip. Sherwood Magee's absence due to injury was also a problem, as his replacement, Pete Compton, was batting a microscopic .120. The train ride home would get them to Boston at 7:00 A.M. for a May 26 game against the Giants hours later.[53] It wasn't the best way to prepare for a very different Giants team from the one that left New York in last place.

As opposed to the other eastern teams, New York headed west with the more modest goal of simply winning a few games. Few teams ever needed a change of scenery or benefited from one more. Since their trip started at the closest western city, Pittsburgh, the Giants actually opened one day earlier than the others, on May 9 at Forbes Field. After six innings of the first game, the Giants trailed, 4–2, suggesting nothing had changed but the scenery. However, New York rallied for three in the sixth and four in the seventh on the way to a 13–5 win, with Christy Mathewson coming on to finish the game. A lineup change of note was the insertion of Dave Robertson in right field, who had four of the Giants' 16 hits. Quickly showing this win was no fluke, New York swept the series, winning, 7–1, and then pulling off two come-from-behind victories on May 11 and 12. This was clearly not the team the Pirates expected, causing Pittsburgh *Press* writer Charles Doyle to wonder, "How on earth did such a team of hitters ever lose 13 out of 15?"[54]

After completing the sweep of the Pirates, John McGraw and his men enjoyed a renewed sense of self-confidence as they boarded their train for a three-game series in Chicago. Although the series was shortened by weather, their confidence continued to build as they won the two games played on May 14 and 15. Along with the hitting, New York's pitching had improved, a clear sign the Giants were now playing "real baseball of the McGraw school." After losing the last game to cold weather, New York was off to St. Louis, having won six straight, and was only five games under .500. It seemed that little could stop the Giants now and certainly not the Cardinals, as New York swept the May 17–20 series, winning every kind of game imaginable. McGraw started the old master, Christy Mathewson, in the finale, and "Big Six" was indeed masterful, allowing only one run on six hits. Finally close to .500, the Giants rode the rails south to Cincinnati, the last stop on the western portion of their trip.[55]

At this point, a rainout was probably cause for a victory celebration by the opposition, and that was all the Reds could manage, falling 11–1, 4–3 and

6–1 in the three games that followed. Having taken all 13 contests from the western teams, the Giants left Cincinnati for Boston on May 24 and a showdown with their co-tenants in third place. It's hard to imagine how two teams could have gone in such different directions on one road trip. Boston headed west just barely out of first place, but suffered through a 5–8 trip to return home tied for third place with the Giants, who had risen from last to third.[56]

To make matters even more challenging for the Braves, they had endured a long overnight train ride to get to the opening game of the series on May 26. Things got off to a bad start when Giants leadoff batter George Burns belted Tyler's first pitch for a triple, the first of 14 New York hits that produced 12 runs for their 14th straight triumph, a 12–1 win. Understandably, McGraw was feeling his oats, "howling his head off" on the coaching lines. Boston may have been more rested for the doubleheader the next day but fared no better, losing 4–3 and 2–1, as the Giants' winning streak reached 16. Now ensconced in second place, the New York skipper and his men enjoyed a restful and blissful Sabbath before finishing off the sweep of the Braves, 3–0. To make things even more enjoyable for McGraw, Christy Mathewson pitched a four-hit shutout for the Giants' first 1916 victory over Dick Rudolph. By winning their 17th straight road game, the Giants had surpassed the Washington Senators' 1912 record of 16 straight road wins and were closing in on Providence's (a National League franchise at the time) 1884 record of 20 straight wins, both home and away. There was, however, no rest for John McGraw's club as they boarded a train for New York City to catch another train to Philadelphia for a 10:00 A.M. opening game of a Decoration Day doubleheader.[57]

Before the Giants arrived, however, the Dodgers and Phillies met in Philadelphia after both had completed successful western trips. Brooklyn still held first place, largely due to a 5–0 record against the surging Phils. All of that changed on May 26 in the first of the four-game set, as Philadelphia prevailed, 1–0, ending for the moment at least the Brooklyn hex and the Superbas' possession of first place. Although both hurlers were hit hard, the game was a pitching duel between Smith and Alexander. In spite of being consistently in trouble, Alexander pitched his fifth shutout, avenging his two earlier losses to Brooklyn.[58]

The reversal of the Superbas' hex over the Phils and Philadelphia's hold on first place were both short-lived, as Brooklyn won the next three games, beginning with a doubleheader sweep the next day, 8–3 and 6–0. Winning both games of the doubleheader meant the Dodgers would finish the overall trip with a winning record and in first place. The first contest began with what Rice called Brooklyn's "daily freak." In this case, the usually reliable Jeff Pfeffer walked the first three batters, all of whom scored without the benefit of a hit. Brooklyn chipped away but still trailed, 3–2, in the ninth, where a combination of three Phillies errors and five Dodgers hits led to an 8–3 triumph. In the second game, Wilbert Robinson went with one of his spot starters, Jack Coombs, who hadn't pitched since May 3. Successful "spotting" of pitchers like Coombs and Marquard was crucial to Brooklyn's pennant hopes since it provided the Superbas more pitching depth. In this case, Robinson picked the spot brilliantly as "Colby Jack" shut the Phils out on four hits. Coombs had to hold on to a 1–0 lead until the eighth when the Brooklyn offense erupted for four runs on five hits. Brooklyn won the last game of the series and the road trip, 3–2, behind Larry Cheney's four-hit pitching, as the Phillies wasted an effective performance by Eppa Rixey. If three straight losses weren't bad enough, the Phils had two games the next day against the express train called the New York Giants.[59]

Brooklyn, on the other hand, was in good spirits as they began the train ride home for a month-long homestand. What was most likely on their minds wasn't the future but the achievements of the past three weeks. By posting a winning record in the West and following that by winning three of four from the defending champion Phillies, Brooklyn was off to a solid start. Jake Daubert, who recorded a .328 average away from home, and Zack Wheat, who hit at a .343 clip, made key offensive contributions on the trip. Mostly, however, it had been the pitching that had put the superb in Superbas, especially the performances of Cheney and Pfeffer.

Equally impressive through the end of May was the Superbas' dominance of Philadelphia, taking eight of the first nine. Offensively, Brooklyn was averaging almost four runs a game against the Phils, with a team batting average of .292. This included two victories over Alexander and at least one victory against each of the Phils' regular starters. Dodger pitchers, on the other hand, had limited Philadelphia to less than two runs per game and a team batting average of .203. Improbably, Wheezer Dell had not only beaten the Phillies twice, he had yet to allow an earned run. Especially noteworthy was that Gavy Cravath, one of the keys to the Phils' offense, was hitting a pathetic .074 against Brooklyn compared to .287 against the rest of the league.[60]

While the Phillies licked their wounds and no doubt wondered what they had to do to beat Brooklyn, the Giants endured their long overnight trip from Boston to Philadelphia. Having lost three straight to the Dodgers and faced with the streaking Giants, Pat Moran went with Al Demaree in the first game, with his ace Grover Cleveland Alexander waiting in the wings. Demaree and his adversary, Pol Perritt, dominated the contest, which was scoreless for the first seven innings. New York almost broke through in its half of the seventh when Fred Merkle hit one out of the playing field, yet failed to avoid Claude

Cooper's glove. In what Nasium described as "one of the greatest catches we have ever witnessed," Cooper reached into the bleachers to rob Merkle and the Giants. Having dodged that bullet, Demaree finished a brilliant performance, allowing only one run on six hits. When the Phils broke through against Perritt for five runs in the bottom of the eighth, the game and the winning streak were over. With Alexander set for the second game, the popular view had to be that New York would soon have a new streak of the losing variety. However, the Giants gave Alexander "the most severe trouncing he has ever received in his young life" in a 10–2 rout. After all this excitement in one day, the rest of the series was anticlimactic, with the two teams splitting 4–2 victories, leaving New York in second place and Philadelphia in third.[61]

Team	Wins	Losses
Brooklyn	22	14
New York	21	15
Philadelphia	21	17
Boston	18	19
Cincinnati	20	23
Chicago	19	23
Pittsburgh	18	22
St. Louis	18	24

With the Phils' victory in the last game on June 1, the Giants ended their road trip with an incredible 19–2 record. Starting out firmly in last place, they were now on the verge of going from worst to first in about three weeks. During the winning streak, the New Yorkers raised their team batting average some 50 points, and as a team they were pushing .300 (.290). One of McGraw's key moves in reversing his team's fortunes was inserting Robertson in the lineup in place of Edd Rousch. Robertson had been a major plus with his bat and his glove. Also important were the contributions of the pitching staff, especially Christy Mathewson, who had apparently regained his old form. In any event, like the Dodgers before them, the Giants took the train back to New York in high spirits. John McGraw and his men would now open a long homestand against the same teams they had just beaten 13 straight times. Logically it seemed they would continue their dominant performance, but logic had little to do with baseball in 1916.[62]

CHAPTER III

"A new order was at hand."

As in the National League, the American League season began with blaring newspaper headlines, such as "Baseball Comes Into Its Own Again Today" and "The Great National Game Is Now On." In Boston, there was the added anticipation of the Red Sox title defense. The weather, however, was unfavorable, as early morning rain gave way to chilly temperatures and overcast skies that continued until game time. But the 5,831 fans would not be disappointed with the festivities nor the game. Among those in attendance were Massachusetts Governor Samuel McCall and Boston Mayor James Curley, as well as 300 members of the Royal Rooters, Boston's renowned fan club. They provided a band, as did the Red Sox.[1]

Fenway Park is one of only two ballparks that currently houses the same team it did in 1916 (Wrigley Field is the other). The home of the Red Sox, however, was distinctly different at that time. First, there was no Green Monster in left field; instead, a 25-foot-high fence kept people from watching the game for free from the roofs of adjoining buildings. Additionally, in front of the left-field wall was a slope that graded upward as high as 10 feet near the fence. Designed to give fans in left field a better view, the slope quickly became an advantage to the Red Sox, whose outfielders, especially Duffy Lewis, learned how to play it. Another new innovation at Fenway included both home and visitor dressing rooms. This ended the practice of visiting teams having to dress at their hotel and then walk in parade-like fashion to the ballpark. Most facilities had become double-deckers, but Fenway had just one tier when it was built in 1912. Seventeen walls gave the park an odd shape, similar to today. The asymmetrical design of the ballpark was due to then-owner John Taylor's unwillingness to buy the end corners of the land that would hold Fenway Park.[2]

Opening Day festivities began when the two teams marched out to the flagpole in center field and hoisted the American flag. Minutes later, manager Bill Carrigan and his team were presented with an eight-foot horseshoe of roses before Mayor Curley threw out the first pitch. Babe Ruth was on the hill for Boston, with Clarence "Tilly" Walker replacing the traded Tris Speaker and Charles "Chick" Shorten substituting for the injured Duffy Lewis. The Red Sox were probably looking forward to an easy victory, but the Athletics had Joe Bush, a promising youngster, on the mound. He matched zeros with Ruth through five innings. In the bottom of the sixth, though, Bush's defense failed him, a problem that would plague the Athletics all season. Third baseman Charlie Pick's errant throw bounded past first baseman Stuffy McInnis to the stands, sending Hoblitzell to second. He then scored on Shorten's single to left field. Pick would go on to make 42 errors during the season, a mark in futility never equaled by another third baseman. His .899 fielding percentage would also be a record until it was matched by Boston's Butch Hobson in 1978.[3]

Two more Philadelphia miscues helped the Red Sox load the bases with nobody out in the seventh, but they scored only once. Trailing 2–0 in the ninth, the Athletics reached Ruth for a run, and had runners on second and third with one out, forcing Carrigan to go to George Foster, who worked out of the jam. Boston was 1–0, and so was Ruth, who allowed only one run on four hits in 8⅓ innings. Walker's eagerly anticipated debut in center field in place of Speaker was a good one. He fielded all four of his chances, displayed a strong arm and made good contact, going 1-for-4 at the plate.[4]

Unlike the fans in Boston, Chicago "bugs" (a Deadball Era expression for fans) didn't have to worry about the weather. Charles

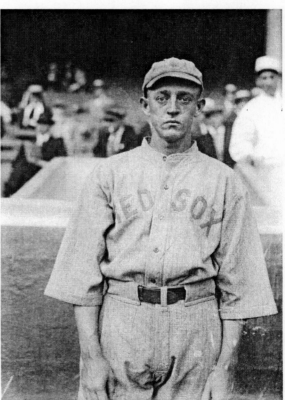

Tilly Walker was in the toughest of tough spots by trying to replace Tris Speaker, but he did little early in the 1916 season to ease the situation (George Bain Collection, Library of Congress).

Comiskey's bank account clearly benefited, as the total gate in the opener against Detroit exceeded 31,000 spectators. Concerns of a long-standing jinx against the Tigers (Chicago had lost 31 of its last 44 to Detroit) clearly hadn't dampened the fans' spirits. They were entertained by two bands while turning out in full force to watch pre-game warm-ups. But the White Sox's problems with Detroit continued on April 12, as Tigers pitcher Harry Coveleski starred on the mound and at the plate in a 4–0 Opening Day victory.[5]

Reb Russell was on the hill for Chicago and got into early trouble by walking Donie Bush to start the game. Ty Cobb doubled, and both runs scored on Bobby Veach's triple to center field. Sam Crawford's sacrifice fly then scored Veach. The Tigers had a 3–0 lead, which was plenty for Harry Coveleski, who pitched a three-hit shutout. In fact, the hurler topped the White Sox hit total by collecting four, while Russell didn't make it out of the second inning. The victory apparently left the Tigers feeling good about themselves, as the Detroit *News* reported, "It seldom has happened that the Tigers have shown as much satisfaction over winning an opener. They are convinced that they can cop the pennant if they keep on their toes and so decisive a victory over the one club they believe they have to beat gave them a lot of ginger."[6]

Insult was added to injury for the fans, many of whom exited the stadium with their clothes ruined. The Chicago owner recently had the seats at Comiskey Park painted green, and much of the paint had yet to dry, leaving it on the spectators' clothes by game's end. Although it was only one contest, the optimism of White Sox fans had apparently taken a hit. I.E. Sanborn of the Chicago *Daily Tribune* wrote that the large throng who "went out to Comiskey Park yesterday prepared to see a christening and came away as long faced as if they had attended a wake."[7]

In his White Sox debut, Terry combined with Weaver to play a strong left side of the infield, which may have been the lone bright spot. Fortunately for the fans' morale, the Pale Hose bats came alive during the remaining three games of the series. The Tigers' George Cunningham didn't enjoy his major league debut, losing 7–2 to Chicago, which was sandwiched between two other Detroit losses, 8–6, and 9–4. Suddenly, the White Sox were 3–1, with the offense coming from across the board. Chicago's early 1916 dominance of the Tigers encouraged White Sox fans to believe the jinx was over.

Meanwhile, the Red Sox were winning methodically and with pitching. Ernie Shore and George Foster followed Ruth's success with 8–2 and 2–1 victories for a three-game sweep of Philadelphia. When Boston opened up a series against the Senators on April 17, Carl Mays, who struggled with injuries in 1915, was supposed to be on the hill. Once again his health was an issue, as he was diagnosed with tonsillitis. With Mays expected to miss two weeks,

Ruth came back to oppose the great Walter Johnson. The early-season duel didn't match the electrifying contests they would have later on, as Ruth easily bested Johnson, 5–1. Throughout April, the Red Sox offense struggled. Following the five-run output against Johnson, Boston failed to score more than three runs in eight of its remaining 11 games that month. The Red Sox hit just .229 in April, far below the output of the Tigers (.269) and White Sox (.247). The team clearly struggled without Speaker in the lineup, as Boston used five different combinations of 3-4-5 hitters and four different cleanup men in April. Clarence Walker, Speaker's replacement, started just the first two games of the month due to a bad cold.[8]

Duffy Lewis had missed Opening Day due to his spring training wrist injury but returned to see most of the activity in center field. With the Red Sox struggling to find an identity for the middle of their lineup, Carrigan dropped Hooper, a prototypical leadoff hitter, to the third spot, where he could team with new cleanup hitter Dick Hoblitzell, who was off to a hot

1916 Boston Red Sox team picture. *From left, top* — Sad Sam Jones, Heinie Wagner, Del Gainer, Vean Gregg, Sam Agnew, Jack Barry, Olaf Henriksen, Weldon Wyckoff, Green (trainer); *middle* — Jimmy Walsh, Harry Hooper, Rube Foster, Pinch Thomas, Bill Carrigan, Tilly Walker, Hal Janvrin, Hick Cady, Everett Scott, Larry Gardner; *front* — Dick Hoblitzell, Herb Pennock, Ernie Shore, Babe Ruth, Glennan (mascot), Carl Mays, Chick Shorten, Dutch Leonard, Mike McNally (National Baseball Hall of Fame Library, Cooperstown, N.Y.).

start. Olaf Henriksen took Hooper's place, leading off in the new batting order. Boston went 3–4 to close the month and let its early-season lead evaporate. However, because of their pitching, the Red Sox finished April tied with the Tigers (9–6) for first place. Ruth, who went 4–0 that month, was starting to emerge as the ace, and Leonard was even better. He pitched two shutout victories and a no-decision in which he allowed one earned run in seven innings.

Carrigan was one of the major reasons Boston's pitching staff excelled. Arguably his biggest strength as a field general was handling hurlers. That ability may have been in part why Carrigan was given the job, since as the team's catcher, he had already worked closely with the staff. Additionally, Bill had a good baseball mind, having learned from the six managers he played under with the Red Sox. One of the most difficult aspects of the situation Carrigan faced was managing players that the week before were his teammates. But then-owner Jimmy McAleer clearly thought a very even-handed Carrigan would be able to handle the transition with ease. Years later, Freb Lieb said, "Rough wasn't the type of man who would stand for cliques and factions on his club. If any players wanted to continue their feuds Bill banged together the heads of the feudists." His nickname, "Rough," came from the aggressive manner for which he played the game, and there were even rumors he fined pitchers a lofty $25 when they refused to dust off a batter. However, Carrigan said this roughhouse reputation was exaggerated since it was simply the way the game was played at the time.[9]

Another positive opinion expressed about Carrigan was his ability to run a fair clubhouse. To that end, his first rule mandated that even the owner wasn't allowed in the clubhouse for fear of a player receiving two opinions. Additionally, during baseball's war with the Federal League, Bill forced owner Joe Lannin to put a deadline on when players had to choose between the two leagues. This even-handed approach could have been one of the things that led to the Speaker deal. Other members of the Red Sox were clearly sick of his salary antics, and Carrigan may not have wanted them to get the impression Speaker was being treated differently. There was also some thought Rough didn't get sufficient credit for Boston's good play because they had the best players. When the Speaker sale appeared to tighten the American League race, it put Carrigan in a position where he was more likely to receive credit if Boston's success continued.[10]

When it came to managing the pitching staff, Rough was certainly ahead of his time. During an era when the only type of player was one who played every day, the Boston manager allowed his pitchers to have personal catchers. He even served in that capacity for Dutch Leonard. It was Carrigan who helped rookies like Leonard, Ruth, Shore and Mays emerge into stars quickly.

He was Ruth's roommate on the road and paid his salary in allowances to curtail the Babe's wild nightlife. Carrigan also sometimes roomed with Leonard, simply because he pitched better in that arrangement. As long as a pitcher had control, Bill wasn't a heavy-handed manager, focusing instead on developing their best stuff.[11]

Boston's final full series in April was against the Yankees, and the Red Sox took two of three to gain a first-place tie. When Dutch Leonard took the mound on April 28 in the rubber game, there were accusations of bean balls, and at one point, Les Nunamaker hurled his bat at Leonard. The game was no less dramatic. Lewis hit his only homer of the season in the ninth inning, a two-run shot to tie the contest, and his groundout won it for the Red Sox in the 11th. The Tigers (9–6) rebounded nicely from their slow start against the White Sox to tie Boston at the end of April. Detroit went 8–2 to close the month despite struggling with injuries to Cobb, Crawford and Bush, all important members of the lineup. Still, the Tigers got the job done with their bats, hitting .269. This was important because even though the pitching staff didn't blow up, it didn't excel either.[12]

After its series in Comiskey Park, Detroit traveled to Cleveland for four games with the Indians that provided plenty of drama. The Tigers, who were hopeful the Speaker trade would help them overcome Boston, saw firsthand what the Red Sox had lost. On April 16, almost 24,000 showed up at Cleveland's League Park, and that didn't include the nearly 8,000 turned away. Speaker, who hit .386 in April, had three hits, an RBI, and saved two runs on separate plays with his defense as the Indians rallied to win, 4–3, in 10 innings. The drama continued the following day when the Tigers' Harry Coveleski refused to pitch against his brother, Stanley, who was on the mound for the Indians. Harry reportedly said to manager Hughie Jennings, "This boy is my brother, and he's trying to make good in the big leagues. If any other Detroit pitcher can beat him, it's all right of course. But I don't want to be the fellow to do it, and to be advertised in that way all over the country." Rallying from his poor debut, Cunningham filled in nobly, allowing just one run in 12 innings as the Tigers won, 3–1.[13]

Coveleski took the mound the following day, and despite his only poor start of April, the Tigers won again. The Jungaleers then went back to Detroit for their home opener against Chicago. Ban Johnson was on hand for the festivities, and Frank Navin had flowers and bunting in place as well as four bands. Detroit Mayor Oscar Marx threw out the first pitch to former Tigers catcher Charlie Bennett, whose career ended when he lost both legs in a railroad accident. The game itself didn't lack for excitement. Coveleski, again on the mound, allowed one run in eight innings but had to settle for a no-decision, as the White Sox's Mel Wolfgang shut the Tigers out for eight frames.

Early in 1916, Harry Coveleski (left) showed the season wouldn't lack for drama, refusing to pitch against his brother, Stanley (National Baseball Hall of Fame Library, Cooperstown, N.Y.).

Bernie Boland pitched a scoreless ninth for Detroit and received the win when Veach and Heilmann drove in the tying and winning runs in the ninth inning.[14]

During this series, Ty Cobb and Sam Crawford fell under the weather. The teams split the next two games, with the Tigers winning the first despite accusations that White Sox pitcher Dave Danforth was doctoring the baseball. Pitcher Red Faber (9 innings, 2 runs) and catcher Ray Schalk (3 RBIs) were the keys for Chicago's win in the third game. Detroit sent Coveleski back for the finale, and he was again phenomenal, allowing just one earned run in a 4–2 victory. Harry Heilmann remained hot at the plate with two hits. In addition to losing the series, the White Sox lost catcher Schalk to an ankle injury. It was unclear how long he would be out of the lineup.[15]

Shortly thereafter, Donie Bush joined Cobb and Crawford on the sick/injured list after being hit by a pitch in the last game with Chicago. Despite playing without three starters, the Tigers swept a two-game, rain-shortened series from the Browns, and then split two games with Cleveland to close the month. Cobb and Crawford returned by the end of April, but Bush was still sidelined as May began. Ty had his first big game in a come-from-behind win against Cleveland. Although forced to work with a patch-work lineup for much of April, Jennings was saved in part by Heilmann, who hit .311 and was consistent all month. Both Heilmann and Vitt were question marks in the spring, but thus far had remained in the lineup and contributed. Cobb (.356), Veach (.270) and Ralph Young (.288) also helped bolster an offense that was the key to their success.[16]

Thus far, the Tigers pitching wasn't as bad as had been feared. Coveleski (2–0) was excellent with the exception of one start, and Hooks Dauss and Jean Dubuc seemed to be rounding into form. Meanwhile, George Cunningham had come on after a rocky start and looked like a promising rookie. The big negatives were Bernie Boland, who had been extremely wild, especially as a starter, and Bill James, who had two poor April outings. In spite of all these challenges, Detroit at least kept pace with Boston.

Part of Hughie Jennings' problems in handling pitchers was his in-game reputation of sticking with a struggling hurler too long. The Tiger manager considered the claim inaccurate, if not unfair, saying, "If I find that the man whom I have started hasn't control or cannot get anything on the ball, I remove him as quickly as anybody would. But as long as he isn't wild and is show-ing his usual amount of speed and his normal curve ball, I see no reason for taking him out." What Jennings may have lacked in the pitching department, he made up in other areas. "Ee-Yah" took over a talented team in 1907, but one that was failing to produce. Two aspects of his managerial style helped the Tigers win pennants the next three seasons. The first was Jennings' upbeat,

1916 Detroit Tigers team picture. *From left, top—* Bobby Veach, Ty Cobb, Burke, Sam Crawford, George Burns, Howard Ehmke, Harry Heilmann, Babe Ellison, Hooks Dauss, Willie Mitchell; *middle—* Ben Dyer, George Boehler, Tubby Spencer, Oscar Stanage, George Harper, Hughie Jennings (manager), Jean Dubuc, Harry Coveleski, Bill James, *bottom—* Ossie Vitt, Billy Sullivan, Ralph Young, Donie Bush, Bernie Boland, Frank Fuller (*Spalding Official Baseball Guide—1917*, Library of Congress).

aggressive, leave-everything-on-the-field style, which helped energize Detroit. In *Hughie Jennings—The Live Wire of Modern Baseball*, John Brown wrote, "Everybody likes Hughie. He is irrepressible, so good natured and deadly in earnest. He is a born scrapper. He fights for all there is in him and he makes his team fight too, but he fights fair, and if he loses, which is not very often of late, he loses gamely."[17]

However, some would argue Jennings' enthusiasm went too far, especially as a player and even as a manager. He used questionable tactics, such as stepping into pitches, being sarcastic to teammates, and baiting umpires. Former Tiger Davy Jones even went so far as to say, "Now I don't know as I ought to say this, but Hughie Jennings was drunk pretty near all the time. He didn't even know what was going on in the ball game. Didn't even know our signals. He'd come out there sometimes and he'd be in a complete stupor. He'd raise cane, you know, and call people names. Oh, the language he'd use to some of the ballplayers." Part of the aggressive strategy Jennings used as a manager was his famous rallying cry. His biographer described it thusly: "In the third-base coaching box the team's new manager pulled up two handfuls of infield grass. With clenched fists raised over his head, he leaned his torso back, raised his right leg with bent knee, let loose with a piercing cry of 'ee-yah' and threw the grass in the air like confetti."[18]

The other key aspect of Jennings' success was the communication lines he opened in the clubhouse. There were open meetings, and players apparently accepted criticism easily. Possibly Jennings' greatest managerial achievement was the ability to harness the talent of Cobb, who simply didn't get along with his teammates. Through open conversations with Ty and the team, he was able to get the relationship to at least the semi-professional level. This could only work one away — allow Cobb to do what he wanted and hope his burning desire to succeed would take over. It did, but it also meant that Ty received preferential treatment. This seemed to be exactly what Lannin and Carrigan wanted to avoid with Tris Speaker. For example, Cobb came and went as he pleased in practice. But Jennings, even though he didn't like it, felt this would enable the difficult Detroit star to put up the best numbers possible.[19]

While Jennings had few problems relating to his players, this wasn't the case for White Sox skipper Clarence "Pants" Rowland. Rowland got his nickname from an umpire in a youth baseball game. Clarence was wearing his dad's pants, which were held up with twine, but he tripped over them, producing the nickname that stuck. Rowland had little major league experience, and in some respects, Charles Comiskey may have hired him in 1915 because he knew Pants would work hard to repay him for the opportunity. The two had first worked together when Rowland was a scout for Comiskey, and in that capacity, he discovered Hap Felsch. Clarence's lack of experience caused constant issues during his tenure with the White Sox, as the media and fans never truly took to Rowland. To make matters worse, many of the White Sox players didn't respect Pants. Years later, Dick Lindberg wrote, "Few of the veteran players listened or took him seriously. His youth and inexperience kept getting in the way. Instructions to players took the form of a well-meaning suggestion, or sage piece of advice. Sometimes they listened, but most of the time the athletes paid no mind. He was, after all, just a 'busher.'" Comiskey, and later assistant coach and future manager Kid Gleason, were the ones who gave the tough instruction to players.[20]

This lack of respect may have forced Rowland's hand in his managerial style, which seemed to be more heavy-handed early in his career. Later in his career, Clarence's theory was to put the chips on the field and let the players decide things. Still, Rowland was keen in some of his baseball thinking. He was ahead of the times when it came to relief pitching, and started to develop Dave Danforth as a reliever in 1916. Pants was more traditional in his ideas of a roster, arguing for 13 position players at the expense of just eight pitchers. After all, a few pitchers did the brunt of the work, making the extras seem like a waste of roster space. Pants was clearly of the thinking that an everyday player was just that, and he distained platoons and lefty-righty match-ups.

Today, Rowland might be described as a player's manager, taking the blames for losses and giving the players credit for wins.[21]

Clarence Rowland did little in April to help overcome his negative reputation. His frequent lineup changes couldn't have helped earn his players' respect. After the strong start against the Tigers, the White Sox went south, finishing the month in sixth place (9–9). Sandwiched in between those eight games with the Tigers, Chicago hosted four against Fielder Jones' St. Louis Browns. Jones had played and managed under Comiskey for eight years, but the two weren't on cordial terms. The White Sox were lucky to salvage a split, as their defense and pitching struggled. For one victory, Chicago had to rally from a 5–0 deficit to win, 6–5, in 11 innings behind key pinch-hits from Byrd Lynn and Jack Ness. Then, Red Faber's outing (2 runs, 9 innings) the next day earned the White Sox the split. Urban (9 runs, 34 innings) was April's brightest spot, going 4–0, with two of the victories stopping mini-losing streaks of three games each.[22]

The next series with the Tigers, in which the White Sox lost three of four, started a 12-game road trip. It was not surprising Chicago struggled so much with Tigers southpaw Harry Coveleski since they had a history of difficulty hitting lefties. The White Sox then dropped the first two games at League Park to the Indians. The second was especially painful when Jim Scott allowed five runs in the eighth inning and let a 2–0 lead get away, making Chicago 1–5 on the trip.[23]

In the third game against Cleveland, on April 27, Rowland decided changes were in order. The meat of the order, with Eddie Collins batting third, Fournier fourth and Jackson and Felsch fifth and sixth, remained the same. But Zeb Terry, who was struggling in the field and at the plate, was benched. Weaver moved back to shortstop but went from second to seventh in the order because of his offensive struggles. As a result, Fred McMullin entered to play third and hit second. Clearly, the questions on the left side of the infield remained. Additionally, Schalk started for the first time since the ankle injury. Rowland made the changes with his ace to date, Faber, on the mound. Once again he was great, allowing three runs in seven-plus innings, while Jackson went 3-for-4 with two RBIs in the victory. Interestingly, though, Rowland seemed to be straying from his theory of letting the players play. And this was only the start. Chicago lost the next day but won the following two in St. Louis to close the month. In the first game, shortstop Buck Weaver and first baseman Jack Fournier turned a triple play. The White Sox also benefited from the Browns' poor defense, and good outings on the mound from Reb Russell and Scott.[24]

The Sox had barely survived a poor April. With the exception of Faber, the starting pitching had been bad, despite its late surge. The left side of the infield continued to be a problem, and the offense, while good in spots, was inconsistent. Although at .500, Chicago (9–9) finished the month in sixth place, behind Boston and Detroit, who were tied for first place at 9–6.

Things wouldn't improve for the pennant contenders in May, as Boston, Chicago and Detroit all faced adversity. That was due in part to the Cleveland Indians. Despite the addition of Speaker, few gave manager Lee Fohl's team any chance of contending for the American League pennant. Cleveland finished April with a record of 8–7, but things changed dramatically in May. By May 9, the Indians were riding an eight-game winning streak and had opened up a 2½-game lead by making a habit of beating up on the White Sox and Tigers. Grantland Rice wrote, "The day that Speaker landed his mates began to feel that a new order was at hand — that the turn had at least arrived — that the new owners meant business. So in place of subsiding gently and doing a high dive at the first blow, the Indians turned and began to fight. So far they are the season's sensations. What they may do later on belongs to the future."[25]

Little did anyone know the Indians would be a fixture in the pennant race into August. Cleveland defeated Detroit on April 30 and also won the next two games at Navin Field to take three of four. Pitchers Stanley Coveleski and Guy Morton allowed a combined one run in the final two contests. Next the Indians traveled to Chicago to take on the resurgent White Sox, who had won four of five. Chicago completed its sweep of the Browns on May 2 when the light-hitting Zeb Terry, although still not starting, used only his sixth hit of the season to drive in the winning runs. After a poor 1–5 start, the White Sox ended their road trip a respectable 5–6.[26]

Like Fenway Park, Comiskey Park was part of the new generation of steel and concrete ballparks built between 1909 and 1915. Comiskey opened his new facility during the 1910 season, and the Chicago owner modeled his park after the Coliseum in Rome. In fact, it was "decorated like a Roman temple." There were interesting similarities and differences between the two relatively new parks that hosted many key games in 1916. An important feature of these venues was better accessibility, especially through downtown locations. Comiskey Park's location in the working class South Side of Chicago served this purpose. At Fenway, Boston's owners addressed the issue by building the facility near subway and street car lines. Chicago's park was double-decked and held 32,000 spectators, slightly smaller than Fenway's capacity of roughly 35,000 in one deck. To help move fans to their seats quickly and orderly, the Chicago owner used ramps rather than stairs, as well as color-coded tickets to direct spectators. A different approach worked in the Fens, as eighteen turnstiles, another new concept, helped keep large crowds organized. Comiskey Park was also spacious, especially in the outfield and behind home plate. Most ballparks had roughly 60 feet of foul territory behind the plate, but the White Sox's field had a gargantuan 98 feet. Fenway's distance to the center field fence (458 feet) was longer than Comiskey's (420 feet), but the latter was significantly further down the lines. Unlike Boston, the shape of Chicago's home field was more symmetrical.[27]

Against the Indians, the White Sox were stopped dead in their tracks, losing four straight by the scores of 2–0, 3–2, 4–1 and 5–2. During the series, I.E. Sanborn highlighted Chicago's inability to score (5 runs, 36 hits) despite hitting the ball hard. By recording more runs, 14, on fewer hits, 29, Cleveland showed a knack for timely hitting. During the third game, there was a near-fight between left fielder John Graney and White Sox catcher Ray Schalk. Sanborn explained:

> The near boxing bout grew out of an argument over a Chill decision while John Graney was at bat. Schalk contended that Chill missed a strike on John, and John contended the ball was both high and wide, illustrated its alleged course by poking his bat into the midst of Schalk's mask. At the same time Graney asked Schalk why he did not join a regular ball team, instead of catching for a bunch of misfits.[28]

Faced with a struggling team, White Sox manager Clarence Rowland seemed to be panicking by juggling his lineup frequently. While there were constants, like Eddie Collins, Buck Weaver, Joe Jackson, Fred McMullin and usually Hap Felsch, Rowland seemed to be changing the top of his lineup on a daily basis. The final game was a match-up of rival aces — Faber (4–1) and Fritz Coumbe. Red suffered his first loss of the season, allowing five runs in seven-plus innings, while Coumbe (1 earned run, 7 innings) picked up his fourth straight victory and second in the series. Speaker was a very respectable 5-for-14 during the set, and with Tris now hitting well overall, Cleveland would head east to Fenway Park to take on the Red Sox in the center fielder's return to Boston.[29]

While Cleveland dominated Chicago, Boston struggled its way through early May, dropping to fourth place with a 1–5 start. It seemed the defending champs never recovered from their sluggish finish to April. Perhaps most disconcerting to the Red Sox and encouraging to the rest of the league were the struggles of the pitching staff, Boston's supposed strength. Babe Ruth (9 walks) and Ernie Shore (5 walks in 6 innings) had poor outings in Washington on May 1 and 2. Returning home to face the Yankees, Carrigan sent his saving grace thus far, Dutch Leonard, to the hill. Leonard (3–0) answered the call, tossing a complete-game, two-hit shutout in a 3–0 victory.[30]

Unfortunately, things got much worse after that. The next day, May 5, Boston blew a 4–0 lead and lost, 8–4. Ruth was again sloppy, walking six batters. Carrigan juggled his lineup on May 6, as Clarence Walker returned for what would be a tough month, leaving fans yearning for Tris Speaker. In fact, there would be a rumor years later that Joe Lannin may have regretted his decision to make the deal (the idea being he only sold Tris to stop other players from complaining about their salaries), and was possibly intent on making Rough a scapegoat. Tilly was installed in the cleanup position, and Hooper went back to his typical leadoff spot, with the ineffective Henriksen landing on the bench. The shakeup didn't work, in part because the struggling Rube Foster (1–4) allowed five runs in as many innings. Showing their frustration, six members of the Red Sox were ejected from the game. Boston was clearly agitated, and the Speaker trade was looking more and more controversial. The situation caused Ralph McMillin to comment, "It looks like a crucial time to us here in the Bean City, the time that we are to prove the fallacy or truth of our Speaker contentions and to make the big fight that will discover whether or not we are to continue as favorites for the Ban Johnson banner."[31]

Ironically, Boston's next attempt to reverse its fortunes came when the Red Sox hosted the much-hyped Speaker Day at Fenway Park on May 9. Cleveland, after a one-day stop at home in which it defeated Detroit, started its long eastern swing and first true test of the season in first place. Speaker was hitting .358 and carrying an Indians team batting only .231 on his back. With a band and roughly 15,000 spectators on hand, "The Grey Eagle" received gifts from the Aleppo Temple of Shriners and a silver cup from Lannin. The two had, at least publicly, smoothed things over. Accepting the gifts, Speaker said, "You may keep your presents, much as I appreciate them, if we can win the game. You all are my friends, but there is no club in the league I would rather beat than the Red Sox." Boston fans cheered wildly for Tris, who tripled in the game. Embarrassingly, the center fielder nearly ran into the Red Sox dugout after one inning. But the Indians, who had spent two straight nights on sleeper trains, finally ran out of gas. Dutch Leonard (1 run, 9 innings), now 4–0, stole the show, even going 2-for-2 with an RBI to snap Cleveland's eight-game winning streak. Ultimately, both teams would split the four-game series.[32]

May 9, however, was a significant day for the other contenders as well. After four straight losses to the Indians, the White Sox got untracked, rallying from a 4–0 deficit in New York to beat the Yankees, 5–4, behind Jack Fournier's three-run homer and Eddie Cicotte's 6⅓ innings of shutout relief. Meanwhile, the Tigers got the best medicine of all — a visit to Shibe Park to face the Athletics. Plagued by inconsistency, Detroit had lost five of six to start the month. Some days the offense was weak, on others the pitching was poor. Jean Dubuc, George Cunningham, Bill James and even Coveleski all had struggles on the hill. In a May 5 loss to St. Louis, the Browns even stole seven bases against Detroit, including three on one play in a triple steal. However, two days after allowing three hits and a run in the 13th to take the loss against St. Louis on May 4, Coveleski (3–2) performed like a stopper, allowing one run in a 2–1 win. The victory snapped a five-game losing streak as the Tigers salvaged the final game against the Browns.[33]

Detroit then took three out of four from the Athletics, but the series was marred by poor pitching, a department where the Tigers clearly were not improving. In the first game, on May 9, both teams combined for a ridiculous 30 walks, a record that shattered the previous mark of 22. Detroit benefited from 18 bases on balls, a twentieth century nine-inning first in utilizing free pass prosperity. All told, Philadelphia pitchers would walk 715 batters in 1916, another record, which stood until 1938. Cunningham, the Tigers' starter, left in the third inning with a 9–0 lead and a no-hitter because he had already allowed six bases on balls. The pitching didn't get much better in the remaining three games. After their 8–6 win on May 12 in the final game, however, the Tigers pushed back over the .500 mark, at 13–12, and in fourth place. The Red Sox (12–13) and White Sox (12–15) were just behind the Tigers, but surprisingly Cleveland, Washington and New York were all in front of the predicted contenders. Although Bush had returned against St. Louis, Detroit lost Bobby Veach to a swollen face caused by a toothache. Injuries were continuing to challenge Jennings' lineup, although the forgotten George Burns, left for dead on waivers, was becoming one of the stabilizing offensive factors. In the Philadelphia series, he went 9-for-15 to bring his average up to .444.[34]

While it seemed the pennant contenders were getting back on track, there was still more than enough inconsistent play to go around. Following a team meeting on May 10, Chicago won for the second straight day as Fournier hit his second homer in as many games. However, the White Sox scored only one run in the next two games, losing both to the Yankees. Chicago then headed to Fenway Park for a series limited to one contest because of rain. The one game was a Boston victory, as Larry Gardner's hit in the 10th inning made George Foster (2–4) a winner. Fortunately for Rube, he was proving to be effective as a reliever.

Meanwhile, most of the action was off the field, and was stirred up by the Boston papers, which might have run out of stories after all of the rain. According to James Crusinberry, the Boston scribes "had it that Manager Rowland and Eddie Collins were at outs and didn't speak, and reported that the members of the Chicago team are all through as ball players and should spend their remaining days in some old people's home." Understandably, the Chicago writer claimed this "stirred up the fighting spirit" of the team.[35]

Rowland planned more changes to his lineup the next day, saying he would move John "Shano" Collins, typically an outfielder, to first and Fournier, usually a first baseman, to the outfield. After utilizing the same lineup for nearly a week (Felsch, J. Collins, E. Collins, Fournier, Jackson, Weaver, McMullin and Schalk), Pants spent the rest of May tinkering with it. It wasn't uncommon for Schalk, McMullin and J. Collins to hit all over the batting order, depending on the day. While McMullin had eased the problems at third base, first remained an uncertainty. There was also never a steady clean-up hitter. On May 20, Schalk's average dropped all the way to .189, and Shano Collins finished the month hitting .221, after being at .345 on May 7. At one point in May, the lineup had scored just two runs in 27 innings for pitcher Eddie Cicotte.[36]

Things got even worse, as Chicago lost its first two games to hapless Philadelphia, dropping to 2–5 on the trip, before salvaging the finale on May 20. Comiskey had seen enough, or so it seemed. On May 22, the White Sox lost, 2–0, to Washington, as the red-hot Senators climbed into first place. The next day, *Tribune* headlines blared, "Rowland's Job Periled; Shakeup For Sox." The story cited a source close to Comiskey, who said if play didn't improve in the next two to three weeks, Rowland would resign and several players would be sold or traded.[37] Instead of fighting for first place, Chicago, 13–19, was in last place — behind even the Athletics.

"Commy" denied the reports the next day, and Rowland, showing all was normal, continued to make changes. Jack Ness, who had just returned to the team and was 0-for-4 since, was sent to the bench for Fournier. Things did improve, and it was Faber who saved the day. After struggling during parts of May following his blazing start, Red led Chicago to a 4–1 win against the Senators on May 24, helping the White Sox to finish their eastern swing at 4–6. Back home, Faber (6–3) teamed with Jim Scott (2–4) on May 28, as each pitcher hurled a 2–0 shutout against the Indians in a doubleheader. In the process the duo handed Fritz Coumbe his first loss of the season (he had already beaten Chicago three times) and also beat the surging Guy Morton, who had won eight in a row. Scott, who had been struggling with his health, picked up his first victory in 1916. Just like that, the White Sox were back in fifth place in the ever-changing A.L. race. The wins came after another players-only team meeting in Washington that Crusinberry said focused on giving maximum effort.[38]

Since Faber as well as the offense had struggled, the Sox pitching staff needed a team effort in May to remain even competitive. Benz, Cicotte, Williams, Russell and Scott all made important contributions both as starters and relievers. That was even true of Dave Danforth, who struggled mightily as a starter amidst continuing accusations he was illegally doctoring the baseball. The irony throughout this turbulent month for the White Sox (Chicago

2

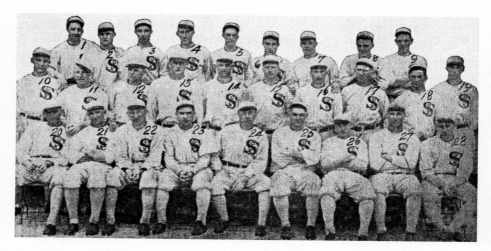

1916 Chicago White Sox team picture. *From left, top*— Eddie Collins, Mellie Wolfgang, Lefty Williams, Jack Lapp, Zeb Terry, Nemo Leibold, Eddie Cicotte, Ray Schalk, Buck Weaver; *middle*— Ted Jourdan, Kid Gleason (coach), Eddie Murphy, Ed Walsh, Dave Danforth, Red Faber, Fred McMullin, Joe Benz, Byrd Lynn, Ziggy Hasbrook; *front*— Joe Jackson, Shano Collins, Jack Ness, Jack Fournier, Clarence Rowland (manager), Reb Russell, Happy Felsch, Jim Scott, Fritz Von Kolnitz (*Spalding Official Baseball Guide—1917*, Library of Congress).

went 8–12) was how Rowland handled his team. Many reports indicate he was a player's manager, not given to over-managing. Typically, that type of manager doesn't make rash decisions when things are not going well, instead letting good hitters play their way out of slumps. This is the exact opposite of what Rowland did early in 1916. Granted, most of the reports that described Pants as hands-off were written later or following his managerial career. But this leads to the conclusion that he gradually became a player's manager over the course of his short managerial career. Also, at times late in May, he used a platoon of Fournier and Ness, furthering supporting the idea that he evolved into a player's manager. Ultimately, Rowland would come to dislike the lefty-righty platoon, possibly because it meant more managing, but at this point it appeared he took a more hands-on approach.

Another aspect of the early-season story of the White Sox was how some sportswriters were putting undue pressure and responsibility on the shoulders of Jack Ness, a much-heralded youngster. For example, in the May 25 issue of *The Sporting News*, beat reporter George Robbins wrote, "The comeback of Jack Ness, one of the most remarkable transactions ever recorded in major league history, is the bright spot in the clouds enveloping the Chicago team, the silver lining, so to speak."[39] For Robbins to argue later in the article that Ness, despite being a promising youngster, was going to be the one to key a resurgence of the White Sox bordered on the absurd. However, it characterized the sports writing of the Deadball Era, which was very different from today. It was often hard to separate fact from opinion, as writers were seldom reluctant to share their viewpoints. Oftentimes these proved to be more hopes and wishes than good analysis.

Another excess of sports writing in 1916 was how defensive plays were consistently described as "out of this world." Writing about sports journalism of a later era, Grantland Rice biographer William Harper cited a source that claimed fielders weren't expected to miss and seldom disappointed. Perhaps in the Deadball Era writers thought the good plays were so exceptional because they expected players to miss. One reason for this could have been gloves were so small that any one-handed catch was considered sensational.[40]

There were also significant differences in game accounts. Modern writers tend to weave player quotes, their own analysis and facts in a personal style. In 1916, most reporters started their stories by mentioning the highlights of the game and their own conclusions. What typically followed was a detailed play-by-play of every key inning and how every run scored. In many cases, every play was included. From writer to writer, the formats were consistently similar. The more detailed descriptions were necessary since few of the readers actually witnessed the game. Most newspapers limited their coverage to one article and a notes section each day on the hometown team. This would only change on such occasions as the World Series.

The growth and expansion of professional baseball in the late nineteenth century occurred simultaneously with the growth of the newspaper industry. Between 1880 and 1900, the number of daily newspapers grew from 850 to 2,000. While this dramatically increased the number of career opportunities, it didn't make sports writing an economically viable profession. A good writer could expect to earn roughly $50-$100 a week. When the New York *Tribune* offered Grantland Rice a whopping $280 per week in 1915, it was considered to be an unheard of sum. In addition, early sports writing, like baseball, had a poor reputation as a career choice.[41]

Since it was the only media outlet, the role of newspapers in publicizing the game cannot be overemphasized. Perhaps speaking for all sports writers for all time, Grantland Rice's biographer added, "Ford Frick, newspaperman, ghost writer for Babe Ruth, and later the baseball commissioner, claimed that no other group advanced American sports more than the sports writers." Frick added, "No group has received less public recognition for the job they have done or the contribution they have made.'" An understanding of this reality, along with the construction of new ballparks, changed working conditions for the better. Before 1900, few baseball parks had press boxes, but in 1916, they were becoming more common, in part due to the formation of the Baseball Writers Association in 1908. Being organized allowed reporters "to demand more press boxes" and require that space be reserved for them. Things were still hit and miss, however, as Ebbets Field was designed and built without facilities for the press. Inside, the press box was a male-only area, featuring an abundance of alcohol, tobacco and cigarettes.[42]

Unlike today, there were two major categories of newspapers, morning and evening. A writer for an evening newspaper would typically arrive in the press box first. However, many were late to their posts, due usually to absurd reasons, such as a round of golf or a few beers at the bar. Some would arrive early to talk to players and managers, in part because organized post-game interviews were years away. The time to speak with players and managers was on the road because reporters traveled with the team. Sometimes clubs would even deal with reporters' itineraries and pick up such travel costs as hotels and meals. The tradeoff was the free advertising the team received from the newspaper articles. While it might seem like an even deal, the familiarity between the two groups could create an interesting dynamic.[43]

Telegraph reporters were a critical part of the newspaper process. Evening writers would dictate a 100-word lead and the lineups to telegraphers, who would relay the information to the papers. This continued with a play-by-play throughout the game. One significant result from the formation of the Baseball Writers Association was the pre-game release of lineups to members of the media. This avoided mistakes and guesswork, which must have been problematic for the P.M. writers, who were under a tight deadline. That was especially important at a time when players didn't wear numbers on their uniforms.[44]

Fred Lieb was an example of a scribe who worked at morning newspapers. Not faced with the tight afternoon deadline, his workday was quite different. Lieb could score the game, take notes, go home for dinner and then return to the office at 7:45 P.M. to write his story. It would be in the editor's hand at 9:45 P.M., in plenty of time for the 1 A.M. first edition of *The Press and Morning Sun*. Lieb's first job as a baseball writer was with the New York *Press* in 1911. Part of the interview process was a writing test, which is still common today. In this instance, Fred was given two, 200-word skeleton reports of the Giants and Yankees activities that evening during spring training, which he had to develop into a column.[45]

There were numerous other interesting aspects of journalism during the Deadball Era. For example, trying to write a game story, or especially a feature, was more difficult without team public relations officials as intermediaries. Secondly, while ghostwriting wouldn't crank into full gear until the 1920s, it was still a very real aspect of baseball in 1916.[46] Newspapers would publish columns and pay a player or manager (Christy Mathewson and John McGraw are examples) for the rights to have his byline or name on it. Of course, the player hadn't actually written the article, but newspapers sure made it seem that way.

Today, scorekeeping is one of the most consistent aspects of baseball. There is an official scorer, whose decisions are final and who produces a standard box score in all publications and records. In 1916, official scorers were rarely the best person for the job, and in some situations, their identity was kept secret, with players not knowing their official batting average until after the season. Additionally, many writers created their own box score, which produced different statistics in different publications. Some, like the New York *Press*, even added categories, such as RBIs, which were otherwise non-existent in 1916.[47]

Impartial as writers might try to be, it was never pleasant covering a struggling team. This lesson was learned anew by Detroit writers during the second half of May. Following the Tigers' final victory against the Athletics, the team lost its next eight games, excluding a 2–2 tie with the Yankees. During that stretch, Detroit hit just .226 as a team. First, there was a four-game sweep at the hands of the Senators in Washington. In the first contest, on May 13, Jennings got Veach back from his facial swelling, finally bringing the Tigers back to full strength.[48] In part, injuries had caused Hughie to struggle to find a consistent lineup, especially when dealing with the middle of the order. Uncertainty about right fielder Sam Crawford hadn't helped either.

Crawford was playing his 18th of 19 seasons, and there was talk in early May about benching him. Sam seemed over the hill, in part due to a 2-for-19 early-month slump. This movement was further magnified by the emergence of players like Heilmann and Burns. However, a couple of good games by Crawford and Veach's injury kept the question open, as Jennings understandably struggled with a difficult decision. But on May 15, he decided to go with Veach, Heilmann and Burns behind Bush, Vitt and Cobb in the batting order. Unfortunately, it didn't pay immediate dividends.[49]

The first day the new lineup was in place the Tigers blew a 5–2 lead in the seventh inning and lost in the 11th. In the third inning, Nationals pitcher Joe Boehling accused Ty Cobb of trying to spike him on a pickoff attempt. Boehling started yelling, and Cobb retaliated by throwing dirt in the pitcher's face. He then defended himself with no small irony, saying, "I come from a country where we cannot stand for that language and I was so incensed at the time that I couldn't help what I did. I always try to play fair, and have never during my baseball career intentionally cut down a man while going into a base."[50]

After moving to New York and the Polo Grounds, Detroit wasted good pitching from both Coveleski and Cunningham, doing no better than a tie and a loss. Failure to take advantage of effective pitching was especially frustrating because the staff's performance was up and down throughout May. For example, prior to those two good starts, Tiger hurlers allowed a total of 27 runs in the final three games in Washington. The offense was no better and couldn't get much worse, scoring just four runs in as many games, not all of them earned. The defeat had Batchelor pushing for Crawford's re-insertion since he wasn't impressed with Heilmann at bat or on the bases. The Detroit scribe also felt that "as a right-fielder he doesn't acquit himself very well either, due probably to the fact that he isn't accustomed to the position and doesn't seem to want very much to learn."[51]

With little going its way, Detroit headed to Fenway Park to meet Boston, which had lost two out of three to the lowly Browns on May 18–20. Rube Foster (2–5) and Dutch Leonard (4–1), at opposite ends of the spectrum thus far, got hit hard in the first two contests, the latter suffering his first loss of the season. Offensively, Jack Barry and Duffy Lewis were struggling at the plate, while Hal Janvrin had come back to earth after his hot start. On May 20, probably in an effort to jump-start things, Carrigan moved Lewis from the five to the three spot, with Dick Hoblitzell again going to cleanup. Barry came to the top of the lineup, batting second, while Janvrin dropped all the way to seventh. Thus far, the bright spots were Hoblitzell and Hooper. Dick had been hot all along, while Harry was in the midst of a stretch that would see his average rise 54 points, to .262 on May 25. A struggling Babe Ruth (4–2) was erratic but combined with Mays to salvage that final game.[52] Still, Boston (14–15) and Detroit (13–17) met for the first time with neither playing .500 baseball.

Since benching Crawford, Jennings had made fewer changes in his lineup, but he seemed to be considering many adjustments. This could have been due to Detroit's current offensive struggles, magnified in light of the pitching's recent success. Most of the rumored changes weren't made, but one of those discussed was moving Crawford to first base in place of Burns, who, while slumping, was still hitting well over .300. Still, Hughie's juggling of his outfield as well as his poor substitution and pinch-hitting patterns raised questions among reporters. Any uncertainty on Jennings' part is curious; he was an experienced manager and had won three pennants. Perhaps, after not winning one since 1909, he was questioning his own abilities.[53]

One of the reasons the Red Sox remained closer to the top of the table than Chicago or Detroit when May ended was their success against the latter two. In reality, all three played poorly all month. Detroit came to Boston having lost five in a row, and their problems continued in Beantown. The slumping Hal Janvrin got key hits in the first and third games, and Ruth

(6–2) tossed a shutout in the middle one, on May 24, for a three-game sweep. It was the Babe's first victory in May. Edward Martin of the Boston *Daily Globe* called the middle game "the best they (Boston) have played this year." For the Tigers, Hooks Dauss, out for two weeks with flu-like symptoms, saw his first action since May 4 in the first contest and was wild but allowed only one run. After the middle game, the Tigers had scored just one earned run in their last 44 innings, and they headed back to Detroit having lost eight straight to finish a 3–10 road trip. This offensive lapse wasn't hard to understand. Much of the lineup, including table setters Bush and Vitt, really struggled. The two hottest hitters — Burns (who had to be pulled off waivers earlier) and Heilmann — performed well, but it wasn't enough. The only positive was Crawford's situation resolved itself, at least temporarily, when he had to sit with back problems.[54]

Back at home, the Tigers won three of four from St. Louis, ending the series with a 17–6 feel-good offensive victory in which Cobb had four hits. His average was up to .331 after dipping all the way to .273 in early May. Off the field, Frank Navin purchased pitcher Earl Hamilton from the Browns in hopes of establishing more consistency in the rotation. The hurler got his chance against Chicago in the opening game of a doubleheader that started a four-game set on May 30, only to be outworked by the White Sox pitching staff in a 3–1 Chicago victory. Things got ugly in the second game for the Pale Hose. Billy Birch, of the Chicago *Daily Herald*, reported, "With another double-header in their grasp and first division staring them in the face, the White Sox pulled up lame at the finish this evening, thereby giving the Detroit Tigers a chance to split the day's double bill."[55]

The Tigers trailed, 8–5, in the ninth, but poor fielding on the part of first baseman Fournier and third baseman McMullin prompted a comeback, and another miscue by McMullin in the 10th gave Detroit an undeserved split. Then, on May 31, trailing 1–0, the Tigers again unnerved White Sox pitcher Dave Danforth in the fifth inning with the bases loaded and two outs. Gamesmanship forced a switch in the baseball, and Danforth threw three straight balls to walk in a run before he allowed a bases-clearing triple to Harry Heilmann. While deflating for the White Sox, which seemed to have righted things a bit, the wins were critical for the Tigers given the way they left the East Coast. Perhaps that hex Detroit had over Chicago was a reality.[56]

The Red Sox sweep of the Tigers earlier in May had done little to lift Boston out of its funk. Carrigan's team went to the Polo Grounds and promptly lost three of four to the Yankees before coming home to face the Senators. Carl Mays (2–0), returning to the rotation after a bout with tonsillitis, had staved off a sweep in New York with a complete-game shutout.

Against Washington, Boston finally received an all-around effort. During the first three games, all victories, the Red Sox recorded 37 hits for 22 runs to support strong pitching efforts by Shore, Leonard and Vean Gregg. After struggling early, Boston's pitching staff seemed to be back in stride, and the Senators scored just six runs. The bigger story was utilityman Mike McNally, who was filling in for an ill Jack Barry in the number two hole and at second base. In four games, McNally hit .467, and in the first three against Washington, he scored seven of the 22 runs, stole three bases and fielded all 26 of his chances at the second station.[57]

Of the three managers, Carrigan was the one who handled his team's May problems successfully. He made one real alteration in the lineup in an effort to jump-start some of his struggling veterans and take pressure off Janvrin. The revolving door at catcher was consistent with Rough's approach when one considers his affection for personal backstops. Most importantly, Carrigan had kept his team in the first division during a tumultuous month when little had gone well for the contenders.

American League Standings
Through May 31, 1916

Team	Wins	Losses
Senators	24	15
Indians	24	15
Yankees	22	15
Red Sox	21	18
White Sox	17	21
Tigers	18	22
Athletics	14	24
Browns	14	24

CHAPTER IV

"I'd like to do it for Rowland's sake."

While there will never be any certainty about the date of the first baseball game, it's fair to say it was followed closely by the first bet. As the sport's popularity increased, so did betting, with professional gamblers determining it a money-maker. At the same time, gambling was not much of a problem until a pool system was devised in the 1800s. As Daniel Ginsburg wrote in his book *The Fix Is In,* "While two individuals with a $100 bet were not likely to fix the game, the pool system put together many thousands of dollars' worth of bets on an individual game, allowing groups of gamblers to place large stakes and motivating them to tamper with games."[1]

During the late 1800s, baseball faced numerous problems with gambling, including the fixing of games. Toward the close of the century, the scandals decreased, prompting the belief and hope that the game was clean. This hope proved unfounded during the Deadball Era, but the bigger problem was how such scandals were handled or not handled by the National Commission. One example is the 1908 National League pennant race between the Cubs and Giants. There were rumors New York tried to buy the pennant in various ways, including one that was verified. This incident concerns an individual "connected with the New York club" who attempted to bride umpires Bill Klem and Johnny Johnstone before the pennant-deciding play-off game, caused by Fred Merkle's bonehead play. It allegedly turned out to be Giants physician Joseph M. Creamer, who more than likely had backers. Creamer was banned from all ballparks in organized baseball, but claiming a lack of evidence, the National Commission didn't look into the issue aggressively, ignoring not only smoke but fire itself.[2] This is just one of numerous examples of the National Commission's "head in the sand" attitude toward clear warning signs.

Regarding that careless and risky attitude, Harold Seymour wrote, "The usual excuse for not acting summarily was lack of evidence, without which the owners would expose themselves to lawsuits." Some bad actors were "quietly banished," but "much of what is now known dribbled out only later, and without doubt there is more that still lies hidden." There were also baseball executives who held the naive belief that players wouldn't give in to temptation. Even more seriously, some higher-ups in baseball openly associated with gamblers, making it difficult for the game to keep its own house clean. Simply put, by the end of the Deadball Era, Organized Baseball "could hardly admit to imperfections in their business after having painted themselves into a corner, so to speak, with years of concealing misconduct, influencing sportswriters to soft-pedal or suppress what was going on, and issuing pious pronouncements of the game's purity." The end of the 1916 National League race would feature a controversy that once again produced little real action by the National Commission. By then, the ground was laid for the volcanic eruption that would rock baseball in 1919 with the Black Sox scandal.[3]

One must wonder how much money had already been lost early in 1916 due to the inconsistent play of pennant favorites Boston, Chicago and Detroit. The stage was about to be set, however, for what would be a heart-pounding pennant race. At the close of May, the first six teams in the American League were separated by 6½ games, and that gap would close even more as June ended. By that time, the three primary contenders would be separated by just a game.

June started with a bang, suggesting it would be an exciting month. Boston was wrapping up a set with Washington at Fenway Park, and pregame festivities included raising the 1915 American League pennant. The feature presentation of Ruth versus Johnson would be even better, as the two prominent pitchers locked up for the second time of the season. On this occasion, both were splendid, matching zeros through seven innings. With one out in the bottom of the eighth, the red-hot Mike McNally, who had already struck out three times, came to the plate. He singled sharply over shortstop George McBride and advanced to second on an error. Dick Hoblitzell then hit a hard grounder to McBride, who thought he might turn two. However, when second baseman Ray Morgan received the throw, he was so shocked to see McNally racing home, he threw there instead. McNally slid under the tag, and Ruth (7–3) had his second straight win against Johnson to complete a four-game sweep and help knock Washington out of a first-place tie.[4]

Meanwhile, in Detroit, the White Sox salvaged a split and returned home in a situation not nearly as bad as it could have been at 18–21. Hap Felsch (stiff knee) and Fred McMullin (twisted instep) were banged up and had the day off, but Red Faber and Joe Jackson carried Chicago to a 6–3 win. Jackson had gone 12-for-15 in the series to raise his average to .313. At one point, he had nine straight hits, an American League record that has since been broken. In McMullin's absence, Buck Weaver moved to third base and was standing just off the bag as Harry Heilmann rounded it in the second inning. Forced to make a wide turn, Heilmann shoved Weaver, and then went back to third after scoring. The two exchanged words but were separated before things became physical.[5]

After the series with Washington, Boston headed to the road, while Detroit and Chicago were happy to be home and not further behind on June 1. The White Sox were six games back and the Tigers seven. Detroit and Chicago were too good not to get hot, and as they did, those same writers that filed such negative reports about them in May soon sang their praises. The Detroit *Free Press'* E.A. Batchelor thought some home cooking would continue to do the Tigers good. His prediction was on target, and then some, since starting on June 3 Detroit sandwiched two seven-game winning streaks around one loss. Sweeps of the Senators, Red Sox and Athletics were included, and on June 21, the Tigers found themselves in first place. In less than three weeks, the Detroit made up seven games and passed five teams in the standings. Against Washington, the Tigers answered Batchelor's call for more clutch hitting, winning the first two games on ninth-inning hits by Donie Bush and pitcher Hooks Dauss. The Jungaleers completed the sweep the following day by defeating Walter Johnson and sending struggling Washington into third place with its seventh straight defeat.[6]

Next into Navin Field was Boston, on its first western swing of the year. Part of the reason the Tigers and White Sox were able to gain ground on the Red Sox was the favorite's struggles from May carried over into June. Boston's trip started in Cleveland, and Dutch Leonard (5–3) and Carl Mays (2–1) were hammered during 11–2 and 9–3 losses. The duo's problems, especially the way Leonard started the season, prompted some concern. But Babe Ruth (8–3) was the stopper in the final game, winning, 5–0, by holding Speaker at bay. Despite the shutout, the pitching staff after Ruth seemed to be struggling, and the lineup was dangerously depleted. Barry remained out with a cold, and leadoff hitter Harry Hooper missed his fourth straight game with a "charley horse." Hooper had been replaced at the top of the order again by Olaf Henriksen, who hadn't excelled in the leadoff spot earlier in the season. In the second game against Cleveland, Hoblitzell and Janvrin were spiked, while Thomas was hit on the collarbone with a foul ball. To make matters worse, pitcher George Foster went home to Oklahoma to be with his sick children. Hoblitzell and Janvrin did manage to play in the final game of the series, but third baseman Larry Gardner was now out with a sore throat.[7]

Another problem that caused Boston to struggle in June was its offense. Hooper, Janvrin and Lewis would all finish the month hitting under .250, while Walker, who was improving, hovered around that mark throughout June. Meanwhile, Hoblitzell, red-hot early in the year, plummeted more than

50 points, to .242. While these players struggled, Hoblitzell's problems, along with Hooper's, may have been the most ominous signs because both performed well in May. What offense Boston did produce was generated by Chester "Pinch" Thomas and Gardner. Thomas was taking advantage of an opportunity provided by Hick Cady, who started June 0-for-22. Gardner also raised his average from .280 to .297, and excelled in a competitive series with Chicago in mid-month. Still, the Red Sox batted just .228 as a team in June while playing barely above .500 baseball.

Yet the victory in the last game in Cleveland didn't signal a turnaround for Boston. When the Red Sox arrived at Navin Field, Dauss (8–4) shut down Boston, 3–0, in the first game on June 6, as Harry Heilmann provided a key two-run, two-out hit in the first inning. Two rainouts didn't change the momentum in the final game, when Detroit rallied from a 4–1 deficit in the eighth inning against Ruth to win, 6–5. Suddenly, the Tigers, who couldn't find any consistency in May, were putting it all together. The only good news for Boston was the return of Gardner and Hooper to the lineup.[8]

Hughie Jennings' pitching staff seemed to be coming around from its May inconsistency, having allowed only five runs in three games for a portion of this early-June stretch. In fact, during Detroit's two seven-game winning streaks in June, the hurlers allowed more than three runs only twice. Batchelor believed the performance "speaks volumes for the increasing efficiency of the mound staff, and gives the fans reason to hope that the big 'drive' toward the top is on at last." After sweeping the rain-abbreviated series against Boston, the Tigers won the first two against the Yankees before having their seven-game winning streak snapped the next day. Coveleski (7–2) on the mound and Veach at the plate led the way on June 11, and another victory on June 12 enabled Detroit to pass Boston in the standings and move into fourth place. Following the end of the streak, the Tigers rebounded on June 14 with a 6–2 victory in the final game against the Yankees. It was again Coveleski (8–2, with a 4–0 record in June) and Veach (4-for-4, one run, two triples, three RBIs) who spurred the win.[9]

Batchelor consistently wrote clever leads in his game reports, not always having to do with baseball. After the last victory, he wrote:

> The local argument was different than the international exchange of verbiage in several respects. In the first place, the weapons used were second-growth ash flails instead of fountain pens and in the second, the Navin field encounter had a definite result, while the bout between our president and the Kaiser was called at the end of the ninety-ninth inning on account of writer's cramp.[10]

This was a reference to growing tensions between the United States and Germany in the days before America's entrance into World War I.

With the four-hit effort, Veach's average was up to .284 after starting

June at .266. It would rise to .292 by month's end, and he, along with Ty Cobb (.327 to .348) and Heilmann (.300+), would carry the offensive load for Detroit. Individually, many Tigers were finding their mark offensively, but there was little change in the team batting average, suggesting it was timely hitting as well as pitching that sparked Detroit. Of the fourteen victories that propelled the Tigers, six were of the one-run variety. By raising an average already well over .300, Cobb rejoined the A.L. batting race, where he was seeking his 10th straight crown. Speaker, hitting .384 in late June, would present a stiff challenge. Keeping Detroit's team average down were table-setters Donie Bush and Ossie Vitt, who had been very ineffective. Additionally, the red-hot George Burns cooled down dramatically in the second half of June. The schedule also worked in Detroit's favor as hapless Philadelphia, now 15–30, came to Navin Field on June 15 for a four-game set following the series with the Yankees. Dauss (9–4) stymied the Athletics in the opener, and Philadelphia's porous defense helped the Tigers to three more victories and a new five-game winning streak.[11]

Navin Field was a major renovation of Bennett Park, which housed the Tigers until 1911. The renovations took place on the original plot of land, but it had been expanded and adjusted. The building now had a capacity of 23,000 and was part of the new era of steel and concrete ballparks. The facil-

Detroit's Navin Field (Ron Selter) (Det Navin).

ity's location at the intersection of Michigan and Trumbell avenues was ideal, just a 10-minute walk from City Hall. Unlike some parks of the day, Tigers ownership prided itself on not being as over the top in terms of decorating Navin Field. The field had a rectangular shape, was deeper than even Comiskey Park to center field, and was much further to right field than left. It certainly wasn't as asymmetrical as Fenway, but the significant differences down the lines produced a less proportional park than Comiskey. One of the oddest aspects was a 125-foot flag pole in center field that was in play.[12]

Victories by the counts of 2–1 and 3–0 against Cleveland on June 20 and 21 continued the winning streak and helped Detroit tie the Indians for first place with identical 32–24 marks. Washington, Boston and New York also had been near or in first place during early June. It was again the pitching of Dauss (10–4), who won for the sixth straight time, and Coveleski (9–2) that got the job done. In light of these performances, it was hard to believe the rumors that circulated in the June 22 Detroit *News*, suggesting Navin was interested in buying Indians pitcher Willie Mitchell. It was also surprising the Indians would consider giving up pitching since Cleveland had just been dealt what many considered a death blow to their pennant hopes by losing Guy Morton, who was having an excellent season, and Ed Klepfer to injury and/or illness. Nevertheless, the transaction occurred the following day.[13] After its seventh straight win, Detroit had thus far racked up a record of 19–4, a critical turnaround considering how poorly the Tigers had been playing.

Considering their ongoing concerns about the Tigers' pitching staff, their phenomenal performance for the first three weeks in June was a hopeful sign to Motor City baseball fans. Coveleski, Dauss and Jean Dubuc did the bulk of the work, starting 17 of 26 games. Coveleski and Dauss had great months, finishing with records of 6–2 and 3–1, respectively. Meanwhile, Earl Hamilton, who also saw significant work, dealt with some bad luck and was sent back to St. Louis. A clause in the agreement allowed the Tigers to return the pitcher for a full refund if they weren't happy with their acquisition. Also contributing was Bernie Boland, who in more than nine innings of relief work allowed just one earned run. Unfortunately, those who believed it couldn't continue were correct because things went south at the end of June. From June 22 on, Tigers starters worked 67⅔ innings and allowed 33 runs for a lofty Deadball Era earned run average of 4.39. Additionally, the defense, typically a strong suit (Detroit ranked third in the American League in fielding percentage in 1915), contributed to a number of unearned runs.[14]

In retrospect, the downturn in the rotation's performance began on June 22 when the Indians snapped their five-game losing streak and re-took sole possession of first place with a 4–3 victory over Detroit. After an off-day, the Tigers looked to win an important final game before heading on another hard-to-believe four-week road trip. After Heilmann and Burns both failed with chances to win it in the 10th inning, Cleveland scored twice in the 11th to record a 10–8 victory.[15] The loss sent Detroit into a tailspin, with the Tigers going just 2–6 for the rest of the month.

The first stop on the road was a six-game series at Sportsman's Park in St. Louis. Bolstered by an opening doubleheader sweep on June 25, the Browns won four of the six contests. Coveleski was hit hard in the first game, and another loss in the nightcap dropped the Tigers all the way to fourth place. But Harry (10–3) returned the next day to stop the Browns, 3–1. The biggest event in a doubleheader split on June 27 was off the field, when Cobb got into it with a fan in the ninth inning. The St. Louis supporter was sitting behind the Detroit bench and harassing Cobb, who finally retaliated. The two exchanged words, and Ty attempted to reach under the railing and grab the fan's leg but was restrained. The *Free Press* never mentioned a physical altercation, but noted the fan was a "youth."[16] With ominous signs abounding, Detroit, in a three-way tie for third and 2½ games back, headed to Comiskey Park for four games with the red-hot White Sox, who were suddenly on the Tigers' heels, only 3½ out.

Whereas Detroit started out hot and then dipped, Chicago made up ground by finishing strong at the end of June. After the White Sox opened the month with a victory at Navin Field, the Pale Hose, like the Tigers, went home looking to gain on the leaders. However, once at Comiskey Park, Chicago lost the opening and closing games of a three-game series to the Yankees on June 3–5 when they were shut down by George Mogridge and Nick Cullop. In the middle game, Chicago opened the floodgates and scored 12 runs on 16 hits. "Savior" Jack Ness and light-hitting Zeb Terry each had three RBIs, but it was a disputed call that caused Yankees hurler Ray Fisher to come unglued. With the White Sox leading, 5–4, Fisher thought he caught a bunt attempt and turned a double play, but the umpire ruled the ball hit the ground. Shano Collins then capitalized for Chicago with a three-run triple. On his way off the mound, Fisher had words for umpire Silk O'Loughlin and American League czar Ban Johnson, who was in attendance.[17]

Rain then wiped out a four-game series with Philadelphia, undoubtedly costing Chicago some easy wins. Once the precipitation stopped, however, the White Sox got going by taking four of five from Washington on June 10–14. Pitching was the critical part of Chicago's success, which was more impressive considering Faber was unavailable due to a thumb injury. Mel Wolfgang, Jim Scott and Reb Russell helped the White Sox to 2–1 and 5–0 victories. Joe Benz then held Washington to three hits on June 12 in a 3–0 win. As in May, a team effort by the pitching staff was continuing to help Chicago. The only negative was McMullin, who was diagnosed with a fractured bone in his left foot and would miss at least two more weeks from an early-June injury that was first thought not to be severe.[18] This development led to further problems on the left side of the infield. It was an impressive string of pitching performances, but Clarence Rowland pushed his luck too far the next day.

There had been talk of a comeback by former White Sox ace Ed Walsh, and Rowland sent him to the mound on June 13. In what was billed as a match-up between the former great and the current great, Walter Johnson, 12,000 exuberant fans were enticed to buy tickets. Johnson, claiming an illness to his visiting father-in-law kept him up most of the night, never went to the hill, although he did warm up during the game. Ban Johnson would later call it unethical to tease fans in this manner. A more likely explanation for Walter's non-appearance was that Nationals manager Clark Griffith didn't want to waste Johnson against Walsh. The latter's greatness was clearly in the past as he didn't make it out of the third inning, allowing three runs with the help of an error in a 3–2 White Sox loss. The game also marked the first time "Shoeless" Joe Jackson had gone hitless in more than two weeks.[19] Chicago got a measure of revenge the next day when Scott came back and mixed his fastball and curve to defeat Johnson, apparently now sufficiently rested. Still, the White Sox were 6½ back and in sixth place, with a struggling Boston team looming.

In between its tough two-game series in Detroit in early June and the trip to Chicago, Boston visited St. Louis on June 10–14 and split four games. The Red Sox won the first game, 4–2, in 10 innings. Boston, continuing to struggle with injuries, was just trying to hold on during a western swing that currently had them at 2–4. The next day's contest was rained out, but off-the-field rumors circulated of a move of Babe Ruth to the outfield to keep his bat in the lineup every day. Ruth, pinch-hitting, did nothing to discourage the idea the next day when his three-run homer in the seventh inning tied the game, although Boston would eventually lose. The Red Sox put themselves in position to win the series on June 13 with a 5–3 win when Ruth hit better than he hurled by homering for the second straight day. During the Deadball Era, most players were lucky to hit two home runs in a season. Things unraveled in the final game when poor pitching by Mays, Shore and Foster, who had returned, blew a 5–1 lead, allowing the Browns to split the series.[20]

One positive note for Boston centered on the team getting closer to full strength. Cleveland seemed to have taken control of the American League, holding a four-game lead over New York and Washington on June 13 after a four-game sweep of Philadelphia. Boston (5 games back), Detroit (5½ back) and Chicago (7 back) were next in line. Mediocre play by the Red Sox continued, however, when Boston visited Comiskey Park, where Boston and

Despite not looking formidable here, Babe Ruth, Ernie Shore and Rube Foster (left to right) were the backbone of one of baseball's dynasties. In 1916, infielder Del Gainer (far right) was just getting started but would go on to play a significant role (George Bain Collection, Library of Congress).

Chicago split a four-game series. It likely meant more to the White Sox, though, who were still trying to get themselves fully back on track and weren't as experienced as Boston. Leonard (6–3) opened the series by driving in the winning run to go along with a great effort on the hill. Vean Gregg, Foster and Ruth (9–4) all struggled in the next two games, both Chicago victories. Boston's pitching staff continued to fail to live up to its hype, allowing an average of 4.6 runs per game thus far in June, high for the Deadball Era. In the first Chicago win, the White Sox broke a 4–4 tie in the eighth inning with the help of Eddie Collins' go-ahead triple. He went 3-for-4, and Chicago fans were hoping an excellent hitter would finally get going.[21] Unfortunately, this was a one-game phenomenon since Collins finished June hitting just .233. It was Jackson and Hap Felsch who instead provided the offense during the month. Jackson was torrid, increasing his average from .299 to .378. In the Boston series, he went 10-for-14 and finished the month on a 14-for-20 roll.

In the third game, on June 17, Joe Benz and Dave Danforth prevailed over Ruth, as Jack Fournier and Nemo Leibold, both substitutes, came up big at the plate. The next day, the Red Sox, despite being outhit, escaped with a series split when they capitalized on a critical error by Weaver. Scott (6–7) was the loser, and Eddie Cicotte pitched in relief, his first action since

May 19. Boston finished the road trip 5–8, while Chicago went 7–5 at home. Against the Red Sox, Fournier, who played part-time for Ness, had hit cleanup but was quickly moved to the sixth spot to get Jackson's torrid bat into the four hole. At the same time, Felsch went to leadoff, and the struggling Collins was dropped to the fifth slot. Interestingly, Chicago writer George Robbins blamed injuries and unexpected results rather than Rowland for the constant lineup changes early in the season. With the victory, the Red Sox had taken sole possession of fifth, five games behind Cleveland.[22]

In spite of the June 18 loss to Boston, the White Sox were playing well and still only six out. Chicago finished June by winning seven out of eight, a stretch that saw its pitching staff allow only two runs per game. Things didn't start out that promising; after a win in St. Louis, the White Sox were swept in a doubleheader by scores of 11–1 and 2–1. The end-of-month run began when Reb Russell's strong effort on June 22 yielded a 2–0 victory, and a three-run fifth two days later gave Chicago a 5–2 lead. When St. Louis rallied, it was Cicotte, whose wife was about to have a baby girl, closing the door with 1⅔ innings of scoreless relief to give the White Sox three of five in the series.[23]

Back home for one game against front-running Cleveland before three with the Indians at League Park, Chicago continued its hot play, taking three out of four in total. Russell won the first contest for the White Sox, with most of the action being extracurricular. In the first inning, Tris Speaker crashed hard into shortstop Zeb Terry. Things escalated from there, and in the fifth, Terry's hand was ripped open by Ray Chapman's spike, an injury that was estimated to keep him out for "several days." It culminated in the eighth inning when both benches cleared after Weaver and Indians second baseman Ivan Howard fought following Buck's retaliatory take-out slide. At home, Cleveland rebounded when pitcher Fred Beebe shut out the White Sox, 2–0, in the second game on June 26. That proved to be an historic date when the Indians became the first team to wear numbers on their uniforms. Chicago bounced back with Jackson and Fournier providing the offense, which along with the pitching of Claude Williams and Reb Russell (6–3) helped the White Sox win the final two games of the series. That knocked Cleveland out of first place and moved Chicago to within 3½ of the top position.[24]

Pitching and to a lesser extent offense were the keys to the White Sox run. Especially surprising was the pitching, since Faber was still out with the thumb injury and made only one June start. Jim Scott, who had struggled with his health early in the season, picked up the load, starting a remarkable seven of the White Sox's 24 games. Even though his record was 4–3 for the month, Scott kept his team in every game he started. Meanwhile, Reb Russell, Joe Benz, Mel Wolfgang and Lefty Williams made effective spot starts throughout the month. Russell was 3–1 as a starter, but he entered in relief on seven occasions, including numerous lengthy outings, and didn't allow a run. Again, it was a team effort by the pitching staff.

One of Wolfgang's effective two spot starts came in Chicago on June 29 against Detroit. After their hot play, the Tigers came into the series just 2–6 in their last eight, and Jennings benched Burns, mired in a 2-for-30 slump, for Crawford. Desperate, Hughie started Harry Coveleski for the third time in five days, and the pitcher was rocked for seven runs in five innings during an 8–2 loss. Not all seven runs were earned, but Coveleski (10–4) made two throwing errors in the fifth inning, including a heave with the bases loaded that allowed three runs to score. This was just part of the pitching staff plummeting back to earth after its strong June start. His counterpart, Wolfgang, allowed only two runs on four hits.[25]

Having only scored more than three runs once in the team's last seven games, Jennings decided it was time for a lineup change on June 30, and the primary move was Vitt and Bush changing places in the batting order. Jennings' thought process was that Vitt, who would now lead off, was good at working counts, and Bush was effective at both sacrificing and the hit and run. Crawford also had recently entered the lineup again, and if he struggled against lefties, Jennings would platoon him with Burns.[26] The moves didn't help when Scott (7–8) capped a strong month with a 5–2 win that put the White Sox in third place. A defensively challenged and wild Hooks Dauss (10–5) also didn't help Detroit, which finished the month in sixth after being in first only 10 days earlier. It's hard to know what was more shocking — how poorly Detroit played after its hot start or the fact they fell six places in the standings in ten days.

After struggling through a tough western swing, Boston finally came home looking to make some noise, and the Red Sox won seven of 10 to conclude June. With the exception of Barry, the Red Sox were back at full strength, and even Jack was getting healthy.[27] The upstart Yankees, just 2½ out of first but in fourth place, provided initial competition. Pitcher Ray Keating brought New York closer to the top when he beat Dutch Leonard (6–4) and the Red Sox in the first game, 4–1. But in a welcome sign, Rube Foster (4–6), Babe Ruth (10–4) and Ernie Shore (4–3) proceeded to toss shutouts for Boston victories. Foster's gem on June 21 was far and away the most significant, as it was the first no-hitter in Fenway Park history. Duffy Lewis drove in both runs in the 2–0 win, and Foster earned $100 from Lannin, while players and newspapermen received gold knives commemorating the event.[28] With the exception of that performance, however, Foster continued to struggle as a starter.

After a tough May, Ruth carried the staff, going 5–1 while throwing a remarkable three shutouts. Leonard returned to earth and was mediocre, while

Mays struggled early and came on late. Shore missed most of the first part of the month but closed with a few good performances. His shutout came against the Athletics in the next series, when Boston took four of five. Not surprisingly, the lone loss resulted from a poor performance by Foster, but Ruth helped the Red Sox rebound with a win on June 27 in the final game. The Senators' Walter Johnson and Harry Harper then shut down the Boston offense in two losses before Carl Mays (6–2) lifted the Red Sox to a 6–1 victory to close June. In that contest, the ever-improving Tilly Walker (3-for-4, 2 runs, RBI) had a big day at the plate in a game marred by extracurricular activities.[29]

According to Stanley Milliken of the *Washington Post*, "Trouble had been brewing between the two clubs for some time, and it started in the third inning, when Carl Mays hit McBride with a pitched ball. McBride responded by deliberately throwing his bat at the pitcher, who almost immediately was surrounded by a score of Washington and Boston players and a few fans, two or three of whom were armed with pop bottles."

By this time Carrigan and Ruth had already been ejected for arguing with the umpire. Things escalated as both benches cleared, and Boston catcher Sam Agnew punched Washington manager Clark Griffith in the face. Agnew, who claimed Griffith shoved him first or called either him or Mays a name, was arrested and then released on $60 bail. Boston had a reputation for beanballs, and Senators batters had already been hit in previous games by the Red Sox in 1916. Additionally, Mays and McBride had a minor mix-up in the previous day's game, and the latter claimed he was told before the June 30 contest that he would be beaned. Mays also appeared to be throwing at McBride earlier in the game as well.[30]

Things were clearly heating up as June came to a close, and it wasn't just the weather. In the July 6 *Sporting News*, White Sox writer George Robbins reported incidents like the one between the Red Sox and Senators had increased dramatically in 1916, and Ban Johnson was trying to put a stop to them.[31] A possible cause of the increased tension was that even this early in the season, it was clear the pennant race was going to be one of the most unpredictable ever. That was evident in the July 1 standings, since none of the contenders ranked higher than third.

Team	Wins	Losses	Games Behind
Yankees	37	26	—
Indians	36	28	1½
White Sox	33	29	3½
Red Sox	34	30	3½
Senators	34	30	3½
Tigers	34	32	4½

Team	Wins	Losses	Games Behind
Browns	29	36	9
Athletics	17	43	18½

This would change in July, however, as all three favorites asserted themselves. The red-hot White Sox, having won the first two against the struggling Tigers, finished the four-game sweep at Comiskey Park. On July 1st, Claude Williams (3–2), another Hughie Jennings castoff, tossed a shutout against his former team, and Hap Felsch hit a sixth-inning home run into the left-field bleachers, one of the longest shots ever at Comiskey Park. The next day pitchers Reb Russell and Harry Coveleski matched zeros until the last of the twelfth. With one out, Felsch doubled, and after nearly being picked off, scored the game-winning run on Eddie Collins' two-out single. Ty Cobb had been ejected in the seventh, and his replacement, Harry Heilmann, was unable to make a good throw to home. Coveleski (10–5), the hard-luck loser, had lost twice in the series, while Russell (7–3) had allowed just one run in his last 39 innings, continuing Chicago's recent stretch of strong pitching.[32]

In Washington, there was a huge gathering at the courthouse on July 1, including Boston players and president Joe Lannin. After much ado, Sam Agnew paid a $10 fine and returned to Boston with a suspension, while Bill Carrigan, Clark Griffith and George McBride also were suspended. Legal charges by both sides could have been pressed, but nothing materialized. On the field, the Senators won, 4–2, to take the series, three games to one.[33] During the series, Jack Barry finally returned to the lineup for the Red Sox, and his presence allowed Carrigan to settle on a steady July lineup. Del Gainer, who would end up playing a significant role in 1916, started to play more in July, but Hoblitzell still saw slightly more time at cleanup. The intra-region road trip continued for Boston with a visit to Shibe Park — again, great medicine after a tough series. The Red Sox responded by sweeping the three-game series against the 17–44 Athletics, who played their trademark awful defense.

The Tigers and White Sox were continuing to go in opposite directions. Detroit was at the beginning of a 31-game road trip, not a good sign for a team with a paltry 10–22 road record. H.G. Salsinger attributed this to the Tigers' inability to put their offense, defense and pitching together — or at least two of the three. Detroit opened the trip by losing two out of three to the second-place Indians, extending their streak to seven defeats in eight games. Poor pitching and defense, with the exception of the sporadic Bernie Boland (4–1), who won the first game of the July 4 doubleheader, hurt the Tigers. That left Salsinger wondering why the hurler wasn't in the rotation. The offense had been just as bad, hitting only .191 during the eight-game stretch. Meanwhile, Ban Johnson handed Cobb a three-game suspension and a $25 fine for his July 2 ejection. Despite the center fielder's history, in this case, he suddenly earned the role of a wronged baseball star, at least in the eyes of his manager.[34] Said Jennings:

> It doesn't seem just that the fans can get away with anything at all in the line of rowdy conduct and everything is all right, yet, whenever a ball player makes a mistake such as Ty made Sunday, he is disciplined. The suspension of Ty at this time is an injustice to the Detroit club which has been having enough bad breaks without the loss of its star. It also is unjust to the Cleveland club, for Ty is a drawing card and his presence in tomorrow's games would have meant a lot of extra money.

Jennings continued, saying he wouldn't blame Cobb if he left baseball for the movie business. Rumors of such a career shift were circulating in the *Free Press*, though Jennings and Detroit stock actor Vaughan Glaser denied them.[35]

Despite dealing with injuries to Red Faber, Fred McMullin, Jack Ness and Zeb Terry, Chicago was hot. This was still due to pitching, specifically Jim Scott, Mel Wolfgang, Claude Williams and Reb Russell. The White Sox defeated the Browns in the first of a three-game series at Comiskey Park for their seventh straight win, and then split an Independence Day doubleheader. After losing the opener, Chicago gave Williams a 4–0 lead, and the hurler struck out eight in the first three innings before faltering. St. Louis rallied to take a 6–4 lead, but in the bottom of the ninth with one on, Joe Jackson drove a ball to deep right-center. He ran through Rowland's stop sign at third base, and collided with Browns catcher Hank Severeid, who had just received the ball. The collision was "awful," and Jackson was called out before Umpire Evans realized that Severeid had dropped the ball, tying the game. Jackson was motionless for a while and had to be helped back to the dugout but played left field in the extra frames. An Eddie Collins two-out single won it in the 13th.[36]

Chicago and Detroit were set to embark on their second eastern swings of the year, with each having struggled on the first one. The third-place White Sox had gone 6–1 on their short homestand and were now three games out of first, having made up 4½ games and three spots in the standings in less than three weeks. First up on what would be a 21-game road trip was a series against the first-place Yankees. New York had won 12 of 14 and remained hot with a pair of 4–3 victories over Chicago, the second one coming in 12 innings. Both Nick Cullop, still undefeated in 1916, and George Mogridge beat the White Sox for the third time that season. Shockingly, in the initial contest on July 6, Rowland yanked Reb Russell, who had allowed just one run in his last 44 innings, due to some first-inning wildness. It wasn't a good decision as reliever Joe Benz struggled. Chicago blew a 12th-inning lead the next day before Eddie Cicotte (3–3) returned to salvage the final game on July 8, 2–1.

Fortunately for them, the Tigers' second eastern swing started like the first one at Philadelphia. Detroit was 3–10 since leaving home and pitchers Jean Dubuc (thumb) and Hooks Dauss (working out "ligament" issues with Bone-setter Reese) were injured.[37] Even with his health issues, Dauss (10–6) had been effective. The result was a Tigers' sweep against Philadelphia. Despite that, Detroit was in sixth, 6½ games behind the front-running Yankees.

Up in Boston, the Red Sox and Indians were starting the first of two important July series on the sixth. In the first contest, Everett Scott was on second with two men out in a 5–5 game in the bottom of the ninth. On the advice of Tris Speaker, the Indians walked Harry Hooper to get to Barry, just back from an injury. Suggesting Spoke might not be an expert on his former teammates, Barry responded with a game-winning single for Boston's fourth straight victory. It was one of the lone bright spots in a month that Barry finished by hitting .197. (While not usually excelling, he typically hit better.) The next day Babe Ruth allowed a first-inning run but then settled down, not permitting another run through seven, and Tilly Walker's two-out sin-gle drove home the eventual winner in the eighth. That same day, Grantland Rice wrote what many were probably thinking, that the standings were so tightly bunched the champion would probably be determined in September. Behind a strong performance from Stanley Coveleski, Cleveland salvaged the final game on July 8.[38] Still, Boston had won five of six (and hit .298 during the five victories), and equally hot Chicago was coming in for seven games (three doubleheaders) in four days.

With both teams playing well and fighting for third place (Boston 4 out of first, Chicago 4½), Clarence Rowland chose a pair of lefthanders in Lefty Williams and Reb Russell to try and quell the Red Sox bats in what was arguably the first important series of the season. Pants reasoned that Boston struggled against southpaws, and Williams (5–2) and Russell (9–3) confirmed that, tossing 4–0 and 3–0 shutouts, respectively, to sweep a July 10 double-header. The victory was Russell's fifth of six straight as the White Sox moved into third place, passing Boston. McMullin finally returned for Chicago from the foot injury, but it was two RBIs, one in each game, by the struggling Buck Weaver that led the offense.[39]

Boston returned the favor on July 11, sweeping a doubleheader from the White Sox to regain third place. Bill Carrigan put Ruth on the mound in the opener, and Rowland tailored his lineup to a lefty hurler. Showing his deft-ness, Rough then replaced Ruth with the righty Rube Foster after one out, foiling Rowland's strategy. The White Sox had chances but couldn't capital-ize, and a third-inning error by first baseman Jack Fournier along with Eddie Cicotte's wildness and Boston's timely hitting helped the Red Sox win, 5–3. Ruth (12–5) came back to pitch the second game, winning easily by a score of 3–1. Sam Agnew returned from suspension in the nightcap of another Boston doubleheader sweep the following day. Rowland sent Williams and Russell back to the hill on one day's rest, and while both were effective, they weren't good enough. Ernie Shore (6–5) and Dutch Leonard (9–6) hurled complete-game, one-run efforts on a sultry, 100-degree day at Fenway Park. Buck Weaver was ejected for arguing a close play at first base in the top of the eighth inning of the first contest. His replacement at shortstop, Zeb Terry, promptly made two errors that provided the winning run for Boston. After being swept in the first doubleheader, Boston had taken the next two twin bills, moving them within two games of first and in third place, while Chicago was 4½ back and in fourth place. The finale was rained out, but the White Sox still lost when Fournier ($8), Felsch ($9) and McMullin ($14) were robbed while they slept in an unlocked hotel room in New York City.[40]

Fans who attended the three twin bills in Boston did so knowing they were expected to return foul balls hit into the stands. This was just one aspect of how the Deadball Era ballpark experience differed significantly from today. The foul ball practice was being reconsidered as a Boston *Herald* article on July 13 stated that owner Joseph Lannin would allow fans who caught a ball to exchange it for a complimentary ticket to the next day's game. Charles Weeghman, the new Cubs owner, would go even further, actually allowing spectators to keep foul balls. Among other things, rushing in employees to retrieve the balls was hurting relationships with paying customers, the primary source of revenue.[41]

Fan behavior was also somewhat different, and there are frequent newspaper accounts of hometown fans cheering good plays by opponents. At the same time, negative fan behavior went to excesses rarely seen today. For example, it wasn't uncommon for the universally hated New York Giants to face flying missiles, such as eggs, rocks and bricks, when they were away from the Polo Grounds. Umpires were also not exempt since they were subjected to aerial attacks with seat cushions, apparently the weapon of choice. While such attacks were spirited, they weren't driven by spirits since no alcohol was sold at the ballpark. Bleacher fans, due to their low-priced and unprotected seats, were considered the most "devout." Low priced meant 25 cents, less expensive than box ($1), grandstand (75 cents) and pavilion seats (50 cents). The latter represented stands down the lines past first and third base. If all seats were sold, owners would place fans behind ropes in the outfield. With beer unavailable, "bugs" expected to spend 10 cents for a hot dog and five cents for cracker jacks, popcorn or a drink, usually root beer. Games started at 3 P.M. and would last 1½ to 2 hours, allowing spectators to go to work, attend the game and make it home for dinner. Also available by 1900 were scorecards (five cents), enabling fans to track game action. Further improvements occurred when lineups and lineup changes were announced via a mega-phone. A 1916 innovation was the Chicago White Sox's use of a flag system to notify fans when a game was postponed. While employed in other cities, it marked the first time a specific flag would designate a postponed game.[42]

While Boston and Chicago slugged it out at Fenway Park, Detroit got its first test on the eastern swing with a series against Washington. Any doubts Batchelor had about the team's success in Philadelphia were resolved when the Tigers took three of four. The writer's call for consistency was answered as Detroit displayed strong offense and pitching. The July 10 contest was rained out amidst rumors the Tigers and Senators were working on a deal that would send Sam Crawford to Washington, despite vehement denials from reporter Joe Jackson. Reportedly, Nationals manager Clark Griffith wasn't offering much in return. Dauss (11–6) came back in the series, but it was strong efforts by George Cunningham in relief, Coveleski (12–5) and Bill James (3–4) that made the difference. Big hits from Burns and even the slump-ing Harry Heilmann also helped. Besides a defeat at the hands of Walter John-son, the only down side for the Tigers was an injury to catcher Oscar Stanage. Since he would be out a week or longer, Del Baker would fill in. The good news was Detroit had made up ground against Washington, climbing to within 4½ of first while residing in a fourth-place tie with Chicago.[43]

Still, the timing of the injury was awful, with a visit to first-place New York for six games upcoming. The Tigers' Willie Mitchell (1–2) won the first contest of a doubleheader, handing Nick Cullop (9–1) his first loss of the sea-son by gamely out-battling him for 12 innings in a 6–2 victory. During the game, the Yankees' Frank "Home Run" Baker crashed into an iron door on the concrete grandstand while chasing a pop fly and suffered "severe lacera-tions and deep bruises on the left side just above the heart." The injuries were said to have him out a week, but there were some reports noting two broken ribs that had him out much longer. Injuries were really hamstringing New York, which was already missing outfielders Frank Gilhooley and Fritz Maisel.[44] Mitchell won again in the final game of the series, 4–0, on July 18. There was a pattern of pitchers leaving the Tigers and becoming effective elsewhere, but Mitchell was doing the opposite after going 2–5 with Cleve-land to start the season. George Burns had six RBIs in the Tigers' third vic-tory, but the depleted Yankees won the other three games and managed a split of the series to barely hold on to first place.

As Detroit and New York were fighting to a draw, Boston had taken three of four from St. Louis. The Red Sox were now just a game behind after winning seven of eight on the strength of a continued strong offense and their vaunted pitching staff getting back in gear. In the opener on July 14, the two teams played to a 0–0 tie after 17 innings. A 17–4 victory salvaged a doubleheader split the next day before the Red Sox won the final two games. Boston tied the last game in the third inning when Ruth (14–5) bowled over St. Louis catcher Hank Severeid, knocking out both the ball and Severeid. Legendary sportswriter T.H. Murnane was pleased with Boston's play, writing, "The all-around fielding of the Champions was exceptionally brilliant during the series, and this morning the Red Sox are in a position very close to the top, and they are very likely to take the lead within a short time." In fact, Carrigan's men were just a game out of first.[45]

The White Sox quickly made up some of the ground they lost against Boston with a series in Philadelphia, which had become a get-well-quick venue for A.L. teams. There were two doubleheader sweeps, and the closest contest saw Benz (4–3) out-duel surprising rookie Joe Bush on July 15. Seeking some off the field excitement the next day, members of the White Sox went swimming in the reportedly shark-infested ocean off of Atlantic City, New Jersey.[46] Although in fourth place, Chicago was only 2½ games out of first while sixth-place Detroit trailed by only 4½ games. Rowland again was having trouble finding a set lineup, but he ultimately settled on Eddie Murphy/J. Collins, Weaver, E. Collins, Jackson, Ness, Felsch, Terry and Schalk. Felsch, who had been leading off, dropped far down in the order for no apparent reason. Ness had won the first base job back from Fournier, and J. Collins would also win the leadoff spot from Murphy toward the end of July. Though Murphy's demotion was less surprising, both situations were again curious because it didn't appear that the losers did anything wrong. In addition, the corner infield spots, a major concern in spring training, were a continuing problem.

For all of the criticism that was heaped on Clarence Rowland for dabbling with platoons and lefty/righty match-ups, Shoeless Joe Jackson finally went to bat for him, saying, "Yes, I'd like to lead the league, and I'll tell you why — I'd like to do it for Rowland's sake, for, if I accomplish the feat he will deserve the credit. I've never seen a single instance since I joined the Chicago team in which the players failed to give Rowland their best effort and he holds their highest respect."[47] Jackson's average dropped in July, but only from .378 to .346. Eddie Collins finally got going, improving more than 29 points to .262, while Hap Felsch was all the way up to .290 at month's end. Yet it wasn't the offense that kept the team hot after its strong June finish. For example, upon returning to the lineup in late July, Zeb Terry suffered a 6-for-46 slump. As in June, it was again pitching, and again, Faber made only one start. The White Sox staff was stellar, and it was a broad-based team effort. Chicago pitchers allowed fewer than three runs per game, and those numbers were even stronger in the first half of July. In one stretch, Reb Russell gave up just four runs in 39 innings, while Eddie Cicotte limited opponents to only two runs in 27 innings.

By month's end, the Red Sox and Tigers had played a number of competitive contests. Neither team dominated, but Detroit won from a psychological standpoint. Detroit, which had been awful on the road, was wrapping up nearly a month-long road trip with its second eastern swing of the season. It started 3–10, but by going 9–4 thus far in the East, the Tigers' overall record was 12–14. In addition, Detroit had done this with a depleted roster. Dubuc and Stanage were still injured, and Dauss had apparently comeback too soon in his start against Washington, possibly ignoring Bonesetter Reese's advice. There were even rumors Detroit might go after Philadelphia rookie pitcher Joe Bush.[48] With the Tigers 4½ out and 12–14 on the trip, the five-game series in Boston was clearly important. A bad result and the Jungaleers could find themselves on the outside of the pennant race looking in. To make matters worse, Detroit's recent history at Fenway Park wasn't good, and though both teams appeared to be playing solid baseball, the Tigers had lost 2½ games on the Red Sox thus far in July. Though not in first place, Boston was still the team to beat.

Things got off to a bad start for Detroit when the Red Sox swept a doubleheader on July 19, nearly the same date Boston took first place for good over the Tigers in 1915. Dauss (11–7), who had a tough month, returned in the first contest but was bettered by Carl Mays (9–3), as pinch-hitter Olaf Henriksen drove in the winning run. In the second game, Hughie Jennings allowed Cunningham to throw three full innings, and in the third, the Red Sox scored four times to take a 6–3 lead they would not relinquish. All four runs scored with two outs, but none were earned. Meanwhile, Carrigan, who was clearly more effective in handling his pitching staff, yanked Shore with one out and the bases loaded in the top of the fourth. Leonard (11–6) worked out of the jam without allowing any runs.[49]

Nearly all month Hughie's batting order had been Vitt, Bush, Heilmann, Cobb, Veach, Burns, Young and a catcher, which lately was Baker because of Stanage's injury. Stanage returned in the doubleheader but still had problems with his finger, and left along with Dauss for Detroit after the twin bill to further recuperate. To start the series, Jennings promoted Burns to the three spot (he had three RBIs there in the second game) and dropped Heilmann to sixth, as both were going in opposite directions. Toward the end of July, Harry would lose his spot to Sam Crawford. The Tigers' offense improved in July, but the efforts, as usual, were hampered by top-of-the-order guys like Donie Bush (.222) and Ossie Vitt (.217). Additionally, Bobby Veach, despite hitting a mammoth home run in that doubleheader at Fenway, started the month 0-for-12 and never recovered, dropping from .292 to .274. Ralph Young did get his average up to .264 from .240, while Cobb improved from .348 to .360. Toward the end of July, Speaker was hitting .391, meaning Ty still had work to do in order to retain his batting crown.[50]

A panoramic view of Fenway Park during its inaugural season in 1912 (George Bain Collection, Library of Congress).

Detroit picked up its first win in Boston in 1916 on July 20. The Tigers staked Harry Coveleski (13–6) to a 2–0 lead in the sixth, but the Red Sox tied it in the eighth. With Boston still rallying, third baseman Vitt turned a critical unassisted double play on Duffy Lewis' liner. Ruth's throwing error in the 13th put Cobb (3-for-6, 1 run, 2 RBIs) on second, and he scored on Young's eventual game-winning single. Coveleski worked out of trouble in the 13th to deny Boston a share of first place.[51] After some struggles, the southpaw was Detroit's workhorse in July. He made eight starts and went 4–4, but the first six were high-quality performances. In those, he allowed only 12 runs in 63 innings and pitched 12 or more innings three times. The other bonus was Bernie Boland, who was coming around and went 3–1 in July.

A rainout the next day gave E.A. Batchelor an opportunity to rip the Tigers for their lack of offense, specifically Harry Heilmann, who would soon find himself on the bench, even though he wasn't hitting terribly. To the contrary it seemed to be the offense that propelled erratic Detroit to an 18–12 record to finish July. The pitching staff had allowed nearly four runs per game while the offense hit .266 and scored more than four per contest. The postponement forced a doubleheader on July 22, which would have a time limit so the Tigers could return to Detroit in time for a game with Chicago. Detroit benefited from some poor Boston defense and clutch hitting in the first game to hang on for a win 4–3 behind Mitchell (3–2). But the Red Sox took three out of five when Dutch Leonard (12–6) hurled a shutout, and Tilly Walker added a great catch in the 1–0 victory.[52]

Detroit had survived, finishing its trip 14–17 and 11–7 in the East. The Tigers were six games out of first in sixth place, and one winning streak away from the thick of the race. Detroit had both hit (.269) and pitched well (fewer than three runs per game) against their eastern counterparts on the road. It was a sign they were either getting things together or continuing to play streaky baseball. Boston went westward in second place, only 1½ games behind the Yankees, but the balance of the schedule didn't favor the Red Sox, especially a tough road trip in September that loomed large. Still, Boston was dangerous, as Grantland Rice noted, "The Red Sox are the people most feared, for unless they are halted in the next three weeks they will not be any harder to overtake later on than a scared coyote."[53] If a western team was to win the pennant for the first time since 1909, the time to make a move was rapidly approaching.

Meanwhile, Chicago had lost two games in the standings during an ugly six-game set in Washington. The White Sox battered Walter Johnson in relief in winning the first game of the opening doubleheader but struggled against him in the nightcap and lost. During a second doubleheader, on July 20, poor fielding, mainly by Shano Collins, contributed to two Chicago losses. The White Sox would split the final two games but had an opportunity to win both, losing a ninth-inning lead in the second contest.[54] Still, Chicago finished the eastern trip a respectable 9–10, and pitching had been the key.

Now 4½ games out in fifth place, the White Sox spent roughly 20 hours on the rails to reach Detroit, while the Tigers outdid them with 21 hours in transit. Even then, the teams were late to the park, and Chicago didn't have clean uniforms. In a sloppy contest, the White Sox used a six-run fourth to out-slug the Tigers, 12–9. Ness led the way with five of Chicago's whopping 20 hits. To end the game, Bush popped a foul ball behind the plate that Schalk may or may not have caught. Bush was ruled out, umpire Dick Nallin was rushed by angry fans, and the players had to escort him to the dugout. Numerous fans, however, still waited, and it took a police escort to get Nallin and the other umpire safely back to the hotel.[55]

Temperatures and tempers remained hot on July 24 in the second and final game of the series. Shano Collins, who had been benched for Eddie Murphy, returned with a lefty on the hill to collect two hits, including the game winner in the 13th for a 3–2 Chicago victory. Williams (6–3), who started the opener on July 23, tossed the final three innings for the victory. There were numerous close calls, and Schalk was ejected in the ninth for arguing balls and strikes. The Tigers were also dealt a blow as Jennings, who was ejected the day before, was suspended indefinitely.[56]

Early in spring training, Jim Nasium had referred to the even-then old adage that pitching was 90 percent of baseball.[57] In spite of similar beliefs today about the importance of pitching, that aspect of the game was vastly different during the Deadball Era. There were few defined roles, it was common to start and relieve, and there was no such thing as a specialist or even a set rotation. The choice of the day's starter seemed to be determined by who was pitching well, and even who warmed up well. Relief work could be handed over to a starter who wasn't pitching well, had a good reputation, or perhaps because there wasn't anyone else available. A hurler would only exit when he really struggled or became injured, and certainly not for a pitch count.

Fastballs, curveballs and changeups or slow balls were standard parts of a pitcher's repertoire, but many also used the spitball, which gained attention in the early 1900s. The basis for an effective spitball is having one area of the ball moist while the remaining parts are dry. The varying frictions in texture caused the ball to behave abnormally. Upon reaching the plate, spitballs had a "fall off the table" type of behavior, which resulted in numerous ground balls. Pitchers typically chewed on lozenges of slippery elm sold in drugstores to produce the necessary saliva.[58]

Chicago's Red Faber was arguably the most significant 1916 spitballer, and years later, he said:

> A spitter has to be thrown moderately fast and the ball slips away from under the two front fingers of the pitching hand and sails up to the batter rotating very slowly. Then it breaks down and to one side ... I never wet the ball but merely the ends of the first two fingers of my right hand. The whole theory of the spitball is to let the ball slide away from a smooth surface. Wetting the fingers gives this smooth surface.

While there were clearly ethical issues about the pitch, other detractors also argued the pitch injured arms, and was difficult to control. For example, the spitball was hard for catchers, pitchers and even fielders to handle because of the moistness. It would be outlawed in 1920, but those spitballers still active, at a rate of two per team, could continue using it until the end of their careers.[59]

Before traveling to Detroit, the Red Sox started their western swing in Cleveland amidst rumors of a potential return for Smokey Joe Wood. The rumors dissipated, as he refused to use 1916 as a tryout. After dropping the first game, the Red Sox won three straight one-run games, and at series' end on July 28, had closed to within a half game of the Yankees. Mays pitched Boston to a 2–1 victory in the second game, and said it was the hottest weather he ever hurled in. Between innings, a Red Sox trainer had to bathe his wrists and neck in ice water. Tilly Walker was another key, and Paul Shannon remarked, "Walker has outshone Speaker in these four games, for while the Texan's bat won the first contest, Tilly did the more effective work in the last two battles. Both yesterday and today he shone in the outfield."[60] Tilly's average improved in July from .256 to .274. Additionally, Duffy Lewis, Del Gainer, Larry Gardner and Dick Hoblitzell contributed during a period where Boston increased its team average from .237 to .245. This equated to the Red Sox hitting .282 while the pitching staff allowed fewer than three runs per game during a recent stretch that had seen them go 13–4 before heading to Detroit. Boston clearly appeared ready to make a big move.

Detroit entered the series against the Red Sox just as hot after taking four straight from the fading Senators at Navin Field. Dubuc, now healthy, picked up three of the victories — two in relief— by throwing 18 straight scoreless innings. Jennings returned, and potentially the only negative occurred when Veach was hit in the eye by a batted ball and was expected to miss a couple days. The best and most important performance by a Tiger wasn't even on the field, however. On the night of July 25, Harry Heilmann, about to be benched, dove into a canal at Waterworks Park and saved the lives of three people whose car had been driven into the water.[61]

Having cut the deficit to five games, Detroit hosted Boston in a six-game series that extended into August. By sweeping a doubleheader on July 29, the Tigers crept to within three games. The night before Boston had traveled by boat to Detroit on an intensely hot, uncomfortable and sleepless night. Then on a parched and ugly Navin Field, another by-product of the heat, the Red Sox performance was equally ugly. Detroit took advantage with key hits, especially by Veach and Vitt, building big leads in 10–8 and 7–3 victories. It was the Tigers' first doubleheader sweep of the season. The only positive for Boston was Gainer, who hit two home runs in the first game to push his average over .300.[62]

Dutch Leonard's performance in the nightcap was the first time all month he allowed more than two runs. Leonard and Mays had been the workhorses in July as Boston's pitching staff got going again. Leonard, back in early-season form, went 5–2 in July, and Mays did the same. Apparently, though, Dutch's workload may have been getting to him, as years later Carrigan said the hurler complained of a sore arm but not until he had already been hit hard against Detroit. Joe Lannin heard about the situation, and this led to a verbal dispute between Leonard and the owner as well as speculation, which never materialized, that Carrigan might be fired. Ernie Shore went 3–1 in July, and while Ruth won four games, he had his share of poor outings, resulting in a 4–4 record over the course of the month. With some rest, Boston responded the next two days and capitalized on big innings each time. Detroit's chances weren't helped by poor defense and sloppy pitching by Mitchell and Coveleski. Mays (11–4) won a 9–3 decision on July 30, and it was Ruth (15–8) prevailing, 6–0, the next day. Carl's victory pushed the Red Sox past the Yankees and finally back into first place for the first time in more than three months.[63] Boston had started its road trip by hitting .281 over the first eight games. Meanwhile, even though the Tigers had lost the final two games in July, they had gone 4–5 thus far during what was a critical 11-game stretch against Boston. At the very least, they were holding their own against the resurgent defending champion Red Sox and well within striking distance at 4½ games out of first.

Now it was Chicago's turn to make a quick move before July concluded. The White Sox had been getting close to first and then falling back. After the brief two-game set in Detroit, Chicago headed home for an extended stand, beginning with a visit from the first-place Yankees. Taking advantage of Ray Caldwell's wildness on July 25, the White Sox won, 13–8. In the following game, Eddie Cicotte hurled a one-hitter in a 2–0 victory. Chicago would drop back again, however, losing the final two games, the first after blowing a 6–1 lead in the seventh inning. Fortunately, an eight-game series with Philadelphia gave the White Sox ample opportunity to rebound. Red Faber (9–3) returned in the first game of a doubleheader sweep on the July 29 and won, showing few signs of a thumb injury that caused him to miss nearly two months. The ever-exaggerating George Robbins noted, "The come back of Faber will round out about the best pitching staff in the American League and with a combination of offensive players that is equaled by none and a defensive that is superior to anything that I have seen in the league this year it must be a prejudiced person indeed who fails to see the White Sox as favorites."[64]

With another doubleheader sweep the following day, Chicago, like Boston, passed New York in the standings and was within a half game of first. And so on August 1, the American League standings seemed to becoming more in line with original predictions.

Team	Wins	Losses	Games Behind
Red Sox	54	40	—
White Sox	55	42	1
Yankees	53	43	2
Indians	51	44	3½
Tigers	52	47	4½
Senators	49	45	5
Browns	48	49	7½
Athletics	19	71	33

Things were undoubtedly jam-packed in the first division, with the Tigers lurking, but the Red Sox had awoken — a very scary thought for Chicago and Detroit. Throughout April, May and June, surprises, like the Indians, Yankees and Senators, had played well, but now the contenders had asserted themselves, creating this logjam. The Red Sox (20–10), White Sox (22–13) and Tigers (18–15) had all enjoyed a good month, but it was no secret why Boston and Chicago, both with very balanced attacks, were a step ahead. The White Sox had been stronger on the mound; the Red Sox tougher at the plate. The latter fact was especially concerning for the challengers since Boston's staff would probably hit its full stride at some point. Inconsistency, however, continued to plague Detroit, especially its pitchers.

CHAPTER V

"A perfect imitation of a
left handed fat lady
sweeping out a dead mouse."

While every game was important, the early results of the 1916 National
League season would be significant only to the extent they were sustained or
reversed. June, therefore, presented the first challenge to early-season success
and the first opportunity to reverse failure. The Giants, for example, had
enjoyed the most dramatic turnaround imaginable — the question was which
performance reflected reality, the April losing or the May winning? As we
have seen, New York began June with a four-game series in Philadelphia that
carried over from the end of May. While the two teams were splitting the
four games, Brooklyn returned home to take on Boston.

The overall priority for the Dodgers was to continue the level of play
that had put them in first place, and more specifically, to reverse their poor
record against Boston, a carryover from 1915. Losing three of the first four to
the Braves after an 8–14 record in 1915 made Rice feel Boston had a hex of
some kind on the Superbas. The Braves, on the other hand, needed a change
in direction after a disappointing road trip, followed by a short but disastrous
homestand against the Giants. The series opened with a separate admission,
morning-afternoon Memorial Day doubleheader. When the Braves jumped
out to a 5–0 lead en route to a 5–3 win, many in the estimated crowd of
12,000 agreed with Rice that the Boston "conjure was in full operation." A
further disappointment was another poor performance by Rube Marquard.
When the Superbas failed to score in the first six innings of the second game,
the situation looked bleak. Fortunately for Brooklyn and an even-larger crowd
of 20–22,000 spectators, however, Sherrod Smith was matching Tom Hughes'
shutout performance. After John Meyers drove in George Cutshaw with the
game's first run, Zack Wheat preserved the win with "one of the greatest

catches ever made on Ebbets Field," robbing Dick Egan of a home run. Things got testy at the end between Wheat and Rabbit Maranville, but ended as nothing more than "wordy combat."[1]

Perhaps motivated by his conflict with Maranville, Wheat took charge the next day with a home run and "two star" catches. Maranville may also have garnered some energy from the exchange, as Rice counted no less than six game-saving plays by the Rabbit. However, Maranville's drop of a potential double-play ball in the bottom of the ninth kept a Dodger rally alive, allowing Cutshaw to drive in the winning run. Although Rice was now confident the Braves' spell was broken, Boston proceeded to sweep a June 1 twin bill, 6–1 and 2–1. In fact, the hex was especially alive and well in the first inning when the Braves scored four runs on only one "dinky" hit. Even more crushing, however, was the second game, as Jack Coombs (2–2) took a shutout into the ninth, only to be beaten when the Braves rallied for two runs. Boston received superlative pitching performances from Ragan and Rudolph (5–5), and reportedly celebrated the go-ahead run in the second game as if they won the World Series. Anticipating future idiom, *Standard Union* reporter Len Worcester commented, "There is much love in Brooklyn for the Braves — not."[2]

Boston's one-game advantage in the series gave the Braves hope that their poor play was turning around, while on the Brooklyn side, they at least held on to first place. Off the field, there was "unadulterated . . rejoicing" by both owners as "the ducats dropped into the dough bag like rain drops into a bucket" throughout the series. Such comments emphasize the crucial importance of gate receipts to team finances in the Deadball Era. Unlike today, the fan at the ballpark, with modest exceptions, was the sole source of revenue, beginning with ticket sales and carrying over to concessions and scorecards. Anything that held down attendance, such as bad weather or disruptions in public transportation, were more devastating than today since there was no television revenue to offset lost ticket sales.[3]

While much of this was different than today's game, two constants remained — uncertainty regarding the actual profitability of teams, and the players' claims they were underpaid. Clearly the reserve clause limited the players' ability to maximize their earnings by "reserving" or restricting them to one team. It was also true, however, that the average salary of a baseball player in 1916 was $4,500, well above the average American worker's $600 annual income. Team profitability is very hard to evaluate, as no reliable figures exist for the period prior to 1920. In 1916, Charles Ebbets claimed the annual cost of running a team was in the $225,000 to $250,000 range. One analysis suggests this latter figure would require an average daily attendance of 4,000.[4] This was probably not a difficult goal for the pennant contenders, but for the western teams it was difficult, if not impossible.

Fresh off their highly successful 19–2 road trip, the Giants opened a three-game series against the Reds on June 2, the beginning of a lengthy homestand. Understandably, optimism reigned supreme, and the players were presented with "loving cups" in recognition of their outstanding road trip. No doubt trying to build on Christy Mathewson's recent success, McGraw chose his veteran right-hander for the first game in front of an enthusiastic crowd of 18,000. However, the Reds shelled Mathewson, taking a 4–0 lead on nine hits. Showing the same spirit that typified the road trip, New York battled back to tie the game, only to fall, 6–4, in 13 innings. The next day the Giants resumed their winning ways by beating Cincinnati, 7–4, in front of a Suffrage Day crowd estimated at 20,000, featuring a large female contingent with their yellow and blue silk banners. In the rubber game of the series, New York again came from behind to tie the game, only to lose once more in extra innings, 3–2. No realist expected the Giants to sweep the western teams at home, but losing two games of the first series in extra innings wasn't a good sign, especially since New York was now 0–6 in extra-inning home games.[5]

While the Giants and Reds played their entire series, their neighbors in Brooklyn lost the middle game of their match-up with Pittsburgh to rain.

Polo Grounds, home of the New York Giants, during the 1913 World Series (George Bain Collection — Library of Congress).

After losing the June 2 opener, 5–2, the Superbas salvaged a split, winning the June 5 finale, 3–2. In the first contest, Brooklyn only managed three hits off Pirate ace Al Mamaux, and had now scored only four runs in three straight losses. One positive note in the latest loss was an impressive relief performance by Rube Marquard. There was also a statistical oddity in the first game, as Pittsburgh had only three assists, one more than the 1906 record of two. The good news was, in spite of losing three of its last four, Brooklyn was still in first place.[6]

Although the Boston Braves had enjoyed a resurgence against the Dodgers, they still had work to do in escaping the second division. Little progress was made in that direction when Stallings' men lost two out of three to the Cubs. Offense had become a major problem, as the Braves managed only five runs in the three games, wasting some very good pitching in the process. After winning the second game on June 3, 3–2, with a veritable offensive explosion, Boston lost the last game on June 5, 1–0, on Heinie Zimmerman's steal of home.[7]

Unlike the Braves, the Phils had enjoyed a successful western trip, but like Boston, had done poorly in the next two home series against their eastern rivals. Philadelphia's western homestand, which began against St. Louis, didn't get off to a good start on June 2, when Mike Gonzalez's ninth-inning double drove in two runs for a 3–2 Cardinals victory. The next day Gonzalez again batted in the ninth, in a similar situation, but this time went quietly, probably because Alexander (9–4) was the pitcher. After losing an early lead in the third game on June 5, the Phillies won, 6–5, in 11 innings on Bert Niehoff's double, his fourth hit of the day. The first series of the western homestand ended in the National League with Brooklyn still in first place, with a 1½ game lead over Philadelphia and New York, while the Braves were two games below .500, in fifth place and five games behind.[8]

As the western teams traded places for the second round of their trip east, rain became a major problem. Three of the scheduled four games in Brooklyn, Philadelphia, and New York were postponed, while Boston managed to get two games in against St. Louis. Boston continued to play .500 baseball, winning 3–2 on June 7 after Dick Rudolph (5–6) suffered a hard-luck 2–1 loss in the first game the day before. While the Braves may have felt fortunate to have gotten two games in, the rain gods had their revenge as precipitation cost Boston not only one game against the Cards, but two versus the Reds in the next series. Play, but not results, resumed on June 13 when the Braves and Cincinnati battled to a 16-inning, 0–0 tie, wasting another stellar pitching performance by Dick Rudolph. Rudolph, however, saved the game with a barehanded stop in the 12th inning, but the resulting injury would keep him from pitching for almost a month. Although it took 12 innings, the Braves finally generated some offense the next day, knocking out 13 hits on the way to a 4–3 victory. Even though they had won two of the three games they were able to play, the Braves fell another game off the pace and were six out with one series left with the western teams.[9]

The Reds were no doubt just glad to play the two games in Boston, as they had suffered three straight cancellations in the previous series at Brooklyn. The one contest the Dodgers and Reds did play on June 6 ended in a 7–4 Brooklyn win, behind 12 Superbas hits, including an inside-the-park home run by Jake Daubert. When Brooklyn finally resumed play against the Cardinals on June 10, the series opened inauspiciously, with a 3–2 St. Louis win in 14 innings. After an unnecessary day of rest on Sunday, the Dodgers came back with a vengeance, sweeping the last three games, twice by 3–1 counts, and once by 8–5. In the first 3–1 win, Larry Cheney (4–4) survived the damage done by the Cards (7 hits) and himself (5 walks). Pfeffer (9–0) was far more dominating the next day, limiting the Cardinals to one run on two hits. Then, in the series finale on June 14, Jack Coombs (3–2) started his

Braves Field, home of the Boston Braves, the "home of big things," during the 1930s (Leslie Jones Collection, Boston Public Library).

first game since June 1. He may have had too much rest, as Brooklyn fell behind, 5–2, before rallying for an 8–5 win, aided by seven St. Louis errors. The game marked another successful relief appearance by Rube Marquard, who allowed only one hit in four innings. Having won four of five in the two rain-abbreviated series, the Superbas were two games ahead of the second-place Phils.[10]

Like Brooklyn, the Giants also managed to get in one game of their second series against the West. Considering how New York was playing at home, that may not have been such a bad thing. Although losing, 3–2, to Pirates ace Al Mamaux on June 6 was probably no surprise, their dismal performance against the Cubs in the next series gave clear indications the Giants weren't as good as their 19–2 road trip suggested. After being shutout, 1–0, by New York in the first game on June 10, the Cubs totally dominated the Giants, outscoring them 17–4 over the next three games. Although it may not have seemed significant at the time, Ferdinand Schupp made his 1916 debut during the series, pitching his first (but definitely not his last) shutout inning. It was probably fortunate for the New Yorkers that all but one of the games against the Cardinals, the last western visitor, were rained out. When the Giants did prevail over St. Louis on June 15, it was only their fourth home win in almost two months. Given that record, it was no surprise New York had lost ground, finishing the homestand against the western teams 4½ games out of first.[11]

After the Cubs pounded the Phils, 8–2, in the opening game of the second series of the western homestand, Philadelphia may not have been that disappointed to lose the last three games to rain. Following the rainouts and one Sabbath in Philadelphia, Pittsburgh arrived at Baker Bowl for an abbreviated three-game series, beginning on June 12. Unlike the Dodgers and Giants, the Phils defeated Al Mamaux in the series opener, 2–1, perhaps because they went with their own ace, the inimitable Alexander (10–4). With the Pirates' best pitcher out of the way, Philadelphia swept the last two games of the series, 5–3 and 3–2, the latter in 12 innings. The final contest on June 14 didn't lack for drama, as Moran's club came from behind to tie the game in the bottom of the ninth, finally prevailing on Bert Niehoff's 12th-inning home run four rows into the left-center field bleachers. Niehoff's blow was timely in more ways than one, as the growing dark would have probably prohibited further play. Eppa Rixey (5–1) went the distance for the Phils, surviving a bases loaded jam in the 11th.[12]

Now two games behind the first-place Superbas, the Phillies welcomed the Reds to Baker Bowl before heading to Brooklyn for a five-game showdown. Not surprisingly, one of the match-ups was lost to rain, and the two teams split the others, the Phils winning, 2–1, and then losing, 1–0. With

Baker Bowl, home of the Philadelphia Phillies, during the 1920s (National Baseball Hall of Fame Library, Cooperstown, N.Y.).

another vintage Alexander performance (11–4), Philadelphia needed only four hits and 1:24 to defeat Cincinnati on June 15. After a day of rain on June 16, Demaree gave up the game's only run to the first batter, the Reds Heinie Groh, on a home run, and Fred Toney shut the Phils out on five hits.[13]

Meanwhile in Brooklyn, the Superbas prepared for Philadelphia by sweeping the two games they were able to play with the Cubs. In cooling off a hot Chicago team, the Dodgers stretched their own winning streak to five. Mike Mowrey was back in the lineup after a knee injury to Gus Getz and drove in both Brooklyn runs in a 2–1 Superbas' victory in the opener on June 15. After suffering through their 15th rainout of the season on June 16, Brooklyn beat the Cubs, 4–3, in dramatic style the next day. Trailing 3–0 in the eighth with two out and no one on, Brooklyn rallied to tie at 3–3. Jack Coombs (4–2) came on to pitch the ninth, and after two hitless innings, drove in the winning run in the bottom of the 11th. Now enjoying a five-game winning streak, the Superbas awaited Philadelphia with a three-game lead.[14]

While Brooklyn improved their league-leading status, the Braves continued to struggle offensively. It didn't help matters that Pittsburgh's Al

Mamaux defeated them, 2–1, in the June 15 opener of what proved to be a two-game series. When a team like Boston is struggling to score, a pitcher's best solution is to limit the opposition's attack. Tom Hughes (9–2) took maximum advantage of that strategy the next day, no-hitting the Pirates in a performance marred by just two walks and one error. Only an estimated 1,500 fans witnessed this historic event, which culminated with Honus Wagner looking at a called third strike. Hughes' dominant performance featured a fastball with three different types of breaks and an equally effective curveball, all of which he mixed with a change of pace. The achievement must have been especially meaningful since Tom had lost a no-hitter in extra innings while pitching for the Yankees in 1910. In fascinating anticipation of the future, at least two newspapers commented on Hughes earning a place in a Hall of Fame that wouldn't exist for another 20-plus years. Despite the outstanding effort, the Braves were still struggling to score as they continued to hover around the .500 level, remaining in fifth place, 6½ games out of first.[15]

The Phils had gotten off to a poor start on their homestand, going 3–5 against the New York teams. Having recovered somewhat with a 6–3 record

Ebbets Field, home of the Brooklyn Dodgers, during the first game in 1913 (George Bain Collection — Library of Congress).

against the western clubs, Philadelphia arrived at Ebbets Field on June 19 for a five-game series. Unfortunately, the rain arrived with the Phillies, making for less than ideal playing conditions. Nasium commented the opener was played "in the midst of a swamp that appeared where Ebbets Field once stood," a surface Wilbert Robinson called the worst he had seen in 25 years of Major League Baseball. An estimated 10,000 fans braved the elements to witness a pitching match-up of rival pitching aces — Pfeffer (9–1) and Alexander (12–4). In the top of the fifth, however, some of the "50 cent boys," exposed to those same elements in the uncovered bleachers, poured onto the field, apparently hoping they could force the game to be called and replayed. With a forfeit to the Phillies the more likely outcome, Robinson and Daubert coached or coerced them off the field. Despite all of that, an exciting game was tied in the seventh inning when with one on, Fred Luderus deposited one of Pfeffer's pitches over the right-field wall. Although Brooklyn rallied, Stengel fouled out with two on and two out in the ninth, bringing the Phils to within two games of first.[16]

With its confidence fortified by Monday's win, Philadelphia erupted for 16 runs to sweep the June 20 doubleheader, cutting the Dodgers' lead to just a half game. It was one of Jack Coombs' (4–3) rare poor outings, as he didn't even make it out of the first inning. The Phils' dominance led Nasium to the conclusion that few in attendance "would bet a nickel on the Dodgers' chances of beating the Phils on the season's play." The Superbas quickly defused that theory when they returned the favor, sweeping a second doubleheader two days later, 5–0 and 8–5. After Pfeffer (10–1) shut Philadelphia out on two hits in the opener, the second game was a back-and-forth affair. Brooklyn led, 4–2, going to the seventh when the Phils rallied for a 5–4 lead. The advantage was short lived, however, as the Superbas scored four times in the bottom half. Marquard came on in the eighth to shut Philadelphia out over the last two frames, another encouraging sign for the Dodger pitching staff. Overall, the Phils won the series but had picked up just one game.[17]

Giants management was smarter or just kinder to its fans and players, for unlike Brooklyn, New York didn't play on June 19, leading to a doubleheader the next day. The first game provided a second straight home victory, the first time the Giants achieved that minimal feat in 1916. Incredibly, New York won 17 straight road games before winning two straight home games. The streak didn't last long, however, as in the second game, Don Carlos Ragan made the only run scored by the anemic Braves offense stand up. Tensions between the two teams also escalated during the second contest. Fiery Johnny Evers sat out the first game amidst claims ownership was trying to muzzle him. Evers made up for lost time in the second game, "brow beat(ing) the Giants one after another" because he would rather "beat a team of McGraw's than eat." By the time the nightcap was over, Johnny had confrontations with Larry Doyle, Art Fletcher and, finally, McGraw. Violence was averted when Rabbit Maranville joined the group and began shadow boxing, ultimately knocking himself out and leading the others to laugh and calm down.[18]

Even though the Giants had won two of three at home, they quickly reverted to the more typical result of extra-inning losses, not once, but twice. After Boston won, 5–4, in 10 innings on June 21, two negative trends collided in the series finale. The Braves' inability to score was matched against New York's inability to win at home, especially in extra innings. Something had to change, and it was the Boston offense, scoring enough runs to win, 3–1, in 11 innings. Both sides quarreled with the umpires, resulting in ejections from both teams and John McGraw's banishment to the bench from the coaching lines. He might have preferred an ejection since it would have allowed him to miss Evers' performance. After singling in the go-ahead run, the Trojan advanced to third, and with the bases loaded, stole home on the front end of a triple steal. Incredibly, after going 19–2 on the road, the Giants had finished their homestand with a 3–10 record.[19]

Although they still weren't scoring runs, three straight wins over New York enabled the Braves to move to Philadelphia on a positive note. After winning nine of their last 12, the Phils' climb to the top had been stymied by the double loss to Brooklyn. However, Philadelphia had Alexander (13–4) ready to go in the June 23 opener against Boston. Although it took 11 innings, he prevailed, 2–1. Alexander's performance was matched by Jess Barnes, and if not for a Braves' error, the Phillies would have lost in regulation. Finally, George Whitted of Philadelphia ended the festivities with a home run that earned him a ride to the clubhouse "on the shoulders of the gleeful fans." It was the last cause for celebration in this series, though, as Boston swept the next four games. Al Demaree pitched well the next day but was beaten when center fielder Dode Paskert "stood in his tracks as though paralyzed" and misplayed a fly ball into a home run on the bounce. Tom Hughes (10–2) came on for the Braves in the fifth and increased his streak of hitless innings to 15⅔ before it finally came to an end during his fourth inning of work. Hughes' dominance was such the Phils kept imploring the umpire to look for an emery board.[20]

The mandatory Sunday off on June 25 didn't slow down the Braves, who swept the next day's doubleheader, 5–1 and 9–5. Both games featured late-inning comebacks by Boston, which was finally starting to generate some offense, while the Phils now had offensive problems of their own. Then to cap off their performance with a flourish, Jess Barnes and the Braves beat Alexander (13–5), 3–0, on June 27 in a rematch of the first game. Had it not been for a Boston error in that initial game, Barnes would have beaten Alexander twice, and the Braves would have swept the five-game series. With a four-game losing streak hanging over them, Moran's club left for New York City, the first stop on a six-city trip. At least they were still in second place, 3½ games back of Brooklyn. Boston, on the other hand, had rebuilt its fortunes off a 7–2 road trip, moving past the Giants into third place, only four games behind the Superbas. As the Braves headed home for five games with Robby's men, Flatley was sure "that fear roosts in the minds of those leading Dodgers."[21]

Before "those leading Dodgers" could worry about the Braves, however, they had a six-game home series against the enigmatic Giants, including two doubleheaders. While the competitive fires between the two long-time New York City rivals probably didn't require much stoking, John McGraw was always willing to assist, apparently claiming the Dodgers weren't a serious pennant contender. Anticipation of large crowds led Charles Ebbets to add 5,000 temporary bleacher seats in left and center. Although only an estimated 10,000 fans made it to opening game on June 23, they probably sounded like 30,000 when Brooklyn took a 4–3 lead into the eighth. However, since the Giants weren't playing at home, anything was possible, and they quieted the crowd by scoring four times to prevail, 7–4. The next day, the "largest crowd in Brooklyn's baseball history" witnessed Wilbert Robinson's skill in picking spots for his pitchers. In the opener, Robby went with his favorite spot starter, Jack Coombs (5–3). Even though he fell behind 3–0 early in this game, Colby Jack went the distance in what became a 6–4 Dodger win, contributing a key hit in the process. In the second game, Robinson made an even more improbable choice, giving Nap Rucker only his second start of the season. Although once considered one of the top pitchers in the game, Rucker, now in his last major league season, had "the slowest ball in captivity." That notwithstanding, he held the Giants at bay for 7⅓ innings before Sherry Smith wrapped up a 5–4 victory.[22]

After a needed off-day on Sunday, the teams returned to Ebbets Field on Monday, June 26, for the second doubleheader of the series. No doubt due to the workday, the crowd was smaller, but was still estimated between 18,000–20,000. Most of them apparently made little use of their seats, since they were on their "feet most of the time rooting wildly for either the Giants or Robins." The early going gave no indication the day would be special, as New York pounded Brooklyn ace Jeff Pfeffer (10–2) for five runs in the fourth after he walked Pol Perritt, the Giants' pitcher, with two out and none on. New York still led, 6–0, in the bottom of the fifth with two out and one on when pitcher Duster Mails, a weak hitter, came to bat. In a triumph of content over style, Mails singled, leading Tom Rice to ungraciously note that the Brooklyn pitcher "gave a perfect imitation of a left handed fat lady sweeping out a dead mouse." As with Perritt's earlier walk, this opened the door, and six straight hits later, Brooklyn had scored eight times for an 8–6 lead. The key blow was a three-run homer by George Cutshaw off Christy Mathewson, now pitching in relief. In the seventh, the Giants rallied, filling the bases for Bennie Kauff. He tripled off Sherry Smith for an 11–8 New York lead that Christy made stand up the rest of the way. It was to be Big Six's last win as a Giant.[23]

Having witnessed a rare Deadball Era slugfest, the large crowd was treated to a classic pitchers duel in the second game. Encouraged by Rube Marquard's effective work in relief, Robinson started him against Rube Benton. Each Rube allowed one run, but otherwise the zeros accumulated into the 12th. As the Giants came up to bat, both growing darkness and gathering fog threatened to end the game. With one out, New York had the go-ahead run on third and Giants catcher Bill Rariden due up, followed by Benton. Robinson had Rariden walked, forcing John McGraw to make a decision regarding his pitcher. McGraw opted to pinch-hit George Kelly, who grounded weakly to Olson. In the bottom half, the New York skipper brought back Pol Perritt, who had started the first game. With one out, Brooklyn had the winning run on third, and McGraw mimicked Robinson's strategy by walking Otto Miller, the Brooklyn catcher, to bring up Marquard. The Superbas' boss countered by sending Lew McCarty to pinch hit, leading the Giants' manager to move his infield back against the slow-moving batter. However, Robinson had one more trick up his ample sleeve — McCarty "bunted prettily," scoring Cutshaw with the winning run. The crowd, which was described as the largest weekday gathering ever at Ebbets Field, had seen 4½ hours of "baseball of class," and some of the most exciting baseball imaginable.[24]

After that performance, it was almost unfair that the two teams had to play once more the next day, June 27. Pitching continued to dominate, as the Giants prevailed, 1–0, behind Jeff Tesreau, who out dueled "Wheezer" Dell. It was to be Brooklyn's last home game for almost a month. They headed off to Boston and the Polo Grounds, followed by the second western trip of the year. Given New York's record at home, it may not have been such a good thing that their second western swing would be preceded by five home games against the Phillies before the series with the Dodgers.

Brooklyn began its second extended road trip, still in first place by 3½ games, visiting a Boston team that had been winning in spite of its lackluster offense. In the first two games on June 28 and 29, the Braves continued to struggle at the plate, and the Superbas took advantage, winning the first, 3–2, and the second, 2–1. Following those defeats, Stallings was so frustrated that he blamed umpire Hank O'Day for the Braves' plight. Fortunately for George's sanity, his men finally generated some offense the next day in a 6–2 win. Contributing to Boston's offensive resurgence were Hank Gowdy and Fred Snodgrass, who combined for five hits. Prior to the game, Stallings continued to complain about the officiating, offering $50 for every close call umpire Mal Eason made in favor of the Braves. While not citing it as a reason for Brooklyn's defeat, several observers said George owed Eason "a lot of money" by game's end.[25]

When Boston swept the July 1 doubleheader, 7–4 and 2–0, Rice (who said he seldom criticized umpires) complained Eason had clearly been intimidated by the Boston manager. Regardless of the complaints about umpires, Brooklyn was clinging to a 4–3 lead in the bottom of the sixth inning of the first game. When the Braves loaded the bases with one out and Snodgrass at bat, Stallings, desperate for offense, ordered what was effectively called a "squeeze and run," with all the runners in motion on the pitch. Edgar Collins, who was on third, "was over the plate almost before Snodgrass left it," followed by Sherry Magee only a few steps behind. The aggressive play seemed to wake up the Boston offense, which added two more conventional runs for the 7–4 win. The second game was another pitchers duel, as Don Carlos Ragan and Rube Marquard matched zeros until the Braves scored twice in the eighth. It was a second impressive performance for Marquard, and he was simply out-pitched by Ragan, who allowed only two hits. As the Dodgers waited for the midnight train back to New York, there had to be others besides Rice who wondered what Brooklyn had to do to beat Boston. In spite of some improvement in the last two meetings, the Braves still led the season series, 9–5.[26]

Although most teams look forward to playing at home, the Giants could be forgiven for not sharing that enthusiasm. However, in the June 28 opener, New York actually won a close game at the Polo Grounds, beating the Phillies, 4–3. Things quickly returned to normal the next day, when the Phils swept both ends of a doubleheader, 4–0 and 5–2, ending Philadelphia's five-game skid. In pitching a 4–0 shutout, Eppa Rixey (8–2) faced the minimum 27 batters, as three of the four who hit safely were wiped out in double plays, and the fourth died stealing. Two losses in one day, followed by the prospect of facing Alexander the next day, June 30, probably convinced more than a few New York fans to save their money. The Giants weren't intimidated, however, as they not only won, but knocked out Alexander (13–6) for the second time in 1916. The key offensive blow for New York was a two-run, inside-the-park home run by Dave Robertson. As June became July, Al Demaree rebounded from losing the first game of the series to limit the Giants to two runs on five hits in a 9–2 Philadelphia victory, his fourth 1916 triumph over his former team. The Phils left New York for Boston before heading west, while the Giants waited for the Dodgers.[27]

As the 1916 season headed towards the midway point, the nature of the opposition changed. Although July began with two series among the eastern teams, the contenders' opposition for the next two months would consist primarily of the western clubs. Moreover, two of the next three rounds of East-West match-ups would be in the West, so Brooklyn, Boston, Philadelphia and New York would spend a considerable amount of time on the road. Before worrying about the western teams, however, the pennant contenders had one more series to play amongst themselves. These series began with Brooklyn leading Philadelphia by 2½, Boston by 3 and New York by 5½.

Philadelphia's visit to Boston was scheduled for four games, but rain wiped out a July 4 doubleheader. The teams split the other two games, the Braves winning a rain-shortened, six-inning affair on July 3, 5–1, with the Phillies rebounding with a 2–1 victory in a pitchers duel on July 5. Although a thunderstorm shortened the first game, there was sufficient time for Boston to score an almost unheard of five runs off Alexander (13–7). The rains on the Fourth produced a "soft field," so the teams were unable to play the regularly scheduled game and make up one of the rained-out games. Excessive rainouts against the Braves would come back to haunt the Phils at season's end. Eppa Rixey (9–2) out-dueled Boston's Jess Barnes on July 5, keeping the Braves off the scoreboard until the ninth.

Although the low score may suggest a relatively uneventful game, any time Johnny Evers was on the field, an event wasn't only possible, but likely. In the bottom of the fifth, the Braves were threatening with runners on first and second, only one out, and Evers at plate. The rally was cut short when Johnny was called out on strikes, and Gowdy was thrown out trying to steal third. Predictably, the Trojan erupted, finally yelling repeatedly that Umpire Byron "ought to be over in the box with the wife of the president of the National League roasting the ball players." According to Evers, on the prior day, National League President Tener's wife made some negative comments about him within earshot of the Crab's wife, probably not knowing she was present. After arguing the call and a subsequent ejection, Evers was on his way to the Braves' clubhouse. While passing, he took a verbal shot at Tener, supposedly saying, "Things are coming to a pretty pass in this league" when the president's wife can criticize a player in front of his wife. Regardless of what Johnny actually said, Tener wasn't amused, suspending the Boston captain for the next ten days. The Braves were now on their way to Chicago, 4½ games in back of Brooklyn, and minus their on-the-field leader.[28]

The Dodgers–Giants series lost only one game to rain, which wasn't good news for New York, as the Superbas swept the other three, winning, 6–1, on July 3, and then sweeping an Independence Day doubleheader, 7–6 and 6–2. Going into the series, Rice wasn't optimistic since Brooklyn had lost six of its last eleven. Even a struggling team, however, can win with dominant pitching, and it was hard to be more dominant than Jack Coombs (6–3) was in the first game. The former A's star held the Giants to only three hits, one after the first inning. During the next day's doubleheader, despite beginning slowly, the Dodgers continued to get strong pitching. After New York lit up Larry Cheney (4–5) for five runs in the first inning, erasing a 2–0 Brooklyn lead, Wilbert Robinson brought on Rube Marquard. He allowed only an unearned run the rest of the way, while the Brooklyn offense fought back for a 7–6 victory. The Dodgers clearly had pitching depth and Robby was using that depth effectively. In the second game, Sherrod Smith was hit hard even though the Giants scored only two runs. After the sixth inning, however, Smith allowed only three balls to be hit out of the infield, much less allow any Giants to cross home plate, as Brooklyn rallied for a 6–2 victory. The Dodgers' offense got a major lift from Jim Johnston, who had four hits in the doubleheader and was on base in eight out of ten trips to the plate. After a rainout the following day, Brooklyn headed west still in first place by four games over Philadelphia and 4½ over Boston. In nowhere near as good a mood were John McGraw and his Giants, now 9–18 over their last 27 games. Other than their record-setting trip, New York was a pathetic 11–31.[29]

The Superbas had a positive start to their second western swing in Cincinnati, taking three of five games. After Brooklyn won the first two, the two teams split a doubleheader on July 9 before the Reds took the final game. Only 1,000 fans witnessed the Dodgers' 3–0 victory on July 8, making it an extremely limited payday for owners Ebbets and August Herrman. Brooklyn came back to earth in the opener of the doubleheader, as the Reds' Fred Toney shut out the Superbas. Offense wasn't a problem in the second contest, however, as the Dodgers pounded Cincinnati, 10–3, for the benefit of Rube Marquard. The final game saw the Reds win, 6–3, before an even smaller crowd of about 500. It's hard to believe total receipts for the contest exceeded $500. If this was the best Cincinnati could do financially when playing the league leaders, changes wouldn't be long in coming.[30]

From there, Brooklyn moved to St. Louis where the financial outlook was no better, as threatening weather on July 11 limited the crowd to about 700 fans. Driven by the finances or lack thereof, changes were also in the offing for the Cardinals. Those in attendance saw Charles Stengel hit a two-run inside-the-park home run to spur Brooklyn's come-from-behind victory. Hardly a week went by in 1916 without a rainout, and this was no exception, as precipitation the following day led to a doubleheader on July 13. The twin bill resulted in another split, the Dodgers losing, 2–1, in the opener, but then easily taking the second game, 7–0. In an effort to deal with their financial problems, the Cardinals sold Slim Sallee to the Giants and their "plethoric bankroll," which from the Brooklyn perspective was better than his going to the Phils or Braves. Apparently tired of pitching for hapless St. Louis, Sallee had encouraged if not forced the trade by claiming he was retiring from baseball. Little went well for the Superbas in the concluding game on July 14, as they fell to the Cardinals, 6–2, thereby splitting the four games.[31]

The Dodgers then began their homeward journey, stopping first in Chicago for a four-game set. In the ninth inning of the first contest on July 15, Brooklyn appeared headed to a 4–3 victory. Unfortunately, Jimmy Archer had other ideas, as his two-run home run gave the Cubs a 5–4 victory, earning him a $100 bonus. It was the second walk-off home run by Chicago in three days. Losing a one-run lead in the ninth was frustrating enough, but it got worse the next day, as the Superbas twice blew three-run leads late in the contest. It was probably only fitting the contest ended in a 16-inning tie, called due to darkness. The length of the game demonstrated the cost of Cubs owner Charles Weeghman's new policy of allowing fans to keep foul balls, as an un–Deadball-like 43 "spheres" were used in the course of the day. I.E. Sanborn of the Chicago *Daily Tribune* felt the Cubs would have won the game, but the temptation of $100 bonuses led them to eschew the bunt for the home run. Chicago had also taken to abusing umpires and inciting the crowd in ways that had the potential to start a riot and/or injure an umpire.

This behavior continued the next day with little success, as Brooklyn triumphed, 2–1. The third straight day of such conduct by the Cubs led to an unusual Dodger win on July 18. Down 4–0 in the sixth, the Superbas tied it at four, sending the game into extra innings. After Brooklyn put runners on second and third with no one out in the top of the 10th, a failed pickoff attempt of Hi Myers caused the Chicago bench to erupt. Seat cushions flew from the stands as fans got into the act. With a 2–0 count on the batter, pitcher Hippo Vaughn "dilly-dallied" to the extent Umpire Byron called ball three without Vaughn even throwing a pitch. Tinker and his players charged Byron, leading to Tinker's ejection. When the Cubs' manager failed to leave the field, the umpire forfeited the game to the Dodgers. Somewhat lost in all of this was four innings of no-hit relief pitching by Jack Coombs (8–4), following 6⅔ shutout innings in the 16-inning tie on July 16.[32]

The momentum built by the Superbas thus far on the trip took a significant hit the next day on July 19 when Pittsburgh swept a series-opening doubleheader, 1–0 and 2–1 in 14 innings. Two consecutive rainouts led to another twin bill on July 22 before the team headed back to Brooklyn. A large crowd estimated at more than 15,000 saw an offensive explosion as the Dodgers prevailed, 7–1, before winning another extra inning game, 3–2, in 15 innings. After the easy win in the first contest, Rice felt there had been "no more bitter struggle" in 1916 than the second game. Cutshaw's fielding gem saved

Brooklyn in the ninth when he batted a ball toward second for a force out. The Superbas then took the lead in the 14th, only to see the Pirates tie the game, turning the grandstand into "an insane asylum." Finally, Zack Wheat's sacrifice fly in the top the 15th put Brooklyn ahead for good. After pitching poorly as a starter in the last game in Chicago, Marquard came on to pitch five effective innings in relief. Once again the Dodgers had enjoyed a winning tour of the West, finishing 9–7–1, to return home with a four-game lead over both Philadelphia and Boston.[33]

When the Giants returned from their record-setting western trip earlier in 1916, the consensus was the New Yorkers had turned their season around. Now, however, as the Giants embarked on their second western swing, there was clarity of a different kind. John McGraw concluded he couldn't compete with his current roster, but New York had the financial resources to do something about it. As a result, this road swing became not just a hunt for wins, but also a shopping trip to upgrade the roster. The Giants began the second western trip in Pittsburgh, pounding the Pirates, 12–6, on July 6. Unfortunately, this wasn't the beginning of a second streak, for by July 10, New York had lost two of the next three games to start the swing at 2–2.

Leaving Pittsburgh, New York made the relatively short trip to Cincinnati where the Giants finally enjoyed some success, taking four of five from the hapless Reds. The first game of a July 13 doubleheader marked Ferd Schupp's first start of the season, and he out-dueled Cincinnati ace Fred Toney, a performance with significant portent for the future. When their next stop in St. Louis began with a Pol Perritt shutout, the Giants may have felt that this trip could be highly successful. That was not to be, however, for in addition to acquiring pitcher Slim Sallee from the Cards, they also acquired three straight losses. Perhaps McGraw should have started by shopping for offense, as the Giants managed only five runs in the three games in St. Louis.

It was at this point in the season the Buck Herzog sweepstakes began. Given the Reds' record on the field, Buck was expendable as a manager, and the poor attendance figures made his high salary equally undesirable. At various times, the Cubs, Dodgers and Giants were reported to be interested in acquiring Herzog, who in spite of his somewhat prickly personality would be an asset to any team. Given its struggles at shortstop, Brooklyn seemed to have the greatest need, but only at the right price. After the Dodgers were unsuccessful in this pursuit, Rice did his own analysis, reporting Ebbets had offered $25,000 to the Reds and a player valued in the $7,500-$15,000 range. Yet that was before paying Herzog, who reportedly wanted $10,000 a season for three years, plus a $5,000 bonus, making the total 1916 price in cash and players could be as much as $55,000, roughly the same amount as the Speaker sale. Obviously the only reason to acquire Buck would be to help win the pennant and then the World Series, but Rice's financial projections suggested a slim profit margin. The last two World Series had lasted no more than five games, and Rice estimated a five-game Fall Classic would net Ebbets less than $40,000, thereby resulting in a loss on the Herzog acquisition. A longer World Series might net $80,000, but there was no guarantee of that happening, or that acquiring Herzog significantly improved Brooklyn's chances to win the pennant.[34]

Against even a successful team like the Dodgers, the Giants' superior financial resources gave them the advantage. New York acquired the Cincinnati shortstop in a deal that involved three future Hall of Famers, none of whom was Herzog. In addition to Buck, the Giants acquired outfielder Wade Kilifer, while Cincinnati received outfielder Edd Roush, third baseman Bill McKechnie and a new manager, pitcher Christy Mathewson. For Herzog, who would play third base, it was his third tour of duty with McGraw. The relationship between the two was cool at best, but the New York manager knew how to get along with players who served his purposes.[35]

While these machinations were in process, the Giants headed to Chicago for five games with the Cubs, a series that began auspiciously on July 19 with an 8–6 win. Even though the next day saw a frustrating 1–0 loss, it marked a second strong performance by Ferd Schupp, who allowed only one run on four hits. On July 21, Herzog was in uniform, paying immediate dividends by driving in the second run in a 2–1 New York victory. Unfortunately, that was the last Giant win of the series and the road trip, as they dropped the next two games. The final defeat on June 23 marked future Hall of Famer Three Finger Brown's last start against New York, giving fans one final chance to remember the days of the heated Cubs-Giants rivalry. Afterward, the Giants headed home nine games behind Brooklyn following a 9–9 trip, but also with a new pitcher and third baseman, moves that began the transformation of McGraw's roster.[36]

Of the four eastern teams, the Phillies once again had the longest trip to start their second western tour, journeying from Boston to St. Louis. This seemed to have little impact, however, as the Phils took three of four from the Cardinals. Of course, it didn't hurt to have Grover Cleveland Alexander (14–7) on the mound for the opener on July 7, especially since he was frustrated, having lost three straight. While offensive support was lacking, Alexander made short work of St. Louis, shutting them out, 1–0, one hour and 35 minutes in just. From there it was on to Chicago, where Philadelphia won the first two games, on July 11 and 12, once again starting the series with Alexander (15–7), who didn't disappoint, holding the Cubs to three singles in a 2–1 triumph. In the third game on July 13, the Phillies trailed but rallied for three in the ninth inning and led, 5–4. George McQuillan came on to finish the game, and with two out and one on, he was within one strike of his goal. This time, however, the "Great Zim" (Heinie) lived up to his nickname, hitting a 3–2 pitch over the right-field wall for a 6–5 Cubs win, earning him a $100 bonus. Perhaps demoralized by this loss, the Phils were listless the next day, losing, 6–3.[37]

Pat Moran and his club then went east to Pittsburgh for a July 15 doubleheader with the Pirates. As usual, Alexander (16–7) started the first game, but the first two Pittsburgh batters hit safely. The Phils' ace was apparently teasing, however, since he allowed only two more hits the rest of the way, winning, 4–0, in just an hour and 18 minutes. Things looked promising in the second game as well when Philadelphia had a 5–2 lead in the seventh, but Pittsburgh knocked out Erskine Chalmers, scoring four times en route to a 7–5 victory. After the Sabbath came three straight days of rain. Weather-related problems were difficult enough at home, but on the road, it meant sitting around a hotel lobby for four straight days, which must have tested everyone's patience. Finally, they left for a five-game series in Cincinnati, with a stop in Pittsburgh on the way home to make up one of the postponed games.[38]

The change of scenery had no impact on Alexander (17–7), who for the fourth straight time won the opening game of the series, shutting out the Reds on two hits in an hour and 34 minutes in the first game of a doubleheader. In the nightcap, Cincinnati knocked out Demaree in the third inning on the way to a 5–3 win. The following day, July 21, marked Christy Mathewson's debut as Reds manager, and it didn't lack for drama, as the also newly-acquired Edd Roush tripled in the tying run for Cincinnati in the ninth. Apparently unfazed by this comeback, Philadelphia scored twice in the top of the 10th, giving Rixey (11–3) a complete-game 6–4 win. The next day's contest was less dramatic, but gave Mathewson his first win as manager. Unfortunately for the Reds, the series had gone on long enough to allow Grover Cleveland (18–7) another chance on July 23, albeit on two days rest. Once again, he won easily, 8–1. Throughout the western swing, Demaree had been as ineffective as Alexander had been effective, and this didn't change during the one-day stopover in Pittsburgh, as the Pirates scored an easy 9–1 win against Al. The Phils had a 9–7 record on the trip, but after wining five of the first six, they went only 4–6 the rest of the way, failing to make up any ground on the first-place Superbas.[39]

As the train carrying the Braves made its way toward Chicago, George Stallings and his players had a number of problems. Most pressing were their struggles on offense, and the 10-day suspension of team leader Johnny Evers couldn't have been far behind. A 1–0 loss to the Cubs on July 7, when they recorded just one hit and wasted a strong performance by Frank Allen, did nothing to allay the concerns at the plate. However, the results at least changed dramatically when Boston swept the next three games. Although the offense didn't improve much in the second game, Lefty Tyler held the Cubs at bay, enabling the Braves to prevail in 10 innings, 3–1. After driving in the winning run that day, Snodgrass continued to wield a hot bat on July 9, getting three hits in a 5–1 Boston win. Having given up only one run and lost in the opener, Frank Allen took no chances in the last match-up, pitching a four-hit shutout to win, 4–0.[40]

Boston continued to play well, taking two of three in Pittsburgh. In the first game on July 11, the Pirates rallied for a 3–2 win, gaining some measure of revenge against Hughes (11–3) for his no-hit performance. Given the frequency with which Hughes pitched, however, he seldom waited long for another opportunity. In this case, it was the next day, as he came on in relief in Boston's 6–5 victory. The game, which saw the Braves rally from a 4–0 deficit against Pirate ace Al Mamaux, also marked Rudolph's return from a month's stay on the disabled list. After a day of rain, Boston won the rubber match behind Don Carlos Ragan, who shut out Pittsburgh, 3–0, on six hits, with the victory moving the Braves into second place, 3½ games out of first and only one in the loss column.[41]

The next stop was Cincinnati, where the Braves had an offensive explosion on July 15, pounding the Reds, 9–2. The surge continued the next day, as a 4–1 Boston win was the Braves' 18th in their last 25 games. Boston wasn't the only thing heating up — the weather was also becoming a problem. There was no relief during the evening hours, as the Braves tried to sleep in hotel rooms without air conditioning. Whether it was the weather or something else, Boston lost the last two games against the Reds. According to Flatley, the weather was "96 in the shade," which was probably part of the reason only 600 fans attended. After two rough days in the Cincinnati heat, the Braves had to endure an overnight train journey to the heat of St. Louis in railroad cars, which like hotels had no air conditioning. The worst part of the two defeats to the lowly Reds was they cost Boston two full games in the standings after Brooklyn won both days against the Cubs. It wasn't the first or the last time bad losses to Cincinnati would hurt the Braves.[42]

After an "all night rattler ride with the 'thermom' up around the 100 mark," Boston must have been in a foul mood upon arriving in St. Louis. A thunderstorm and some cool breezes on July 19 gave temporary relief, and the Braves took out their frustrations on Miller Huggins' team, winning, 10–1. With Brooklyn in the process of losing a doubleheader to Pittsburgh, Boston closed back to within 2½ games of the Dodgers. Flatley, never one to avoid a chance to get ahead of himself, said the Braves played "like the champions they are going to be." Although Boston suffered a 5–2 defeat the next day, he remained confident that "first place seems inevitable sooner or later." Flat-ley's optimism may have been slipping on July 21, though, since the Braves trailed, 3–2, in the eighth inning. In one of those hunches that pan out, Stallings chose not to pinch-hit for pitcher Lefty Tyler, who rewarded his manager's confidence by hitting a home run onto the right-field roof. Maranville then tripled and came home on Evers' single so that Hughes (11–3) could come in and bring "affairs to an end in his usual efficient way," with two innings of shutout relief. Even after this come-from-behind win, Boston continued to struggle against the Cards, losing the next day, 6–4, before win-ning the July 23 finale, 2–1. The latter contest began 20 minutes early to allow the Braves to catch the 5:45 train in order to arrive back in Boston at 10:00 the next night. Apparently no one bothered to tell the Cardinal fans, who weren't pleased to have missed some of the action, although they cer-tainly couldn't have missed much scoring. Rudolph (9–6) pitched a six-hit-ter and was aided by fine defensive plays from both Maranville and Evers as well as Wilhoit's home run. Flatley felt Boston was going home in good posi-tion for "a climb to the roof." If all the Braves players had Flatley's confi-dence, that ascent wouldn't take long.[43]

Team	Wins	Losses	Games Behind
Brooklyn	48	32	—
Boston	43	34	3½
Philadelphia	44	36	4

Of the challenges facing the four contenders entering this part of the season, Brooklyn's task was the simplest — to maintain the level of play that had put the Dodgers in first place. Wilbert Robinson and his Superbas more than met that challenge by increasing their lead from 1½ games on May 29 to 3½ games on July 24. Throughout the period, they played .500 ball against the eastern teams, but took advantage of the weaker western clubs, posting a 16–9 record. Not surprisingly, this last mark was better at home (7–2), but Brooklyn had just completed a second above .500 western trip. Consistent hitting was one of the factors in this success, as the Dodgers' team batting average remained in the .255 –.260 range the entire seven-week period. Jake Daubert (.322) and Zack Wheat (.302) continued to lead the team, but the situation in center field illustrated Brooklyn's depth. Through the June 24 doubleheader with the Giants, Hi Myers had been the regular center fielder. After a slow start to the season, he began hitting, batting .295 over his last ten games, with at least one hit in nine of those contests. During the first match-up on July 24, Myers injured his ankle, bringing Jim Johnston (an Ebbets' off-season acquisition) into the lineup. Hitting only .227 at the time,

Johnston batted almost .286 through the end of the second western road trip, keeping Myers out of the lineup even after he recovered.

The other key to Brooklyn's success was its pitching. Although Larry Cheney had been inconsistent and Wheezer Dell had tailed off after some impressive early starts, the Dodgers didn't lack for good performances. Sherrod Smith was 5–2 during this time frame, while Jeff Pfeffer was even more dominant, racking up eight wins against only three losses. Also important was the work of Jack Coombs and Rube Marquard, a tribute to Robinson's ability to handle pitchers. The Brooklyn skipper continued to use Coombs, both as a spot starter and a relief pitcher, and since May 29, Colby Jack was 5–3, including two hard-luck losses. Even more impressive was the turnaround of Rube Marquard. After some poor performances early in the season, Robinson used Rube exclusively in relief, allowing the left-hander to gradually regain his confidence. After five very effective appearances in which he allowed only three runs in 17⅔ innings, Robinson started Marquard in the second game of a June 26 doubleheader against the Giants. The left-hander allowed only one run in a 2–1, 12-inning victory and went on to win two more games, his only defeat coming in a 2–0 shutout loss to the Braves. Looking forward, Brooklyn's challenge was simply to maintain their level of play.[44]

Like the Dodgers, the Phils saw no change in their position in the standings. Unfortunately for Pat Moran and his team, this meant they were in third place, four games back. Offensively, there had been little change in the team's performance, as they were still scoring nearly four runs per game, and their batting average dropped off only slightly, to .249. Fred Luderus and George Whitted both raised their averages by more than 30 points during the stretch, but this was more than offset by the horrendous slump of Gavy Cravath. Hitting only .205 from June 2 through the end of the second western trip, his average fell from .310 to .258. By the middle of the western swing, Moran even decided to bench Cravath, at least for a while. This was especially of concern, since much of Philadelphia's 1915 success had been built on the offense of Cravath and the pitching of Alexander. Fortunately, the latter was holding up his end of the bargain; even though Alex had lost three straight, this followed and preceded five straight victories, giving him a 10–4 record with a 1.56 ERA since June 2. That meant, however, that the rest of the Phils' pitching staff had been below .500. The biggest problem was Demaree, who was 4–7 with a 4.29 ERA, astronomical for the time. Without the pitching depth of Brooklyn, Philadelphia had to get Demaree turned around and get at least some help from the rest of the staff.[45]

While Brooklyn and Philadelphia had basically maintained their positions, Boston and New York had gone in opposite directions. In fifth place on May 20, the Braves had gone 28–17 to move into second, only four games out of first. After a mediocre 4–4 record at home against the western teams, Boston first went 11–5 against the other eastern teams and then 10–6 on their road trip for a 21–11 record since June 20. This is even more impressive since Braves ace Dick Rudolph was injured on June 13 and didn't pitch again until July 12. In fact, Boston posted a 16–8 record during this stretch, sparked by Don Carlos Ragan, who went 5–0 with a 1.60 ERA. Like Brooklyn, the Braves had considerable pitching depth, as Barnes, Nehf, Reulbach, Allen and mainstay Tom Hughes made contributions during the period. Upon returning, Rudolph made up for lost time, winning his next four starts. Somehow, Boston also improved offensively during its 21–11 run, slightly increasing its runs scored per game from 3.4 to 4.1. The Braves did this despite a team batting average that remained almost constant, with only two players, Magee and Snodgrass, showing any significant improvement. During this time frame, the Braves scored runs on a triple steal and squeeze bunt and run. To be successful, Boston would have to rely on continued strong pitching plus creative offense.[46]

Little had gone right for the Giants since returning from their 19–2 road trip. Just 1½ games out of first on May 29, they were a distant fourth, nine games behind Brooklyn, on July 22, and two games below .500. Indeed, after a 2–7 homestand against the western clubs, followed by a 6–12 record against the eastern teams, it had taken a 9–9 western trip to get their record for this period to just 17–28. New York's pitching staff was in shambles, as even workhorse Jeff Tesreau was only 3–6 with a 4.60 ERA during this time span. Mathewson's success on the first western trip had clearly been a farewell tour, and he was now the manager of the Reds. The only bright spots from a pitching standpoint were the acquisition of Slim Sallee from the Cardinals and the impressive beginning by Ferdinand Schupp, who had allowed only three runs in two starts. Offensive production had dropped off as well; at least four Giants had seen their batting averages fall by 30-plus points, including Doyle and Rariden, who had dropped more than 50. Only Dave Robertson was still hitting over .300. Not surprisingly, New York's run production was down as well, from 4.8 runs to 3.4 per game over the last 45 contests. While Brooklyn, Boston and Philadelphia had met the challenges of June and most of July, the Giants hadn't. Nevertheless, there were still another six weeks of similar challenges facing each of the contenders before September and the home stretch of the pennant race.[47]

CHAPTER VI

"Imbued with the idea the pennant is theirs."

With the completion of the eastern teams' second visit to the west on July 24, all eight National League teams headed east for a return engagement. The second western invasion of the East began with Brooklyn leading Boston by 3½ games and Philadelphia by four. Rain interfered with the contests of July 25, and only the Braves and Chicago were able to play. Boston probably wouldn't have minded a rainout as they again generated little offense in a 3–2, eleven-inning loss. Playing for the first time since his suspension, Johnny Evers wasted no time earning an ejection, followed by a fight with Cubs third baseman Rollie Zeider.[1]

Although the Braves' offense didn't improve over the course of the series, the results did since Boston proceeded to win two, with one ending in an extra-inning tie. The match-up on July 26 was a brilliant pitching duel between Frank Allen and Chicago's Hippo Vaughn. Hippo was more dominant, but Boston scored on a squeeze bunt and once again relied upon the relief pitching of Tom Hughes to preserve the 1–0 victory. Much as they had in the last series with Brooklyn, the Cubs tried to intimidate the umpires. Since this was already the Braves' standard operating procedure, one can only imagine how umpires felt about being assigned to a Boston-Chicago game. After the July 27 contest ended in a tie, Art Nehf pitched the Braves to a 2–1 victory the next day in spite of "support" that recorded as many errors as it did hits.[2]

In typical baseball irony, New York opened the homestand on July 26 against the Cincinnati Reds and their new manager, Christy Mathewson. The legendary Giant star was greeted warmly by his old fans, and then enjoyed a 4–2 victory over his former team. After that disappointing start, however, the Giants actually won two consecutive extra-inning home games. The wins were New York's first extra-session victories at home of 1916 and ended an

John McGraw (left), Buck Herzog and Christy Mathewson after the Reds-Giants trade, the first step in McGraw's in-season rebuilding of his team (George Bain Collection, Library of Congress).

eight-game home losing streak in extra-inning affairs. In the first, new/old Giant Buck Herzog had the honor of scoring the winning run. After he crossed the plate, Buck supposedly looked over at the Reds' dugout and had a "laugh at Matty's expense." Then on July 28, after a Rube Benton wild pitch allowed Cincinnati to tie the game in the ninth, the Reds returned the favor in the 10th when New York scored the winning run on a wild pitch.[3]

After their games on July 25 were wiped out by rain, Brooklyn and Philadelphia played doubleheaders the next day. The Superbas started on a losing note, dropping the first contest to St. Louis, 3–2, before winning the second game, 5–0. Much like Alexander for Philadelphia, Pfeffer (15–4) was becoming Brooklyn's stopper, and he responded with a five-hit shutout. With this as a starting point, the Dodgers proceeded to sweep the remaining two games of the series, 4–2 and 9–5. The latter also saw Jack Coombs (8–4) give up five runs in the second inning, but seven shutout innings by Wheezer Dell (six frames) and Rube Marquard (one inning) bailed out Colby Jack and the Superbas. Even though Brooklyn had won three straight, defense, especially that of Ollie O'Mara, was becoming a concern. Ivan Olson replaced O'Mara at shortstop on July 28 and for one game at least played well.[4]

Like Brooklyn, the Phillies split the July 26 doubleheader and went on to win the last two games of the series. The only difference was Philadelphia won the opener of its doubleheader, 7–1, when Alexander (19–7) scattered 10 hits in a game that took all of one hour and 25 minutes. In the nightcap, Pirate manager James Callahan successfully went the platoon route, using nine right-handed batters, who hit Phillies southpaw Eppa Rixey (11–4) hard in Pittsburgh's 5–2 win. After the doubleheader split, the Phils won the last two games, the first 5–4 on a seventh-inning home run by Dode Paskert and then a 5–2 July 28 win behind Charles Bender. One series into the western homestand, Boston and Philadelphia both trailed Brooklyn by four games while the Giants had fallen 10 off the pace.[5]

For Giants fans clinging to hope, the series victory over the Reds may have sparked a small flicker. That flickering flame must have come fully ablaze when New York took five out of six games from the visiting Pirates. Clearly, there was plenty of hope among the 30,000 fans (the largest crowd in three years) who paid their way into the Polo Grounds for the opening double-header. The "hordes of men crowding the bleachers in their shirtsleeves" consumed an estimated 300,000 peanuts, no doubt complimented by soda pop. In the first game, the large throng saw the Giants win their third straight extra-inning home game, 4–3, while in the second contest Fred Anderson pitched a five-hit shutout. Sunday's off-day did nothing to slow down New York; they swept another doubleheader on July 31 by identical 7–0 shutouts that took almost the same amount of time (1:47 and 1:44). The much smaller crowd, estimated at 12,000, must have seemed immense to Slim Sallee, given his experiences in St. Louis. The new Giant threw a shutout in the opener, only to be topped stylistically by Tesreau's two-hit gem in the second game. Pittsburgh snapped the six-game winning streak the next day, beating the New Yorkers, 4–3, in 10 innings. Pirate manager James Callahan used his ace, Al Mamaux, in the final game on August 2, but the Giants weren't impressed, knocking out 13 hits in a 6–2 victory. Although winning seven of ten may have kindled some hope for New York and its fans, it didn't narrow the distance to first place as the Giants remained 10 games out.[6]

Hope may have been less important in Philadelphia, where the Phils could rely on Alexander (19–8) to open a July 29 doubleheader against the Cubs. As in New York, a large crowd turned out, but unlike their peers at the Polo Grounds, their hopes and perhaps expectations were dashed, as Grover Cleveland was denied his 20th win. Fortunately, Al Demaree, who had been as cold as Alexander had been hot, picked his team up, dominating Chicago in the second game. Buoyed by that fine effort, the Phillies won three of the next four, making it four out of six in the series and seven out of ten on the homestand. Sunday's off-day was followed by a 4–2 victory on July 31, sparked by Gavy Cravath's two-run home run. Demaree's victory the next day salvaged a doubleheader split for the second time in the series. The

August 2 finale was Alexander's opportunity for revenge, and although frequently in trouble, he kept the Cubs off the scoreboard for 12 innings before the Phillies scored the game's only run. It was Alex's 20th victory, one more than the entire Philadelphia Athletics team had recorded to this point in the season.[7]

The eastern teams were dominating their western counterparts, and the Braves-Cardinals series was no exception — Boston took four out of the six games. On July 29, before one of the biggest crowds of the year, estimated at 20,000 plus, the Braves won 4–3 and 8–5 behind Dick Rudolph (10–7) and Tom Hughes (12–3), who had switched into a starting role. Both pitched well, and for a change received offensive support. Unfortunately, Boston catchers Henry Gowdy and Walter Tragesser went down with injuries, and the only replacement, Arthur Rico, wasn't even under contract. A second doubleheader on Monday, July 31 didn't go quite as well since St. Louis won the first game, 4–3, but the Braves bounced back to win the second, 2–1. Rudolph finished things in relief, but still had enough energy to pitch 11 shutout innings the following day in a 1–0 Boston triumph. From the Braves' point of view (or at least that of the Boston *Herald*), the story of the August 2 series finale and 5–2 loss to the Cards was summed up in the sub-headline, "Same old story: Braves get worst of decisions," and it wasn't referring to managerial decisions.[8]

Umpiring wasn't a concern for Brooklyn, at least not against the Reds, as the Superbas showed Christy Mathewson the challenge he faced. After losing the first game of a July 29 doubleheader, Brooklyn proceeded to win five straight from the Rhinelanders. As with all the other July 29 National League twin bills, there was a large crowd inside Ebbets Field in addition to some non-paying customers (to Ebbets' chagrin) outside, who watched from a "hill and nearby rooftops." Convinced that bigger crowds would be the norm, Ebbets planned to increase the capacity of the ballpark's temporary bleachers by another 2,000. Many in the Saturday crowd apparently came directly from a half-day's work, planning to lunch on one of "Harry Steven's sandwiches." To their surprise, the price of a ham sandwich had escalated to 15 cents (a delicacy Rice thought to be worth no more than a nickel), with the accompanying soft drink costing another dime. This occurrence produced no little "wailing and gnashing of teeth" among the fans.[9]

After a disappointing performance by Marquard in the opener, Jeff Pfeffer (16–4) was again the stopper in the second game. The big right-hander had allowed just three runs in his last 36 innings of work, and although the Reds scored twice, Pfeffer prevailed, 3–2. The estimated 8,000 plus at the second doubleheader was supposedly the biggest Monday crowd of the year, but the drop of over 50 percent in attendance from Saturday indicates how much money was being lost to the Sabbath. Those who did make it to the park saw a Brooklyn sweep, 8–3 and 4–0, behind Sherrod Smith and Larry Cheney (7–7). Although watching the games in "terrible" heat, the gathering clearly enjoyed themselves, cheering for several minutes when they learned Boston had lost. The heat was so oppressive that almost all of the Reds players personally paid for cars to take them back to their hotel rather than ride "the crowded and super-heated subway."[10]

The Brooklyn onslaught continued as the Superbas won the last two games from Cincinnati, 5–2 and 5–4, the second in 13 innings. In the first contest, with the Reds teeing off on Wheezer Dell's fastball, Wilbert Robinson reached deep into his bullpen for Nap Rucker, who no one believed had a fastball any longer. He got out of a jam in the fourth and tossed shutout ball the rest of the way, which was exactly what Robby said he expected would happen. In the series finale on August 2, the Dodgers prevailed, 5–4, in 13 innings, even though Brooklyn could only score five runs on 21 hits (19 singles) and four walks. The Superbas' offense didn't help their cause in the fifth when they failed to score even though all four batters singled. They managed this rare and undistinguished feat because the first three batters were thrown out stealing or trying to advance on a hit. Fortunately, Pfeffer (17–4) was on the mound, and he weathered both the ineffective offense and some shaky defense to hold the Reds at bay through the 13th, when Daubert drove in the winning run. A major part of the defensive problems were three "screaming errors" by Olson, showing that the problems at shortstop hadn't been solved. Hard-earned as it may have been, the Superbas' success against Cincinnati added to their lead, which was now five games over both Boston and Philadelphia.[11]

August is traditionally a hot month, but the play of the Brooklyn Superbas was even hotter, as they followed their success against Cincinnati by taking three out of four from Pittsburgh. After winning the first two games, 7–2 and 2–0, the Dodgers won the first game of a doubleheader, 4–0, for their eighth straight victory. Even when a 7–1 loss in the nightcap snapped the streak, it couldn't have depressed anyone, including Tom Rice, that much. The first game of the series on August 3 didn't start auspiciously, as the Dodgers were still struggling to solve Pirates pitcher Frank Miller, who had already beaten them twice. In fact, it took what Rice termed "the daily freak" for Brooklyn to score in the seventh and break a scoreless tie. When George Cutshaw attempted a sacrifice bunt, the ball landed fair and took a crazy bounce, rolling all the way to the fence in foul territory. The hit drove in a run, putting Cutshaw on second with one of the shortest doubles in baseball history. He could now add this feat to one of the weirdest home runs ever seen on May 6. This opened the flood gates, with key hits by Mowrey and

Stengel putting the game away for Brooklyn and pitcher Larry Cheney (8–7). The streak reached seven the following day when Sherrod Smith shut out Pittsburgh on five hits, the only dark cloud being an injury to Jake Daubert. In the first game of the August 5 twin bill, Rube Marquard also threw goose eggs at the Pirates, holding them scoreless on six hits. Daubert was in the starting lineup, but left during the game due to what was now described as a charley horse. The second contest looked to be a match-up of rival aces, with Pfeffer (17–5) opposing Al Mamaux. Although Mamaux suffered from indigestion before the contest, it was the Dodgers who looked sick during the game, as Pfeffer was shelled and Mamaux was "invincible."[12]

After another Sunday off, the series finale was rained out, as was the August 8 opener against the Cubs. Daubert's injury continued to defy diagnosis, now being listed as a pulled ligament. Regardless of the exact nature of the ailment, it was projected the Brooklyn star wouldn't return during the homestand. Rain would also claim another game against Chicago, but nothing slowed down the Dodgers, who swept the abbreviated three-game series. The postponements allowed Wilbert Robinson to start a well-rested Larry Cheney (9–7) on August 9, and he threw the Superbas' third shutout in four games, a two-hitter. Jim Johnston's hitting streak had reached nine games, while catcher Lew McCarty filled in adequately for Daubert at first. When the next day's game was washed out, Brooklyn management opted to play a doubleheader on Friday, August 11, rather than wait until the Cubs' next visit in September. It turned out to be a wise decision, as the Dodgers won both games, 2–1 and 4–1, behind strong pitching performances by Wheezer Dell and Rube Marquard, completing a 14–3 homestand against the West. A four-game series against second-place Boston, five back of the Superbas, was next before Brooklyn hit the road for nearly a month.[13]

Across the river in Manhattan, things were also going well for the Giants, who were 7–2 in the first two series against the West. As with Brooklyn, the good times continued, as New York finished the homestand by taking three of four from both the Cubs and the Cardinals. On August 3, Hippo Vaughn limited the Giants to three hits, but Fred Merkle's home run was enough for Pol Perritt to beat Chicago, 1–0. After losing the second game of the set, 6–2, New York won the last two by identical 3–2 scores, even though they managed only four and three hits, respectively. A Saturday, August 5 crowd of 7,000 (limited by the weather) saw two Cubs errors compensate for the Giants' offensive woes. In the final game on August 7, a bases-loaded double by pinch-hitter Hans Lobert generated enough runs to win before 15,000 brave souls, who battled the hot, dark and wet conditions.[14]

Two postponements in the series against the Cardinals resulted in doubleheaders on August 9 and 11. New York's offensive problems finally caught up with them in the first game on August 9, as the Giants were shut out. Their easy 8–4 victory in the second contest provided some comic relief when Fred Merkle fell victim to the hidden ball trick. Although base coaches Hans Lobert and John McGraw apparently "dozed placidly" while Bruno Betzel tricked the unsuspecting Merkle, the blame, of course, went to him. One observer commented, "It does seem queer that whenever they have to find a goat in a baseball game they pick out Merkle." Perhaps the incident only served to annoy Merkle and his teammates, who swept the August 11 double-header from the Cardinals, 5–3 and 2–0. The two victories yielded a 13–4 record on the homestand and seemed to position New York well for a road trip of almost four weeks.[15] However, as impressive as the 13–4 record was, the Giants actually fell a game further behind Brooklyn, which went 14–3 against the same opposition.

The Phillies may have helped the Giants by softening up the Cardinals when they took three out of four from St. Louis. In the opener on August 3, Philadelphia scored 10 runs for Charles Bender in an easy 10–4 victory. Eppa Rixey (13–4) didn't receive that level of support the next day but didn't need it, as he limited the Cards to one run. Having won the first two without difficulty, there must have been few doubts on August 5 that Alexander (20–8) would make short work of the Cardinals. Confidence levels must have been even higher when St. Louis started virtual unknown Milt Watson, whom the Phils had already pounded. Since everything clearly pointed to an easy Philadelphia victory, the result, of course, was exactly the opposite, a 2–0 Cardinals win as Watson hurled a seven-hit shutout. Shocked as they may have been, the Phillies recovered quickly, taking the last game of the series, 5–3.[16]

Philadelphia's final western opponent was Cincinnati, which had just lost six straight to the Braves. Unfortunately for the Reds, the change of scenery made no difference, as they lost their seventh straight on August 8, 5–1. On top of this, Cincinnati faced Alexander in the first game of the next day's doubleheader, and he couldn't have been in a good mood after his loss to the Cards. Leaving nothing to chance and taking little time to do it, Alexander (21–8) shut out the Reds, 2–0, allowing just two hits in one hour and 24 minutes. After scoring only two runs in the previous two games, Cincinnati finally erupted for eight runs in the second game for an 8–7 win. Two contests still remained in the series, and both were heartbreaking for the loser. This was the case for Reds ace Fred Toney on August 10, as he allowed only three hits and lost, 1–0, to Erskine Mayer. His five-hit shutout was a hopeful sign for the Phils in their desperate search for an effective fourth starter.[17]

The next day, however, was the Phillies' turn, not just to be frustrated, but furious after a 3–2 loss. Down by that score in the ninth, Philadelphia had two on with one out when Bill Killefer drove the ball off the left-field wall, sending home what appeared to be the tying and winning runs. However, when Christy Mathewson claimed a fan had interfered with the ball, umpire Charles Rigler concurred and sent the two runners to second and third and awarded Killefer first base. When the next two batters were retired without incident, the Reds had an improbable win. Moran and the Phils were furious, claiming no one had seen the interference and that the call should have been made by home plate umpire Pete Harrison. Despite the complaints and a planned protest, Philadelphia had to swallow a bitter loss in a close pennant race where every game mattered.[18] The game also marked the end of a 13–6 Philadelphia homestand against the western teams.

After compiling a 6-3-1 record in the first half of the homestand, the Braves' third series began on a negative note with a 3–1 loss to the Reds in an August 3 doubleheader. Things shifted quickly, however, as Boston swept the next six games, beginning with a 5–3 victory in the second game of the twin bill. All was not well with the Braves, though, starting with mercurial Mr. Evers, who after fighting opponents and umpires now shifted his attention to teammates. Even though Boston jumped out to a quick lead in the second game on Red Smith's first-inning grand slam, Evers and Smith fought in the Braves' dugout in the fourth inning. After Umpire Byron ejected the Crab, the fight resumed in the clubhouse, with Evers reportedly getting the worst of it and "sobbing like a child." On top of this, Stallings had been suspended for three games for using "bad language" directed at umpire Charles Rigler. Naturally, George claimed he didn't understand the reason for the suspension since the worst thing he had said was that Rigler should be in jail.[19]

The next day the Braves focused on the game instead of fighting or quarreling with the umpire, earning a 5–2 come-from-behind win. In addition, there was reconciliation when Evers met with Stallings and Haughton, and then apologized to Smith. Boston continued its winning ways on August 5, sweeping the first of two doubleheaders from the Reds, 1–0 and 4–3, before a crowd of 15,000. Apparently taking full advantage of the intervening Sabbath's rest, the Braves finished off Cincinnati with two shutouts on August 7. It was fortunate Boston's pitchers were on form, as the hitters generated little offense, especially in the first game, when Stallings' club got only two hits off Fred Toney. Without much offense, Flatley attributed the Braves' success to its pitching and the "glorious Boston defense."[20]

The only negative was an injury to Ed Fitzpatrick, who was filling in for Evers while the latter recovered from injuries suffered in his pugilistic endeavors. Even the weather was favoring the Braves; after three doubleheaders in five days, three straight rainouts provided badly needed rest for the pitching staff. The postponements meant only two games of the Pirates series would be played, in a doubleheader on August 11. In order to allow both teams to catch trains, the opener started at noon and resulted in a 2–1 Pittsburgh victory. Apparently, the "glorious Braves defense" took the initial contest off since both Pittsburgh runs scored on errors by Arthur Rico and Earl Blackburn, replacements for injured backstop Hank Gowdy. Fortunately, Lefty Tyler out-pitched Al Mamaux, 4–1, in the second game, as Boston benefited from six walks and a balk by the losing pitcher. Continuing his campaign to rebuild the Braves' image, Flatley proudly noted that even though provoked, Boston had refrained from any umpire baiting throughout the twin bill. After the game, the Braves boarded the train to New York and a four-game series with the Superbas, the first stop on a 20-day road trip.[21]

Perhaps at no other point during the 1916 season was the disparity between the East and West as clear as it was after the second round of games in the East. Brooklyn had the best record at 14–3, but Boston, Philadelphia and New York each won 13 times. In effect, the Dodgers had played over .800 ball and didn't add significantly to their lead. However, the Superbas at least maintained their position, while the Phils, Braves and Giants were losing time to catch up. Indeed, despite a 13–4 record on the homestand, New York had lost ground and was 10½ games off the pace, not a good position with less than 60 to play. Boston (five games out) and Philadelphia (six games out) were much closer, but couldn't afford to fall any further behind. All of this made the next series even more important since it was the only head-to-head competition until Labor Day weekend. This was especially true for the Braves, who would face Brooklyn for four games at Ebbets Field.

Given the Superbas' league-leading position and a Saturday, August 12 doubleheader against the second-place Braves, it was no surprise a record-breaking crowd of 30,000 was expected. Although Ebbets claimed the actual attendance was less, there were reportedly some 4,000 people still in line when the ticket windows closed. As usual, some of those who couldn't get inside or chose not to pay watched from the roof tops of adjoining houses. Each team scored an early run in the first, and it was 1–1 going to the bottom of the fifth in a match-up of rival aces Pfeffer (17–6) and Rudolph (12–6). With two out, Jake Daubert, who was back in the lineup, singled, scoring Jim Johnston, before crossing the plate himself a few minutes later on Zack Wheat's home run over the right-field fence. No doubt frustrated by allowing three runs, Rudolph tried to "quick pitch" Cutshaw, but the ploy failed as the Brooklyn second baseman singled. George was soon picked off first, but the quick pitch raised the ire of Wilbert Robinson, and he and Rudolph had words that briefly threatened to escalate into something more.[22]

Brooklyn maintained its 4–1 lead heading to the ninth, and when Pfeffer retired the leadoff hitter, there had to be many Dodger fans who considered the game won. Instead, the next two batters reached base, and former

Superba Red Smith singled, scoring one and putting runners on first and second. Pinch-hitter Joe Connolly then hit a ball to center that should have only loaded the bases, but Johnston tried and failed to make a shoestring catch, allowing one run to score and the potential tying and winning runs to move to second and third. At this point, managerial strategy intervened, and for once Wilbert Robinson came up empty. Stallings sent pitcher George Tyler, a left-handed batter, up to hit for Blackburn, and Robinson countered by pulling Pfeffer for seldom-used veteran lefty Nap Rucker. The choice of Rucker is more than a little surprising since Robinson had to know Stallings had a move of his own remaining. No doubt wearing out his suit pants on the Braves' bench, the Boston skipper sent up right-handed-hitting Ed Fitzpatrick. Since first base was open and the potential winning run was already on, it's also a little perplexing that Robinson didn't change pitchers again and/or walk Fitzpatrick intentionally to load the bases. Whatever his reasoning, Robinson stayed with Rucker, and Fitzpatrick singled in both runners, giving the Braves a 5–4 lead they preserved in the ninth.

Without question, the silence from the big crowd was almost palpable, and it got no better when the Braves scored in their first two at-bats of the second game to lead, 2–0. Brooklyn tied it in the second, knocking out Frank Allen and bringing Tom Hughes (13–3) into the game. The score remained tied into the sixth, when with two on, Dodgers center fielder Hi Myers tried to make a shoestring catch on a ball Rice felt he should have played more conservatively. Unfortunately, Myers, like Johnston, didn't make the catch, and the ball got by him into the vast expanses of center field for a three-run home run. Myers' judgment looked even worse when Brooklyn scored twice in the bottom of the inning, closing the margin to 5–4. The afternoon must have been extremely frustrating for a baseball purist like Rice, and the final events made it worse. With the score still 5–4 in the bottom of the ninth, Lew McCarty led off with a single, and Gus Getz was inserted as a pinch-runner. When Zack Wheat singled sharply to right, Getz violated one of the cardinal rules of baseball, making the first out of the inning at third when he was cut down on a strong throw from Joe Wilhoit to Red Smith. To make matters even more painful, Cutshaw followed with a single that could have tied the game. Robinson let Jack Coombs, a good hitting pitcher, bat for himself, but with a one-strike count, Stallings brought in his ace, Dick Rudolph, to do for Hughes what Hughes usually did for others. Rudolph was more than willing to oblige, shutting the door for a doubleheader sweep.[23]

Two contests of this intensity naturally lent themselves to post-game analysis, especially with an intervening off-day. Rice attributed the two losses to the Dodgers being "rattled" and "wildly over anxious," leading to the bad judgment by Johnston and Myers. To make matters worse, Jake Daubert was re-injured in the second game, and it would be a long time before he would play again. Nick Flatley, on the other hand, was ecstatic, as he had feared a Brooklyn sweep that would have knocked the Braves out of the race. In lauding the many Boston heroes, Flatley mentioned the obvious, like Fitzpatrick, Rudolph and Hughes, but reserved his highest praise for Rabbit Maranville. The Braves shortstop reportedly made so many nice defensive plays that even the partisan Brooklyn fans cheered him. All in all, it was a good day for Boston. At risk of being virtually eliminated from the pennant race, the Braves now trailed by only three games.[24]

While all of this was going on in Brooklyn, the Phillies and Giants opened their four-game set at Baker Bowl. Pat Moran's team had a golden opportunity, since by winning they would gain ground on one of the teams ahead of them. Things didn't get off to a good start, though, as New York led, 2–0, and put men on second and third with none out in the third. At that point, however, Dave Robertson hit a hard liner right at shortstop Davy Bancroft, who caught both Giants runners off base for a 6–5–6 triple play. Even though New York still had a two-run lead, the Giants looked beaten after losing this chance. The Phils quickly tied the game in the bottom of the third and broke it open in the bottom of the fifth when George Whitted hit a three-run home run over the fence "on the hop." Although Al Demaree had been hit hard in the first, he was in command the rest of the way. Even worse for New York, catcher Bill Rariden suffered a broken finger.[25]

Now 1½ games closer to first, the Phils weren't about to let up on the Giants, who appeared to be coming apart at the seams. That was especially true with Alexander, available to start an August 14 doubleheader, and he pitched a four-hit shutout for his 22nd win. Grover Cleveland then retired to the press box to watch the second game, but he was spotted by the sellout crowd, who cheered until he stood up and took a bow. Any hope New York had for a split died when Philadelphia scored five times in the second inning en route to an easy 7–4 win. Reflecting on the doubleheader, *Globe and Commercial Advertiser* correspondent Sid Mercer felt the sweep "practically eliminated the Giants from the race." In Mercer's view, the Giants were going through the motions, and he believed a disgruntled McGraw was going to clean house. Doyle, Robertson, Kauff and Merkle were described as "in a trance."[26]

In sweeping the twin bill, the Phils gained only a half-game on Brooklyn, since the Superbas finally found a way to win a game from the Braves on August 14. Having attributed much of Boston's success on Saturday to the Braves getting the breaks, Wilbert Robinson had no such complaints about Monday's 5–2 Brooklyn win. Although Rabbit Maranville led off the game with a home run against Larry Cheney, things changed quickly in the second, as three Boston errors and two Dodger hits led to four runs. The key sequence came with one run in and Jim Johnston hitting with two on. According to Rice, Johnston hit the ball "viciously" at third-string second baseman Dick Egan. Somehow, the ball got past not only Egan, but also center fielder Fred Snodgrass, bringing in three Brooklyn runs, including the batter, in what was scored as a four-base error. Eyewitness descriptions of the "hit" range from Rice's "vicious" liner to a ground ball "that looked like an easy out." Since it got by both Egan and Snodgrass, the latter accounts seem somewhat suspect. The Superbas went on to win, 5–2, behind Cheney (10–7), who won his fifth straight while allowing just three hits.[27]

Any hopes the Monday victory meant a change in Brooklyn's fortunes against Boston didn't last long when the Braves won the next day, 4–1. In fact, there was plenty of evidence the Boston hex was alive and well since the Superbas registered 10 hits off Rudolph (13–6) but scored only once. Also of concern was the weak-hitting Braves pounding out ten hits against Rube Marquard, including five for extra bases. Yet even with losing three of four to the Braves, Brooklyn departed for its last western trip with a three-game lead over Boston and Philadelphia. However, this was a trip, and then some, since Robby's club would play 28 straight games away from home in seven different cities. They would also start the adventure without first baseman and leading hitter Jake Daubert (.321). The Braves, on the other hand, took great comfort from their 12–6 overall record against Brooklyn, and headed west "imbued with the idea the pennant is theirs." In a sign of Deadball Era finances, Boston began its western trip by dividing into two groups, with both squads playing not one, but two exhibition games en route to St. Louis.[28]

Before heading west themselves, the Phils picked up another game on Brooklyn on August 15 with a 1–0 win over the Giants. Al Demaree allowed just three hits, one more than Philadelphia managed off of Jeff Tesreau. Rariden's injury in the first game of the series came back to haunt New York when his replacement, Brad Kocher, had a throwing error that allowed the only run. Demaree had now beaten the Giants six times in 1916, not to mention twice in this series, which did nothing for McGraw's already high frustration levels. Having lost four straight and two of the last three by shutouts, it was hard envisioning things getting worse for New York. Yet that would be the case until John McGraw's final personnel moves wreaked havoc on the home stretch of the pennant race.[29]

Team	Wins	Losses	Games Behind
Brooklyn	63	38	—
Boston	59	40	3
Philadelphia	61	42	3
New York	52	50	10½

While the schedule makers allowed a day for travel at the beginning of the trip, club owners wouldn't pass up an opportunity for some additional revenue. Even though the teams had played close to 100 games and were now on the road for at least three weeks in the heat of August, both the Braves and the Dodgers played exhibition games on their way west. It seems hard to believe there was financial justification for this, but since salaries were a fixed cost, owners apparently believed any additional revenue was important. Still, since there was only so much baseball in each player, the additional traveling and games had to take its toll. The contender's departure for the West also saw the first speculation about the future of Heinie Zimmerman, who had worn out his welcome in Chicago. Zimmerman was a controversial figure who combined impressive offensive numbers (a .372 batting average in 1912) with misbehavior on and off the field, including rumors of dishonesty. Nicknamed "the Great Zim" by Chicago sportswriters, Zimmerman adopted the name for his own use.[30]

From the Dodger perspective, there was no uncertainty about the significance of the impending 28-game marathon. One reporter claimed this was the most important Brooklyn road trip since the last pennant-winning season in 1900 under Ned Hanlon. The Dodgers were fortunate to draw the shorter journey to Pittsburgh, but awaiting them on August 17 was Pirate ace Al Mamaux. Facing Pittsburgh's best pitcher didn't faze the Superbas, though, as they knocked out the dreaded Pirate hurler in a 5 -1 win. Pfeffer (18–6) showed no ill effects from his ninth-inning failure against Boston, turning back Pittsburgh on six hits. George Cutshaw, who hadn't missed a game all year, provided a scare when he was hit in the head with a throw while stealing second. It was feared he had suffered a fractured skull, but showing toughness and possibly not the most rational thinking, Cutshaw remained in the game.[31]

The first full day of the western trip occurred on August 18 with the Dodgers leading the Braves and Phillies by 3½ games and the Giants a distant 12½ back. Brooklyn and Philadelphia maintained the pace that day, but Boston suffered a setback on the way to a pennant "imbued" to be theirs. The Dodgers and Phils both won via shutouts, Brooklyn, 6–0, over Pittsburgh, while Grover Cleveland Alexander threw his 13th shutout for his 23rd win, white-washing the Reds, 3–0. The Dodgers had enjoyed a dominant performance from Cheney (11–7), his sixth straight win since July 13. Boston opened in St. Louis in very hot conditions, which alone might have enervated the Braves, but Flatley sensibly wondered if the exhibition games en route contributed to Boston's loss of "fire and fight." Although the Braves tied the game in the ninth, they lost, 4–3, in ten innings. Johnny Evers had rejoined the club but couldn't play due to an injured left arm and emotional issues.[32]

Due to some type of a quirk in the schedule, Philadelphia and Boston played only two games apiece at their first stops in Cincinnati and St. Louis. Two games against the Cards were more than enough for the Braves, who followed their strong performance against Brooklyn with two straight losses to a seventh-place team. In the second defeat on August 19, they led, 3–0, but the Cards rallied to win, 7–4, in what Flatley called "one of the worse ball games known to science." The only good news for Boston, as they endured "a hot night on the rails" en route to Cincinnati, was the Dodgers managed only a split in their doubleheader in Pittsburgh. Both games were close — the Superbas lost the first, 2–1, in 10 innings before winning the second, 1–0. George Cutshaw's poor judgment in the form of a bad throw when he should have held the ball made Sherrod Smith a hard-luck loser in the opener. Cutshaw redeemed himself, however, by driving in the only run in Marquard's five-hit shutout of the Pirates that salvaged a split. Speculation about potential deals for Zimmerman had Rice thinking Brooklyn might offer Getz, O'Mara and a pitcher for the Cubs star. The Phils were more fortunate than the Braves, picking up a half-game on Brooklyn, with a 6–1, 14-inning victory over the Reds as Eppa Rixey (15–5) went the distance. One series into the western trip, Brooklyn led Philadelphia by three and Boston by four.[33]

Since the second series in the West began on a Sunday, August 20, the Phils enjoyed a day of rest in Pittsburgh. In looking at Philadelphia's situation, a columnist in the *Inquirer* pointed out that Alexander, Demaree and Rixey were a combined 49–22, but the rest of the staff was only 14–20. Obviously, if the Phillies were to defend their championship, they needed more help from the rest of the rotation. Brooklyn's rotation endured an extremely scary moment that same day when the Superbas opened their second western series in Chicago. Pitching to the Cubs' leadoff batter, Rollie Zeider, in the bottom of the first inning, Jack Coombs' (9–4) spikes "hung in the rubber," causing him to fall flat on the ground. It was an exact repetition of the injury Coombs suffered in the 1911 World Series and also during the 1915 season. While the 1915 injury put him out of action for a month, the World Series one, as described earlier, came close to ending his life.

Understandably, the Superbas crowded around their fallen hurler, concerned about both his health and their pennant chances. Fortunately, Coombs was up almost immediately, saying unlike the prior incidents "he had merely tripped and had not wrenched himself." Zeider immediately tested Jack's condition with a bunt, but Colby Jack fielded the ball and tagged out the Cubs batter. Having passed that test, Coombs went on to pitch one of the most dominant games of 1916 or any other season, allowing only one hit and one walk. Those two base runners, along with one who reached base on a Mike Mowrey error, were either thrown out stealing or eliminated in a double play.

Jack was extremely economical, retiring the side on three pitches once and using only five pitches in both the eighth and ninth. According to Rice, no one kept a pitch count, but he felt Coombs had to be close to a record. To say the least, the 1–0 victory got the series off to a good start. Jake Daubert was with the team but still out of action with what was now diagnosed as sciatica.

After their debacle in St. Louis, the Braves traveled east to Cincinnati. Boston got off to an early 4–0 lead, but the Reds closed to within one. Tom Hughes once again came to the rescue, shutting out Cincinnati the rest of the way. The win featured another strong performance by Maranville, who went 4-for-5 while playing good defense. After the game, Stallings left Fred Mitchell in charge of the team as he went off to join Charles Ebbets for the Heinie Zimmerman sweepstakes in Chicago.[34]

When the Phils got back into action on August 21, their six-game winning streak ended in Pittsburgh. Shockingly, it came about with an Alexander loss (23–9), 6–3, in the first game of a doubleheader. Things didn't improve in the second game when Al Demaree lost a 2–1 pitchers duel, turning a six-game winning streak into a two-game losing steak. Key in the twin defeats was Bert Niehoff, who made errors at crucial times in both games. Fortunately for Philadelphia, the double defeat only cost the Phils a half-game in the fight for first place. It didn't look as if the Phillies would get any help from the Cubs when the Dodgers took a 3–1 lead into the eighth behind Jeff Pfeffer (19–7). However, in an alarmingly similar repeat of his meltdown against the Braves, Pfeffer blew up "higher than Gilroy's kite" in the ninth, losing, 5–3. Tom Rice now believed Cheney had replaced Pfeffer as Brooklyn's ace because of his 6–0 record since July 13. During that period he had allowed just seven runs over 70⅔ innings. Cheney was clearly worth the $3,000 and outfielder Joe Schultz that Brooklyn had paid for the right-hander in 1915.[35]

The Braves weren't about to miss this opportunity to pick up ground on both Brooklyn and Philadelphia, and they defeated the Reds, 2–1, with Rudolph (14–7) chalking up his ninth straight win. The victory shouldn't have been a surprise as Fred Mitchell was now 8–0 as interim manager. When the series with Cincinnati ended the following day, Boston would again split into two groups for exhibition games in Indiana on the way to Chicago. Flatley noted the Cincinnati newspapers were critical of the "Braves money making polices," but it was "mild compared to what the players themselves have to say."[36] This wasn't a good sign for team morale in the heat of the pennant race.

Now ahead of Boston by four games and Philadelphia by 4½, Brooklyn maintained its lead by scoring early and often on August 22 to defeat Chicago,

9–4. The Superbas tallied four times in the first for Cheney (12–7), who got the win under the scoring rules of the day, even though he only pitched three innings. Daubert pinch-hit in the contest, prompting hopes he would soon be back in action. His return was now even more important since Jim Johnston had suffered a broken nose; it was projected he would be out for two weeks or more. Boston also kept pace, winning a rain-shortened 1–0 game over the Reds. Even though he couldn't play, Johnny Evers also couldn't stay out of trouble. The Trojan was suspended indefinitely for his words in the third-base coach's box against St. Louis the previous Saturday. Since he was injured and unlikely to play for some time, the suspension was meaningless. That alone was enough to feed Flatley and no doubt others' paranoia that the league was out to get the Braves and their captain.[37]

After being swept in the August 21 doubleheader with Pittsburgh, Philadelphia's 6–2 win in the first game of its second consecutive doubleheader may have suggested things were back to normal. It was, however, an illusion. Even though the Phils won the game behind George McQuillan's relief effort, there were ongoing disputes with the umpires, Charles Rigler and Al Orth. Ultimately, Pat Moran was ejected for the second straight day and had to sit out the second game. Captain Fred Luderus was put in charge, but when the Phillies took a 7–0 lead in the nightcap, it didn't seem like he would be faced with many difficult decisions. Yet things changed quickly when both the Phils' defense and Charles Bender unraveled in the fifth inning. Luderus decided to replace Bender with McQuillan, who had already pitched three innings in the first game. Bender wasn't pleased with the decision and had "to be shoved off the field by his team mates." Without doubt, second-guessing abounded when McQuillan surrendered a double to Pirates pitcher Wilbur Cooper. It was the Pittsburgh hurler's second hit of the inning, driving in what proved to be the tying and winning runs. To add injury to insult, Niehoff was spiked in the first game and projected to be out for the rest of the trip.[38]

To make matters worse, Philadelphia's problems with the umpires weren't over. In the final game of the series, on August 23, the Phils lost to the Pirates, 2–1, in 16 innings. On top of the loss, Philadelphia missed the 6:00 P.M. train to St. Louis, which meant they would arrive just in time for the next afternoon's match-up with the red-hot Cardinals (five wins in a row). Moran's club led, 1–0, in the ninth against Pittsburgh when star rookie Max Carey singled with one out and stole second — or at least that is what the umpire ruled. According to various accounts, Carey was out by distances ranging from two feet to "a block." Understandably, Philadelphia argued with George Whitted, reportedly earning an ejection for the first time in his career. Carey then scored all the way from second on Rixey's wild pitch to tie the game. Matters then dragged on to the bottom of the 16th, when Moran chose not to walk Alex McCarthy, who already had three hits, with the winning run on the third. McCarthy's game-winning hit sent the Phils on a long and unhappy trip to St. Louis. In the four games, the Pirates had beaten Philadelphia's big three, including an unlikely victory over Alexander. It wasn't a good sign for a team so dependent on a limited number of arms.[39]

As painful as the loss had to be, the Phillies at least didn't lose any ground to the Superbas, who fell to the Cubs, 7–6, on August 23. Horrible Brooklyn defense led Rice to call the game the worst contest since the first road game in Boston in early April. Additionally, news came that Heinie Zimmerman's career as a Cub was over after a fifth-inning temper tantrum. Zimmerman was thrown out trying to advance from second base against the direction of manager Joe Tinker, who was coaching third. Criticism from Tinker led to an argument that, in turn, led to a suspension for "the Great Zim." Both Tinker and Chicago owner Weeghman vowed Heinie's Cubs career was over. As a result, the Zimmerman sweepstakes went into high gear, with John McGraw the latest to visit Chicago for that purpose. Given the Giants' recent play, it was hard to visualize what New York players would be of interest to the Cubs or anyone else for that matter. Amidst this excitement, the second series of the final western road trip ended with Boston moving past Philadelphia into second, 3½ games out (one in the loss column). The Phils were now 4½ games back, in third place, after losing four out of five in Pittsburgh.[40]

Team	Wins	Losses	Games Behind
Brooklyn	68	41	—
Boston	62	42	3½
Philadelphia	64	46	4½
New York	53	56	15

After a long, hot and frustrating train ride that lasted all night and well into the next day, Philadelphia might have been expected to have difficulty with the Cardinals. However, resiliency was one reason the Phils were defending National League champs, and they bounced back to defeat St. Louis, 7–2, on August 24, ending the Cards' five-game winning streak. Pat Moran had a powerful weapon to use in these situations — Grover Cleveland Alexander (24–9), who pitched on two days rest. The win also helped Philadelphia climb within three games of the Dodgers, who lost in heart-breaking fashion to the Reds, 2–1. Down 1–0 in the top of the ninth, Brooklyn rallied to tie the game, only to lose in bizarre fashion in the bottom half of the inning. Sherrod Smith lost the contest on four pitches — a hit batsman, two first-pitch bunts and a wild pitch. Like the Phils, Boston also picked up a full game on the Dodgers, closing within 2½ and tying Brooklyn in the loss column by defeating the Cubs, 5–1. Tom Hughes (14–3) allowed a run in the first and then settled down to shut Chicago out the rest of the way on six hits. Always the optimist, Flatley reported that every Brave expected to catch the Superbas upon their return to Boston. Even if Stallings shared that confidence, he was well into the Zimmerman sweepstakes, meeting with Weeghman and Tinker. Some speculated the Braves manager offered Red Smith, Ed Fitzpatrick, Joe Wilhoit and Jess Barnes in exchange for the difficult Cubs star.[41]

Having recovered from a poor showing in St. Louis, Boston was now the hot team, winning their fifth straight on August 25 when Dick Rudolph (15–7) shut out Chicago, 1–0. It marked the 10th straight victory for "the bald pated pitching marvel" or the "thin thatched farmer," this in his hometown newspaper. Typical for 1916, a good pitching performance was accompanied by speculation regarding the use of an emery board to doctor the baseball. Even Flatley acknowledged Rudolph's pitches had "a lot of funny breaks." Injuries were starting to become a problem for the Braves, as Wilhoit was now out for a week with a knee injury. Boston didn't gain any ground on the Superbas with its win since Brooklyn also had a red-hot pitcher in Larry Cheney (13–7), who won his eighth straight against Cincinnati. One of the keys to the Dodgers' success all year was their ability to bounce back from a poor performance; remarkably, thus far they hadn't lost three straight all season. Jake Daubert was still injured, and Robinson switched to Gus Getz at first in place of Lew McCarty. There was also speculation Brooklyn would acquire Fred Merkle from the Giants in exchange for McCarty. Philadelphia didn't keep pace with Brooklyn and Boston, losing to the Cardinals when St. Louis' Mike Gonzalez beat the Phillies with his bat for the second time in 1916.[42]

Stallings club won again on August 26, this time picking up ground on both the Dodgers and Phils. After falling behind early, Boston rallied and pounded the Cubs, 8–3. In spite of the rare offensive outburst, the Braves' pitching was, as usual, the major factor, with Tyler hurling seven innings of shutout relief. Connolly, in the lineup for the injured Wilhoit, also had three hits. Not surprisingly, Flatley's confidence soared, claiming the "Stallings stars" believed they would catch Brooklyn before their road trip ended. Still having little respect for the Dodgers, Nick named the Phils as the team to beat. Meanwhile, Brooklyn followed Cheney's one-hit shutout in Chicago with a six-hitter by Coombs (9–5), but he was out-pitched "a wee bit" by Pete Schneider in a 1–0 loss. Philadelphia endured another tough day in St. Louis, losing a 3–1 lead before seeing the Cards score once in the ninth for a 4–3 victory. The loss cost the Phillies (4½ out) a game on Boston while the Braves were now only 1½ games back of the Superbas and actually one game ahead in the loss column.[43]

Flatley, who never seemed to learn, got another lesson about the dangers of over-confidence on August 27 when the Cubs beat Boston, 6–1, to end the Braves' six-game winning streak. Pat Moran was in Chicago during the contest to make his pitch for Heinie Zimmerman. After the game, Boston took an overnight train ride to Pittsburgh, where they were scheduled to arrive at dawn for the first of three straight doubleheaders. Unfortunately for the Braves, the end of their winning streak also cost them the game they had made up on Brooklyn the day before, as the Superbas routed the Reds, 13–6. Fred Merkle, who had indeed been traded to Brooklyn for Lew McCarty, was in the lineup for the first time and had two hits in the win. Apparently according the Superbas more respect than Flatley, the Cincinnati crowd gave the league leaders a "rousing sendoff" as they left Redland Field for the last time. The Dodgers' final western stop would be St. Louis, and Brooklyn had a 2½ game lead over Boston and five over Philadelphia. The weather played a cruel trick on the Cards as their last game against the Phillies was rained out. The

combination of St. Louis' recent good play and a final chance to see Alexander had excited Cardinal baseball fans, and a crowd of 18,000 was expected. Given their attendance problems, the rainout was a huge financial loss for St. Louis, with the game slated to be made up in Philadelphia on September 12.[44]

In Pittsburgh for the first of three straight doubleheaders beginning August 28, the Braves were unpleasantly surprised to find Al Mamaux, back from a suspension, on the mound. He took his frustrations out on Boston, winning easily, 5–1, ending Rudolph's 10-game winning streak. Fortunately, Frank Allen came back and won the second game, 8–2, which was called after seven innings because of darkness.

Dick Rudolph, Boston Braves ace pitcher, was known as "the bald-headed farmer of West Nyack" and similarly unflattering monikers (National Baseball Hall of Fame Library, Cooperstown, N.Y.).

Meanwhile, in St. Louis, Wilbert Robinson brought back Jeff Pfeffer (18–8) after a week's rest to overcome his "staleness." Whatever the problem, rest wasn't the solution, as he gave up three runs on ten hits in a 4–0 loss. Anticipating the Dodgers' trip back east, the teams agreed to end the August 30 finale early so Brooklyn could catch its train. This would allow the Superbas to arrive in Philadelphia on Thursday evening instead of spending two straight nights on the rails. Moran's men picked up a game on Brooklyn, defeating the Cubs, 8–2, on August 28, in Alexander's 25th win, which earned him a $1,000 bonus. Brooklyn now led Boston by two and Philadelphia by four.

The other news from Chicago was the Giants had won the Zimmerman sweepstakes, acquiring the talented but problematic player for Larry Doyle, Merwin Jacobson and Herb Hunter. With the little-known Jacobson and Hunter clearly throw-ins, the key part of the deal was the exchange of Doyle and Zimmerman. Although the Giant second baseman had begun his major league career earlier, he was actually a year younger than the Cubs star. After hitting .320 in 1915, Doyle had hit well early in 1916, owning a .300 average as late as June 30. Since that point, however, he hit only .228 and was named by Sid Mercer as one of the Giants who appeared to be playing "in a trance." At this point McGraw probably felt he had little to lose by taking a chance with Zimmerman, as he already had with Herzog.[45]

Clearly, the Giants needed help of almost any kind. New York had begun this last long road trip in the worst possible way by losing four straight to the Phils. The western part of the swing was no better — the team lost eight of the first ten before winning the last two games in Cincinnati. Perhaps the low point was four straight defeats to St. Louis that included three straight shutouts. At one point, McGraw tried to literally wake up his players, requiring them to rise each morning by 8:00. This led one observer to comment that the players looked like they were making up for their lost sleep on the field. At another point in the swing, they were said to be playing "as if baseball was a drudgery." Given how badly New York was performing, it's no surprise "the Great Zim" made them a better team, almost by default, driving in the winning run in the last game of the trip. Offensively, the Giants had given the Braves some competition for ineptitude, hitting just .234 on the swing while scoring fewer than three runs per game. New York was a seemingly insurmountable 15 games out of first and two games below .500. The Giants' season was obviously over.[46]

Having moved to within two games of Brooklyn (and tied in the loss column), it was time for Stallings to pull out all the stops to catch the Superbas. On August 29, that meant going with the hot hand, or in this case, the hot arm, to try to win both games of the second doubleheader with the Pirates. In the opener, George "Lefty" Tyler dominated Pittsburgh in an 8–1 Braves win. His performance and the Pirates' predominately left-handed batting order inspired Stallings to start Tyler in the second game as well. He took a 4–0 shutout into the seventh before tiring and Pittsburgh tied the game at 4–4 in the eighth. Things were still knotted up in the top of the ninth, but the Braves were threatening with two on and one out when Pirates manager James Callahan literally played his ace, bringing Mamaux on in relief. This time, however, Boston was ready, pounding the Pirates pitcher on its way to a five-run inning and a 9–5 win. Tom Hughes (15–3) had relieved Tyler in the eighth and was the winning pitcher, which upset Flatley, who felt the latter to be more deserving. Although this was the first time in 1916 that a National League pitcher attempted to hurl both ends of a doubleheader, it would by no means be the last. Since the poor start in St. Louis, the Braves had been red-hot, winning 10 of their last 12.[47]

Further west that afternoon, the Dodgers came to bat in the top of the eighth, down 4–2 to St. Louis. They couldn't have missed the final score of Boston's victory in the second game, which had been posted on the Robison Field scoreboard. Unless Brooklyn rallied quickly, the Superbas would lead by only a half-game and trail in the loss column. Thus far, it had been what Rice described as a "weird contest," with Robby's team unable to do anything against Milt "Mule" Watson for the first five innings before knocking him out in the sixth. With runners on first and second, Wheat singled on an 0–2 pitch, allowing Stengel to score on a close play at the plate. St. Louis manager Miller Huggins then brought "Steamboat" Bill Williams on in relief to try to quell the Brooklyn rally. The first batter, George Cutshaw, bunted, and Williams fielded the ball, only to throw wildly to third, allowing Merkle to score the tying run. The other runners advanced and scored when Hi Myers singled, giving the Superbas a lead they would not relinquish in a 7–5 victory. Over in Chicago, the Phils kept pace by pounding the Cubs for the second straight day, winning, 8–3, behind Rixey (16–6) and a 17-hit attack.[48]

Having dodged a huge bullet on August 29, Brooklyn ended the western portion of its odyssey successfully the next day with a 4–1 victory over the Cards, making the Dodgers the only eastern team to take a series from St. Louis. Marquard threw a five-hitter at the Cards and benefited from three hits by Zack Wheat and two from Cutshaw. The Superbas had gone 9–6 in the West, which Rice found "somewhat disappointing," but given injuries to Daubert and Johnston as well as Pfeffer's slump, things hadn't gone all that badly. The Dodgers managed to catch the earlier train, but they still had to hustle out of their sleeping car in Pittsburgh early on August 31 to make the day coach to Philadelphia. Unfortunately, the Superbas didn't get the desired private day coach, having to settle for a parlor car that wasn't as conducive to their comfort or for card games. The win allowed them to increase their lead on the Phils, who lost, 2–0, to the Cubs, to five games. Since hosting the western teams in a homestand that began on July 26, Brooklyn had received good production from its offense, averaging nearly four runs per game. Even though Daubert had missed more than two weeks, Stengel, Wheat, Miller and Olson all hit .300 or better over the period. The pitching had also been effective, ranging from Cheney's winning streak to Rucker's 10 surprising scoreless innings in relief. Brooklyn seemed well prepared for its five games in Philadelphia, followed by visits to New York and Boston.[49]

In spite of Brooklyn's win in St. Louis, it appeared at least for a while the Braves would pick up another half-game on the Superbas. Dick Rudolph (16–8) took care of the first game of the August 30 doubleheader, pitching a six-hit shutout and driving in the only run of the game. Boston had now taken four of five from the Pirates, but this homestand was Pittsburgh's turn to be a factor in the pennant race. In the second contest the Braves fell behind, 2–0, and then rallied for a 6–2 lead, but Pittsburgh loaded the bases in the bottom of the sixth against Frank Allen, who was making his second appearance in three days. At the plate was Pirate second baseman Don Baird — no great offensive force, as he would finish 1916 with a .216 batting average and 28 RBIs. When he did reach base, which wasn't often, Baird wasn't a threat to run since he had been thrown out on 16 of 36 attempts to steal. None of that mattered at this point, however, as Baird tripled in three runs and then scored on a squeeze bunt to tie the game. Yet Don wasn't done. With the scored still tied in the bottom of the eighth, he doubled off Jess Barnes, successfully stole third and scored the winning run on a sacrifice fly. As a result, the Braves ended up losing a heartbreaking half-game to Brooklyn. Although it couldn't have provided much solace, Boston picked up a full game on the Phils. Flatley, however, still not willing to take the Dodgers seriously, found the gain on the Phillies important, as they were the "much more dangerous contender."[50]

While the Dodgers, Giants and Phils headed east, the Braves still had one more game to play in Pittsburgh, which was shortened to eight innings by mutual agreement so Boston could catch its train. That turned out to be a questionable move on the Braves' part, as the Pirates held on for a 3–2 win behind Al Mamaux, who was apparently weakening. Still, Boston finished 13–7 on its road trip, making up 2½ games on Brooklyn and putting them 2½ back of the league leaders. The significance of losing the last two games to the Pirates can't be underestimated, however. The Braves entered play on August 30 tied with Brooklyn in the loss column and only 1½ games out of first. Now Boston trailed the Superbas by 2½ games, and two in the loss column. The Phillies, on the other hand, had lost ground on the trip, primarily because they lost six of eight games to Pittsburgh and St. Louis. Their 6–7 mark in the West left them five games behind Brooklyn heading into a critical five-game series against the Superbas at Baker Bowl.[51]

Team	Wins	Losses	Games Behind
Brooklyn	72	44	—
Boston	69	46	2½
Philadelphia	67	49	5
New York	56	58	15

At some point, every National League team would have an impact on the pennant race. Pittsburgh and St. Louis had done so during this final western trip for the contenders. The Pirates had taken four of five from the Phils in addition to three vital games from the Braves. The Cardinals hurt the same teams, taking both games from Boston and two of three from Philadelphia. August was now over, and the National League race was headed for its climax over the next five weeks. On August 28, a Philadelphia *Inquirer* columnist, writing under the "Old Sport's Musings," noted that after the western trip, the Dodgers had 11 straight games against the eastern teams, all on the road. The columnist felt this would be an "acid test" for Brooklyn. In fact, everyone would be well tested before the curtain came down on the season.[52]

CHAPTER VII

"All of them were wild with enthusiasm."

August began with Boston and Chicago in a nip-and-tuck struggle for the top of the American League. The Red Sox began the month by finishing an important six-game series with Detroit. After showing signs of life and winning the first two, the Tigers dropped the next two contests to conclude July. This negative trend would continue into August.

On the first, the Jungaleers had the Navin Field crowd in a frenzy after rallying to tie the game. In addition, the scoreboard in left field showed the White Sox were hammering the Athletics in a doubleheader, warning Boston that its half-game lead was in jeopardy. With imminent danger staring them in the face, the Red Sox went to work in the eighth. Dick Hoblitzell's go-ahead run-scoring double eluded the diving Sam Crawford in right field, highlighting a 6–2 victory. The Detroit *Free Press* blamed poor fielding for the loss, but Ty Cobb also was 0-for-4 and left multiple runners on base. Dutch Leonard (13–7) came on in relief to pitch the final three innings for Boston to earn the victory.[1] Chicago finished its sweep of Philadelphia on August 1, and also won the next day. Though two back in the loss column, the White Sox were in a virtual tie with their hose counterparts.

Back in Detroit, Rube Foster (8–8) relied on a devastating curve on August 2, keying Boston's fourth straight victory over the Tigers. The improved pitching suggested the Red Sox mound staff might be catching up to the bats. E.A. Batchelor commented, "The Tigers couldn't hit Foster hard enough to keep the Red Sox interested in their work." By that time, Boston had a 5–0 lead due to wildness from the recently effective Bernie Boland and Hoblitzell's second key hit in as many days. The biggest rally-killer for Detroit was again Cobb, who tried to score on a single to left field with two out in the eighth but was thrown out at the plate. The Red Sox strong finish suggested traveling in the heat may have caused Boston to be swept in the open-

143

ing doubleheader of the series. However, Batchelor claimed Detroit always started strong against Boston before falling apart.[2]

Potentially the biggest factor in the pennant race thus far was the inconsistency of the three contenders. At points, all looked like world-beaters, and at other times, played poorly. This trend would continue in August, and it wasn't uncommon for a sportswriter to argue the pennant was lost one week and won the next. Part of this is certainly due to the sportswriting of the time, but it was also a result of streaky play. Before August was over, the failure of any of the contenders to take control would turn the A.L. race into a six-team dogfight for first.

Boston headed for St. Louis with an excellent 7–3 start to its western swing. The Red Sox had finished July hot, and now in first place, they were looking to put distance between themselves and the other contenders. In St. Louis, Joe Lannin's first concern was the outfield grass at Sportsman's Park, which was nearly knee-high. He quickly wired a protest to Ban Johnson.[3] Regardless of the impact of the high grass, the winning stopped at Sportsman's Park, where the Browns were hotter than the summer heat in St. Louis. After a 1–0 loss to the Yankees on July 22, Fielder Jones' team was in seventh place, 13½ games out; by the August 3 opener with Boston, St. Louis had reeled off 12 straight wins. The last six came against the Yankees, who started the set in first place and ended it in fourth. The Browns were still in seventh but had cut six games off the lead to put them in the middle of the race. And St. Louis wasn't done yet.

The Red Sox were sloppy in the first two games and lost both, and suddenly, Chicago was in first. St. Louis was also in a sixth-place tie. In the Boston *Daily Globe*, Grantland Rice noted it was exactly a decade earlier that Fielder Jones (now the St. Louis Manager) led the White Sox back from exactly the same deficit the Browns now faced at exactly the same time to win the American League pennant and the World Series. A doubleheader with Boston was slated for August 5, and though still in sixth place, St. Louis had caught pennant fever. Probably not used to describing large throngs watching the Browns, J.B. Sheridan wrote:

> The boxes, grand stand and pavilions were filled to the last seat and many hundreds of spectators stood back of the seats. The bleacherites will not pack up close in hot weather and the bleachers were some 2000 shy of their theoretical seating capacities. About 1000 persons were on the field in front of the pavilion in left field. The writer does not remember seeing a larger crowd at Sportsman's Park.[4]

The Boston *Herald* estimated the crowd at 26,000, but what they saw didn't rate high marks for style. St. Louis was sloppy in the first game and Boston the second, leading the teams to split the twin bill. At least the Browns' onslaught had been slowed, and the Red Sox also won the final game on August 6 to take two out of five in the series. In that contest, Rube Foster (9–8) tossed a three-hit, 1–0 shutout, his second straight exceptional outing. He also started a two-out rally in the fifth, with Harry Hooper and Jack Barry following with infield singles for the game's only run. Unfortunately, extracurricular activities marred the contest. Browns third baseman Jimmy Austin accused Foster of attempting to bean him, and after striking out on the next pitch, Austin turned around and took a swing at catcher Pinch Thomas. It was an action Austin would soon regret. The Boston *Post's* Paul Shannon reported, "Before help could reach the scene Chester (Thomas) swung three times on Austin and he didn't miss once. Every blow found Austin's face, and before the umpire and players of both teams could pull the men apart the hot-headed St. Louis man was pretty badly mussed up. None of the other players were engaged, as the timely rush of a dozen policemen quickly ended the trouble." Not as lucky was Umpire Chill, who also caught a punch before ejecting both players. Lannin supported Thomas, saying he would fire a player who didn't respond the way the catcher did and defend himself after being "assaulted."[5]

Unlike Austin, Boston (58–43) escaped relatively unscathed and was just a half-game behind the White Sox. After taking full advantage of the Athletics by sweeping all eight games, Chicago split four with the Senators. Now in first place, Chicago began the Washington series by dividing an August 4 doubleheader at Comiskey Park. Enthusiastic and large crowds were becoming the norm in A.L. cities. James Crusinberry claimed, "It was one of the greatest baseball days the Sox have had this season, even if they did get only an even break. There were at least 22,000 fans present, and all of them were wild with enthusiasm. It was probably the biggest weekday crowd Comiskey ever entertained unless some special feature was on the books."[6]

Red Faber (10–3) out-dueled Walter Johnson, 3–2, in the first game, but six White Sox pitchers weren't able to replicate the effort in the second. Chicago's Eddie Cicotte (7–4) tossed a 7–0 shutout the next day, and Shoeless Joe Jackson went 3-for-4 with a run and two RBIs. But the White Sox dropped a tough, 10-inning decision on August 6, Faber losing in relief. Shano Collins allowed the winning run to reach base when he misjudged a fly ball. Boston was next into Comiskey Park, with a meager half-game separating the two teams.[7]

After losing the last two games with Boston on August 1 and 2, Detroit was in fifth place, 6½ games out, and trying to make up ground in a limited amount of time. Fortunately, the Tigers were catching the Yankees at the right time (following that awful series with St. Louis), and Detroit won the first three to push New York's losing streak to nine games. Harry Coveleski and

Bernie Boland combined to allow just one run in the opener on August 3, but New York's Allen Russell was just as good. Tied at 1–1 in the last of the ninth, the Tigers' Bobby Veach led off with a triple. With one out, second baseman Joe Gedeon fielded Ralph Young's grounder, and his throw home was in plenty of time, but catcher Roxy Walters lost the ball and the game in a collision with Veach. Poor fielding cost New York the second game as well, and the third game went into the fourteenth inning tied at two. At that stage, Paddy Baumann's throwing error allowed Harry Heilmann to reach third base, and Del Baker drove him home with the game winner. Seven teams were separated by eight games, leading the Detroit *News* to comment that even though it was August, "The most hectic pennant chase in years is still in its infancy."[8]

The Tigers were stopped in the fourth game by Nick Cullop, who made his return after tearing a stomach muscle on July 18. He was excellent, matching zeros with Hooks Dauss until the ninth when the Yankees pounded the Detroit hurler for four runs. Hughie Jennings allowed Dauss to pitch the entire game, while Bill Donovan removed Cullop when he got into trouble in the bottom of the ninth. Once again, this raised questions regarding Jennings' handling of pitchers. The Tigers scored twice, but it wasn't enough. Detroit catcher Oscar Stanage caught another foul tip on his hand, which reopened the previous wound, but was expected to miss only a few days. He would soon be diagnosed with a broken thumb on this throwing hand, leading to a significantly longer stint on the bench.[9]

Next up for Detroit were the Athletics, who hadn't won a game in the West (0–29) and were about to tie the 1906 Red Sox's American League record of 20 straight defeats. Their typical sloppy play in the first two games "earned" Philadelphia a share of that dubious mark. The Athletics had also lost 19 straight on the road, another A.L. record. Understandably, Connie Mack was facing criticism, but Chicago reporter George Robbins disagreed. In an argument perhaps even further off the mark than his excessive praise of Jack Ness, Robbins argued Mack was competing against teams he helped to make better. Since every 1916 club was improved, according to Robbins, the Athletics were worse only by comparison. Fortunately for Mack and the A's, they had one competent pitcher in Joe Bush. Before Philadelphia could set the overall mark for losses, Bush stopped Detroit and the losing streak on August 9. The A's had only two victories since July 11, and Bush won both of them. A five-run fifth spurred the Tigers to a victory in the final game to take six of eight from New York and Philadelphia. While still trailing the Red Sox, Indians and White Sox, Jennings' club had climbed into fourth place, five games out.[10] This recent stretch of good play had been bolstered by both offense and pitching. If Detroit was going to make a run, the Tigers would have to get hot on multiple fronts.

The Tigers and Athletics finished their series on August 10, as Boston and Chicago were completing a four-game series at Comiskey Park. Though the Red Sox led by a game in the loss column when the series began on August 7, Boston trailed by a half-game overall. The White Sox were playing excellent baseball during the current homestand against the eastern teams. Chicago was hitting .278, and the pitchers were holding the opposition to fewer than three runs per game. As the Red Sox had done previously in Cleveland, Detroit and St. Louis, Boston opened the set with a bad loss. A large Monday crowd of about 10,000 showed up at Comiskey Park with first place on the line to watch the White Sox pound Dutch Leonard (13–8). It was his second poor start of the trip, while Reb Russell (12–6) put forth a supreme effort in a 7–1 victory. Making George Robbins look good for at least the moment, Jack Ness went 3-for-4 with a triple, home run, two runs and three RBIs. With another tough, hot, sleepless trip on the way to Chicago, the Red Sox could only hope they would bounce back as they did on their previous stops. Although things did improve on August 8, numerous Red Sox were briefly chased from the dugout for sarcastically singing love songs. However, Carl Mays (12–6) was brilliant, and Boston's offense was steady in building a 5–0 lead as Carrigan's team hung on for a 6–4 victory. Faber (10–5) exited in the fifth, trailing 1–0, but the Red Sox achieved their big lead by battering Lefty Williams.[11]

The series turned in Boston's favor the next day in a game that was tied 1–1 in the twelfth. Chicago scored its run in the fourth on a questionable call, and Red Sox manager Bill Carrigan spent most of the afternoon inspecting baseballs for evidence of tampering. Apparently eager to assist, White Sox catcher Ray Schalk pegged one of the spheres at him in a not-so-gentlemanly fashion. Finally, in the twelfth, with two Boston runners on base, Cady and Hooper came through with run-scoring singles that put the Red Sox back in first place by a half-game. Shoeless Joe Jackson went 0-for-5 and failed to deliver with runners on base on three separate occasions. Comparing what he considered to be the top two teams, Grantland Rice favored Chicago, noting, "As between the White Sox and the Red Sox the latter have a slight shade in pitching, but man for man the Chicago club has the call. The White Sox have a far stronger attack, a better catcher, a better infield and a harder-hitting outfield." While Rice focused on Boston as the primary competition, Chicago also had to worry about the Indians, since Cleveland's 5–3 victory over New York put the Tribe just a half-game behind the White Sox in third.[12]

The series finale on August 10 was a rare Deadball Era slugfest, with Boston again getting out early and hanging on for an 11–5 victory. Chicago committed five errors behind Reb Russell (12–7), but the pitcher wasn't without fault. At one point, he stood and watched, then reacted far too late while

Duffy Lewis and Jack Barry executed a double steal. The game was played in a rainstorm, with mud ankle-deep by the finish. Rube Foster (10–8) was again effective for the Red Sox but worked with a big lead. His only challenge was in the seventh, and Chicago's Dave Danforth gave up a crucial first out by sacrificing with his team trailing by three runs. At one point during the game, an advertising flag went skyward, promoting tickets for a White Sox-Dodgers World Series. While probably not officially sponsored by Comiskey, the message couldn't have been lost on Boston. Even though the Red Sox missed their train and wouldn't arrive home until 10:00 P.M. the following night, with first place in hand and a 12–7 western swing in the books, it was a happy ride. After losing three out of four, the White Sox fell to third during a series in which 50,000-plus spectators had come out to support them.[13]

During the trip, Carrigan's club outscored its opponents, 86 to 72, but the pitching staff held the opposition to a measly batting average of .215. Meanwhile, the Red Sox hit .270 as a team, with Larry Gardner (.403), Del Gainer (.316), Dick Hoblitzell (.308) and Tilly Walker (.307) all hitting over .300. Boston would be at Fenway Park for the rest of the month. It was critical for the Red Sox to take advantage of this homestand since they would spend most of September on the road.[14] Fortunately, Boston seemed to be playing the kind of baseball that would enable them to do just that.

Although the White Sox dropped into third place, 1½ games out of first and a half-game behind the Indians, Chicago was still playing good baseball. They next would be tested by a hot Detroit team, five out and eager to make up more ground, at Comiskey Park. Harry Coveleski (16–8) opened things up on August 11 by blanking the White Sox, 2–0, for his third 1916 shutout of the Pale Hose. This prompted suspicion that the jinx against the Tigers might have returned. White Sox pitcher Mel Wolfgang (6–5) was effective, but not quite good enough. His most questionable pitch was an 0–2 spitter he threw to Cobb in the sixth inning that Ty slammed for a triple to the fence in left-center and a 1–0 lead.[15]

Warm-ups for the second game yielded a torn finger nail for pitcher Bernie Boland and probably a week on the bench. Once the contest started, Red Faber's spitball stopped Chicago's troubles, as he allowed only four hits to lead the White Sox to an important 3–0 victory. Faber had struggled against Detroit through 1915, but had been much better during the current campaign, meaning the Tigers had no hex over him. Nemo Leibold and Buck Weaver produced the first two runs, and Fred McMullin, who replaced Zeb Terry, singled home Hap Felsch on a squeeze play for the final tally. The squeeze had failed twice earlier in the game, but Clarence Rowland didn't hesitate to go back to it. That same day St. Louis used a nine-run first inning to pound Cleveland and pass the Tigers in the standings. Almost miraculously,

St. Louis had won 23 of 25 games to put the Browns just 4½ out of first, making them a major factor in the race. Though their offense was certainly producing, pitching seemed to be at the heart of the run, as Browns pitchers allowed more than two runs in only four of the 23 victories.[16]

On August 13, 25,000 fans showed up on an unseasonably chilly day for the White Sox final home game until September 5. Hughie Jennings benched Harry Heilmann for George Burns, and Tubby Spencer saw his first action at catcher. Chicago rallied from a 4–0 deficit, but porous defense late in the contest helped Detroit pull away for a 9–4 win. Zeb Terry's seventh-inning error put Cobb on base, setting the stage for Sam Crawford's go-ahead triple. The blow gave Coveleski, in relief, his second win of the series. In the bottom half, the White Sox had two on and one out, but Bobby Veach caught Shano Collins' long drive to left. Veach then followed by doubling off Fred McMullin, Detroit's fourth twin-killing of the game. The fact that three of these had come on blows to the outfield suggested poor judgment on someone's part. Chicago's performance drove G.W. Alexson to write, "It seems as if the Sox will nurse every little misplay into a full-grown panic. With some confidence injected into the erratic bunch the team most likely would walk through the rest of the contenders. Eastern critics have contended all season that the Hose lack gameness. There may be something in this." After an 11–2 start to the homestand, Chicago staggered to a 14–9 finish, with the final eastern swing about to commence. During the end of that homestand, the White Sox had come back to earth, hitting .254 and allowing more than four runs per game. On the way to its first stop in Boston, Rowland's team played a couple exhibitions, and after the first one, Buck Weaver fell off the back of an automobile. He was not injured, but the event illustrated how things were going.[17] Through August 13, the standings read:

Team	Wins	Loses	Games Behind
Boston	62	44	—
Cleveland	61	48	2½
Chicago	62	49	2½
St. Louis	60	52	5
Detroit	60	52	5

Boston returned east to battle Washington in the teams' first meeting since the brawl. The Red Sox scored two ninth-inning runs against Walter Johnson in relief in the August 12 opener to rally for a 2–1 victory. An especially feisty crowd of 16,000–17,000 saw Boston comeback on Chick Shorten's game-winning force out (center fielder Clyde Milan may have had a play at the plate but threw to second instead) to defeat the A.L.'s premiere right-hander. Turn about was apparently fair play, though, since two days later it was Washington's turn to rally for a 2–1 victory. In the rubber match, Babe Ruth and Johnson hooked up in another classic duel. The Senators were hoping to make a quick getaway from Fenway Park, but the pitchers matched zeros through 12 innings. In what his Nationals' teammates called Johnson's best game in nearly a month, the Big Train even earned the consistent cheers of the Boston home crowd. However in the 13th inning, Johnson deflected Jack Barry's infield knock rather than let third baseman Eddie Foster field it. The Red Sox leadoff man reached first on the play, went to third on Tilly Walker's single, and then scored on Larry Gardner's base hit for the victory.[18]

Stanley Milliken of the Washington *Post* argued Gardner should have been walked; it was a reasonable point. The struggling Everett Scott was up next, while Gardner was nearing the end of a stretch that saw him go 16-for-28 with seven straight multi-hit games. In fact, Scott would go just 1-for-24 over the last nine games in August, dropping his average to .207. It was Johnson's third loss to Ruth in 1916, and maybe the toughest, since the Senators had two men thrown out at the plate. The length of the game also had a price because Washington would have to wait for the midnight train.[19]

In the midst of all this, Bill Carrigan's father-in-law passed away, and he would keep a low profile during the second August series with the White Sox. That set would open in front of 25,227 fans (second largest of the year) at Fenway Park on August 16, many of whom were probably there to see Boston's second flag raising of 1916, this time the 1915 world championship banner. "Great preparations had been made for the unfurling of the world championship pennant won last year, but this incident paled before the titanic struggle that was waged in the curtain raiser," wrote John J. Hallahan in the Boston *Herald*. As a result, "The raising of the banner between the two games did not create much enthusiasm."[20]

To that end, the first game was managed like the seventh game of the World Series, with Carrigan, who used all 21 players, staying out of sight and directing traffic from the dugout in respect for his late father-in-law. The game was tied at four after 15 innings, and Rowland was on his third pitcher, with Eddie Cicotte (7–5) in his seventh inning of relief. Harry Hooper drew what seemed to be a meaningless two-out walk in the 16th, stole second, and then scored the winning run when third baseman Fred McMullin threw wildly to first. It was easy to blame McMullin, but Buck Weaver ran the White Sox out of a potentially big fourth inning when he fell down rounding third and was tagged out. Despite four hits in the stanza, Chicago scored just one run. After pitching 8⅔ innings of scoreless relief, Ernie Shore (10–5) earned the win.[21]

Due to the lengthy contest, the flag raising didn't get underway until 5:30 P.M. Mayor James Curley and Joe Lannin were joined by bands and the teams as they processed out to the flagpole in center field. Upon arriving,

White Sox manager Clarence Rowland joined Heinie Wagner, who was taking Carrigan's place, to hoist the flag as the band played, "The Star Spangled Banner." The flag had gold lettering and read, "Boston Americans, 1915, Champions of the World."[22]

All this meant the nightcap wouldn't start until 5:40 P.M., immediately provoking a controversy. It was just over an hour before sunset at 6:40 P.M., and according to the rule book, games weren't to start less than two hours before sunset. Chicago had the bases loaded in the second inning, but Hap Felsch was doubled off second base. Walker and Gardner then put Boston on the board in the fourth with two-out, run-scoring singles. Trailing 2–0 with darkness quickly falling, the White Sox mounted a threat in the sixth, and a two-out double from Joe Jackson cut the deficit to one. With the tying and go-ahead runs in scoring position, Dutch Leonard relieved Rube Foster (11–8) and struck out Fritz Von Kolnitz. The game was then called, and Rowland quickly filed a protest (which he would lose), as his team fell 4½ games out of first. Boston also had a 3½-game advantage over second-place Cleveland, six over St. Louis and 6½ over Detroit.[23]

Foster was having his first stellar month of the season with a 4–0 record to date. More importantly, those wins came early in August when Mays was struggling and Ruth wasn't producing at his usual rate. Ernie Shore also provided help during the first half of the month. When August 17 dawned, Bill Carrigan and the experience-laden Red Sox must have been sensing a knockout punch. The White Sox were the only widely recognized pennant contender close to Boston. Two more wins would put Rough's squad 6½ ahead of Chicago, with little more than a month remaining. After being right with Boston at the end of July, the White Sox had dropped well back. While only 3½ out, few experts believed the Indians could hold their own in September, and St. Louis and Detroit were already six or more behind as well. Boston was playing the best baseball of the three and had continued right where July left off. This scenario unfolded despite fairly similar statistics for all three contenders, even though the Red Sox were allowing the fewest runs per game, at 2.81. More telling, however, is Boston's 7–1 record against the other two teams, significantly better than Chicago (2–7) and Detroit's (2–3) marks.

White Sox stopper Red Faber was unavailable for the third game of the series, but Chicago battered Boston starter Carl Mays (12–7) for an easy, yet critical 7–0 victory. Reb Russell (13–7) came through with another clutch effort for the White Sox, allowing just five hits. That was important because Chicago's pitching had been awful of late. Leading the offense was Shoeless Joe Jackson, who went 2-for-4 with a run scored and four RBIs. Eddie Collins and Hap Felsch also added key hits in a three-run first, while Jackson highlighted a four-run fifth inning with a three-run double.[24]

Things continued to go Chicago's way the following day, as the White Sox hammered Dutch Leonard (14–10) on their way to a 6–0 lead after one inning. Boston rallied and got as close as 7–5, but the Pale Hose put the game on ice with four runs in the ninth. Leonard's sloppy fielding of a Buck Weaver bunt helped start the trouble in the first, and the Red Sox starter didn't survive the first inning.[25] Though he went 4–4 overall, Leonard wasn't effective as a starter in August. However, he was excellent in relief, allowing just a single run in 10⅔ innings. Red Faber entered in the eighth to finish the job for Lefty Williams, who improved to 7–7 with the victory.

There were some excellent offensive performances against the favorites, as some hitters got especially hot. Eddie Collins went 17-for-40 against the Red Sox and Tigers on his way to increasing his average from .262 to .288 at month's end. Jackson was also successful, but for obvious reasons, was only able to up his average seven points, to .353. Finally, in that second series against Boston, Felsch had gone 8-for-17. Since the Sox actually increased their team batting average during August, their struggles may have been due more to poor pitching. The increase in team batting average occurred despite the weak performances of the offensively challenged Buck Weaver, John Collins and Ray Schalk

With victories in the final two games of the series, the White Sox were back to within 2½, and any Boston dreams of a knockout punch were just that. Suddenly, the pressure seemed to be on the Red Sox, since Grantland Rice believed Boston would need a five-game advantage to survive its lengthy September road trip. Cleveland (3½), St. Louis (4½), New

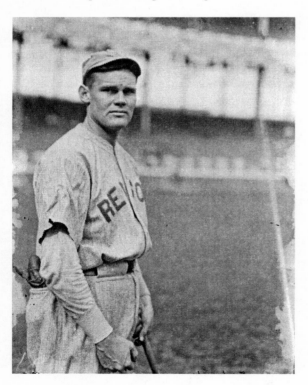

Dutch Leonard, no stranger to controversy, was a savior early in 1916 and went on to fire Boston's second no-hitter of the year (George Bain Collection, Library of Congress).

York (5) and Detroit (5) were all within five games of the favorites. Unfortunately for Detroit, while Chicago and Boston were splitting their four-game series, the Tigers weren't able to make up any significant ground. Before heading east, Detroit stopped for one game in Cleveland on August 14 and went to the bottom of the ninth tied at two before a pair of errors on one play sealed the Tigers' doom. The Indians' Elmer Smith played a big role in the victory but was only in the game because Bobby Roth had been suspended for an incident in St. Louis. Fans were throwing bottles at the Cleveland outfielder, who finally had enough and decided to throw one back.[26]

Five back (eight in the loss column), Detroit headed east for a trip that could potentially end the Tigers' pennant hopes. E.A. Batchelor believed Detroit couldn't fall any further behind since "early next month, the Jennings clan has three tough engagements — or rather has three series with clubs that heretofore have been troublesome. At the same time, the Red Sox will be fattening up at the expense of the sad and dejected east..." The beginning of September included games with Cleveland, Chicago and St. Louis. Fortunately for Detroit, the Tigers opened their trip against Washington, which had fallen out of the race. The Jungaleers got off well, sweeping an ugly doubleheader on August 17. Ty Cobb went a combined 6-for-10 with four runs and seven RBIs before the Senators salvaged the final game of the series, 2–1.[27]

Teams	Wins	Losses	Games Behind
Boston	65	46	—
Cleveland	62	50	3½
Chicago	63	51	3½
Detroit	62	53	5
St. Louis	61	53	5½
New York	59	52	6

Although they had slipped somewhat in the last two games against Chicago, the Red Sox were still in first place, having earned that position on the road. Evaluating Boston's performance, reporter Ralph McMillin argued that Bill Carrigan had played a major part in the team's success. He noted his

refusal to get ruffled under the most trying circumstances and his calm way of sizing up the season in its entirety have proved his best assets. Where other managers might have taken the Speakerless Sox and forced them beyond their endurance for half the race, Carrigan laid back and nursed them along. You can't hurry Bill in this respect, but his reward is in the lasting power of his ball club and its reserve strength...[28]

McMillin, taking a page out of George Robbins' notebook, also added Lannin must be happy with the Speaker sale because it helped keep the team profitable by making the pennant race more competitive and drawing added interest.

With its pitching struggling, the Indians acquired hurler Joe Boehling from Washington as part of a four-player trade. Three and a half games back and still surprisingly in the race, Cleveland was the next visitor to Fenway Park for what was a unexpectedly meaningful August series with Boston. Meanwhile, the White Sox were in New York, and Detroit in Philadelphia. All three series would play a big factor in the pennant race, but Boston's pitching keyed a four-game sweep and virtually knocked the overachieving Indians out of the race. Boehling walked in the winning run in the first game on August 19, the loss making Cleveland just 16–23 in one-run games. Babe Ruth was effective, allowing just one run in six innings in front of 18,000-plus fans, the third largest Fenway Park crowd of the season. However, he was overcome by what was claimed to be a mysterious heart ailment in the sixth and had to be relieved by George Foster (12–8). The *Post* was the only newspaper to mention the heart problem. The *Globe* claimed he left because of the heat, while the *Herald* noted a problem in the Babe's side.[29]

After an off-day, Ernie Shore (11–5) and Carl Mays (13–7) tossed a pair of complete-game shutouts. Hooper went 2-for-3 with two runs in the first game, and Gardner, having a standout season, notched a 2-for-3, two-RBI performance in the second. In the first three games of the match-up, Speaker was just 1-for-10 before going 2-for-4 in the final game. Still, it wasn't enough. Cleveland took an early 2–0 lead before Boston rallied for a 7–3 victory again on August 23, helped by a four-run seventh inning that was highlighted by Dick Hobliztell's two-run single. The Indians had lost seven in a row and were suddenly in sixth place, 7½ games out, and for all effective purposes out of the pennant race.[30]

The news would soon be nearly as bad for Chicago. Like Boston, the White Sox had also won on August 19 behind a great effort from Eddie Cicotte, the same day Kid Gleason was named a coach. Due to Gleason's strong pedigree, rumors immediately had to be dispelled he was taking over for Rowland, whose managerial abilities were constantly criticized. One writer felt that due to so many suspensions in 1915, Pants had calmed down, costing the White Sox some of their fighting spirit. It was hoped that the feisty Gleason would infuse more life into Chicago for the stretch run. Even Rowland-backer George Robbins acknowledged the new coach would handle more of the on-field strategy. Meanwhile, Jim Scott, Eddie Cicotte, who had beaten New York five times thus far in 1916, and Reb Russell were all hammered in three losses to end the series with New York, which left Chicago 5½ games out of first.[31]

In Philadelphia on August 19, the Tigers were facing a surprisingly feisty Athletics team. The Tigers had to score five runs in the 10th inning to win the first game, and then in the third, Joe Bush shut out Detroit, 1–0, for his second straight victory over the Tigers. Bush was tied with Babe Ruth for shutouts in the American League with six, and had racked up an amazing 13 of the Athletics' 24 victories. For obvious reasons, he was the subject of trade rumors. In the other two contests, Detroit received effective pitching from Hooks Dauss (14–8), who was fighting for his job, and George Cunningham (5–10) in 7–1 and 10–3 victories, respectively.[32] In addition to wounding if not killing Cleveland's hopes, the Red Sox had built a more comfortable margin over the other contenders. Time was getting short in the American League, and the Red Sox were still in the driver's seat.

Team	Wins	Loses	Games Behind
Boston	69	47	—
Chicago	65	54	5½
New York	63	53	6
Detroit	65	55	6
St. Louis	64	55	6½

Thus far, Detroit was 7–4 on the road trip, and 5–2 on the eastern portion of it. Still six games back, however, the Tiger's next stop was Fenway Park for a critical three-game set, a place where Detroit hadn't won a series since 1913. Coveleski, Dauss and Bill James were all scheduled to start against Boston. While Dauss was currently struggling, Jennings hoped Hooks could regain some of his previous magic against the Red Sox. A slight drizzle fell most of the morning of the first game on August 24 and continued into the afternoon, providing extremely poor light for the players and nearly a rainout. Coveleski got the start in the

Named for the pinpoint control of his curveball, Hooks Dauss won 19 games in 1916 (National Baseball Hall of Fame Library, Cooperstown, N.Y.).

opener, but Babe Ruth (17–9), who had apparently overcome his health problems, was the story. He threw a three-hit, 3–0 gem against the Tigers for the southpaw's league-leading seventh shutout. Additionally, Boston had posted three shutouts in the past week.[33]

It is unlikely the Tiger players enjoyed that night's performance of "The Amber Empress" at the Colonial Theatre, where the Boston and Detroit teams were guests. Now seven games back, the Jungaleers figured to be in a must-win situation the next two days. Noting Coveleski always had bad luck against the Red Sox, Detroit *News* reporter Joe Jackson commented, "There's no reason to doubt now that Carrigan's team again will represent the American League in the World Series." Henry Salsinger of *The Sporting News* agreed and had already turned his attention to the following year, noting Detroit simply wanted to finish second. The Boston *Herald* even ran a breakout box, headlined "Have The Red Sox Got Flag Clinched," but *Sporting News* correspondent Ralph McMillin still thought there was a lot of baseball to be played.[34]

There was indeed a lot more baseball to be played, and Hooks Dauss (15–8) started it the following day for Detroit, allowing just a sixth-inning run during a 2–1 win. With George Burns on second, the Tigers rallied against Ernie Shore in the seventh, getting a pair of two-out doubles from pinch-hitter Harry Heilmann and Dauss to overcome a 1–0 deficit. Tilly Walker may have had a play on the latter double but broke the wrong way. Walker, who historically owned Dauss at the plate, had a shot at redemption with a runner on third in the eighth but struck out. Even with the loss, Carrigan's team was still 9–4 thus far on the homestand and winning with leadership, pitching and defense. Although Red Sox batters were hitting only .247 since the beginning of August, the Boston skipper had stuck with nearly the same lineup all month, consisting of Hooper, Barry, Lewis, Hoblitzell or Gainer, Walker, Gardner, Scott and a catcher. T.H. Murnane noted on August 25 that Duffy Lewis, who had suffered a steady decline in batting average during the month, didn't seem to be comfortable in the three spot.[35] Oddly, Lewis had been hitting there since May. Poor play by the likes of Lewis, Scott, Thomas, Barry and Gainer had to be offset from somewhere. Fortunately, Hooper had increased his average 11 points, from .244 to .255, while Gardner, with his strong streak earlier in the month, had gone from .282 to .306.

A large crowd of 23,321 showed up for the rubber game on August 26, forcing three rows of spectators to stand behind the seated crowd. The offense still hadn't returned for Boston, as Bill James (6–8) shut the Red Sox down in a second consecutive 2–1 Tigers win. After seven scoreless innings took only 58 minutes to play, Detroit scored single runs in each of the last two frames. Sam Crawford drew a walk in the eighth, but Carl Mays had him picked off, only to see Hoblitzell muff what would have been the pitcher's third pickoff of the game. Crawford went to third and then came around to score on Ralph Young's single. Young hadn't been great in August but showed some improvement, including this clutch hit. Detroit made it 2–0 in the ninth when Ossie Vitt led off with a triple and scored on Donie Bush's sacrifice fly. The Red Sox scored a run in the ninth, but Hick Cady struck out to end the game with runners on first and second, making Carl Mays (1 unearned run, 8 innings) a hard-luck loser. Jackson wrote, "On this trip there have been some tough ball games. There has been none that was harder to win than this one." The Tigers won a series in Boston for the first time in three years to move into sole possession of second place, but still trailed the Red Sox by five games.[36]

Detroit closed August in even better position after finishing its road swing with a four-game set at the Polo Grounds. The first game of the series was rained out on August 28, producing a doubleheader the next day. Since it is more difficult to sweep a doubleheader than to win two single games, Hughie Jennings wasn't keen on twin bills. This time, though, the extra day off would allow him to use Coveleski and Dauss on August 29. It also meant he would be unable to bring the southpaw back for a second start in the final game, which was his initial plan. Home Run Baker and Fritz Maisel also returned to the injury-plagued Yankee lineup, as New York remained on the fringe of the race, just six games out after a recent stretch of good play. However, Detroit won easily behind Coveleski (20–9) and Dauss (16–8) in the doubleheader. Bob Veach, Ralph Young and Tubby Spencer, who seemed to be jumpstarting Detroit, ignited the offense; the Tigers were suddenly only three out.[37] The Detroit bats had gotten hot toward the end of the month and hit .266 on the road. Likewise, the hurlers performed well, allowing just 2.43 runs per game during the swing. Harry Coveleski and the inconsistent Hooks Dauss keyed the pitching side of the August run. The former was 6–1 overall, 4–1 as a starter, and allowed just seven earned runs in 54 innings. Hooks' final three starts in August were complete-game victories, where the hurler allowed only one run in each outing. Although the rest of the starters were mediocre, excellent relief pitching by George Cunningham, Jean Dubuc, Bernie Boland, Bill James and Willie Mitchell more than made up for it. Overall, the relievers allowed just 10 runs in 54⅓ innings.

The Tigers offense was being helped by the middle of their lineup. Ty Cobb was in the midst of a stretch that would see him go 9-for-16 and finish the month at .363. Veach steadily increased his average and got it as high as .290 due to five games with three or more hits. This occurred despite the same poor production from Donie Bush (.230) and Ossie Vitt (.211) at the top of the order. Consistent playing time for Sam Crawford helped the aging outfielder, but it didn't last. He was hitting .313 on August 17 before he bottomed out to .274, in large part due to a five-game hitless streak. If Detroit could continue this success into September, the Tigers just might have a chance to cop the pennant.

The Tigers obviously needed help to make up so much ground quickly and received it from St. Louis, which swept a doubleheader from Boston on August 29. The Red Sox were awful in losing their third and fourth straight, with Dutch Leonard, Babe Ruth and Ernie Shore all performing poorly. There were additional mental errors with poor coaching at third base and pitchers forgetting to cover first base. Leading 3–2 in the first game, two walks and an error by Ruth, who was working in relief, set the table for a three-run sixth that won it for St. Louis, 5–3. The Browns built a 7–0 lead in the second game and never looked back in an 8–2 victory. Even worse, Jack Barry broke a bone in his hand when he was hit by a pitched ball. He was expected to miss two weeks, but the actual result would be much worse.[38]

A few days earlier it appeared Boston was in control, but now Detroit had closed to three back and St. Louis four. Making matters worse, Carrigan and his team learned on August 30 that Barry would be out a month, a severe blow to the champions. The Red Sox added outfielder Jimmy Walsh from the Athletics the same day, and rumors surfaced of a blockbuster deal that would have sent Harry Hooper to St. Louis. Carrigan warmed up Rube Foster for the game against the Browns, but instead sent Leonard to the hill. Seldom has a pitcher rewarded his manager's confidence so well. Tilly Walker, who still had fans calling for his head after a tough start to August, tripled in the second and scored on Larry Gardner's single, the latter coming home on Leonard's base hit. Gardner drove Walker home again in the sixth, and Boston tacked on another for a 4–0 lead. As important as winning the game was in its own right, there was something special going on, due in large part to some brilliant Red Sox defense. No play was more spectacular than Hooper pulling down George Sisler's first-inning drive just a few feet from the right-center field fence. Just a day after getting hammered by St. Louis, Leonard no-hit the Browns, the Red Sox second 1916 no-hitter.[39]

Boston also picked up a game on Detroit when the Yankees received a great effort from Bob Shawkey and hit Bill James hard to beat the Tigers. However, the added margin was short lived. On August 31, Detroit, with the help of sloppy play by New York, built a 7–0 lead for Willie Mitchell, and he cruised to a 7–3 victory. That same day Boston lost to St. Louis, 2–1, an error by Mike McNally (in for Jack Barry) and a hit batsman by Ruth leading to both runs. Ernie Koob allowed just a run; he had held Boston to just two runs in 35 innings in 1916. This time, the Browns pitcher had unexpected help. Red Sox runners were thrown out at third three times, and a great catch by left fielder Burt Shotton in the fifth may have saved two runs. In losing five of six to close the month, Red Sox hitters batted just .213. [40]

Following its poor performance in New York that ended with the third straight loss on August 23, Chicago lost two out of three in Washington. Red Faber and Mel Wolfgang got hit hard, and poor fielding and missed opportunities on offense didn't help the White Sox's chances. Rowland had made some minor lineup changes thus far in August, but in an effort to jump-start the lineup, he switched Weaver and J. Collins at the top on August 26. Jack Lapp had also been seeing some time at catcher, and Pants inserted him in place of the fatigued Ray Schalk.[41] The lineup was: Weaver, J. Collins, E. Collins, Jackson, Ness, Felsch, Lapp and Terry. Rowland would make some additional minor changes over the next few days before settling back into a set lineup in early September. Something worked, and the White Sox salvaged the final game in Washington before going on to Philadelphia and taking three of four — albeit no great feat. The games against the Athletics couldn't have come at a better time because the series with New York and Washington cost the White Sox three games in the standings. During that period, the offense hit just .241 and the pitching staff was worse, allowing five runs per game.

After being strong in June and July, Chicago's pitching staff struggled in August. Things would have been worse had it not been for two excellent spot starts by Benz, coupled with two more from Wolfgang. Eddie Cicotte had been inconsistent and Jim Scott struggled, while Reb Russell (4–2) and Red Faber (3–3) had both good and bad starts. In relief, Dave Danforth made seven appearances and

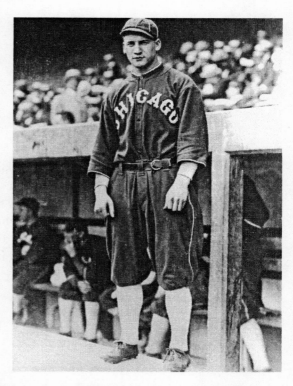

Known for his happy demeanor, Happy Felsch appeared to be on his way to a promising career in 1916. Unfortunately, it would come crashing to a halt three years later (National Baseball Hall of Fame Library, Cooperstown, N.Y.).

allowed runs in five of them, and Lefty Williams also struggled in that same role. Other factors made the White Sox even harder to read as the race headed toward its climax. Ever since Kid Gleason was appointed coach, rumors had increased that Rowland would be fired if he didn't win the pennant. To add unneeded and unwanted turmoil, Pants was also at odds with Jim Scott. Rowland suspended him for missing curfew after a season-long disagreement about the pitcher's role.[42]

After taking three of four from Philadelphia while Boston was losing four of five to St. Louis, Chicago was only 3½ back of the Red Sox and a half-game behind second-place Detroit. The Tigers were three games back of Boston, while St. Louis, four games back in fourth, was surprisingly still in the mix. Additionally, both New York and Cleveland were still not out of it at six games back, but Washington and Philadelphia were simply playing out the string.

Team	Wins	Loses	Games Behind
Boston	71	52	—
Detroit	70	57	3
Chicago	69	57	3½
St. Louis	69	58	4
New York	66	59	6
Cleveland	67	60	6
Washington	60	62	10½
Philadelphia	27	94	43

Boston had finished its long homestand at 10–8, while Detroit and Chicago had gone 12–6 and 7–8 on the road, respectively. The Red Sox had started their run at Fenway Park by going 9–3 before faltering at the end. Boston now faced the prospect of a month on the road, trying to protect a small lead from multiple contenders, most of whom would be playing at home. Reports began to surface that members of the Red Sox didn't think they would win the pennant.[43]

But there was bizarre off-the-field news as well when on the last day of the month a New York *Times* headline blared, "Strike May Mean No World's Series." The impending rail strike could begin as soon as September 4, leaving boats, automobiles and trolleys as the only means of intercity transportation. That was manageable for intersectional battles, but it presented a seemingly insurmountable problem when eastern teams went west in the A.L. in September and vice versa in the N.L. The slower modes of transportation could push the season back a month, meaning cold weather and/or the interference of the college football season could possibly wipe out the World Series.[44]

There truly never was a dull moment in 1916.

CHAPTER VIII

"Third in the National League, this day and date, with much thirdness."

When poet T. S. Eliot wrote, "April is the cruelest month," he was invert-ing the world of Major League Baseball. For owners, managers, players and especially fans, April is not cruel but full of promise and hope. In 1916, Sep-tember and early October were the cruelest months, the time when some teams would just play out the season and others would have their hopes and dreams crumble and die before their eyes. This was especially true in a time before divisional play, wild cards and playoffs, when no matter how close the race, only one team in each league experienced joy at season's end.[1]

As the four contending teams ended their last western swing and headed east, baseball's cruelest month was indeed here. Brooklyn was still in first place, as the Superbas had been since May, while Boston and Philadelphia trailed by 2½ and five games, respectively. New York, though still in the first division, was under .500, 15 games out and sinking fast. After two months with almost no head-to-head competition, the contenders would now play three intense series against each other.

The Dodgers and Phillies began with a five-game set in the City of Brotherly Love, and the Giants and Braves played four times at the "home of big things" in Boston. The Superbas would then return to New York City for four games at the Giants, as the Phillies and Braves went at it in Boston. Finally, the Dodgers would go to the Hub city for the final stop on their seven-city, 28-game odyssey, while the Phillies would visit the Giants.

Although they probably wouldn't have admitted it, Robinson, Moran and Stallings likely saw their games with slumping New York as an opportu-nity to pick up ground while the other two teams knocked each other off. The Braves would have the first chance to test this theory, facing the reeling

Giants while the Phils and Brooklyn battled it out in Philadelphia. For Moran's club, the series against the Dodgers was much like Boston's match-up against the Superbas in August. Down five games in the loss column, the Phils had to make up some ground. Falling behind even one more game in the standings would make the defending champions' task problematic. Meanwhile, having beaten Philadelphia ten out of fourteen times, Robby and his team had reason to be optimistic, and if past was prologue, Rice felt Brooklyn would take four out of five. However, the *Eagle* reporter was no neophyte, recognizing "it is never safe to predict what will happen in baseball." This statement would prove to be prophetic for Rice and the Superbas.[2]

Although Wilbert Robinson spent much of the train ride from Pittsburgh to Philadelphia regaling his audience with tales of the old Orioles, he also gave some thought to his pitching match-ups for the five games in four days at Baker Bowl. One of the main reasons the Dodgers were still in first place after almost 120 games was the depth of their staff. Curiously, however, with only 36 games remaining, Robinson's decisions were more complicated than those of Pat Moran. Since the Phils' pitching staff lacked the depth of Brooklyn's, the Philadelphia manager's choices were limited, but clear. After all, Alexander in Nasium's words was "an entire pitching staff by himself," while Rixey and Demaree had also performed well. Moran had received little help from the rest of his staff, but almost every Brooklyn pitcher had made some contribution. Because he had more choices, however, the Dodger manager had to pick and choose the right spots. Thus far, he had done so brilliantly, but Robinson had to repeat the feat with more on the line. Moran's choice of Alexander (26–9) and Rixey (17–6) for the September 1 doubleheader was no surprise. Robby was also fairly predictable in his choice of Coombs (9–6) and Pfeffer (18–9). While it was unclear which team would profit on the field, both would clearly do so at the box office. Even though it wasn't a Saturday or holiday, a capacity crowd in excess of 20,000 "frenzied and wild eyed fans packed into every nook and cranny" of Baker Bowl. One observer claimed the throng was larger than any that attended the 1915 World Series, with as many as 5,000 fans turned away.[3]

Alexander began the game by retiring the Superbas without incident, bringing the Phils to bat against Jack Coombs. Moran had a clear offensive strategy against the Brooklyn veteran. Philadelphia batters weren't to let Coombs go deep in the count, instead swinging at the first good offering. It didn't take long for this line of thinking to pay dividends, as Dode Paskert hit Coombs' first pitch into the left-field stands for a home run. Knowing that playing from behind against Alexander wasn't a good strategy, the Superbas tried gamely to recover in the top of the second. Wheat and Cutshaw led off with singles, putting runners on first and second for Mike Mowrey. His

Brooklyn Superbas infield (left to right): Jake Daubert, George Cutshaw, Ivan Olson and Mike Mowrey (George Bain Collection Library of Congress).

job was to bunt them over, but Mowrey failed, fouling out to Bill Killefer. The importance of that failed sacrifice became clear very quickly. Ivy Olson followed with a single down the left-field line, but George Whitted crammed two good plays into one, first stopping the ball from going by him, and then turning completely around to throw Wheat out at the plate. When Otto Miller flied out to left, Brooklyn had racked up three singles with nothing to show for it. Mowrey's failure to bunt successfully was crucial — had he done so, there would have been runners on second and third, at least one of whom would have scored on Olson's single. Teams received few opportunities to score against Alexander, and failing to take advantage of one was a bad sign. To that end, Philadelphia added runs in the fourth and eighth innings, and Alexander did the rest, recording his 14th shutout to establish a major league record. While neither Coombs nor the Dodgers could appreciate the irony, the previous record holder was Colby Jack Coombs, who set the mark with the Philadelphia Athletics in 1910.[4]

Things got off to a promising start for Brooklyn in the second game, though, when Hi Myers led off with a triple against Rixey. He died there, however, another bad sign that would prove to be all too prophetic when Rixey also shut out the Dodgers. George Whitted, who was the defensive star of the first game, provided the spark to the Phillies offense, driving in two of the six runs. For at least the second time in 1916, Alexander watched the night-cap from the press box, generating another loud ovation from the fans. While it is unlikely Tom Rice joined in the applause, he was realistic enough to note the Superbas never had a chance against the pitching of Alexander and Rixey. Another unfortunate reality was the Dodgers were now on the verge of falling into second place, depending on the results of Saturday's single game with Philadelphia and the Giants-Braves doubleheader in Boston.[5]

If the first inning in Boston on September 1 was any indication, return-ing to the East wasn't going to improve New York's play, for McGraw's team handed the Braves their first run on an Art Fletcher error. Boston maintained the 1–0 lead behind Don Ragan, who was replaced by Tom Hughes when the starting pitcher weakened in the seventh. The reliever not only finished the game but doubled to start a two-run rally in the bottom of the eighth. That more than offset Bennie Kauff's home run to the "flag pole in the centrefield," supposedly the "longest hit ever made on the grounds." The Braves' 3–1 win enabled them to pick up 1½ games on the Dodgers, putting them only a half-game out of first and tied in the lost column.[6]

Saturday's September 2 doubleheader, however, demonstrated Stallings' men still had work to do, and also gave the first vague rumblings that New York's season might not be over just yet. A large crowd, estimated at 20,000, saw McGraw's team score three times in the top of the second — "the most consistent hitting the Giants have done in months" — on the way to a 4–1 win. The contest also saw a return of the Braves squabbling with the umpires, in this case Bill Byron and Ernie Quigley, prompting booing from the crowd. The fans' reaction was conclusive proof to Flatley that something was wrong, as "Boston is admittedly the fairest baseball corner of the continent." The Braves also reverted to their lackluster offensive production, managing only two hits and one run. Even though it didn't result in a loss, the second game may have been more frustrating. Boston took a 5–1 lead behind Rudolph (16–8), only to see the Giants tie it in the eighth with darkness ending play after the 10th. Another positive sign for New York was Fred Schupp's four shutout innings in relief. The tie would be replayed during Boston's visit to New York on the last weekend of the season, which would prove to be a bad time to add games against the Giants. It was also announced that Johnny Evers was out for the rest of the season due to neuritis in his left shoulder. Although the Braves hadn't picked up more ground on Brooklyn, manage-ment was apparently as confident as Flatley since they decided to put World Series tickets on sale.[7]

Events in Philadelphia that same day may have given some credence to Flatley's belief the Phils were Boston's most serious competition. The game featured a pitching match-up between Pat Moran's third starter, Al Demaree, and Brooklyn's current ace, Larry Cheney (14–8), who had won eight straight. Threatening weather in the area limited the crowd to an estimated 14,000. The fans saw a game eerily like the opener of Friday's doubleheader. Once again, Philadelphia scored first, this time on Milt Stock's fourth-inning home run into the left-field bleachers on one bounce. As on Friday, the Dodgers threatened to tie things up in their next at-bat, but once again a throw from the outfield, this time by Dode Paskert, nailed a Brooklyn runner at the plate. At that point, to at least one observer, it appeared the Dodgers "spirit seemed to ooze out of their fingertips," taking Cheney's eight-game winning streak with it. Moran's team put the game out of reach in the bottom of the fifth by scoring three times while Demaree limited Brooklyn to only five hits. The only blot on Demaree's record was the first run the Dodgers had scored in the first three games of the series, which was far too little, far too late. The only good news for the Superbas was they expected both Daubert and Johnston to be back for Monday's morning-afternoon doubleheader.[8] Philadelphia was now only two back of Brooklyn, while Boston, which had missed a golden opportunity to take over first, was still one out.

With the Phils this close to first, baseball fever reached epidemic proportions in Philadelphia. The fans' enthusiasm combined with the separate-admission doubleheader on Labor Day, meant a huge financial payoff to both teams. Numerous Philadelphia newspapers labeled the crowd for the morning game as the largest in the city's baseball history. The gates closed long before the start of the first contest, leaving thousands of fans in the streets to receive the results from those fortunate enough to be inside. Since those in the ballpark far exceeded the seating capacity, some stood on the rafters of the grandstand and pavilions, while others climbed onto the roof before being chased off by the police. The rooftops of adjacent buildings were crowded with those trying to get some glimpse of the action, and speculators and ticket scalpers, accompanied by assistants with megaphones, were circulating in the streets and demanding $10–15 for a $1 ticket. Baker Bowl hadn't even completely emptied from the morning game when a crowd estimated at 1,000 lined up for what would be a 1½ hour wait in the "broiling sun" to get tickets for the afternoon game. Clearly, "Philadelphia was baseball mad."[9]

On the field, manager Pat Moran took a chance with his choice of pitchers. This was partially driven by the schedule, since after playing two doubleheaders in four days against Brooklyn, the Phillies would play another doubleheader in Boston the next day. In addition, Philadelphia had already chopped three games off the Dodgers' lead, and there was reason to save either Alexander or Rixey for Boston. It turned out to be a brilliant move, the kind that can decide pennant races, as Erskine Mayer took a 2–0 lead into the ninth inning. Both runs had come via the long ball — one by Killefer on the bounce and another by Fred Luderus over the friendly right-field wall. Frank O'Neil of the New York *Tribune* groused that both were due to the Phillies' "ballroom-sized arena," but that fact was irrelevant. Each blow came at the expense of Rube Marquard, who had otherwise pitched well enough to win. In the ninth, however, Brooklyn threatened when doubles by Cutshaw and Miller produced a run and put the tying score on second with two out. Moran was smart enough not to push his luck too far and brought Alexander in to get the final out in a 2–1 victory.[10]

Having scored two runs in four games, the Dodgers startled everyone by scoring in the top of the first of the afternoon contest. Any hopes of a Brooklyn recovery were short lived, as Cheney (14–9) and his team collapsed in the bottom half. A series of hits, as well as two errors by Gus Getz, led to six Philadelphia runs, and Cheney exited after retiring only one batter. Rixey (18–6) coasted the rest of the way to an easy 10–3 win, forcing Robinson to use his entire pitching staff with the exception of Coombs in the double-header. It is hard to overstate the Phillies' dominance over these five games; Philadelphia had outscored Brooklyn 25 to 5. Those especially effective with the bat included Stock (.474), Whitted (.467) and Luderus (.500), as the team hit .329. On the Dodgers' side, it was not hard to compile a list of the shortcomings, beginning with a team batting average of .209. Of special concern was the poor performance of Larry Cheney, especially his failure to get out of the first inning in the last game. The sweep had brought the defending champions into a flat-footed tie with the Superbas. If Philadelphia had been baseball mad beforehand, insanity must have pervaded the crowd leaving Baker Bowl that day.[11]

In Boston, where the Giants and Braves also squared off in a morning-afternoon doubleheader, Stallings chose Tom Hughes (16–3) to start the opener. Staked to a 2–0 lead in the third, he made it stand up. Unlike the first contest, which was well played, the second was a nightmare for baseball purists, with the teams combining for 11 errors — five for Boston and six for the Giants. Four of New York's miscues came in one inning, but the Braves only managed to score once. With the game tied, 3–3, in the eighth, the Giants loaded the bases, and McGraw sent Hans Lobert to pinch-hit. Lobert, who had already pinch-hit three times in the series, striking out each time, came through with a single, driving in what proved to be the winning run in an 8–3 victory. While a second loss to slumping New York had to be a disappointment, the split of the twin bill put Boston in first place. The Braves, who had played two fewer games and had one fewer loss than Brooklyn and Philadelphia, held a slim percentage point lead. Flatley apparently was incapable of celebrating the Braves' success without taking a shot at the Dodgers, noting there was "little glory in the passing of the Robins."[12]

Team	Wins	Losses	Games Behind
Boston	71	48	—
Brooklyn	72	49	—
Philadelphia	72	49	—

This negativity toward the Superbas wasn't unique to Flatley. Even before the Labor Day sweep, Philadelphia sportswriters had little good to say about Wilbert Robinson and his men. An unsigned column in the Philadelphia *Record* claimed there was a "good foundation" for the low opinions of the Superbas. Incredibly, the writer went on to say that while Brooklyn had both

"wonderful hitting strength" and "fine pitching," the Superbas weren't a great ball club because they were "almost stupid" in the field and on the bases. Furthermore, the writer believed the Superbas lacked the "fighting spirit" of the Braves and Phils. Apparently, some New York writers shared this view; James Sinnot of the *Evening Mail* claimed Brooklyn was "slow of foot and brain on the bases" and this might cost them the pennant.[13] Regardless of the accuracy of such analysis, Brooklyn was out of first place for first time since May 26. Faced with possible elimination, Pat Moran and his men performed brilliantly and were back in the thick of the pennant race. However, those dismissing the Dodgers were missing an important point. The three teams had played about 120 games out of a 154-game schedule and were nearly in the

Tom Hughes of the Boston Braves led the National League in performances in 1915 and was headed for a similar record in 1916 when a September injury ended his season and seriously damaged the Braves' pennant hopes (National Baseball Hall of Fame Library, Cooperstown, N.Y.).

same place as on Opening Day. The National League pennant race would be determined by how Boston, Brooklyn, and Philadelphia played over the next 30-plus games, not how they had gotten to this point or how things had gone in one series. With two more head-to-head match-ups among the contenders immediately forthcoming, the Dodgers had a chance to recover quickly. Indeed, when these two series were over, one of the three teams, while still in the race, would be on the outside looking in. That team wouldn't be the Brooklyn Dodgers.

During all this excitement, an event of note was taking place on Chicago's north side. As planned and announced, Christy Mathewson and Mordecai Three Fingered Brown faced each other on the mound for the last time. A crowd of some 17,000 braved threatening weather to take in the event, which wasn't by any definition an artistic success. The Reds prevailed, 10–8, as Brown gave up 18 hits, while Mathewson was only slightly better, allowing 16 Cubs to hit safely. It wasn't a day to be concerned about purity of play, however, but rather a time to honor the achievements of two worthy hurlers who had provided countless thrills to baseball fans. Reporter I. E. Sanborn found the event sufficiently moving enough to remark "the dollar sign has not driven all the sentiment out of the nation's pastime."[14]

Pat Moran and his players didn't have long to celebrate their sweep of the Dodgers. They traveled to Boston on Labor Day evening for their second doubleheader in as many days. While the Braves were happy to be leading the league, all wasn't well at the "home of big things." Starting pitchers Allen and Nehf were on the sick list, joining Evers, who was already out for the season. On top of everything else, Rabbit Maranville, the team's shortstop and spark plug, suffered a broken nose when he was hit with Zimmerman's ground ball in Monday afternoon's game against the Giants. While Brooklyn's Jim Johnston had missed about two weeks with a similar injury, Rabbit underwent surgery that night, and in spite of the doctor's warnings, played both games of the Tuesday doubleheader against Philadelphia. As a result of the injury and/or the cure, Maranville also had two blackened and partially shut eyes, couldn't talk, and had difficulty breathing. This was one occasion where Flatley wasn't exaggerating when he called Maranville the hero of the day.[15]

Like Philadelphia, Boston was also caught up in pennant fever, as a crowd estimated at 15,000 braved cold, dark, windy and rainy conditions on September 5 to see the two games. The fans were encouraged by a band that led them in "Tessie," a long-time favorite of Boston baseball fans. Since Moran's Labor Day gamble of starting Mayer had paid off, he now had his ace, Alexander (27–9), ready for the first game against Jess Barnes. Stallings once again decided to avoid a duel of aces, saving Rudolph for the second contest. Under-

Philadelphia Phillies outfield (left to right): Gavy Cravath, Dode Paskert, and George "Possum" Whitted (National Baseball Hall of Fame Library, Cooperstown, N.Y.).

standably, the Phillies had been re-energized and were "on their toes" throughout the day with "constant chatter" as they ran "out every play." Philadelphia took the lead in the top of the first inning when Niehoff and Cravath (two of the slowest Phils) pulled off a double steal. Alexander made this stand up until the bottom of the fifth when the Braves tied things on three singles and a ground out. Philadelphia came back in the sixth, however, with Whitted providing a clutch two-run single before scoring a few minutes later on a sacrifice fly. Although Boston threatened after that, Alexander kept things under control by winning his 27th game, and the Phils took their sixth straight, all against their main rivals.[16]

The second game lasted only five innings and didn't reach a decision, but it didn't lack for drama. When the game began, what was described as "unnatural" darkness" to go with rain, strongly suggested the contest wouldn't go the distance. With two good pitchers in Demaree and Rudolph on the hill, this also meant one run could decide an important game in a very close pennant race. Rudolph (16–8) was dominant, allowing just one hit, but

Philadelphia nearly found a way to score. In the top of the second, the afore-mentioned slow-running Gavy Cravath reached first on an error. With two out, on a hit-and-run play, Bancroft grounded to Maranville. Perhaps because of his impaired vision, the Rabbit's throw to first was well over Ed Konetchy's head and bounded beyond the reach of the scrambling Braves. Cravath tried to score on the play, and it was "an eyelash decision," but umpire Bill Klem called him out, prompting an argument and Cravath's ejection. Regardless of whether the call was correct, it didn't cover up Gavy's ill-conceived decision not to slide, which would have eliminated the need for any decision on Klem's part.

That was the only Philadelphia threat, and it occurred after the Braves had already lost an opportunity when they were turned back on some good defensive work by Phils third baseman Milt Stock. Boston was by no means finished, however, threatening again in the second when J. C Smith tripled. Egan then hit a "wicked shot," once again at Stock, who made a great stop, catching Smith too far off the bag and tagging him out, with enough time to also throw the batter out. Reportedly, even the Braves' fans applauded the double play, which included a new method of making the first out of an inning at third base. If saving the Phillies' fortunes two straight innings wasn't enough, Stock still had one more defensive gem in his repertoire. Threaten-ing again in the bottom of the third with two out, Boston put runners on second and third with Joe Connolly was at the plate. He popped a pitch foul toward the Braves' dugout, which Stock caught by way of a "flying leap" down the stairs. After two more uneventful innings, the "unnatural dark" ended the game in a 0–0 tie, to be made up as part of another doubleheader on Thurs-day, September 7.[17]

Both Brooklyn and the Giants had ridden the rattlers to their Septem-ber 5 meeting at the Polo Grounds, the opener of a four-game series. Not coin-cidentally, it began with a distinct lack of energy, which William Hanna of the *Herald* ascribed to "train weariness." Although the Superbas had made the shorter of the two trips, they understandably seemed the worse for wear. Sid Mercer noted the Dodgers "started the game as if they were attending their own funeral." Pushing the boundaries of eruditeness, Rice said Samuel Coleridge's poetic description of "the painted ship upon the painted ocean" wasn't much more "a study of still life" than the first six innings of the game. Given the anemic offense displayed by Brooklyn in Philadelphia, it wasn't a promising sign when the Superbas didn't score in the first six innings. The Giants had a 2–0 lead at that point, including a fourth-inning home run by Bennie Kauff. Fortunately for Wilbert Robinson and Brooklyn, both Jake Daubert and Jim Johnston were back in the lineup, but when the first two batters in the Dodger seventh were retired, things indeed looked bleak. However, consecutive singles by Johnston, Daubert and Stengel produced one run and left runners on second and third for Zack Wheat. He came through, doubling in both runs before scoring on an error. Now the beneficiary of more runs than in his last three games combined, Coombs (10–6), although described as "wobbly," shut out the Giants the rest of the way for a 5–2 win. The Dodgers' win, coupled with the Phillies' victory over Boston, put Brooklyn and Philadelphia in a first-place tie. The Braves had been knocked out of first after a one-day stay, but they were tied in the loss column and only two back in the win column.[18]

Team	Wins	Losses	Games Behind
Brooklyn	73	49	
Philadelphia	73	49	—
Boston	71	49	1

Back in August, George "Lefty" Tyler tried to pitch both ends of a doubleheader, lasting into the seventh inning of the second contest. While there may be a tendency to identify this tactic with "Iron Man" Joe McGinty and the Giants of the early 1900s, the feat would be performed more successfully in 1916 than any other season. The next attempt came on September 6 in a Giants-Dodgers doubleheader at the Polo Grounds. In the first game, Rube Benton pitched New York to an easy 6–1 victory. Rice attributed the loss to "the general cussedness of the Superbas play" as well as "Cheney's wildness and ineffectiveness." After falling apart in a six-run first inning during his last start in Philadelphia, this time the Brooklyn spitballer (14–10) blew up in the second, allowing four costly runs on two walks and three hits. At bat, the Dodgers were completely dominated by Benton, who allowed only four hits and an unearned run. Apparently, he wasn't the least bit tired and volunteered to start the second game as well, against former Giant Rube Marquard. Rice did give the Superbas more credit for their energy in the second contest as they scored twice, just enough for Marquard to beat his former manager for the third time in 1916.[19]

Apparently some observers, perhaps those in the press box, questioned the appropriateness of Benton pitching both games since the second meant little to the Giants, and a tired pitcher might benefit Brooklyn. Rice dismissed this notion, however, pointing out Benton allowed only one earned run on nine hits in the second game. Of more concern to the *Eagle* correspondent was that McGraw played former Dodger Lew McCarty in the first game. It was well known he would receive a share of the World Series money if the Dodgers were that fortunate, which might provide him with a financial motive not to play his best against Brooklyn. McCarty played well and New York won easily, but Rice worried about the potential scandal, calling for a rule prohibiting players in McCarty's situation to play against their former teammates. Little did anyone know that in spite of their heated rivalry, the significant inter-relationships between the two teams would lead to a different and much larger outcry of scandal in the final days of the pennant race.[20]

Meanwhile, the weather in Boston was still a problem, or from Stallings' point of view, served as a solution to the exhausted state of his ball club. Citing the morning rain and threatening outlook for the afternoon, George postponed the September 6 doubleheader. This was in spite of claims from Philadelphia that the teams could have at least played one game. The Phils had won eight of their last ten, including six straight, and for that reason alone wanted to play. Since the two teams already had a doubleheader scheduled for Thursday, September 7, they would have to make up the two remaining games during the last week of the season in Philadelphia. Although this gave Boston the ability to go back to Rudolph as well as Tyler and/or Hughes on Thursday, it also created a situation calling for six games in four days in the waning moments of the pennant race.[21] The Dodgers-Giants split and the postponements in Boston created more confusion in the standings.

Teams	Wins	Losses	Games Behind
Philadelphia	73	49	—
Brooklyn	74	50	—
Boston	71	49	2

Although it wasn't obvious at the time, the games of September 7 marked turning points for the Giants and Braves, both of whom were going in opposite directions. At the Polo Grounds, Brooklyn had one more contest before a four-game showdown against its nemesis, Boston. The good news was the Superbas would be at full strength for that series. In order to have his full pitching resources at his command in Boston, Wilbert Robinson decided it was time to pick a spot for one of his most seldom-used hurlers, veteran Nap Rucker. Damon Runyon saw humor in this because it meant "Brooklyn's most historic ruin Napoleon Rucker was taken from the archives of the borough yesterday afternoon, unwrapped, dusted off and brought to the Polo Grounds, where he was set to pitch his biennial game of baseball." Even though it hadn't been seen recently, Runyon said there was documentation for the "claim that Rucker had a fastball in the seventeenth century." John McGraw also dug deep into his staff, calling on Ferdinand Schupp, who had pitched almost exclusively in relief. Schupp allowed a home run to Wheat in the second inning, but it was one of only two Dodger hits. The Giants pitcher used a "sweeping curve" or "baffling hook," as well as an effective fastball to great benefit. Rice, at least, was surprised by Schupp's performance, which he called "one of life's little mysteries."

Equally mysterious was the Giants' failure to do much of anything with

Rucker heading to the bottom of the sixth. New York did tie the score in that frame and had the bases loaded with two out. At bat was first baseman Walter Holke, who was new to the team, and according Runyan, he had to wait "several minutes" for Rucker's pitch to arrive. When it finally did, Holke singled, driving in two runs and sparking a 4–1 Giants win in an Alexander-like one hour and 25 minutes. While there may not have seemed to be anything special about the victory, neither New York nor Schupp would taste defeat for a very long time. Afterward, Runyon unkindly claimed Rucker was "taken back to his sarcophagus" in Brooklyn. Equally unkind, but perhaps more accurate, was William Hanna's complaint about what he perceived to be the Dodgers' poor attitude, arguing "their play was spineless. They need stiffening of these vertebrae and need it badly." In some ways, it was remarkable Brooklyn had managed a split because its team batting average for the series was an anemic .195, producing just over two runs per game. One positive was the pitching, where both Coombs and Marquard had come back with strong performances. Even so, Tom Rice, for one, was concerned, calling the overall situation "distressing."[22]

Not surprisingly, Flatley predicted a sweep by either Philadelphia or Boston in the September 7 doubleheader "practically means the National League pennant." In spite of speculation, Stallings would come back with Rudolph. The Boston skipper named Ragan and Hughes as his starters. Don Carlos was opposed in the opener by Rixey (19–6), who drove in three of Philadelphia's four runs as the Phils held on for a 4–2 win. For the second game, Moran decided Erskine Mayer's performance against Brooklyn on Labor Day had earned him another start. Stallings, on the other hand, went with Tom Hughes, who had been the Braves' stopper just as much Rudolph. The match-up was scoreless in the bottom of the third when Boston had runners on the corners, creating a prime opportunity for a double steal. Niehoff and Bancroft were more than ready for the play, as the Phils had changed their strategy against this highly popular tactic. Using what was referred to as the "Collins and Barry bluff," Niehoff charged in, as if to cut off the throw to second and come home with the ball. However, at the last minute he ducked, allowing the throw to go through to Bancroft, who tagged out a surprised Hughes at second before Fitzpatrick could go home. Apparently, the Braves didn't fully understand the change in strategy, and tried the same thing in the fifth with the same result.

Later in the fifth, Boston had runners on second and third with two out and Hughes up. When he swung at Mayer's first pitch, disaster further struck both Hughes and the Braves' pennant chances. The ball hit his finger, injuring him so badly that he had to leave the game with an initial prognosis that the Braves pitcher would be out for three to four weeks. In fact, Hughes wouldn't pitch again in 1916. At the time, he had a 16–3 record with a 2.35 ERA. Boston failed to score in the inning, and the game remained scoreless into the ninth when the Braves were betrayed by their defense. Errors by Maranville and Smith, sandwiched around a walk to Cravath, loaded the bases for Philadelphia, and two runs scored on Luderus' single. Mayer finished his second fine pitching performance of the month, a 2–0 shutout, this time without help from Alexander. It had been a remarkable week for Pat Moran and his men, featuring eight straight victories over the two teams ahead of them in the standings. During this stretch, Phils pitchers had allowed all of nine runs, slightly more than one per game. It was no wonder they had moved from five off the pace to a 1½ game lead on Brooklyn and a three-game advantage over Boston. Flatley, swinging from optimism to the other extreme, recognized the seriousness of the situation. He noted a different kind of "unnatural gloom" descending on Braves Field, such that Boston would need a miracle "more miraculous than the hectic surge of 1914."[23]

Boston was clearly reeling from a sweep at the hands of the Phils, particularly the previous day's doubleheader and the loss of Tom Hughes. The last thing the Braves needed was another twin bill, but that was what they had. Even though Brooklyn had recovered slightly from its debacle in Philadelphia, the Dodgers had a high level of anxiety going against the team that had dominated them all season long. According to Robert Ripley of the *Globe and Commercial Advertiser*, there was little optimism in the Brooklyn locker room, as the Superbas were "silently and sullenly donning their uniforms." Clearly, "discouragement prevailed" when veteran Jack Coombs stood up and said he wanted to speak. According to Ripley, both Robinson and Ebbets had spoken to the players ad nasuem, which meant they weren't excited about another pep talk and "looked askance at Coombs." However, Colby Jack was a veteran of multiple pennant winners with Connie Mack's Philadelphia Athletic teams, so they listened. According to Coombs, the problem was simple — a lack of spirit the Dodgers could and should reverse by simply holding up their heads and fighting. Promising to lead by example, the veteran pitcher said, if necessary, he would have himself ejected from every game for the rest of the season, even though one of his goals was to finish his career without such a blot on his record. It is impossible to know whether this happened exactly as reported and, if it did, how much it affected the Brooklyn players. What is clear, however, is a number of observers noticed a change in the Dodgers' attitude, as evidenced by such comments as there was "more life on the Brooklyn bench than there had been for a month."[24]

Perhaps part of what these observers noticed was the contrast with the Braves, who appeared listless, possibly due to their numerous injuries and illnesses. In addition to those casualties previously mentioned, Smith, Maranville,

Egan and Fitzpatrick were all playing hurt. Even so, the only regular out of the lineup in the doubleheader was Evers. Hughes wasn't available for the first time all year, but he certainly couldn't pitch every day, even though sometimes it appeared he had. Brooklyn, on the other hand, was back at full strength, allowing Wilbert Robinson to play a right-handed platoon of Merkle and Myers in the first game against Tyler, a lefty, and then switch to a left-handed duo of Daubert and Johnston against Rudolph (16–9), a right-hander, in the second. Ironically, the starting pitchers for both teams were the same as those in Boston's fateful doubleheader sweep at Ebbets Field in August. In the first game, Brooklyn enjoyed a balanced attack, scoring six runs, one at a time, while everyone in the lineup recorded at least one hit. Pfeffer (19–9), meanwhile, regained his earlier form, limiting the Braves to two runs as Brooklyn won easily, 6–2.[25]

Having lost five straight, the Braves were counting on their ace, Dick Rudolph, who had already beaten Robby's team three times in 1916. After a scoreless first, Zack Wheat put the Superbas on top early with a home run to left-center, which supposedly "took the steam out of Rudolph." Two more hits and a stolen base put runners at second and third with pitcher Sherrod

Brooklyn Superbas outfield (left to right): Casey Stengel, Jim Johnston, Hi Myers, and Zack Wheat (George Bain Collection Library of Congress).

Smith coming up. Smith, who knew a 3–0 lead when he saw one, singled in both runs. Having supplied the bulk of his own offense, Sherrod took care of his pitching responsibilities, shutting out Boston on four hits in a 4–0 win. Reportedly, the Dodgers were happier about the second contest than any other that season since they finally "got Rudolph and got him good." Wilbert Robinson enjoyed the sweep, delaying his exit from the field to yell rhetorically at the Boston bench, "Who's cracking now?" Another reason for Robby's high spirits was the success of his strategy to use second-string pitchers against the Giants (and still split the series), thereby saving his stars for Boston. One observer said this demonstrated Robinson "is the greatest handler of pitchers in the league."[26]

Extremely depressed on the Boston side of the ledger was Flatley, who felt all was lost, even with the "miracle man" at the helm. Resorting to gallows humor, he commented that the Boston ownership's plan of taking the team out to dinner after being swept by Philadelphia to take their minds off baseball had worked all too well. Instead of doing so for just one evening, Flatley felt the Braves also forgot to play baseball against Brooklyn. Meanwhile, Rice was extremely pleased to find the Superbas in a virtual tie with Philadelphia, and that "Boston may be the Hub of the Universe and the Athens of America, but it is also third in the National League, this day and date, with much thirdness." One can imagine the satisfaction Rice took in writing those lines.[27]

If the Dodgers had any doubts things were going their way, they were removed after seeing the score of the Phillies' first game in their September 8 doubleheader against the Giants. Pat Moran hoped to build on his recent success behind Alexander (27–10). Instead, the reconstructed New York team erupted for nine runs on 14 hits against the Phils' ace, giving him his worst beating of 1916. Perhaps the only good news for Philadelphia were thunderstorms that occurred in the top of the ninth, prematurely ending the opener and preventing the Giants offense from continuing the attack in the second game. In addition to losing the contest, the Phils seemed to be picking up the Braves' habit of ripping the Superbas, as it was reported Moran wasn't upset by the Dodgers' doubleheader sweep of Boston since he believed "the Robins would be easier picking than the Braves." In words that would prove even more ominous, the unidentified *Inquirer* correspondent then claimed McGraw and his players wanted Brooklyn "to win this rag."[28]

This probably wasn't the first comment of this nature during the season, and it certainly wasn't the last. Part of the problem for even objective observers of the 1916 National League season was what to make of the Giants. Through the beginning of the last western trip in August, their performance had been consistently inconsistent. Then, on that swing, New York began to have trouble scoring, much less win games. At the end of the trip, it seemed they were on a free-fall into the second division, their only safety net being the weakness of the western teams. However, in the midst of these disasters, John McGraw was completing a rebuilding of his team for the second time in one season. During the winter of 1916, the Giants, more than any other National League team, had brought in Federal League players with limited major league experience. In this second phase, he traded the right side of his infield, Merkle and Doyle, replacing them with the tried, but temperamental Zimmerman and prospect Walter Holke. On the left side, New York still had the capable Art Fletcher, now playing alongside Herzog, who no matter what his baggage was a significant upgrade. Amazingly, in all of these moves, McGraw hadn't given up any pitching and even added one competent major league starter in Slim Sallee.

While it should have been clear these changes strengthened the Giants, given past disappointments, writers were reluctant to jump to conclusions. Thus, while the Giants' splits with Boston and Brooklyn were creditable, they didn't produce much in the way of accounts noting a revitalized New York team. When this was followed by the unexpected shelling of Alexander in the opener of the series against the Phillies, it wasn't surprising a Philadelphia writer looked for an alternative explanation — a desire to help Brooklyn win the pennant. These comments were more than a little ironic given the longstanding feud between McGraw and Robinson.

Those who were skeptical regarding John McGraw's motive in starting Benton in both ends of a doubleheader against Brooklyn on September 6 would've been hard pressed to explain New York's doubleheader against the Phils on September 9. Before a huge crowd estimated at 37,000, Pol Perritt, who some felt had been a "rank in and outer" all year (also not a bad metaphor for the Giants), pitched and won both games, allowing only one run and eight hits over 18 innings. This was the fourth 1916 attempt at the feat, and Perritt joined the St. Louis Browns' Dave Davenport as the only two thus far to accomplish something unimaginable today. The size of the crowd was nearly as impressive as Perritt's effort. At a time when attendance figures were almost always speculative, New York president Harry Hempstead came into the press box to tell reporters this was the largest regular-season crowd ever at a Giants' home game. Supposedly New York even had to borrow some extra safes from Harry Stevens to hold the receipts. Given the crowd's enthusiastic reaction to the posting of the Dodgers-Braves score, Fred Lieb thought there were many Brooklyn fans in attendance.[29]

In the first game, the Giants picked up single runs in the fourth and fifth innings and held off a Phils' rally in the seventh to prevail, 3–1. In addition to winning, New York broke the jinx of former Giant Al Demaree, who had beaten the New Yorkers six times in 1916. Philadelphia manager Pat Moran played a hunch in the second contest, starting Charles Bender for the first time since August 22. The layoff clearly hurt, as Bender was his own worst enemy by walking two, hitting one and throwing two wild pitches in the first inning, all of which resulted in two Giant runs. Bender settled down after that, limiting New York to an unearned run in what was described as his best performance since the 1913 World Series. The damage had been more than done, however, since the Phils could do nothing with Perritt, who shut them out on four hits.[30]

Since hitters tend to do better against a pitcher the more times he works through the batting order, the utter failure of the Phillies' batters in seven to eight at-bats makes Perritt's performance more impressive. Damon Runyan suggested while the "lean and lank and hollow flanked Perritt wasn't exactly the ideal sculptor's model," Brooklyn should put his statute at the entrance of Prospect Park, constructed appropriately of "enduring iron." Having seen Pol's dominating performance and the overall play of the Giants in the twin bill, the Philadelphia writers had gotten the message about New York's transformation. The *Inquirer's* unidentified correspondent noted the Phils were simply no match for a "newly constructed" Giants team. More prophetically than he could have known or imagined, that writer predicted New York "should go clear through the western hordes" during the upcoming homestand.[31]

Up in Boston, anyone who needed a reminder of the changes in fortunes for the Braves and Dodgers got one in top of the first. After Brooklyn's first batter was retired, Jake Daubert singled to center, with the ball going by Fred Snodgrass all the way to the wall, allowing Daubert to circle the bases. That was all the resurgent Larry Cheney (15–10) needed, as he shut the Braves out on three hits in a 5–0 win. The Superbas' final run scored on a single by Zack Wheat, extending his hitting streak to 22 straight games. To make matters worse for the Braves, Maranville was spiked (some thought intentionally) by Johnston. The Boston shortstop suffered two dislocated fingers and was expected to miss an undetermined amount of time. The dramatic collapse of the Braves brought a flood of explanations and excuses. Sherwood Magee claimed Boston's inability to hit was due to the lack of a background in center field. Stallings fell back on the more reasonable problem of injuries, especially to the pitching staff. In any event, regardless of the causes, the Braves had lost 10 of their last 12 and were even more firmly ensconced in third place. The team in first, however, was no longer the Phils; the Brooklyn win, coupled with two Philadelphia losses, put the Superbas back on top.[32]

Teams	Wins	Losses	Games Behind
Brooklyn	77	51	—
Philadelphia	75	52	1½
Boston	71	54	4½

Before the western teams arrived, one game remained in the current series, and prior to that another obligatory Sunday's rest, which gave the writers time to reflect on recent events. Some in New York were clear the Braves were finished due to a combination of exhaustion and injuries. In Philadelphia, at least one columnist claimed New York's three straight wins over the Phillies "proves that McGraw overlooked nothing to help out his old friend, Wilbert Robinson." In Brooklyn, there was understandably a lot of excitement. Tom Rice, who clearly knew better, felt winning the last game in Boston "should be a simple matter." He went on to predict the Dodgers would win enough games against the western teams to increase their lead before the final series with Philadelphia and New York. Wiser counsel in the Brooklyn *Daily Times* noted the surprising results since September 1, specifically Philadelphia's sweeps of the Dodgers and Braves, followed by New York's and Brooklyn's sweeps (thus far) of the Phils and Boston. This showed that never in National League history had "more dope gone wrong in a similar period than since September 1st." Lester Rice, writing in the Brooklyn *Citizen*, agreed, calling the season, "the most frenzied six months in the history of the national sport." It was a period of time where "hope has been at constant play with black despair," a state of affairs far from over.[33]

When play resumed on Monday, September 11, at the Polo Grounds, Pat Moran had one more ace to play in Eppa Rixey (19–7), who on most teams would have been the top starter. Now, however, with Alexander having been shelled a few days earlier, Rixey had a chance to be the stopper. The Giants scored in the second inning and led, 1–0, heading to the bottom of the fourth, when the Phils once more tumbled into the realm of "black despair" that Lester Rice had written about. The bases were loaded when New York catcher Bill Rariden hit a Texas Leaguer to center field. Center fielder Dode Paskert tried to make a circus catch, only to see the ball go by him and allow three runs score. Two more runs scored on a single by the Great Zim, ending Rixey's day early. Moran's team did come back to score four in the seventh, but New York added two more for a comfortable 9–4 win and a sweep of the four-game set. The four runs scored by the Phillies were exactly half of the total they scored in the entire series, compared to 24 for the suddenly hard-hitting Giants.[34]

In mid–August, Sid Mercer observed Philadelphia's sweep of the Giants had begun the New Yorkers' tailspin that had effectively ended their pennant hopes. Now Mercer noted there was no little irony in the Giants returning the favor this time, especially since McGraw loved to beat the Phils because of indignities suffered at their hands in 1908 and 1914, not to mention earlier 1916 defeats. Some writers still harped on the help the Giants were providing the Dodgers, but there was also some recognition New York was playing championship ball, and perhaps the best in the National League. After playing so well and winning eight straight from Brooklyn and Boston, the Phils had been caught in a buzz saw, averaging only two runs per game and seeing both Alexander and Rixey get hit hard, while Demaree and Bender allowed just enough runs to lose.[35]

As the Phillies boarded the train home amidst rampant gloom and despair, they could at least take some consolation they had fallen no further behind. The 1916 pennant race clearly had no intention of providing clarity until the end, so it was no surprise Boston finally came out of its doldrums by beating Brooklyn, 5–1. With few other options, Stallings went with former Dodger Don Carlos Ragan, perhaps hoping the revenge factor might provide him with additional motivation. Whatever the reason, Ragan was in control, especially after Stengel and Wheat "whiffed woefully" with the bases full in the third. The Boston battery also provided offense by combining for seven hits. Flatley felt the cool autumnal temperatures reminded Gowdy of the 1914 World Series when he hit .545. In spite of the defeat, Robinson and the Dodgers had to be in a good frame of mind as they boarded the "rattlers" for the last time in the regular season. Their collective positive mood was due to finally dominating a series against Boston. After hitting roughly .200 as a team against the Phils and Giants, the Superbas had rebounded to bat .295 against the Braves while scoring an average of four runs per game. Since Dodger pitching had allowed only two runs in first three games of the series, it was no wonder they finally found a way to beat the Braves. Brooklyn had broken even (14–14) on their 28-game trip, surviving with a slim 1½ game lead. The Dodgers would play their last 25 games at home, where at least metaphorically, "the smell of roasting peanuts and newly-raked grass is pervading the atmosphere of rural Flatbush."[36] If Wilbert Robinson and his men did take another railroad journey in 1916, it would be for the World Series, and that was a trip they would gladly make.

Teams	Wins	Losses	Games Behind
Brooklyn	77	52	—
Philadelphia	75	53	1½
Boston	72	54	3½

CHAPTER IX

"A less courageous outfit would have curled up and died."

Had there been sports talk radio in 1916, one topic would have been on the minds of American League fans. Would Boston preserve its lead during a nearly month-long September road trip while the other contenders, Detroit and Chicago, just three and 3½ back, spent virtually the entire month at home? The Red Sox advantage had been cut from 6½ games to three, as the champions lost five of six home contests to close August. That gap would narrow further during the first half of September, setting the stage for a dramatic finish.

Boston's road trip started on September 1 against the Yankees, while Detroit and Chicago had the day off. The Red Sox provided Carl Mays (13–9) a 3–0 lead, but he failed to survive the sixth inning. After indifferent fielding by Mays gave the Yankees a second run in that frame, Wally Pipp hit a two-run home run to the right-field bleachers. The blow gave New York a 4–3 lead, and the Yankees won, 7–3. Pipp would finish the season with 12 round-trippers, and the American League home run crown. He also tied for the Major League lead with the Giants' Dave Robertson and the Cubs' Cy Williams. Boston really needed to right the ship before heading westward in mid-month, and the Red Sox gutted out a 5–3 victory the next day. Rough, playing a rare game at catcher, beat out two important infield singles, and Rube Foster (13–8), back from arm trouble, labored through 5⅔ innings before Dutch Leonard came on to shut the door. By defeating southpaw George Mogridge, Boston also proved it could defeat lefties.[1]

The Tigers managed to stay 2½ back by defeating the White Sox, 2–1, in the teams' final meeting of the season. Clarence Rowland sent Reb Russell to the hill to face Harry Coveleski, who E.A. Batchelor claimed was at his best against Chicago. In front of 12,945 at Comiskey Park, the left-handers hooked up in a pitchers' duel. First baseman Jack Ness' error allowed Ossie

Vitt to score in the first, but the White Sox tied it in the seventh when Ray Schalk tripled and scored on Shano Collins' squeeze bunt. Otherwise, the two pitchers were in control until Ralph Young led off the tenth by doubling over left fielder "Shoeless" Joe Jackson's head. Young went to third on a sacrifice, bringing up Coveleski. Hughie Jennings had a decision to make, and he lifted the pitcher for a pinch-hitter, Harry Heilmann. The move paid off when Harry singled to drive in the winner. Detroit won the game to keep pace with Boston; Chicago won the season series, 13–9.[2]

Over the next two weeks, Boston's play was marred by lapses that allowed Detroit and Chicago to draw closer. After an off-day on the third, Babe Ruth took the hill in the opening game of a Labor Day doubleheader against the Yankees. New York was six out, lurking in the wings along with the Browns, who were five back. With his wife in attendance, Ruth (18–10) overcame a heel problem and was splendid, allowing just two hits in the first six innings in a game Boston easily won, 7–1. The second contest was a loss that would haunt the Red Sox if they didn't win the pennant. Although New York led, 3–0, Boston rallied for three in the ninth to tie. The Red Sox would have had the lead, but pinch-runner Mike McNally was tagged out after missing the plate. Thus reprieved, the Yankees won the game in the bottom half on a passed ball by Hick Cady.[3]

While the Red Sox split four games with New York, Detroit and Chicago were looking to take advantage. The Tigers were hosting the Indians for three games that featured Speaker and Cobb fighting for the batting crown. Tyrus was closing the gap at .359, and at the end of August was 19 points behind Speaker's .378. Chicago's Joe Jackson (.353) had also joined the race. In spite of Cobb's improvement, E.A. Batchelor argued one of the reasons the Tigers hadn't hit their full stride was because he was hitting a soft .359. Detroit was ready for the Indians and swept the three-game set that started on the third, the same day Oscar Stanage returned at catcher. Cobb continued his "light hitting" in the opener, playing table-setter while collecting four hits, two runs, two stolen bases and an RBI in Detroit's 5–3 come-from-behind victory. Now even Batchelor was convinced the old Cobb had returned. The Labor Day doubleheader was sloppy. The Tigers used big innings in both games to sweep, 7–5 and 11–8.[4] With the twin killing, Detroit was only a game behind Boston; the Tigers actually had one more win but trailed by three in the loss column.

Also making their move were the White Sox, who swept three games from the Browns in St. Louis. The story of the first was Red Faber (13–6), who pitched like an ace, tossing a complete-game 1–0 victory. "Faber had a noble big curve that broke smartly and of which he had complete and perfect control. His fastball had a shoot a foot wide on it. He had a spitball and a good change of pace," wrote J. B. Sheridan. Ray Schalk's double brought home the game-winning run in the ninth. It was more of the same during the holiday doubleheader when an estimated 25,000–30,000 turned out at Sportsman's Park. The St. Louis *Post-Dispatch* said the crowd was probably the largest ever to witness a ball game in the city. And the fans were all over the place — in the seats, behind the seats, in the aisles and in roped-off areas on the field. The difference was again the White Sox pitching, as Lefty Williams (8–7) and Joe Benz (9–4) won 3–2 and 2–1 victories, respectively. While striking out six and allowing two runs (1 earned), Lefty also led the offense, scoring one run and driving in another. Benz struck out 10 and had only been scored on twice in the past eight days on his way to three victories.[5]

While Red Faber was the White Sox ace in 1916 and won 17 games, he came up empty in two of his biggest starts (George Bain Collection, Library of Congress).

Team	Wins	Loses	Games Behind
Boston	73	54	—
Detroit	74	57	1
Chicago	72	58	2½

Chicago was pennant mad, and fans were questioning why this team was playing catch-up instead of leading by a comfortable margin. To those inclined to blame the manager, Rowland's vehement defender, George Robbins, responded, "Rowland doesn't carry a team superior to his competitors all things considered. Still he may win the pennant and should be given credit if he does. If he doesn't, give him credit for making a great fight in the greatest race the American League has known."[6] The White Sox had finished their last lengthy road trip of the season just over .500 (10–9).

The three teams remained in the same position on the fifth, when Boston suffered a bad defeat while splitting a doubleheader with the Athletics (at this point in the season, any loss to Philadelphia was a bad one). Ernie Shore (11–8) and Ruth both struggled on the hill, and Dick Hoblitzell and Duffy Lewis failed to hit in the clutch, as the Red Sox lost, 5–2, in the opener. Lewis rebounded in the second game, a 7–1 win, by going 2-for-3 with two runs and an RBI, while Carl Mays was exceptional on the mound.[7]

Hoblitzell had just begun a stretch that would see him go five games without a hit. The mediocre baseball the Red Sox played over the first half of the month seemed to be due in large part to a lackluster offense — Boston hit just .233 through September 16. The Red Sox copped the final two games against Philadelphia, winning 5–2 and 2–0. Carrigan, however, was hit with a three-game suspension for an ejection in a previous game. Rube Foster tossed an "ineffective" shutout in the second game by throwing well when the situation merited, while Dick Hoblitzell's ground out and Everett Scott's single provided the runs.[8] There was nothing wrong with three out of four, but the Athletics were so bad any loss was a missed opportunity when chances were running short.

In the series with Philadelphia, Boston made some lineup changes. Lewis, who was struggling in the three spot, dropped to five, and Walker, still suffering from a neck injury suffered during a collision at the Polo Grounds, went to the bench. There were other reports, however, that suggested Tilly had been benched by manager Bill Carrigan. In turn, new pickup and speedster Jimmy Walsh moved into the vacated three hole. On the seventh, Gardner left the lineup, forcing Everett Scott into the six spot, with Mike McNally taking the seventh position. Gardner, in the midst of a career year, had injured the big toe on his right foot (fortunately, it wasn't broken) against Philadelphia. His absence was a problem, and forced Carrigan to use even more of patchwork lineup, including Hooper, Janvrin, Walsh/Shorten, Hoblitzell, Lewis, Scott, McNally and a catcher. This depleted roster contributed to the team's offensive struggles. Fortunately, Joe Lannin appealed to Ban Johnson, and Carrigan was re-instated earlier than expected, providing some help behind the plate.[9]

The Tigers and White Sox clearly weren't going away quietly. Detroit had won five straight, and with St. Louis coming to town, Joe Jackson in the Detroit *News* posted the new odds for the pennant, listing the Tigers as the favorite at 7 to 5, ahead of Boston (2 to 1) and Chicago (9 to 2). A small crowd at the first game on September 6 became excited when the scoreboard indicated Boston had lost to Philadelphia, only to be disappointed when the score was corrected. It looked like they would be even more disappointed when the Tigers trailed St. Louis and were down to their final strike. However, a Jean Dubuc single tied it and Cobb won it, 6–5, in the 10th by wreaking havoc on the basepaths. Ty stole second, went to third on a bad throw, and scored on a grounder when Browns first baseman George Sisler failed to adequately look him back to the base before going to first. The Tigers had even beaten long-time nemesis Carl Weilman, extending their winning streak to six. It would go no further, however, when 12 walks and two hit batsman contributed to a 6–5 loss on September 7.[10]

Detroit had pulled to within a game, but the Tigers fell two back with the September 7 loss when the Red Sox won that day. Boston's win created no such problems for Chicago, which won the first two against Cleveland upon its return to Comiskey Park. On the sixth, Jack Fournier and Ray Schalk were ejected early for arguing balls and strikes. With Ness injured, Rowland had to turn to Robert Hasbrook, a recruit from the Central Association, to play first base. Leading 2–1 in the eighth, Jackson's triple ignited a two-run inning, essential runs since Reb Russell (15–9) allowed two in the ninth before retiring the side. Overall, the defense was strong, and Hasbrook handled all of his opportunities. Unfortunately, scoreboard watching wasn't an option for Chicago fans because "vandals had cut and appropriated fifty feet of cable" connecting the Comiskey Park scoreboard to the press box.[11]

Chicago rallied for a 5–3 victory in the second game on September 7 on the strength of a four-run eighth inning. The final two scored when a slightly off-line throw pulled Cleveland first baseman Chick Gandil off the bag. Umpire Bill Dinneen had first called the batter, Hap Felsch, out, but then reversed his decision upon seeing Gandil throw home. Dinneen assumed Gandil would have thrown home only if he had come off the bag or dropped the ball, but Chick maintained this was his standard practice. Having dropped to nine back, the Indians were understandably upset, argued vociferously and protested the game.[12] The call stood, however, putting Chicago just 2½ back of Boston and a half game behind Detroit.

The Indians appealed to Ban Johnson on the eighth regarding the previous day's game. He admitted Dinneen made a mistake but couldn't order the game to be replayed because the protest was based on an umpire's judgment. In that day's contest, the score was tied at two in the 11th when Zeb Terry drew a leadoff walk. He was on second with one out when reliever Al Gould struck out his counterpart, Eddie Cicotte. Unfortunately, catcher Steve O'Neill couldn't hang on to the ball and his ensuing throw to first was wild and went into right field, allowing Terry to score the winner. This was a rare offensive contribution for Zeb, who saw his average drop below .200 in September. Despite that, Terry was seeing significant time, leading to continued woes on the left side of the infield. Hap Felsch, who had just ended a three-game stretch that saw him go 6-for-12, strained his leg, forcing him temporarily out of the lineup. Chicago won its seventh straight and completed the four-game sweep when Lefty Williams (9–7) buckled down late to help the White Sox hang on to a 5–4 win on the ninth. While the four-game sweep was obviously good news for Chicago's chances, Cleveland had lost seven straight to fall 10 behind. The only real positive for Cleveland was that through September 7, Speaker was hitting .378, good enough for a 19-point lead on Cobb in the batting race.[13] Even though the Indians had certainly added a lot of drama to the race, their pennant hopes were clearly over.

A day after the ugly outing in which Detroit pitching walked 12 and hit two, Willie Mitchell (6–3) allowed just four hits, leading the Tigers to a 3–0 victory. In a case of turnaround being fair play, Detroit's offense benefited from eight walks by St. Louis hurler Bob Groom. Bobby Veach's two-run single broke the game open in the seventh. The left fielder was beginning a stretch that would see him hit a torrid 20-for-41. The offense carried Detroit in the series finale on the ninth, as four triples and two doubles helped the Tigers to a 12–0 lead, making Harry Coveleski's (22–9) job easy. Detroit, which took three out of four and was just one back, also knocked out supposed nemesis Carl Weilman early and defeated him for the second time in less than a week.[14]

Boston left the door open again on September 8. With Gardner still unable to play in Washington, the Red Sox and Senators battled to a 0–0 tie

When Bobby Veach helped propel the Tigers to first place in September, he was just beginning to show the type of offensive force he would become, despite standing just 5' 11" (George Bain Collection, Library of Congress).

when the game was called for rain in the sixth inning. Carrigan's team wasted many opportunities, especially when Hooper was thrown out at home in the first, even though he claimed he wasn't tagged. With writers pestering Rough for answers, the Boston skipper offered his own analysis of the race, saying, "Despite the loss of Jack Barry, most likely for the remainder of the year, and the fact that my team is otherwise crippled and in a bad batting slump, I believe that the Red Sox will win the pennant provided the pitchers hold up during the remainder of the grind."[15] However, Detroit was now only 1½ back and Chicago trailed by two.

The rainout caused a doubleheader on the ninth, the first game featuring another Ruth-Johnson showdown. For the fourth time in 1916, Ruth won, and it was another classic. With the score tied at one in the sixth, Hooper singled, and went to second on a wild pitch and to third on Hoblitzell's infield hit. Carrigan then went for the jugular, calling for a delayed double steal, and before the Nationals could tag out Hobby, Hooper scored what proved to be the game-winner in a 2–1 victory. The Big Train seemed to be frustrated and was reported to have been dusting off Red Sox hitters. Johnson, despite having been unsuccessful thus far against Ruth in 1916, would go on to lead the American League in wins with 25. However, Boston couldn't sustain the success, letting a 3–2 ninth-inning lead slip away in the second game and losing on an unearned run in the 10th.[16]

The day's results meant both Detroit and Chicago were only two back in the loss column, providing some tangible hope for a western champion. At 6–4 in September, Boston wasn't playing poorly — they just weren't matching the Tigers' and White Sox's results. Chinks in the Red Sox armor included a struggling offense (clean-up man Dick Hoblitzell was a prime culprit, hitting only .129 so far on the trip) and injuries to players like Gardner, Walker and Barry.[17] Additionally, Boston had lost two games in which it had been leading or tied in the ninth inning. Despite some poor starts, pitching was still the strength. Leading the way was Ruth, who was 2–0 and had allowed just two runs in 18 innings in September.

Team	Wins	Loses	Games Behind
Boston	77	56	—
Detroit	77	58	1
Chicago	76	58	1½

The Tigers, 7–1 thus far in September, were being carried primarily by their offense, which hit a whopping .291 through September 17. Though still inconsistent, even Donie Bush and Ossie Vitt were making a contribution on offense. Bobby Veach was on fire early in the month, while Cobb was steady with clutch performances in certain games. Sam Crawford and Oscar Stanage provided further spark at the plate. Also 7–1 to start September was Chicago. While not as powerful as the Tigers, the White Sox still hit significantly better than the Red Sox, racking up a .268 average through September 16. The most notable offensive performance came from Eddie Collins, who was back with vengeance and would soon have his average over .300. Chicago also had the pitching staff that allowed the fewest runs per game among the contenders at 3.20. Staff ace Red Faber was 4–0 in the first half of the month, allowing just nine runs in 36 innings, with five of those tallies coming in one start. Reb Russell, Joe Benz and Lefty Williams were also off to good September starts. Boston's hurling corps was second at 3.27 runs per game, but that clearly wasn't enough to overcome its offensive inefficiency. Even though the Tigers pitchers allowed 3.65 runs per game, their offense was so much stronger than Boston, and it clearly made up for the difference. In half of its games, Detroit had scored five or more runs. The numbers for the defending champions certainly weren't bad, but enough to allow the Tigers and White Sox to draw even closer.

The Red Sox had the usual eastern Sabbath on September 10 to regroup before continuing their series with the Nationals. Meanwhile, Chicago would host St. Louis while Detroit traveled to Cleveland. At League Park, Bill James and George Cunningham were ineffective as the Tigers lost badly, 8–2. Things weren't much better at Comiskey Park, where an estimated 27,000 turned out to watch their White Sox suffer a sloppy 5–2, 10-inning decision to the Browns. Chicago's defense was porous, and George Sisler's two-run single provided the go-ahead markers in the tenth inning.[18] Both teams fell back a half game, while Chicago's seven-game winning streak was snapped.

The Tigers were convincing in the remaining two games at League Park, winning 9–1 and 10–2 decisions on September 11 and 12. George Burns missed the first contest with an upset stomach, and his replacement, the somewhat forgotten Harry Heilmann, went 5-for-5 with three RBIs to lead the offense. Just days after suffering a drubbing by the Browns, Hooks Dauss' nine innings of one-run ball were more than enough. The following day Hughie Jennings gave the ball to Howard Ehmke, who had made his Major League debut on the tenth. Two days later, Ehmke, using the wide variety of arm angles he used to throw the ball, mowed down the first 10 batters he faced, struck out four and allowed just two runs (one earned) in a complete-game victory. E.A. Batchelor was impressed, noting Ehmke "had the aplomb and equipment of a veteran in the big show. He was cool and collected at all times..." Cobb provided the offense on September 12 by swatting two home runs while going 4-for-5 with four runs and four RBIs. Veach also collected four hits and scored three times. The duo combined with Crawford to register 11 hits for 21 bases, which Batchelor believed to be an offensive record for an outfield in one nine-inning game. At a half game out, Detroit was well positioned upon returning to Navin Field to face the eastern squads. New York and Philadelphia came in first, with Boston and Washington to follow. The other three eastern teams had nothing of their own to play for, but would play a significant role in the race because of their head-to-head match-ups against Chicago and Detroit. Since these teams were weaker than their hosts, this could be an advantage for the White Sox and Tigers.[19]

How Ehmke got to Detroit with a chance to play a role in the race is a fascinating story. After a successful season in the Pacific Coast League in 1914, Washington signed Ehmke, but he defected to the Federal League. His performance there was lacking, and he struggled with injuries. After the dissipation of the rival league, Ehmke, who had no other suitors, was forced to sign with Syracuse in the New York State League. He had extraordinary success there, establishing league records in shutouts and wins. The new marks broke the previous records set by Grover Cleveland Alexander. When Detroit signed Ehmke, Washington also claimed his rights, but the Tigers won the prized recruit.[20]

The White Sox kept pace on September 11 behind Red Faber (15–6), who didn't allow an earned run in a 5–2 win over St. Louis. The red-hot Eddie Collins went 3-for-5 with a run and an RBI. The next day, and for the second time in three days, the defense was atrocious, committing four errors in a 5–3 White Sox loss. Chicago had dropped two of the three games to St. Louis, putting the team two back.[21]

Meanwhile, the Tigers clawed closer to Boston when the Red Sox split their two remaining games in Washington. The victory occurred on the eleventh when Dutch Leonard (18–12) allowed only two runs and recorded two RBIs in a 4–2 win. Bigger news arrived off the field, however, by means of a Boston *Daily Globe* report that Bill Carrigan would retire at the end of the season. Rumors had cropped up previously but were always dismissed by Rough. This time, his denial was clearly a façade, especially after it was learned Carrigan had told president Joe Lannin of his decision a month earlier.[22] The bombshell may have finally sunk in on September 12 since the newspapers were full of retirement stories the following day. The Boston *Post* reported, "(Carrigan) gave business interests and a desire to replace active athletics and much travel with the comforts of his home, but the Red Sox prexy (Lannin) is of the opinion that Boss Bill will find it very difficult to renounce the pastime in which he has enjoyed such singular fame."[23]

The decision may have been based in part on the death of Carrigan's father-in-law, who left a business that would require Rough's management. The *Globe* and *Herald* were much more concerned with how the timing of the report might impact Boston's play. Lannin had clearly wanted to table the

Joseph Lannin (left) and ballplayer Bill Carrigan (right) certainly made their share of news off the field in September of 1916 (an unidentified man stands between them) (George Bain Collection, Library of Congress).

issue until season's end, and now he was quoted as saying, "It is likely to affect the men who should have no distractions at this time. The fans of Boston and myself are more interested in the Red Sox winning the championship than in what Manager Carrigan may do at the end of the season." The Boston owner also tried to deflect the issue further by saying he expected Carrigan, who was more than financially stable, to stay.[24]

The poor timing of the leak showed on September 12 in Washington. Speculation was rife about possible replacements, including current Red Sox players Jack Barry and Dick Hoblitzell, as well as Heinie Wagner. Connie Mack and even John McGraw were also suggested as possible replacements for what may have been the most high-profile managerial job at the time. The issue could be a major distraction just before key match-ups with Chicago and Detroit that would probably once and for all determine the pennant race.[25] These two critical series were just days away.

Before that, Babe Ruth and Walter Johnson came back on two days rest on September 12, and Ruth held a 2–0 lead in the last of the ninth. This time he couldn't close the deal, as a pair of two-out walks loaded the bases, and John Henry's double tied it, forcing Carl Mays into the game. Boston scored once to take the lead in the 10th. With Shore taking the mound in the bottom half, a series of hits tied it, and when the typically sure-handed shortstop Everett Scott botched a force play at the plate, the winning run scored. While Ruth didn't take the loss, Johnson, in the Nationals' final home game of the season, had finally beaten the Red Sox ace in a contest both had started. As a result Boston headed west clinging to a precarious half-game lead.[26]

Chicago, two back, still had to finish its series with St. Louis on the thirteenth. While it wasn't pretty, the White Sox won to split the four-game set. Fittingly, for a contest that saw a combined eight errors and nine pitchers, the White Sox scored the winning run in the 10th inning on a wild throw by St. Louis hurler Carl Weilman. The bottom of the fifth inning was even described as "a regular orgy of misplays." Unfortunately for Chicago, Ray Schalk injured the middle finger on his throwing hand and was expected to miss "considerable time." This forced Rowland to insert the seldom-used Jack Lapp into the lineup at a critical time. To make matters worse, pitcher Reb Russell injured his ankle and might miss a "turn or two" in the rotation.[27]

Team	Wins	Loses	Games Behind
Boston	78	57	—
Detroit	80	59	—
Chicago	78	60	1½

Since Boston had an off-day on September 13, the White Sox were back within 1½ games but still three out in the loss column. Washington was the first eastern team to visit Comiskey Park, and the Nationals' trip to Chicago was a nightmare. First, around 10 P.M., the train passed over a deposit of pig iron, a liquid form of the element. That brought the train to a sudden stop, and the players were "hurled out of their seats." A two-hour delay for repairs followed. Then at 8:00 A.M., the train struck a brakeman, who reportedly fell asleep on the side of the track, probably fatally injuring him. This delay was followed by another because a freight train was in the way.[28]

The weather didn't cooperate either on September 14, with dark clouds and high winds enveloping Comiskey Park, causing numerous delays so players could rub dirt from their eyes. Despite the conditions, Chicago built a big lead and held on for a 7–5 win. Hap Feslch returned, and Lapp made his presence known with an RBI single in the fourth. The White Sox built a 7–0 lead, but Red Faber (16–6) had to quell rallies in the seventh, eighth and ninth. The following day, with the score tied at two in the ninth, a wild pitch allowed Zeb Terry to score the winning run for a 3–2 victory and a two-game sweep.[29] Three straight wins obviously helped the White Sox — the question was how much.

Beginning September 13, Detroit hosted New York for a three-game set. Based on his past success against the Yankees, Jennings sent Coveleski to the mound. He was protecting a 4–0 lead behind key hits from Veach, Crawford and Heilmann when he weakened in the eighth. Hooks Dauss was sloppy in relief but worked out of the jam to maintain the 4–1 victory. Coveleski (23–9) was now 3–0 in September and performing in a manner reminiscent of his efforts in the 1908 pennant race. Another key factor was the Tigers' left side of the infield, as shortstop Donie Bush and third baseman Ossie Vitt came up with a number of key stops. Unfortunately, Tub Spencer injured his finger stopping a wild pitch.[30]

While Chicago (78–60) was still 1½ games back, Detroit (80–59) had effectively tied the mighty Red Sox (78–57), though the Tigers were two out in the loss column. Salsinger wrote, "It is on this stretch of games that Detroit is counting for its chance. Eastern clubs have been meat for Jennings' athletes on the local lot this year and if the Tigers are consistent in their work at home it is a cinch that they will be in the fight right up to the last game of the season."[31] At the same time, Boston was playing this entire stretch with games in hand — three on the White Sox and four on the Tigers — which was a distinct advantage.

The noose that seemed to be tightening around Boston's neck loosened a bit the following day when Urban Shocker, in a homecoming, shut down Detroit, 4–2, at Navin Field. The key play was a successful double-squeeze by New York, caused in part when Ralph Young and Harry Heilmann both attempted to field the bunt and no one covered first. Young attempted to run to the bag, but with his back turned, he didn't see the second runner coming home. Offensively, Ty Cobb went hitless for the second straight day and failed to reach base.[32]

The loss came at an inopportune time for the Jungaleers because a win would have given them sole possession of first. Boston, meanwhile, was just starting the most important part of its trip — a swing through the West — without Jack Barry. Walker replaced Shorten on September 14, and Gardner and possibly Foster were nearing a return. The Red Sox didn't respond, though, looking terrible in a 6–1 loss in St. Louis. The bonehead play of the day came from Bill Carrigan. Everett Scott had been hitting sixth and Mike McNally seventh while Gardner was out. On the fourteenth, Rough reversed it, but in the game, Scott continued to go to bat ahead of McNally. The Browns either didn't catch the mistake or conveniently didn't bring it up until the fourth inning when McNally registered a hit, and he was ruled out. Both Boston and Detroit had lost, but Chicago beat Washington to get within a half game of the effectively even Red Sox and Tigers. Both Detroit and Chicago still trailed by two in the loss column.[33]

Team	Wins	Loses	Games Behind
Boston	78	58	—
Detroit	80	60	—
Chicago	79	60	½

Chicago defeated Washington again on September 15, but this time Detroit matched it. Hooks Dauss (19–9) allowed two first-inning runs but settled down and pitched eight straight innings of shutout ball. The Tigers rallied for a 4–2 victory, the winning run scoring when Bush tripled and came home on Cobb's double. Detroit's catching corps was further depleted, however, when Oscar Stanage was badly spiked on his toe.[34] Like Coveleski, Dauss was exceptional in the first half of September and had just one bad start, leaving him with a 3–1 record. Jennings may not have been a good handler of pitchers, but his staff was certainly making a real contribution to the Jungaleers' pennant run. Although Detroit pitchers allowed more runs during the first half of September than the other two pennant contenders, this was skewed by three occasions in which the Tigers' opposition scored eight runs.

Victories by Chicago and Detroit left Boston in desperate need of a win. Following the final game at Sportsman's Park, the Red Sox headed to Chicago and Detroit for six games. To make matters worse for Boston, while they visited Chicago and Detroit, the two western contenders hosted the hapless Athletics. If either team could win the series with Boston and sweep Philadelphia, it would greatly improve their chances to take the flag. Before returning home, the Red Sox still had four games in Cleveland — and Speaker, dominating the American League offensively, certainly wouldn't lack for motivation.

There is more to the story, though. Carrigan was hoping to line up his pitching rotation for the series with Chicago and Detroit. His goal was to get a victory in the St. Louis series from someone other than Shore, Ruth, Leonard or Mays. Shore had pitched the first game and lost, but Carrigan seemingly wanted his "big four" to have at least one day off. That left Rube Foster, Vean Gregg, Jack Wycoff and Sam Jones to hurl a contest the Red Sox really needed to win. Foster was the most likely candidate, but many years later, Carrigan recalled he was "hardly able to lift his arm."[35]

When Rough asked Foster if he could go, the hurler replied, "I can't put anything on the ball, but I might hold them off with slow stuff for six or seven innings." Carrigan would later say, "He called the turn exactly. I had to take him out, after seven innings. He couldn't have rolled the ball to the plate any longer. But he had fooled the Brownies with his 'nothing' ball long enough for us to take a lead and I had the relief pitching to protect it."[36]

Carrigan's memory wasn't entirely accurate, since Foster lasted only 4⅓ innings. However, Boston built an 8–0 lead, and Carl Mays probably didn't have to work that hard for the last 4⅔ frames. Larry Gardner returned in the victory and went 3-for-4 with four RBIs, including a key two-run single in the second.[37] While Carrigan did have to use one of the big four, Mays, in relief, the shortened pitching rotations of the Deadball Era would easily allow him to return for Chicago or Detroit. The same was true of Shore. Although it may not have been exactly what Carrigan wanted or remembered years later, it was close enough. Most importantly, Ruth and Leonard would be able to make two starts each against Detroit and Chicago.

During the series, Browns manager Fielder Jones had a conversation with Carrigan regarding the Red Sox chances. Bill responded by saying, "We certainly didn't show much here, but this club never looks good against weak opposition. It just won't bear down unless there's a lot at stake. It will be different in Chicago and Detroit. The boys know they must win those games, so they'll win 'em, if the pitching stands up as well as I expect. That's the kind of a ball club this is."[38]

Both Chicago and Detroit had gone 11–3 during the first 15 days of September, while Boston was 8–6, leaving a microscopic difference between the three teams.

Team	Wins	Loses	Games Behind
Red Sox	79	58	—
Tigers	81	60	—
White Sox	80	60	½

The Red Sox still had games in hand, but the race was certainly down to these three and would most likely be decided in head-to-head match-ups over the next week.

On September 15, the National Commission announced it might allow all three teams to start printing World Series tickets within the next week as a time saver. A second off-the-field issue was Carrigan's job status, which in an odd piece of timing, Lannin planned to discuss with him in Chicago. Rowland's pitching rotation wasn't lined up like Boston's, but the White Sox were still in reasonably good shape. The big question was whether Reb Russell, still hampered by that ankle injury, would be available. He, Faber and Williams had been the most effective hurlers in September. Faber pitched the first game in Washington but figured to see a start against Boston, and Benz and Williams had more than enough rest. The forgotten Jim Scott was still suspended, while Eddie Cicotte, in his first September start, pitched a complete-game victory on the fifteenth against the Senators.[39]

In *The Sporting News*, the opinion of potentially biased Chicago beat writer George Robbins seemed to suggest the race was down to the White Sox and Tigers. Somehow, the first-place Red Sox, even with games in hand, had been forgotten. Robbins wrote, "Boston will have to battle to keep in the race on four hostile grounds of the West, meeting a quartet of fast teams. The Boston pitchers aren't quite so effective as they were last year. They are encountering faster clubs in the West and they feel the loss of Barry, while the Sox and Tigers are in the best trim of the season and fighting on their home grounds." Still, Rough's team appeared to have a distinct advantage in the opener when Dutch Leonard (18–12) opposed Lefty Williams (9–7), who has not been successful in that role. Leonard, however, had struggled against Chicago in 1916. Even though there was rain in the forecast, an estimated 15,000–18,000 fans turned out. In a hopeful sign for Chicago, Reb Russell warmed up before the game, suggesting he might be available during the series.[40]

Williams worked out of a jam in the first, and the White Sox came to bat. With one down, Buck Weaver "bounced the pill over the picket fence between the left field bleachers and the pavilion for a home run." Reporter John J. Hallahan argued the ball bounced not over but through the "picket fence," a bad "break" in favor of Chicago. It quickly got worse, as Eddie Collins tripled and scored for a 2–0 advantage when Tilly Walker muffed Joe Jackson's fly ball. Shoeless Joe went to second on the play and then scored on a Hap Felsch single. Eddie Collins' sacrifice fly in the following frame gave Chicago a 4–0 lead.[41]

G.W. Axelson wrote that Boston "seemed to be a crew broken in spirit, shy of pep and base hits, which faced the Sox (Chicago) in the 'croocial' series." Things did get tighter when a couple of misplays brought Boston to within 5–3 in the sixth, but the Red Sox never got closer than two in a 6–4 loss. Shano Collins (2-for-3, 2 runs, 1 RBI), Weaver (2-for-4, 1 run, 1 RBI) and Eddie Collins (3-for-4, R, 2 RBIs) had provided the offensive punch for Chicago. "(Williams) pitched a game that was full of courage and brains and a lot tougher than it looked, considering the fact the White Sox gave him a lead of four runs in the first two innings." Ring Lardner, a columnist for the Chicago *Daily Tribune*, sat on the White Sox bench during the game and reported Leonard was the subject of much taunting by Jack Fournier. Whatever the cause, Dutch (18–13) was hit very hard in just four innings of work. Over the past month, there had been times when it appeared Boston had taken over first place permanently. But Detroit's 4–3 victory over the hapless Athletics at Navin Field on September 16 coupled with Boston's loss suddenly thrust the Red Sox into third place. Perhaps "whistling in the dark," Edward Martin claimed Carrigan and the team remained confident.[42]

Against Philadelphia, Hughie Jennings made a gutsy decision and sent Ehmke back to the hill for the rookie's Navin Field debut. Both the teams scored two runs in the first, and it remained that way until the bottom of the fifth, when Donie Bush drew a walk, stole second and scored on Bob Veach's single to center field. Ehmke fought through first and third and no one out in the sixth to preserve the 3–2 lead. In the bottom half, Sam Crawford reached on an error and eventually scored on Ehmke's infield single for a 4–2 advantage. Philadelphia scored in the ninth, but the Tigers hung on for a 4–3 victory after Ehmke struck out a hot Socks Seibold with runners on second and third. Duly impressed, E.A. Batchelor wrote, "There were several situations that sorely tried the soul of a young man whose big league experience is measured by the span of only a week, but for all the signs Howard ever gave of being nervous, he might have been in the upper stratum of baseball society as long as Eddie Plank, and that is so long that the memory of man runneth not to the contrary."[43]

Ty Cobb had gone 2-for-3 with a run scored and an RBI, while Veach went 2-for-4 and knocked in two runs, including the go-ahead tally. As usual, the Tigers benefited from Philadelphia's horrific fielding. Ehmke, now 2–0, walked five and allowed eight hits (Detroit was outhit 8–6), but the rookie also struck out seven and was effective when he had to be. Unfortunately, the promising youngster wouldn't be eligible for the World Series due to his late start in 1916. Even though Detroit (82–60) still trailed in the loss column, the Tigers had a one-game advantage over third-place Boston (79–59). Chicago (81–60) was in second, a half game back of Detroit. With the Tigers in first, Frank Navin had to spend $50 on a suit for each player, honoring a deal he made earlier in the season.[44]

Things were at the point that Detroit might have preferred Boston win the final two games against Chicago. The Tigers would have an opportunity to defeat the Red Sox, but the Pale Hose might be more dangerous, with a series against the Athletics looming. The dangerous Joe Bush opposed Harry Coveleski the next day, but it wasn't a pitcher's duel. Bush (seven walks, one hit batsman) was wild, and Coveleski's support (six errors) was horrendous. After Detroit lost an early lead, Ty Cobb's double in the seventh put the Tigers back on top, 5–4. Philadelphia rallied in the eighth, but the day was thought to be saved when the tying run was thrown out at the plate on a tough catch by Stanage, who redeemed some poor defense earlier. Stanage may have been redeemed, but Detroit wasn't, at least not yet. Second baseman Ralph Young fumbled a game-ending double play just long enough to allow Jim Brown to score the tying run. Coveleski (24–9), who allowed five runs (one earned) and had navigated his way around mine fields all afternoon, worked out of a two-on jam in the ninth to preserve the tie. Cobb was up in the 10th and worked a walk, went to second on a sacrifice and advanced to third with his aggressive baserunning when the throw to first was just a bit off-line. After Sam Crawford was intentionally walked, Harry Heilmann's (1-for-4, 3 RBIs) sacrifice fly to center won it, 6–5.[45]

The Tigers were sloppy in both games but had escaped. Despite the victories, there was bad news for Detroit. Ossie Vitt was hit on the wrist, and though he said it wouldn't cost him any time, this was clearly uncertain considering how the injury "handicapped" him later in the game. In addition to the six errors, Coveleski was pounded for 12 hits, and probably only a team as inept as Philadelphia would have scored only five runs. Bush was worse, though — of the eight he walked or hit, four scored. As a result, the Tigers would hold on to first place for at least another day. Maybe this was Detroit's year after all.[46]

The September 17 game between the Red Sox and White Sox was awe-inspiring. Just a half game back, fans in Chicago were rabid, coming out in droves for the second contest with Boston. A record 40,000-plus packed every nook and cranny of Comiskey Park, possibly one of the largest crowds in baseball history. According to the Chicago *Daily Tribune*, it was the largest ever to see a game in that city. G.W. Axelson described the scene:

> Yesterday the fans started to besiege the park at noon. Surface and elevated cars from then on swelled the mob to constantly larger proportions and at 2:30 o'clock it was worth one's life to get through the crowd in front of the main entrances. The bleachers had long before that been filled to overflowing and the fans started to vault the fences, a thousand or more gaining entrance that way.[47]

In need of a win, Rough sent Babe Ruth to the hill, and Pants Rowland countered with Red Faber. In the first, the White Sox received two-out singles from Eddie Collins and Joe Jackson, both of whom advanced on a wild pitch, and then Hap Felsch capitalized with a two-run single.[48] If anyone on the Red Sox bench knew Detroit had a 3–1 lead, he might have felt the pennant slipping away. The atmosphere in Chicago bordered on bedlam.

It is in such situations, however, that champions dig deep inside themselves, and Boston did just that. Ruth settled down, Faber came unglued, and the Boston offense ignited. Larry Gardner and Everett Scott drew one-out walks in the second, and the bases were loaded when center fielder Hap Felsch wasn't able to catch Pinch Thomas' drive. Ruth hit back to Faber, but the pitcher's throw home was too late to nail Gardner, and Harry Hooper followed with a two-run single. Suddenly, Boston was up, 3–2, and Chicago's ace was out of the game in favor of Dave Danforth. Both were wild, as Faber walked two, both key, and Danforth five. Felsch left an inning later, apparently injuring his leg on the play in center field.[49]

After the first inning, Ruth allowed just two hits and improved to 20–10. Larry Gardner added a pair of sacrifice flies later in the game, but Harry Hooper was the offensive star, going 4-for-4 with two RBIs, three stolen bases and a key catch in the seventh inning. Although Boston appeared to be in control on the way to a 6–2 win, it wasn't that simple. As the game went on, Comiskey Park officials (if there were any) failed to handle the overflow crowd. Paul Shannon reported, "In the eighth and ninth rounds the fans saw defeat staring the White Sox in the face and they did their utmost to help the home players by tactics which were a disgrace to any big league city." It was especially difficult for outfielders Walker and Lewis, who were pelted with cushions and shoved by out of control fans. By the time "the last man flied out to short left Duffy could never have caught the ball as a dozen maniacs rushed out and interfered. Happily for Boston, Scott was able to get under it." It was a miracle the Red Sox didn't win by forfeit, especially since Ban Johnson watched the proceedings in person. Feeling little was done to control the situation, Bill Carrigan, Joe Lannin and Boston writers cried conspiracy. Lannin voiced these feelings and then some, saying, "It looks as if everybody is after the Boston club and didn't want it to win. The poor handling of the crowds and the umpiring on Sunday were a disgrace. It is pretty hard to say what might have happened if we had had a close game. It is very clear that Boston is not wanted as a pennant winner. If it doesn't win, I will have something to say." Lannin added he would retire if the Red Sox were "robbed of the championship."[50]

Despite all of the adversity, however, Boston (80–59) had improved its position, trailing Detroit (83–60) by a game and now leading Chicago (81–61) by a half game. If the Pale Hose lost the rubber game on September 18, they would be three games behind the Red Sox in the loss column and potentially two back of the Tigers, with no head-to-head contests remaining. Chicago would play without Hap Felsch, who was replaced by Nemo Leibold. In a curious decision, Rowland went back to Claude Williams. Lefty was pitching on just one day's rest, but he had handled Boston in the first game of the series. Bill Carrigan's selection was Ernie Shore, who was an ineffective 0–3 on the trip thus far.[51]

Boston got on the board quickly in the second inning. Duffy Lewis singled and went to third on Larry Gardner's one-base knock. With two out, Gardner attempted a steal of second, and on the throw down, Lewis broke for home. Eddie Collins' return throw to the plate was low and got away from rookie catcher Byrd Lynn. Lynn, who had seen shockingly little time in 1916, was taking the place of Jack Lapp, just 1-for-7 in the series. Chicago argued in vain that Lewis was out of the base line. The White Sox had a chance to get even in their half of the second, but Joe Jackson was thrown out at the plate by Everett Scott, who's overall play, especially his fielding, was exceptional throughout the road trip. Chicago scored the equalizer in the fourth when Jackson redeemed himself by driving home Shano Collins on a sacrifice fly. The White Sox, however, left runners on the corners, and it would come back to haunt them.[52]

Hal Janvrin walked in the fifth, and Walker hit to Zeb Terry on what should have been a double-play ball, but the shortstop booted it. It was a bad play at a critical juncture by the precarious left side of the infield. With two outs, Lewis came through again, driving a two-run double to left field for a 3–1 lead. Boston knocked Williams (10–8) out of the game in the sixth, and Hooper greeted reliever Reb Russell with a sacrifice fly for a 4–1 advantage. The White Sox would close the gap but never caught up, losing 4–3.[53] The Comiskey Park crowd booed Boston all game, and White Sox coach Kid Gleason, who was on the coaching lines, tried to distract Shore. Eddie Collins went so far as to dig his spikes into a darkened ball that Shore was using effectively. This stunt brought a new ball into play, preventing Shore from reaping the benefits of a discolored ball that was hard to see.[54]

Boston had taken advantage of Chicago's mistakes (only one Red Sox run was earned), while the White Sox had been unable to do the same on two Boston errors. Rowland's team also struggled to string hits together, enabling Shore (12–10), who allowed three runs on six hits, to match Ruth's performance of a day earlier. Lewis was the offensive star in the rubber game, going 4-for-4 with a run and two RBIs. In both wins, Boston had a large supporting cast, including Tilly Walker, Everett Scott and Larry Gardner. Boston had demonstrated for all to see how championship teams produce in the clutch. The only downside was Del Gainer and Heinie Wagner, who drew three-day suspensions when they were ejected during the second game.[55]

The White Sox ranks were obviously depleted, which certainly didn't help matters. Schalk played only the final inning of the third game, Felsch missed the last game and most of the second, Russell was out of the first two, and Scott was still suspended. Rowland could legitimately be questioned as to why Russell didn't start the third game. Reb had previous success against the Red Sox and threw 2⅔ innings of relief, which meant he was probably available to start. Additionally, previously in 1916, Williams had started twice in one series against Boston, and the Red Sox handled him on that occasion as well.[56] The length of Scott's suspension at such a critical time is also curious. In the end, though, Faber wasn't himself and the White Sox's defense was weak. Chicago did receive strong offensive performances from E. Collins (5-for-12), Jackson (4-for-9), Felsch (2-for-6) and Shano Collins (5-for-12), but in the final two games, as a team, the White Sox hit a paltry .179. Chicago (81–62), now 1½ out, trailed Boston by three games in the loss column with only 11 remaining.

The news for Boston got even better when the Red Sox learned Detroit's supposedly questionable pitching had been betrayed by its allegedly superior offense and defense. Philadelphia got on the board early in the top of the first due to poor defensive plays by catcher Stanage and center fielder Cobb. More loose play by right fielder Crawford, third baseman and substitute "Babe"

Reb Russell won a team-leading 18 games but, like Faber, he did not measure up at the most critical juncture of 1916 (George Bain Collection, Library of Congress).

Ellison and pitcher Willie Mitchell in the third inning provided the Athletics all of the runs they needed in a 2–0 win. Although Mitchell (6–5) pitched well for Detroit, the Tigers were shut out on three hits by Elmer Myers (who finished the season with a 14–23 record). Since Myers was wild, however, Detroit didn't lack for base runners, leaving the bases loaded in the fifth and ninth.[57] Of all the upsets of contenders by bad teams, this has to be one of the worst of all-time.

Stanage, who shouldn't have even been in the lineup, had been playing with a bad hand, but "Tubby" Spencer's injured finger didn't leave Jennings much choice at catcher. Both Spencer and Vitt hoped to return during the crucial series with Boston that started on September 19. The Red Sox were percentage points ahead of the Tigers but had four games in hand, two in the loss column. Chicago was 1½ back but three out in the loss column.[58]

Team	Wins	Loses	Games Behind
Boston	81	59	—
Detroit	83	61	—
Chicago	81	62	1½

Still, Detroit was ahead of Chicago and could make real progress with a big series against Boston. E.A. Batchelor sized up the situation, noting Dauss, Ehmke and Coveleski would probably pitch in that order against the Red Sox. He also hoped the city of Detroit would be ready, writing,

> So far as can be gathered from the fragments of conversation that you overhear on the streets and in the cars, business is going to be entirely suspended while the Carrigans are in town and everyone is going to devote himself exclusively to rooting the Tigers into the championship. This is as it should be, for a man who would work at a time like this would show himself lacking in patriotism to the extent that he would hire a substitute if war broke out and the conscription method of acquiring food for the guns were resorted to.[59]

When the Red Sox arrived at Navin Field on September 19, there was extra motivation for the visitors. Almost 30 years later, Carrigan recalled, "In fact, so confident were the Tigers that they had the flag in the bag that a new press box and temporary outfield stands were being erected, in the park in preparation for a world's series, on the day we arrived. I pointed out to my gang that the time had come for them to put up or shut up." Regardless of whether time constraints forced Detroit to start preparations (the Chicago White Sox had also started getting ready), Carrigan used it motivationally to his advantage. A crowd of nearly 15,000, the largest weekday crowd of the year, turned out for the series opener, and Rough selected Carl Mays, who hadn't pitched since his relief stint in St. Louis, to oppose Hooks Dauss. With Vitt still out, the Tigers used a makeshift lineup that included Young at third base and Heilmann at second, with George Burns, who had seen very limited action in the past week, hitting seventh and playing first.[60]

Both pitchers had to work out of jams. Much of Dauss' trouble was due to wildness. He walked three in the first, two of them setting the table for Duffy Lewis' two-out, run-scoring single. Detroit might have tied it in the second, except Harry Heilmann was thrown out by Harry Hooper while trying to stretch a double into a triple. The Tigers did equalize matters in the fifth when Sam Crawford singled and came around to score on a base-knock by Burns. Play was intense, and Paul Shannon wrote, "The Jennings men fought like real Tigers for the decision, slid frantically for first base on almost every play and played with the desperate earnestness that showed their realization of the importance of getting first blood." Not surprisingly, Ty Cobb had a confrontation, this time exchanging words with Joe Lannin.[61]

Substituting for Tilly Walker, Chick Shorten, a Red Sox youngster who had been effective, scored Boston's first run, and followed that by doubling down the left-field line in the seventh. Residing on third base after Dick Hoblitzell's sacrifice, Duffy's Lewis' sacrifice fly scored Shorten for a 2–1 lead. Detroit put two on base in its half of the seventh for Red McKee, but as in the prior game against Philadelphia, he failed in the clutch. Helping his own cause, Carl Mays singled with two out in the eighth and scored on Hooper's triple to left-center, giving Boston an important insurance run. Mays (16–10) worked out of another two-on jam in the eighth, as the Red Sox won the series opener, 3–1. Praising Carl, Shannon described his performance as "a display of wonderful head work, splendid control and an alertness never before shown by him (Mays)." The Red Sox hurler also received errorless support. Dauss dropped to 19–10 with the loss. Detroit had received offensive contributions from Crawford, Burns, Cobb and Heilmann, but failed to get the big hits that Boston received

A Boston *Globe* cartoon captures the end of the 1916 American League race (Boston *Daily Globe*, October 2, 1916).

from Hooper and Lewis. It was reminiscent of the duo's clutch contributions during the stretch run in 1915. The untested Shorten chipped in with two runs, and Mays had a big hit as well.[62]

Boston (82–59) was 11–7 on its daunting road trip thus far, including 4–2 on the western portion, and held a one-game lead on the Tigers (83–62), three in the loss column. Although the difference in the loss column wasn't considered as significant as today, some experts felt Detroit was in desperate straits. Still the optimist, E.A. Batchelor was one of the few still favoring the Tigers, noting a clean sweep wasn't expected. Detroit hoped Vitt could return on Wednesday, September 20, but effectively in a must-win situation, the Tigers would put their season in the hands of rookie Howard Ehmke.[63]

The White Sox did manage to keep pace with Boston on the nineteenth, but just barely. Chicago had a 2–1 lead against Philadelphia in the eighth with Joe Benz, who had dominated the Athletics, on the mound. Feisty Philadelphia, however, knocked Benz out in the eighth and suddenly took a 4–2 lead. Thankfully, Chicago had a rally left. Pants Rowland went to his bench for four straight pinch-hitters, starting with Eddie Murphy. Murphy and Jack Fournier singled against Tom Sheehan, and after a sacrifice by Ray Schalk, Hap Felsch drew a walk. It was 4–3 on Shano Collins' sacrifice fly, the second out, and with Sheehan starting to come apart, Buck Weaver drew a walk to reload the bases. I.E. Sanborn described what happened next: "One bad ball went by before (Eddie) Collins swung at what he liked and sliced it off the end of his bat at top speed past third base well inside the foul line. Past (Wally) Schang (LF), too, the ball sped, giving Fournier and Hasbrook, who ran for Felsch, plenty of time to register the runs that converted defeat into victory." A loss might have been fatal, but Chicago survived. Even at the most crucial time of the season, Rowland's status was in question amidst reports that Kid Gleason had already signed a contract to manage next season and was effectively the current skipper. It was a dramatic win, but the White Sox were still three back in the loss column, 1½ out overall.[64]

Team	Wins	Loses	Games Behind
Boston	82	59	—
Detroit	83	62	1
Chicago	82	62	1½

It was more of the same for the White Sox on September 20—another sloppy victory, this time by a count of 8–7. Chicago had five one-run leads during the contest but never fell behind. Reb Russell (17–9), who somehow earned the win, was hammered for 11 hits and seven runs in seven innings. After Philadelphia had closed the gap to 8–7 in the top of the seventh, Dave Danforth shut the door in two hitless frames. If there was a positive, it was the offense, which rapped out eight runs on 14 hits, even though it was against Philadelphia. Eddie Collins led the attack, going 4-for-4 with a run scored and three RBIs, while Shano Collins (1-for-4, 3 runs) and Buck Weaver (3-for-4, 2 runs) also contributed.[65]

Chicago and Detroit needed Boston to start losing and soon since the Red Sox had three games in hand on the White Sox and four on the Tigers, and Boston would finish with three against the Athletics. As expected, rookie Howard Ehmke took the mound for the Tigers that same day. Detroit had Ossie Vitt back and put two on base in the second. One run scored on an Oscar Stanage sacrifice fly and two more came home on throwing errors by Dick Hoblitzell and Everett Scott, putting the Jungaleers ahead, 3–0, in front of 16,192. To the South and West, the Comiskey Park crowd let out a roar upon hearing the news.[66]

Dutch Leonard, on the mound for Boston, was victimized by a bad break and a pair of errors. Then he tightened up, and Carrigan's team rallied against Ehmke in the fourth. Chick Shorten, again in the lineup, singled, and Duffy Lewis doubled down the right-field line to put runners on second and third. A Larry Gardner sacrifice fly scored Shorten, and Lewis came home on Scott's single. Boston trailed, 3–2, and with the seldom-used Bill Carrigan up next, Ehmke probably figured he would get out of the frame with a lead. However, Rough hit the ball sharply to center field, and Ty Cobb tried to make a shoestring catch. The ball bounded past him, causing John J. Hallahan to write, "Ty Cobb made a sorry exhibition of playing the ball. He actually quit when the sphere bounded past him and he refused to chase it. He just looked at it, and allowed Veach to retrieve it. Carrigan landed at third base and the score was tied."

Later on, Cobb would be forced from the coaching lines at third for arguing but would return to argue even more vehemently before leaving at the pleading of Donie Bush. Detroit threatened in the sixth, but Dutch worked out of a bases-loaded, no-out jam. Ehmke struck out for the final out, and Jennings would again be criticized for not pinch-hitting, especially considering Howard had already fanned twice. Ehmke returned the favor, coming back to work out of a bases-loaded, no-out jam in the seventh. Yet the youthful Detroit hurler struggled with command all afternoon and paid for a seemingly innocent two-out walk in the top of the eighth. With the right-handed Carrigan up (Ehmke was also right-handed), Scott stole second. Carrigan then lifted himself for a pinch-hitter, lefty Olaf Henriksen, who hit the first pitch into center field with the game-winning single. Numerous writers considered it a heady, gutsy decision by Rough, who was given much of the credit for the victory.[67]

The win came a year to the day Boston put the finishing touches on a similar important series with Detroit. Ehmke (2–1) had allowed four runs on eight hits while walking four. The Tigers had their opportunities with a 3–0 lead and a chance to go back in front in the sixth. But after his poor perform-ance against Chicago, Leonard (19–13) was excellent, striking out six and giv-ing up just three runs (one earned) on eight hits. The offense came from many of the same sources as the day before, with Shorten (1-for-5, run), Lewis (1-for-4, run), Gardner (0-for-3, RBI) Scott (2-for-3, 2 runs, RBI), Carrigan (1-for-3, RBI) and Henriksen (1-for-1, RBI) all stepping up. In a win that may have symbolized where the race was headed, the Tigers hadn't played badly but still lost to a highly efficient Boston team. The Boston *American* was confident, noting, "The Carriganeers have slid over the rough sledding of the tough road grind without losing their lead more than momentarily, and in the big show at Chicago and here in Detroit have smeared their rivals with the elimination brush. Only by falling dead can they now fail to bring the world's title to Boston."[68]

Like most of the A.L., the White Sox had feasted on the Athletics in 1916 with an 18–3 record. Suddenly, though, and much like Detroit, the two sloppy wins caught up with them, and Chicago was blitzkrieged in the September 21 finale, 8–0. Philadelphia led, 4–0, after five innings against Red Faber, who continued to struggle as he did against Boston, before tacking on four more in the ninth. In all, the Athletics racked up 16 hits, seven of them com-ing against Faber (16–8), who lasted just 4⅓ innings. Offensively, the White Sox didn't take advantage of the six walks issued by Joe Bush. Chicago hoped to gain ground against Philadelphia but could now only hope for an even break in the standings. Incredibly, both the White Sox and Tigers hadn't only lost a crucial game to the pathetic A's, they were both shut out.[69]

For the final game at Navin Field, Bill Carrigan sent Babe Ruth to the hill against Harry Coveleski. Like Faber, the ace of the Tigers was pounded by Boston and lost his cool in the process. The problems started in the first inning when Tilly Walker hit a two-run home run to the deepest corner of center field.[70] According to Paul Shannon, Harry Coveleski's response to adver-sity "manifested itself in the use of the 'bean ball,' with which he hit both Lewis and Gardner and came near causing a row with the good-natured Duffy." Not surprisingly, the Tiger hurler "was driven from the mound in the third, after the Sox had piled up four runs on passes and five hits."[71]

With Boston already up, 4–0, Walker went back to work in the fourth. Bernie Boland, in relief of Coveleski, issued walks to Ruth and Hal Janvrin, who both came home on Walker's triple. Tilly then scored on an infield sin-gle by Lewis. Detroit would cut the lead to 7–2, but with Ruth pitching, the Tigers had little chance and lost, 10–2. Coveleski allowed four runs on five hits in 2⅓ innings, while Ruth, even though he wasn't spectacular, tossed a complete game (7 hits, 2 runs). Most importantly, the Babe completely shut down Ty Cobb and Bobby Veach, who went a collective 0-for-7.[72]

Walker was the offensive star, going 2-for-3 with two runs and four RBIs, all of them critical, along with two great catches in center field. Once again, Lewis was a big factor, driving in two runs on two hits, while Hooper (2-for-5, 2 RBIs) and Gardner (2-for-4, RBI) also played a part. Boston's lead was 2½ over Chicago and three over Detroit, but that was again deceiving. The Red Sox had 11 games to play to Chicago's eight and Detroit's seven. Carrigan and his team left Navin Field for Cleveland, their last stop before heading home.[73]

Team	Wins	Loses	Games Behind
Boston	84	59	—
Chicago	83	63	2½
Detroit	83	64	3

Boston's thorough domination of Detroit and Chicago in the most critical games of the season was due to sound, well-balanced baseball. The pitching, specifically Ruth, Shore, Mays and Leonard, was splendid, the defense was solid, and the offense took advantage of opponents' mistakes and consistently came up with key hits. After struggling for the first half of the month with a depleted lineup, the Red Sox bats returned to hit .323 during the critical five victories. Harry Hooper (12-for-25, seven RBIs) and Duffy Lewis (11-for-23, seven RBIs) were nothing short of spectacular. Both played a key role in 1915, and despite some struggles in 1916, had risen to the occasion when it mattered most. Larry Gardner and Tilly Walker were the leading members of a strong supporting cast. The Boston *Herald* noted how Boston had out-hit its rivals in the key match-ups (.293 to .222 against Chicago and .314 to .235 against Detroit).[74]

The Tigers hadn't played badly, but the weakness of their pitching staff finally ruined their chances. The wildness of Hooks Dauss and Howard Ehmke and the all-around poor performance of Harry Coveleski, who continued where he left off against Philadelphia, never gave Detroit a chance to win. The offense also struggled (after their strong September start, the Tigers hit only .206 in losing four games to Philadelphia and Boston), but some of that could have been due to Boston's pitching. Harry Heilmann and Sam Crawford had solid performances, but poor ones were much more abundant. Donie Bush went 0-for-14 in the series, Ty Cobb 3-for-12, Bobby Veach 1-for-11 and Ralph Young 1-for-10. As with Chicago, Detroit's injury problems also can't be underestimated.

While Boston traveled to Cleveland, Chicago would host New York and Detroit would entertain Washington. The White Sox and Tigers needed the

Red Sox to start losing, and with Boston's trip nearing its end, few were feeling confident. Those doubts were well-founded, as the Red Sox won the first two games, on September 22 and 23. Boston runners only reached base in the second and ninth frames in the first game, but the Red Sox got a pair of runs each time, aided by some sloppy Cleveland defense. Ernie Shore (13–10) worked out of a bases-loaded, one-out jam in the eighth to preserve the 4–1 victory. The next day Boston won, 5–3, behind Carl Mays (17–10), while not surprisingly, Hooper (2-for-4, RBI) and Lewis (5-for-5, 2 runs) provided the offense.[75]

Detroit and Chicago kept pace by winning on September 22, but both teams were dealt a near death blow the next day in 6–3 and 7–2 losses that featured poor pitching by Bill James and Reb Russell. With Chicago 3½ out and Detroit four back, Boston, winners of seven straight, started making World Series preparations in earnest.

Team	Wins	Loses	Games Behind
Boston	86	59	—
Chicago	84	64	3½
Detroit	84	65	4

The White Sox had just six games left and Detroit five. Boston needed to win only five of its nine remaining to clinch, and that assumed the White Sox finished 6–0. The Red Sox left the door slightly ajar on September 24 when Marty Kavanagh's grand slam keyed a 5–3 Indians win. While both Detroit and Chicago won, time was not on their side. The Jungaleers virtually sealed their fate the next day. In front of just 1,510 in the final 1916 game at Navin Field, the Nationals knocked Hooks Dauss (19–11) out in the second inning and held on for an 8–5 victory. Behind Babe Ruth, now 5–0 on the trip, the Red Sox capitalized with a 2–0 win to complete their road trip 16–8, 9–3 in the West. Duffy Lewis' sacrifice fly drove in the only run Boston needed.[76]

Boston hadn't only survived its lengthy road trip, the Red Sox had dominated the trek. Ruth led the Red Sox pitching staff in September and would finish the month with a 6–1 mark. Mays, Foster, Leonard and Shore had been inconsistent at times, but also made some effective starts, especially on key occasions. The Red Sox didn't have any outstanding month-long offensive performances, but clutch hitting, such as that of Harry Hooper and Duffy Lewis against Chicago and Detroit, were critical. Hal Janvrin, who didn't hit well overall, had some key knocks and filled in admirably for Jack Barry. Overall in the second half of the month, the offense hit .277 compared to .233 in the first half.

The White Sox, also playing their final home game on September 25, did keep pace with Boston, with Hap Felsch, now back from injury, driving in three runs.[77] While still four out in the loss column, Chicago (86–64) cut the deficit to 2½ behind the 87–60 Red Sox. The Tigers (85–66) were four out with only three to play against St. Louis.

The following day was an off-day for all three teams. Boston's return home was all business, and with the pennant not officially wrapped up, there was little fanfare. E.A. Batchelor decided to give credit to the Red Sox, who won in the face of injuries to key players like Larry Gardner and Jack Barry, writing, "A less courageous outfit would have curled up and died under the circumstances, but instead of doing so, Carrigan's men just naturally went out and gave their best exhibition of the season. They did not lose a single series on the road." In fact, Boston had out-hit its opposition in the West, .314 to .203.[78]

The Boston *Daily Globe* reported on September 27 the Fall Classic would probably start on October 7, and the Red Sox would use the more sizable Braves Field for their home games. With Chicago and Detroit both off again that day, Boston won a dramatic, 3–2, 10-inning decision from New York in front of an appreciative crowd of 10,000 that welcomed the Red Sox home. After losing a 2–0 lead in the ninth, pinch-runner Mike McNally scored the game-winner on a Dick Hoblitzell squeeze bunt. Having almost closed the door, Boston reopened it slightly on the 28th, losing a 4–2 decision to the Yankees in 10 innings when New York rallied against Carl Mays (18–11). Detroit was again off, while the White Sox were rained out in Cleveland. It only brought the deficit down to 2½ for Chicago, three in the loss column, but the White Sox and their writers seemed to be holding on to increasingly unrealistic hopes for the pennant.[79]

The White Sox and Indians were scheduled to play a doubleheader on September 29, but once again they were rained out. Fortunately for Chicago, which needed to play every remaining game, Ban Johnson announced he would allow western teams until Wednesday, October 4, to finish their schedules. Even with the rainout, the Pale Hose were pushed to three back, as Babe Ruth mowed down New York in a 3–0 shutout. It was the Babe's 23rd win and ninth shutout, the latter an A.L. record for lefties that would stand until Ron Guidry tied it in 1978. In 324 innings pitched, Ruth hadn't allowed a home run and had compiled an ERA of 1.75 that would be the standard in the American League. The Red Sox win also officially eliminated Detroit, which posted a meaningless 4–1 victory over St. Louis. Just two more wins in four games and Boston would clinch the pennant regardless of what Chicago did.[80]

The White Sox did keep the pressure on the next day by sweeping a doubleheader in Cleveland. Reb Russell (18–10) cruised to a 7–2 victory in the first game, which saw a triple steal. Hap Felsch made four great catches in the second contest and hit a game-winning grand slam in the 12th inning for a 7–3 win. The Red Sox, meanwhile, reduced the magic number to one in front of 14,000 at Fenway Park. Dutch Leonard (20–14) was magnificent, not allowing a run through 10 innings, and pinch-runner Mike McNally scored the winner in daring fashion in the bottom half on a sacrifice fly to short right.[81]

The Red Sox were off the next day before hosting Philadelphia for three games to finish the season. Boston could clinch that day, however, if Chicago lost one game in its doubleheader with Cleveland. Pants Rowland sent Red Faber (16–9) to the hill in the first game, which remained scoreless into the fifth inning. Then, a hit batsman, an error and a hit loaded the bases, before Bill Wambsganss scored on pitcher Fred Coumbe's sacrifice fly. Since Coumbe was in the process of hurling a complete-game, two-hit shutout, one run was all that was needed to end the 1916 American League pennant race. The dramatic season had finally come to a conclusion, with Boston once again on top of the mountain.[82]

The Red Sox could take justifiable pride in their accomplishment, since as Paul Shannon wrote, "never in the history of baseball has a team facing such discouragements from the start and handicapped at various stages in the race by serious injury come through such a terrific fight with such glowing colors. Well do the Sox deserve their title as champions. All Boston looks to Carrigan and his men to bring home another world's championship now." Most writers heralded Boston's toughness and gameness, but Chicago's I.E. Sanborn went a step further, claiming that with seven of eight teams alive so late in the season, it was the "most sensational" pennant race in A.L. history.[83]

Team	Wins	Loses	Games Behind
Boston	91	63	—
Chicago	89	65	2
Detroit	87	67	4
New York	80	74	11
St. Louis	79	75	12
Cleveland	77	77	14
Washington	76	77	14½
Philadelphia	36	117	54½

Chicago's offense had been led by Eddie Collins (.308–0–52), Joe Jackson (.341–3–78) and Hap Felsch (300-7-70), but the team had struggled with inconsistency in its lineup all season. In fact, two of the players typically at the top, Shano Collins and Buck Weaver, hit just .243 and .227, respectively. In addition to his offensive woes, Weaver had played the majority of the games at third and committed 20 errors (he racked up an additional 16 at short-stop). First base had been another question for Chicago, and there Jack Fournier, who saw the majority of the action, hit just .240 and made 22 errors. In fewer attempts, Ness had an additional 15 miscues, while batting .267. Intriguingly, George Robbins' favorite prospect never played again in the major leagues. Though the team hit better in September, led by Eddie Collins, it just wasn't enough. By the crucial phase of the race, the defense and pitching also struggled. Specifically, Faber and Williams had performed poorly at key junctures. Faber (17–9, 2.02), Russell (18–11, 2.42) and Cicotte (15–7, 1.78) led the pitching staff, but Williams (13–7, 2.89) and Benz (9–5, 2.03) contributed as well. The mysterious Jim Scott finished just 7–14 (he had won 24 games a year earlier) but still had a 2.72 ERA. Later in 1917, Rowland would say regarding the 1916 season, "We were not dependable at first base and third was a source of much worry. Two of my best pitchers (Faber and Scott) failed me in the pinch.... And Eddie Collins started very, very slowly and didn't get into his proper stride until way late."[84]

Detroit's pitching wasn't nearly as deep. Harry Coveleski (21–11, 1.97) and Hooks Dauss (19–12, 3.21) were the two central figures. After that it was anybody's guess, and Harry Salsinger said he thought pitching was ultimately the cause of the Tigers' demise. Detroit hurlers had higher ERAs than either Boston or Chicago. Coveleski had gone 4–1 in September but struggled late, especially in the third game against Boston, while Dauss had been 3–3, but two of the losses came at critical junctures. Howard Ehmke added some much-needed depth, but another promising youngster, George Cunningham, didn't even get a start in September. Much like Chicago, Detroit struggled at the top of the order with weak performances by Donie Bush (.225–0–34) and Ossie Vitt (.226–0–42). Neither performed well in September. Ty Cobb (.371–5–68) and Bobby Veach (.306-3-91) were undoubtedly the only two consistent anchors to the Detroit offense. Cobb had closed the gap late but still fell short of Tris Speaker's .386 average to have his streak of nine straight American League batting titles snapped. The Grey Eagle would also lead the A.L. in hits (211), on-base percentage (.470) and slugging percentage (.502). Cobb, who obviously lost to a worthy competitor, still won the league title for runs (113) and stolen bases (68). Most of Detroit's best offensive performances came in the first half of the month when the Tigers were making up ground, with Veach leading the way. Unfortunately, this didn't continue when it was needed the most.[85]

On the morning of the second, Boston newspapers were packed with stories celebrating the Red Sox triumph. The Boston *Daily Globe* headline read, "Red Sox Champions Again Through Cleveland's Win." A cartoon below showed an Indian simultaneously throwing a member of the Pale Hose off the mountain while boosting a Red Sox player, holding a flag that read "Red Sox Champions," up to the top. As this was occurring, the Boston player said, "Thanks for the boost old chap."[86] Numerous other stories depicted reaction from Bill Carrigan and Joe Lannin and praised the Red Sox for not folding under trying circumstances. With a strong early September, Chicago and Detroit were in position to win the pennant (and it appears they had the talent), but though challenged, the Red Sox were not to be denied. At the heart of Boston's success was its 14–8 record against the White Sox and Tigers and the Red Sox's now-proven ability to win without Speaker. In the end, it came down to pitching, good defense and clutch hitting, where Boston's previous pennant-winning experience was no small factor. Detroit and Chicago, much-less experienced in comparison, didn't get the job done when the pennant was on the line. In the final analysis, there were good reasons why the Red Sox were headed to the World Series.

CHAPTER X

"Like a thunderstorm, the riot broke out."

There is no doubt the Superbas left Boston at the end of their long journey through the National League both satisfied and tired. Regardless of fatigue, the Dodgers were coming home, not to rest but to play a September 12 doubleheader against the Pirates. The twin bill and the homestand got off to a good start when Pfeffer won his twentieth game before an estimated crowd of 15,000. Supposedly about a third of those in attendance wore their straw hats in a "farewell tour of the summer headgear." The second contest was a different story, however, when Jack Coombs (10–7) suffered another tough defeat, losing, 2–1. Zack Wheat hit safely in both games, pushing his hitting streak to 25 games.[1]

Heading into the ninth inning that same day in Philadelphia, it didn't appear the Phillies were going to take advantage of the Dodger loss. St. Louis, which had already beaten Alexander (28–10) once before, jumped out to a 3–0 lead and still led, 3–2, in the ninth inning. While some of the faint hearted "tottered out through the exits," clutch hitting by Wilbur Good, Dode Paskert and Bert Niehoff tied the game. Milt Stock's long drive to deep center field then drove Paskert across the plate with the winning tally. The Phils were now tied with the Superbas in the loss column, trailing by only a half game overall due to the differential in games played.[2]

Up in Boston, the Braves weren't quite ready to write off 1916. Strapped for pitching in a doubleheader with the Cubs, Stallings resorted to what was becoming a standard 1916 strategy — have the same pitcher, in this case Dick Rudolph (17–9), start both games. In the opener, the Boston ace tossed a shutout, a good thing since his teammates collected only one run in a game that lasted only an hour and 15 minutes. Rudolph then returned to the mound for the second game, "continuing to flash his sarcastic smile" at the Chicago hitters. The Braves' offensive woes continued, but trailing 3–1 in the ninth, a Fred Snodgrass double tied the game at 3–3. Earlier that inning, Rudolph had exited for a pinch-hitter, so he couldn't win the doubleheader. In fact, no one would win it, since the game was called for darkness after 13 innings. The draw meant another twin bill the next day, so at the very least, Rudolph had limited the drain on Boston's already-depleted pitching corps.[3]

A tired pitching staff wasn't a problem for the Giants; their hurlers had thrown seven consecutive complete games. After the sweep of the Phillies, a letdown might have been expected against the last-place Reds. However, New York rallied for a 3–2 win in the series opener behind another complete game, this time from Rube Benton. The Brooklyn split, combined with the Boston and Philadelphia victories, narrowed the gap between the contenders.[4]

Team	Wins	Losses	Games Behind
Brooklyn	78	53	–
Philadelphia	76	53	1
Boston	73	54	3

Incredibly, things became even tighter on September 13, since Brooklyn was in the process of losing its second straight to Pittsburgh, 6–3. Before a small crowd of only 4,000, Sherrod Smith was unable to repeat his strong performance against Boston. Although the Superbas' loss gave the Phils another golden opportunity, Pat Moran and his men only managed a split against St. Louis. Rixey (19–8) was knocked out for the second straight time in a 7–4 opening loss, and Philadelphia was in danger of being swept when the Phils trailed 2–1 in the second game. Gavy Cravath hit a three-run home run over the right-field wall, giving Al Demaree the support he needed to hold on for a 5–4 win. A Philadelphia split accompanied by a Brooklyn loss meant the only difference between the two teams was the Dodgers had played and won one more game.[5]

Nearly as close were the suddenly resurgent Braves, who after losing seven straight had now won four in a row. Stallings' team probably surprised itself in using its offense to sweep the Cubs, 7–3 and 11–6. The offense and defense received a big shot in the arm with the return of Rabbit Maranville, who had five hits in the doubleheader along with some of his typically great defensive play. Boston racked up 18 runs on 28 hits in the twin bill, which enabled Stallings to use his limited pitching resources creatively. Reulbach started the first game and lasted into the fifth inning before being relieved by Lefty Tyler, who shut the Cubs out the rest of the way. When Chicago knocked out Jess Barnes in the first inning of the nightcap, Stallings came back with Reulbach, who pitched the rest of the way for the victory. Boston now joined the Phils and Dodgers with 54 losses, trailing Brooklyn by only the two additional games the Dodgers had played and won. This was no small accomplishment given the Braves' injury problems, and Flatley had reason to call Boston the "gamest team in baseball" in "the most maddening baseball melee in history." The Braves weren't the only team to sweep a doubleheader on the thirteenth as the Giants, bolstered by Ferd Schupp's three-hit shutout of the hapless Reds, also won twice. Amazingly, the eight straight wins, coinciding with the Dodgers' slump, brought John McGraw's team to within eight games in the loss column.[6]

After another win on September 14, it was clear the New Yorkers were playing the best baseball in the National League. Attempting to make up an 8½ game deficit this late in the season reminded Damon Runyan of the old story about the man in jail asking a passerby the time. Back came a question as to why it mattered since the "jailbird" wasn't going anywhere. In Runyan's opinion, the Giants weren't going anywhere either. Given the performance of the leaders that day, it seemed uncertain whether anyone was going anywhere. After being thrown out of two consecutive games in Philadelphia, Bob Bescher of the Cardinals decided to stick around for the entire contest. That was bad news for the Phils since the St. Louis outfielder won the game with a grand slam home run, while Philadelphia suffered its second loss to Mule Watson, a former Class D minor league pitcher.[7]

The caliber of play in the major leagues was supposed to be far above the Southern Association, but that premise seemed very questionable on September 14. In Boston, the Braves' offense reverted to form, suffering a 2–0 blanking by Hubert Scott Perry, fresh from the league's Atlanta franchise. At the same time, Brooklyn was struggling with the Pirates' Burleigh Grimes, up from Birmingham, also of the Southern Association. Tied 2–2 in the bottom of the ninth, the Dodgers had a man on second with two out. Just as Larry Cheney (16–10) came to bat, the score of Boston's loss was posted, joining the news of Philadelphia's defeat. Although the crowd was calling for Fred Merkle as a pinch-hitter, Robinson made another good decision by staying with Cheney, who doubled in the winning run. Brooklyn had an easier time the next day, September 15, when the Dodgers exploded for eight runs in the second inning of a rain-shortened victory over the Pirates. Zack Wheat hit an inside-the-park grand slam home run, extending his hitting streak to 28 games. Everything else was rained out, including the Giants-Reds contest, which was stopped just in time to prevent Cincinnati from ending New York's winning streak.[8]

Team	Wins	Losses	Games Behind
Brooklyn	80	54	—
Philadelphia	77	55	2
Boston	75	55	3

The Dodgers' second series against the western teams opened in Brooklyn on Saturday, September 16, where the Reds and Superbas played to a 1–1 tie in the second game of a doubleheader after Robby's team won the first game, 4–3. Jack Coombs (11–7) finally won a close affair in the opener with help from Rube Marquard, who got the last out on one pitch. The "enormous crowd" of 20,000 fans then sat through a 12-inning pitcher's duel between Pfeffer (20–9) and Toney before the game was called on account of darkness. The second contest also saw Zack Wheat's hitting streak end at 29. The tie was bad news since another doubleheader would be necessary on Monday. Still, it was a day for big crowds in New York, as more than 22,000 saw the Giants extend their winning streak to 11 games by sweeping the Pirates, 8–2 and 4–3. Meanwhile, down in Philadelphia, another large gathering watched the Phils easily sweep two games from the Cubs. Alexander (29–10) won the first, while in the second Demaree pitched a shutout, aided by two home runs from Gavy Cravath. Although his 10 round-trippers for the year were well behind Gavy's 1915 totals, a hot bat for the Philadelphia slugger could greatly improve the Phillies' pennant chances. In Boston, the Braves also got off to a quick start, leading 5–0 in the second before coasting behind Dick Rudolph's (18–9) four-hitter.[9]

Sunday was a day of rest for the players but not the writers, who had plenty of material for their columns. Fred Lieb believed the Braves had overachieved to the extent Stallings deserved the title "Miracle Man" more in 1916 than in 1914. Lieb, more prophetic than he knew, felt on paper even the last place "Reds have it all over him (Stallings)." The writer was also very impressed with John McGraw's rebuilt club and would prove even more prophetic when he said, "It is easier to tell who will win the 1917 National League pennant (New York) than the 1916 gonfalon." In Philadelphia, the concern about some less-than-honest play surfaced in James Isaminger's column in the *North American*. Sharing the concerns of some Boston writers, the scribe felt that if the Dodgers had promised Lew McCarty some World Series money before trading him to the Giants, "It will throw a stain on the 1916 pennant."[10]

Stained or otherwise, Brooklyn first had to win the pennant, and the Dodgers made little progress in that direction on September 18, splitting another doubleheader with the last-place Reds. After winning the first game, 6–1, behind Larry Cheney (17–10), they scored only one for Rube Marquard in a 2–1, 10-inning loss in the nightcap. With that result, Philadelphia closed to within one game (tied in the loss column), beating the Cubs for the third straight time, 6–1, as Rixey won his 20th. Also tied in the loss column was Boston, which defeated the now-passive Cardinals, 2–0. It was an impressive performance by Lefty Tyler, who not only threw a three-hit shutout but drove in both runs. Flatley pulled no punches, saying the Cards were "not trying."

Although supposedly out of it, the Giants also picked up ground with a 2–0 win in the opener of a doubleheader against Pittsburgh before rain ended the second game as a 1–1 tie. In the victory, Ferd Schupp had another impressive performance with a three-hit shutout.[11]

The tie didn't slow down McGraw's team, as they won the replay the next day in addition to the regularly scheduled September 19 game. After an easy 9–2 triumph in the opener, Jeff Tesreau went the distance, New York prevailing, 5–1, in the second game. In spite of the two victories, New York picked up only a half game on the Dodgers, who beat the Reds, 3–1, despite being out-hit 12–7. Boston also kept pace, completing a sweep of the Cards with a 6–3 win, sparked by a three-run, inside-the-park home run by Maranville. The Phils weren't so fortunate because even Alexander (29–11) couldn't overcome an offense that scored only one run and a defense that handed the Cubs two unearned scores. The standings of the contenders now had to be expanded to include the Giants.[12]

Team	Wins	Losses	Games Behind
Brooklyn	83	55	—
Philadelphia	80	56	2
Boston	78	55	2½
Giants	73	62	8½

In praising Stallings' 1916 managerial performance, Fred Lieb said on paper the last-place Reds were as good as the third-place Braves. He was probably exaggerating for effect, but the results of the three-game series against hapless Cincinnati were too painfully real. Mathewson's club may have been as surprised as anyone on September 20 when the Reds erupted for 12 runs on 17 hits against Rudolph (18–10), and according to Flatley, once again effectively put Boston out of the race. One reason for his negativity was the Superbas, who broke a 2–2 tie in the seventh inning to win, 4–2, against St. Louis. Meanwhile across the bridge, the Giants rallied for a 4–2 victory behind Ferd Schupp. Pitching for the second time in three days and not as dominant as he had been, the hurler still limited the Cubs to an earned run.[13]

Meanwhile, down in Philadelphia, an estimated 15,000 fans showed up for a weekday doubleheader against the Pirates. Having lost the day before with Alexander on the mound, the Phils needed a strong performance from Al Demaree in the first game. They got more than they could have imagined, as the hurler joined a very select group. The first contest was scoreless in the bottom of the sixth, but with two out, Philadelphia scored seven times, and Demaree completed the shutout. During the 10-minute break between games, Erskine Mayer warmed up, but Demaree asked to pitch the second game as well. Aided by some Pittsburgh errors and misplays, he took a 2–1 lead into the ninth inning before the Pirates rallied to tie the score. Moran's team, however, loaded the bases in the bottom half and won the game on Mamaux's wild pitch. The fans, who had been transformed into a "howling mob of pennant fanatics," stormed the field and tried unsuccessfully to carry Demaree off on their shoulders, settling instead for Pat Moran. A more tangible reward was awaiting the pitcher in the clubhouse, as Phils president William Baker presented him with a $100 check for the feat, which enabled Philadelphia to pick up a half game on Brooklyn.[14]

The last thing any of the contenders needed was a distraction, but when the Superbas, Phils and Braves were authorized to print World Series tickets, it became just that in Brooklyn. The top price of $5 produced significant outrage from Dodger fans, especially since that cost applied to the first seven rows of the second level in addition to the first level. Things calmed down a bit when it became clear the prices weren't set by Brooklyn owner Charles Ebbets but by the National Commission. On the field, a World Series was looking more likely for the Superbas when they defeated the Cards, 6–3, on September 21, while both Philadelphia and Boston lost. The victory saw an atypical poor performance by Jack Coombs (11–7), who didn't make it through the second inning. Fortunately, Larry Cheney (18–10) was ready to step in, and allowed only an unearned run the rest of the way. In the Hub City, World Series tickets were probably the last thing on anyone's mind when Hal Chase's triple in the seventh broke a 4–4 tie, sending the Braves to their second straight loss to the cellar-dwelling Reds.[15]

Things were no better in Philadelphia, where the Phils followed the prior day's strong showing by taking the day off against Pittsburgh, or at least that was Nasium's view. Both Brooklyn and New York had been fortunate to avoid defeat at the hands of rookie Burleigh Grimes. The Phillies and Eppa Rixey (20–9) weren't so lucky, as Pittsburgh scored three times in the first and went on to an 8–3 victory. Back in New York, it was business as usual; the Giants "simply overran and crushed the opposition," shutting out the Cubs, 4–0, behind Pol Perritt for their sixteenth consecutive win.[16]

Little changed in the standings on September 22, as Brooklyn, Philadelphia and New York all won while the Braves suffered through the end of an ignominious sweep at the hands of the Reds. The Dodgers won easily, routing the Cardinals, 11–1, behind Marquard. The only bad news for Brooklyn centered on Zack Wheat, who was out of the lineup with a bruised hip. It was uncertain how long that would remain the case. Philadelphia also won relatively easily, 7–4, in a game that featured Gavy Cravath's 11th home run. But in what was supposedly the "home of big things," Stallings' team lost again to the lowly Reds. Cincinnati won, 8–5, in a debacle that included five Boston errors. With Flatley's negativity undoubtedly at its boiling point, Boston was closer to fourth place than first. That was partially because the Giants won their 17th straight with a second consecutive shutout of the Cubs. Chicago manager Joe Tinker apparently considered the upcoming series with Brooklyn a higher priority, holding back his ace, Jim Vaughn, for the opener at Ebbets Field. This was part of a grudge dating back to 1913, and the Cub manager wanted "above all things to beat Brooklyn." He would certainly have his chance in a six-game set against the first-place Superbas.[17]

Even if Phillies manager Pat Moran didn't know of Tinker's supposed animosity toward the Dodgers, he was probably well aware Vaughn was a likely candidate to pitch in the September 23 doubleheader in Brooklyn. The doubleheaders in these final series against the West presented both challenges and opportunities. Philadelphia was fortunate to have only one twin bill, while Brooklyn and New York had two with a Sunday off in between. The Braves and their overextended pitching staff, meanwhile, would play three in four days. Faced with two games on September 23 and a reasonable probability of at least one Brooklyn loss because Vaughn was pitching, Moran's challenge was to figure out how to win both games against the upset-minded Reds.

Given Al Demaree's doubleheader victory on September 20, he didn't have to look far for ideas. Since Alexander (31–11) was already slated to start the first game, it seems reasonable to believe the Phils' manager was already thinking of trying the same thing with his ace. The Reds put men on against Alexander in the first contest but couldn't score, and the Phils broke it open on Bert Niehoff's three-run home run, winning, 7–3. During the 10-minute respite between games, Philadelphia retired to the center field clubhouse. One of the first to appear outside was Demaree, who took a few warm-up pitches. Shortly thereafter, Alexander returned to the field in uniform. Since earlier in the season he watched second games from the press box, it wasn't hard for fans to figure out what was going on, and a loud cheer went up. Grover Cleveland took a few practice throws and signaled he was ready. And was he ready, shutting the Reds out on only 78 pitches to win the contest, 4–0, against Cincinnati ace Fred Toney. Incredibly, both games took all of two hours and thirty-six minutes to play after the second went an hour and seven minutes. When Alexander arrived at the clubhouse, the now customary $100 check was awaiting him. Two Phils pitchers had now pitched complete-game wins in both ends of a doubleheader in the same week. Moran's gamble had paid off, and Alexander would have four days off before the first game in Brooklyn.[18]

At one point during the twin bill, "the big throng rose and cheered madly," even though nothing special was taking place on the field. "The fans cheered for fully five minutes ... hats were thrown on to the field and there was a tremendous demonstration." The crowd in Baker Bowl was reacting to the score of the first Dodgers-Cubs game at Ebbets Field. As feared by Brooklyn and hoped for by everyone else, Vaughn defeated the Superbas, 3–1. An estimated 20,000 fans saw a doubleheader consisting of "two madhouse games." Jack Coombs (11–8) opposed Vaughn in the first one, and once again lost a close match-up, although this time Colby Jack had to bear a lot of the responsibility. A poor decision by Coombs in the eighth, followed by his wild pitch, led to two Cubs runs that broke a 1–1 tie.

"Colby Jack" Coombs was a key member of the Brooklyn pitching staff (George Bain Collection, Library of Congress).

Fortunately for Wilbert Robinson, he had more than one stopper; Jeff Pfeffer allowed just one run in the second game for his 23rd victory, which was stopped after seven innings due to darkness. Throughout the twin bill, there was constant arguing with the umpires, who in the view of Chicago sportswriter James Crusinberry, seemed to favor Brooklyn. Crusinberry had an explanation for this as well, suggesting Charles Rigler's spring training job as the Dodgers groundskeeper led him to favor the Superbas.[19]

Fan interest also remained high in Manhattan, where more than 25,000 traveled to the Polo Grounds for a September 23 Giants-Cardinals doubleheader which at this point had little significance in the pennant race. The interest, of course, was in New York's winning streak, and the fans weren't disappointed since McGraw's team swept reeling St. Louis, 6–1 and 3–0. Playing the "boldest baseball," which featured aggressive baserunning, both wins tied the modern record of 19 straight set by the 1906 White Sox. Tesreau held the Cards to one meaningless run in the first game, while Benton shut them out on three hits in a rain-shortened second game. In Boston the Braves were concerned about a different kind of streak — three straight losses to the last-place Reds. In the first of three consecutive doubleheaders against Pittsburgh, Boston jumped on Mamaux for four runs in the first two innings of the opener and held on to win, 4–2, behind Rudolph (18–10). If the prospect of three doubleheaders in four days wasn't bad enough, the two teams played to a 1–1, 13-inning tie in the second contest, leading to speculation of a tripleheader on Tuesday.[20] As the teams headed into the last two weeks of the season, the gap in the loss column continued to shrink.

Team	Wins	Losses	Games Behind
Brooklyn	87	56	—
Philadelphia	85	57	1½
Boston	79	58	5
New York	78	62	7½

Once again, the Saturday doubleheaders gave sportswriters plenty of material for their columns. Understandably, the main topics were the impending last two series between the contenders and the Giants' winning streak. Joe Vila believed Pat Moran would pitch Alexander on Thursday and Saturday, with Demaree starting the middle game. Meanwhile, Sid Mercer felt the schedule favored the Phils, as they would play Boston in the last series while the Dodgers faced red-hot New York. Moreover, Mercer had no concern about the Giants' effort in those games due to the enmity between John McGraw and Brooklyn owner Charles Ebbets. Watching New York attempt to tie the 1906 Chicago record on September 23 was Art Irwin, shortstop of the 1884 Providence Grays, who held the Major League record of 20 straight wins. According to Damon Runyan, Irwin seemed to think the Giants might be the superior team with one exception — Providence's pitching ace, "Old Hoss" Radbourn, who had won 18 of the 20 games in the streak. Radbourn's record that year made Alexander's 1916 season look like a vacation, as the pitcher started 73 of his team's 114 games, working 678 innings and compiling a 59–12 record. Over in Brooklyn, one question was why the Dodgers hadn't emulated the other three eastern teams and tried to use one hurler in both games of a doubleheader. According to Tom Rice, Robinson said there was no need since there was little drop off among his five starters. In another interesting aside, given earlier comments about Tinker's desire to beat Brooklyn, Rice reported Cubs manager Joe Tinker denied having a grudge against the Dodgers.[21]

Grudge or not, Chicago was doing its best to destroy Brooklyn's pennant hopes. Trailing, 3–0, in the first game of the September 25 doubleheader, the Cubs tied it in the eighth and won, 7–4, in ten innings. When booing broke out in the 10th from the Superbas' faithful, Ebbets rose and tried to say something. It is hard to imagine what he could have said that would have made any difference, but no one ever found out since the crowd shouted him down. Fortunately Brooklyn's pitching depth again paid off, as Marquard "pitched a masterly game," winning the nightcap, 4–2.[22]

Down in Philadelphia, Pat Moran started Eppa Rixey (21–9) in the Monday, September 25, match-up with Cincinnati. It was the right choice, as the pitcher threw a shutout in a 4–0 victory. According to one source, Eppa was now the likely starter of the Friday game in Brooklyn since Demaree would apparently not pitch due to a lack of prior success at Ebbets Field. Meanwhile in Boston, Flatley, who had written off the Braves, changed directions after their sweep of the Pirates put Boston back in the race. After winning easily behind Tyler, 5–0, in the first game, the Braves went with ancient Ed Reulbach in the second contest. Trailing, 2–1, in the sixth, the pitcher tripled to start a two-run rally that put Boston ahead, 3–2. Then, in the top of the eighth, after the leadoff batter tripled, Reulbach turned back Pittsburgh without a run. The victory brought the Braves to within one game of Brooklyn in the loss column, while Philadelphia was now tied with the Superbas in the loss column and trailed by only a half game overall.[23]

While the pennant race was becoming even closer, history was made at the Polo Grounds. In the first game, the Giants parlayed an unearned run and a two-hit shutout by Schupp to defeat St. Louis, 1–0. Having squeaked that one out, McGraw's team took no chances, taking a 5–0 lead after four innings and coasting to a 6–2 record-setting win. The biggest challenge for the sportswriters was finding new superlatives for the Giants, who were "playing the most sensational baseball imaginable." After two contests filled with "breathless moments," the estimated 10,000 fans had just enough energy left to issue a huge, collective sigh of relief. A moment later they apparently recovered their collective voice, giving a "cheer that boomed from Brush Stadium and reverberated across the prosaic Harlem." It was, indeed, a historic moment, and the New York *Times* writer couldn't have realized how prophetic he was when he predicted the new record "will probably stand for many more years than the Providence mark."[24]

Anyone who thought things couldn't get closer or more dramatic wasn't paying attention. Boston enjoyed its doubleheader sweep so much the Braves decided to do it again on September 26, winning, 3–0 and 2–1, over the Pirates. Art Nehf and Fred Allen, both just back from the sick list, pitched complete games. Meanwhile, at the Polo Grounds, in what was probably an anticlimax, the Giants won easily again, defeating the Cardinals, 6–1, behind Slim Sallee. The real drama that day was provided by the Phils, who trailed the Reds, 2–1, with one out and no one on in the ninth. To make matters worse, the latest update from Brooklyn showed the Dodgers ahead, sending a large part of the crowd toward the exits. However, aggressive baserunning by Cravath (of all people) and his pinch-runner, Claude Cooper, tied things up. Moments later, Bert Niehoff laid down a bunt to drive in the winning run and sent those who stayed home happy. The win wasn't just dramatic, but crucial because the Dodger score held up as Jeff Pfeffer (24–9) defeated the Cubs, 4–1. Brooklyn and Philadelphia were tied in the loss column, Boston had one more defeat, and unbelievably, the Giants were only 6½ out.[25]

Team	Wins	Losses	Games Behind
Brooklyn	89	57	—
Philadelphia	87	57	2
Boston	83	58	3½
New York	81	62	6½

From a financial standpoint, it might have been better for the Braves and Pirates to have played a tripleheader on September 26. The idea, however, had been vetoed, leaving the teams with an extra game to play and no convenient time to play it. As a result, Boston's last home game of 1916 was conducted on "gray and gloomy" Wednesday morning of September 27 before a reported "crowd" of 642 fans. At least anyone who had snuck out of work wasn't gone long since it lasted all of an hour and twenty-seven minutes, as Tyler shut out the Pirates on four hits. Clearly, Boston hadn't quit after being swept by the Reds, winning six straight from Pittsburgh due to dominating performances from its starters, who gave up only six runs in seven games, including the 1–1 tie. Amazingly, the Braves were still in it, but their remaining 10 games would be on the road.[26]

Boston had gotten no closer than three games overall because Brooklyn defeated the Cubs, 2–0, on September 27 in what Rice felt was Sherrod Smith's best performance of the year. Tinker came back with Vaughn, who could've benefited from a few more warm-up tosses because Myers and Daubert each tripled on the first pitch to provide Smith the only run he would need. The Dodgers' win ensured the Phillies had to sweep the upcoming series in order to take first place. At the Polo Grounds, the Giants trailed St. Louis, 2–0, going to the bottom of the ninth, causing most of the crowd to head for the exits. However, with two on and two out, Buck Herzog hit a two-strike pitch to the right-field wall for a triple, tying the contest. New York went on to win its 23rd straight contest on a wild pitch an inning later, and those who had kept the faith, justifiably went wild.[27]

On the concluding day of the final western homestand, Philadelphia enjoyed an unusual open date. However, it wasn't a day off, as Moran had his players out at Baker Bowl for a morning workout. Many of the Phils, including their manager, then went to watch the hapless A's at Shibe Park; at least part of their motivation was to keep track of the Brooklyn-Cubs game. After learning the disappointing result, the Phillies boarded an 8:00 P.M. train at North Philadelphia Station, with a well-rested Grover Cleveland Alexander slated to pitch games one and three of a three-game set. Joe Vila spoke for most observers when he said, "Alexander stands between the Robins and the pennant, therefore, and it will require the hardest kind of baseball to conquer him."[28]

Vila had further speculated that four days of rest might hurt Alexander. A "seething mass of wildly excited humanity" at Ebbets Field on Thursday, September 28, may have had the same thoughts or hopes once Grover Cleveland (32–11) unleashed his first pitch. The ball "hit the grandstand on the first bound," and Alexander uncharacteristically went on to walk Hi Myers, but nothing came of it. Cheney (18–12), who struggled in the first, wasn't so fortunate in the second. Aided by his throwing error in that frame, Philadelphia got off to a three-run lead, never a good thing with Alexander on the mound. Brooklyn got one back in the third, but things got totally out of hand in the fourth when Cheney lost his control. Having seen more than enough, Robinson brought in Coombs, who allowed a two-strike, bases-loaded single to Alexander. Bad went to worse when the ball rolled past Wheat in left field, allowing all three runners to score. Colby Jack pitched well after that, suggesting perhaps he, not Cheney, should have started. Unfortunately, Coombs was probably now unavailable for the rest of the series. It seemed the pressures of the pennant race were getting to Tom Rice. In a comment directed specifically at Jim Nasium, Jim Isaminger and other Philadelphia writers, Rice claimed that despite the loss, the Phils "did not get the goats of the Superbas a darned bit." The Philadelphia scribes obviously drew different conclusions. Nasium reported Brooklyn was "shrouded in gloom," while William Brandt of the *Record* claimed, "It is admitted all over New York that the Dodgers are done."[29]

Brandt was exaggerating when he wrote "all New York went to the ball games" that day, but baseball fever had certainly seized the city. The estimated 35,000 fans who made their way to Coogan's Bluff saw the Giants extend their winning streak to a mind-boggling 25 with a pair of shutouts, dealing a major, if not fatal, blow to the Braves' pennant hopes in the process. In the opener, Tesreau and Rudolph (18–11) hooked up in a pitchers duel that saw New York prevail, 2–0. The Giants broke open the second contest in the third when Benny Kauff hit an inside-the-park grand slam home run. The crowd celebrated in "a riot of joy," prompting veteran reporter Sam Crane to say, "I have never seen a more demonstrative crowd." William Macbeth of the *Tribune* claimed the atmosphere exceeded that of the Fall Classic, saying, "Nothing at a World Series approached the ardor spilled through Brush Stadium yesterday afternoon." The crowd cheered their heroes to what Macbeth described with unknowing foresight as "a record that will outlive the century." Although he had a safe lead, Schupp never let up, pitching a one-hit shutout for his sixth straight win that included four shutouts and a total of just three runs

Ferdinand Schupp of the New York Giants won six straight games in dominant fashion during the Giants' 26-game winning streak before facing Coombs in a crucial October 2 contest (George Bain Collection, Library of Congress).

allowed on 17 hits. And while the Braves lost twice, they still didn't quit, the *Times* noting, "The players acted as if the future of the universe was at stake." Perhaps speaking for not just this day but for all of 1916, Walter Trumbell of *The World* wrote, "There were fine weather and breathless moments and peanuts and rows with the umpires and everything that goes to make up baseball and brings a fan to the end of a perfect day."[30]

Team	Wins	Losses	Games Behind
Brooklyn	90	58	—
Philadelphia	88	57	½
Boston	84	60	4
New York	84	62	5

Once again, the day's results brought the four teams even closer together. Brooklyn actually trailed the Phils in the loss column but remained in first since the Dodgers had two more wins. Especially hard to believe was that McGraw's team, 15 games out at the end of the last western swing, was now only one game out of third and only five out of first. Just in case anyone had missed the point, Sam Crane told his readers, "Do not think for a moment the Giants are out of it." Given the impact of the weather on the 1916 National League schedule, it should have come as no surprise that rain would intervene one more time. Both the Phillies-Dodgers and Giants-Braves games on Friday, September 29, fell victim to precipitation that blanketed the New York area. In Brooklyn, the mandatory day off on Sunday and no open dates the following week left no alternative to a Saturday doubleheader. The only choice was between a morning-afternoon separate-admission twin bill or two games in the afternoon. Since reserved seats for Saturday were supposedly sold out, rain checks from Friday's game couldn't be honored for a single admission doubleheader; Ebbets understandably wanted to play morning and afternoon games. This required the agreement of the Phils and team president William Baker, and Manager Moran left the decision to the players, who voted unanimously for separate admissions. The morning game would start at 10:30 A.M. The pitching match-ups were unclear, other than the fact that Alexander would start the second game.[31]

The rain had an even greater impact at the Polo Grounds since the Giants led 1–0 with only three outs between an official game and consecutive victory number 26 when the contest had to be called. Boston and New York already had a doubleheader scheduled for Saturday, which generated speculation of a tripleheader. McGraw vetoed the idea because he didn't want to put the winning streak at risk by trying to win three times in one day. Not playing the contest made it almost impossible for New York to win the pennant, but given the long odds, the Giants manager was apparently more concerned with finishing third.[32]

Including the game stopped by rain, New York's pitching staff had a streak of 22 shutout innings against the Braves, and the hurlers weren't finished. In the opener of Saturday's doubleheader, Rube Benton threw a one-hit shutout for the Giants' 26th straight win. The scoreless streak then lasted three innings into the second game before Boston finally broke through with two runs in the fourth. However, New York came back to tie it in the fifth, and the game remained knotted in the seventh. Ed Konetchy led off with a single against Giant starter Slim Sallee, and then with an 0–2 count, J. Carlisle Smith hit a home run into the left-field bleachers. Magee followed with another home run even further than Smith's blast. The Braves had three runs, but they also weren't done, scoring twice more for an 8–3 win. Finally the streak was over, after 26 straight Giant victories, a string that saw them defeat each team at least once. The defeat also marked New York's final home game, played in front of a crowd estimated at 38,000-plus, some of whom "stood ten deep in the rear of the two tiers."[33]

Across the East River, two smaller crowds saw the Dodgers and Phils play for much higher stakes. Whether it was the early hour, cold weather "with a brisk raw wind" or annoyance over the separate admissions, only an estimated 7,000 fans attended the morning affair. Perhaps they had a premonition of bad things, with Philadelphia scoring early and often on its way to a 7–2 win and first place. Fred Luderus continued to feast on Brooklyn pitching, hitting two doubles and a home run. A number of reporters commented on the Dodgers' listless play and lack of aggressiveness, which led to boos from the hometown crowd. The one negative for the Phils was a leg injury to their shortstop, Davy Bancroft.[34]

When the first game ended around noon, the two teams adjourned to their locker rooms for rest and refreshment. It would be hard to imagine two more contrasting atmospheres. The Phils, back in first place for the first time since May, had to feel their long quest to win the pennant was nearly over. Even better, with their ace Alexander going in the afternoon game, Philadelphia players had every reason to believe they would return home with a 1½ game lead. Reportedly, the Phils were "whooping it up" with a quartet of players rehearsing "Tessie" in anticipation of a World Series rematch with the Red Sox. Things even looked hopeful for Bancroft; after trainer Mike Dee worked on his leg, the shortstop's name was inserted in the starting lineup for the second game. The situation was much different in the Superbas' locker room, but the mood was determination, not despair. The players' faces were "set" as they "talked in the tone of men resolved to retrieve themselves." At one point, Robinson addressed his team, and mincing no words, he "read the riot act to them" and "demanded a victory." The players reportedly "answered in one voice" with a terse "you'll get it Robbie."[35]

As was reported all week, Alexander started the second contest on one day's rest, a decision that merits some second guessing. Since the Phils had won the first two, it might have been better to save him for the upcoming six games in four days against the Braves. Moran's team had limited pitching depth and would need all of it against Boston. In any event, it was Alexander for Philadelphia, and the Dodgers countered with Rube Marquard. The game began in "cold and blowy" football-like conditions in front of roughly 16,000, less than a sellout.

The top of the first did little for Brooklyn's morale since the Phils took a 1–0 lead. Unfortunately, Philadelphia again lost Davy Bancroft, who suffered another leg injury. He was carried to the locker room, done for the game and probably longer. Sometimes, one run was all Alexander needed, but fortunately for the Superbas, they tied the contest in the bottom of the first. Suddenly things changed, with Marquard shutting down the Phils, while the Superbas threatened twice but failed to score. Finally in the bottom of the fifth inning, as Tom Rice joyfully reported, Casey Stengel "fell upon the second pitch, and the second pitch fell upon the pavement outside of the right field wall" for a 2–1 Brooklyn lead. Brooklyn added single runs in the sixth and seventh, and Moran finally removed Alexander (32–12) for a pinch-hitter in the eighth inning. Brooklyn put the finishing touches on a 6–1 win when

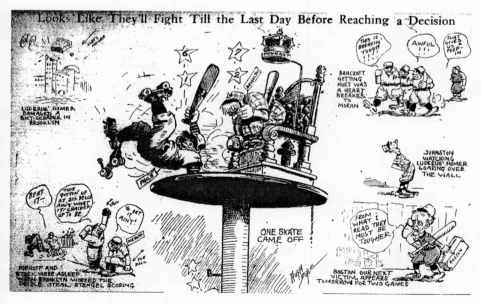

Hugh Doyle's commentary on the Phils-Dodgers September 30 doubleheader (Philadelphia *Press*, October 1, 1916).

Zack Wheat caught a fly ball for the last out, and the fans poured on to the field to mob Marquard, who managed to retreat to the dugout. It was the only retreating he did all day, allowing just one hit and two base runners after the first inning. Alexander, on the other hand, had been touched up for four runs on 11 hits in the biggest game of the year. It marked the third time the Superbas had quickly regained first after having been knocked into second. However, the margin was only a slim half game, meaning the "apoplexy breeding National League race" would now come down to the final series — Brooklyn at home against New York and Boston in Philadelphia.[36]

Team	Wins	Losses	Games Behind
Brooklyn	91	59	—
Philadelphia	89	58	½
Boston	85	61	4
New York	85	63	5

The last mandatory Sunday respite of the season provided the sportswriters a final opportunity to speculate about the outcome of the pennant race. Since Stallings had postponed two September games with the Phillies, the two teams had to play six games in four days, beginning with two doubleheaders. At the same time, the Dodgers and Giants would play four single contests. The math was relatively simple at this point — Philadelphia had to win two more games in its six-game set than Robinson's team won in its four-game series. For example, if Brooklyn won only once, the Phils would have to split with the Braves. Meanwhile, Boston could win the pennant only if the Braves won five of six from the Phillies while the Giants swept Brooklyn. All that was left for New York was the spoiler's role, as the Giants couldn't catch the Superbas. Joe Vila believed the Phils had a difficult task since the Braves had greater pitching depth. Adding to their burden was the injury to Bancroft, as his absence would require Philadelphia to play with an infield that hadn't played together before. The other unknown was the Giants, or more specifically, how well New York would play. Throughout the Giants' winning streak, the "dope" or analysis was the Dodgers would be at a disadvantage playing against the New York juggernaut at season's end. Now that the streak had ended, some felt a letdown was inevitable. There was also the issue of how hard the Giants would try. As noted earlier, there was a consistent theme in the 1916 sports pages that once out of contention, John McGraw might want to see his old friend, Wilbert Robinson, capture the flag. Also of interest were comments by W. J. Macbeth in the New York *Tribune* and Sam Crane in the New York *Evening Journal* that McGraw would have his team play hard because of the amount of money bet on the Giants to finish no lower than third.[37]

Friendship, imagined or real, was apparently considered a more powerful motivator or corrupter than dislike or grudges. In contrast to all the speculation that the Giants favored the Dodgers, an unsigned article in the *Eagle* seemed to be the only show of concern about how hard the Braves would play against the Phils, given Stallings' dislike for Brooklyn. Also mentioned in this piece was the role of gambling, citing a rumor that some of the Giants had bet on an unnamed team (not the Dodgers) to win the pennant. Of more tangible interest was a story in the New York *Tribune* that reported a wealthy guest at the Hotel McAlpin in Brooklyn had wagered $1,000 on the Superbas once Marquard and Alexander were announced as the starters in the second game of the crucial September 30 doubleheader. Supposedly after collecting his winnings, the man gave $250 to Marquard, who shared some of the money with John Meyers (in the form of a suit) and Casey Stengel ($35). Another somewhat less discrete account in the *Record* put the bet at over $500, the gift to Marquard at $200 and named the gambler as Percy Weise, an oil magnate. Weise was supposedly a friend of Jack Coombs and had followed the Dodgers on the last western trip.[38]

Before the Dodgers-Giants match-up, both teams played exhibition games on Sunday. At Ebbets Field, the Superbas' exhibition was between their reserves and some September additions to the roster. New York, however, traveled to Paterson, New Jersey, to take on the Paterson or Doherty Silk Sox, a local semipro team. The Silk Sox had enjoyed an excellent season but lost their two prior major league exhibition games to the Yankees and Philadelphia A's. Not surprisingly, a large crowd of 10,000 gathered to see the record-setting Giants. New York played its regulars with the exception of the catcher and pitcher against Paterson's star hurler, Otto Rettig, who had already hurled the day before. In one more 1916 surprise, Rettig used his "slow ball" to shut the Giants out on three hits while striking out 13. Predictably, there was some questioning of New York's effort, but the Giants had been given a financial incentive for runs and home runs, none of which they collected. Ironically, Rettig had a very brief Major League career, but his only win was a 1922 victory over the St. Louis Browns, a crucial contest since the Browns finished one game short of the top that season.[39]

After this ignominious defeat, McGraw's team arrived at Ebbets Field on "Nap Rucker Day" with newly discovered star pitcher Ferdinand Schupp on the mound. Supposedly, Rucker had been given the option of starting, but declined in favor of Jack Coombs. A relatively large October 2 "washday" crowd, estimated at 15,000, was on hand, although it was reported nearly half of the fans were rooting for the Giants. In the top of the first, New York loaded the bases with two out, bringing Benny Kauff to the plate. Coombs fell behind 3–0 but came back to strike him out on a slow, waist-high pitch that "suddenly dropped into Miller's big glove." Considering Schupp had won six straight games in which he allowed a total of three runs, this was a key out.

The contest remained scoreless in the bottom of the fourth. In light of the controversy that was to erupt over the next few days, this half-inning merits special attention. With one out, Jake Daubert reached first on a ground ball to short that was ruled a hit, but Rice noted "many scorers gave Fletcher an error and they were not all wrong." At least one scribe attributed Fletcher's failure to make the play to a hand injury he suffered in the third inning. The next batter, Hi Myers, struck out, but Daubert was running on the pitch. Rariden's throw to second was perfect, but Buck Herzog dropped the ball, putting a runner in scoring position. Zack Wheat wasted no time taking advantage, "crackling a whistling single to left," and providing Brooklyn a crucial run. Giants left fielder George Burns didn't field Wheat's hit cleanly either, ending any chance of getting Daubert at the plate. Coombs then continued to hold the Giants at bay, aided by George Cutshaw's great catch of a pop fly, to preserve the lead.[40]

Down one run in the eighth, McGraw went to a pinch-hitter for Schupp, but the Giants still failed to score. The Dodgers then added an insurance run off Fred Anderson for a 2–0 win. Schupp was once again brilliant, allowing only an unearned run on four hits. However, this was Coombs' day (13–8), as he shut out New York on six hits for his sixth victory over McGraw's team since 1915. James Sinnot claimed it was the greatest game of Colby Jack's career. Mention should also be made of Wilbert Robinson's decision to pitch Colby Jack in this crucial match-up. No doubt aware of his record against New York, Robinson chose his veteran right-hander even though Cheney and Smith had at least equal rest. Coombs' success in changing speeds, coupled with the off-speed success of the semipro, Rettig, the previous day, suggests that exhibition game could have hurt the Giants' timing. Still, some "disgruntled" fans claimed New York "did not play their best" due to their friendship with Robinson. The complaints included Bennie Kauff's strikeout in the first, even though he never played for or with Robinson. Other observers said the Giants played as if they had a collective hangover and might have been "pulling their punches." However, most writers believed Coombs was simply too dominant.[41]

When the Brooklyn right-hander took the mound earlier that afternoon, the Dodgers were actually in second place because the Phils won the opener of their doubleheader against the Braves. Although some thought Alexander (33–12) was suffering from overwork, he pitched his 16th shutout, even though it was Alex's third start in five days. The loss finally eliminated Boston from the race, but that didn't mean the Braves would quit. While some fans thought

Grover Cleveland would start the second game as well, Al Demaree instead faced off with Ed Reulbach. The score was 1–1 until Stallings' team scored once in the sixth and twice in the seventh while Reulbach held off the Phils. The Braves' win coupled with Brooklyn's victory seriously damaged the Phillies' remaining pennant hopes. Some of the Philadelphia writers were quick to put the blame on Bancroft's absence, but the Phils' lack of offense was equally important. At day's end, Brooklyn was on the brink; if the Dodgers beat the Giants on Tuesday and the Phils lost twice, the Superbas would win the pennant. However, there was little room for error, as the opposite result would put Brooklyn in second place. Nasium captured the mood perfectly, saying the "nerve shattering strife for the baseball supremacy of the National League continued unabated."[42]

Team	Win	Loss	Games Behind
Brooklyn	92	59	—
Philadelphia	90	59	1

Since Boston and Philadelphia were playing their second straight doubleheader on October 3, the first game began before the Giants-Dodgers match-up in Brooklyn. The Phils scored once in the fourth, and when Paskert hit a home run in the fifth, things were looking good. Although the Braves cut the lead in half in the seventh, it looked like Philadelphia would survive after Fitzpatrick hit an "ordinary" ground ball to Stock. However, the ball got by the substitute shortstop before hitting Snodgrass' of the Braves glove on the outfield grass (opposing players typically left their gloves on the field while at bat), causing Paskert to also muff it. The tying run scored on the play, followed shortly thereafter by the go-ahead tally. Boston put two more on the board in the inning to break open a 6–3 victory.[43]

As the Phils' last pennant hopes started to crumble in the seventh inning, Nasium noticed the posting of a "one-sided and suspicious looking score" from Brooklyn. "Suspicious" is a subjective term, but if the game was "one-sided" at the outset, it was in favor of the Giants. In the first, New York got three hits and benefited from three Dodger errors en route to a 3–0 lead, highlighted by Fletcher's two-run home run. While the Superbas made up one run in the second, the Giants got it back in the top of the third, aided by another Brooklyn error. Down 4–1 in the bottom of the inning, the Superbas scored four times to take a 5–4 lead and knock Rube Benton out of the game. New York wasn't done, however, as the Giants rallied against Jeff Pfeffer (25–10), who had relieved Sherrod Smith in the fourth. Perritt (who had come in for Benton) led off with a single but was thrown out at third while trying to advance on Burns' single. Burns went to second on the throw and scored on Robertson's one-base knock to tie the game at five. Things didn't stay that way for long, though, because with two out in the fifth, Olson drove in Mowrey for a 6–5 Brooklyn lead. At some point during the bottom of that inning (accounts differ), John McGraw stormed off the field and wouldn't return for the rest of the season. He wasn't the only unhappy Giant. Fletcher and Benton had words earlier in the contest, and Herzog was reportedly so annoyed with New York's pitching that "it looked as if he was going in and pitch himself."[44]

With a 6–5 lead and Pfeffer now in command, the Superbas added single runs in the next three innings while holding the Giants to a meaningless tally in the ninth. At the end of Brooklyn's 9–6 win, the Phils and Braves were tied in their second game. Erskine Mayer had started against Lefty Tyler, and the Phils took a 1–0 lead on George Whitted's home run. He sprained his ankle in the first game and was basically playing on one leg since this was literally the last chance for Philadelphia. In the sixth, Mayer struck out the first two Braves, but Wilhoit hit one that Whitted could only limp after. The batter ended up on third and scored the tying run on Bert Niehoff's "inexcusable boot." Even though the Dodgers' game was over, many Brooklyn fans waited in the stands while the Superbas changed into their street clothes and sat in the locker room "silent and watchful." Another gathering, this one at the Brooklyn *Daily Times* offices, had followed the Dodgers game on the playograph, hoping for final word of a pennant won. The waiting must have seemed to have lasted an eternity, but finally there was good news; in the Boston seventh, a double by Egan and a throwing error by Phils third baseman Byrne allowed the Braves to take 2–1 lead. Any hopes of one last comeback ended in the eighth when Boston scored four times.[45]

At about 5:30 P.M., in the time it took for the score to reach Brooklyn by telegraph and for a reporter to run to the locker room, the Superbas learned they had indeed won the 1916 National League championship. "Like a thunderstorm, the riot broke out," as some players threw things, while the eyes of others welled up with tears. In response to a demand from his players, Wilbert Robinson tried to say something but "just gurgled." Outside in the gathering twilight, the fans didn't wait for the final result to start celebrating. When the Braves scored in the seventh, "pandemonium broke loose." Most of the crowd left "laughing, grinning from ear to ear," while some staid businessmen were reported to have "skipped along merrily." It was an "inspiring scene," but supposedly nothing like the "demonstration" at the Brooklyn *Daily Times* plaza. The news that Boston had taken a 6–1 lead was greeted with a roar so loud "the air was shattered." Those who swore "swore hard," and those who laughed "laughed hard." Finally, the growing darkness and thoughts of supper and "angry wives and mothers" sent "the devotees of the only game in the world away from the most pleasant sight of the ages for them."[46]

The joy and happiness in Brooklyn was matched by depression and despair in Philadelphia. A number of Phillies fans "quit in disgust" during the second game, some leaving, others staying and jeering. Upon reflection, the fans would most likely recognize how hard and well the Phils had played all year, but that was for another day. Jim Isaminger laid the blame for Philadelphia's failure to repeat on Bancroft's injury, but as damaging as that may have been, the Phils' bats had gone cold at the worst time, producing just seven runs in the first four games of the final series. Perhaps the last words on the Phillies' season properly belonged to Nasium, who said the team reminded him "of a game and courageous gladiator — who has put up a hopeless struggle against greater odds, but has refused to quit."[47]

Ideally, the story of the 1916 National League season would end with the Dodgers' victory while the other contenders were defeated with honor. Unfortunately, that ending wasn't to be. As noted earlier, John McGraw had stormed off the Giants' bench in the Brooklyn half of the fifth. After the game, the New York manager called in reporters and made a statement. McGraw specifically noted he wasn't saying his team didn't play to win the game. At the same time, however, the Giants' skipper claimed the players failed to follow their manager's instructions, and he refused to be associated with such poor baseball. The only specific incident cited by McGraw was Pol Perritt's working from a full wind-up with runners on base.

There was also a lack of specifics provided by writers, who felt something was wrong but weren't sure what. James Sinnott used the phrase "weird baseball," claiming the Giants fielded "miserably" and ran and hit as if they didn't care. Their style of play was so "indifferent" the entire press box commented on it. Sinnott went so far as to demand N.L. President John Tener investigate the game, and if he concluded New York hadn't done its best, order it replayed. Exactly how Tener was supposed to objectively measure the Giants' effort wasn't stated. According to the *Times*, the difference between New York's play during their record streak and this game was outs had become infield hits. This apparently referred to the Dodgers' four-run rally in the third inning. A play-by-play account in the *Evening Mail* indicated the rally began with Johnston beating out an infield single, followed by Zimmerman's "fumble" of Daubert's grounder, which was apparently scored a hit. Myers then forced Daubert at second, but Fletcher's throw was wide, failing to complete the twin killing. Next, Wheat beat out a bunt, which "Smith" (a misprint of some kind since no Giant named Smith was in the game at that point) failed to field. It was only after loading the bases without hitting the ball out of the infield that solid hits by Cutshaw and Mowrey enabled the Dodgers to take the lead.

In a counter argument, both Fletcher and Daubert attributed the failure to complete the double play to a hard slide on Jake's part. The Giants' shortstop also claimed his fielding problems were due to a hand injury suffered the day before. A more specific claim was made by Sam Crane, who wrote New York wasn't trying "to make safe hits" when the Giants had a runner on second and one out in the eighth. A review of the *Evening Mail* play-by-play indicates that two batters, Fletcher and Zimmerman, grounded out to second base at that point. In spite of his first-inning home run, Fletcher's name comes up repeatedly, and Joe Vila claimed it was the shortstop's worst game of the year. For all the talk of poor defense, however, the majority of the box scores list only an error for Fletcher and one for George Smith (in relief of Perritt), with no other listing having more than one additional Giant miscue.[48]

Other writers echoed McGraw's claim regarding full wind-ups with runners on base, but while this suggested images of the Dodgers running wild on the base paths, the *Evening Mail* play-by-play lists three stolen bases, all of which came after the Giants' manager left the field. Perritt denied making a full wind-up with runners on base. Pol also claimed the game presented the opportunity to win his 20th of the season, and his failure to do so cost him a bet of about $100. Joe Vila, for one, didn't recall Perritt's inappropriate wind-up, and after talking to him, felt the pitcher's protests of innocence were sincere. However, one aspect of Pol's performance not so easily explained was his lackadaisical baserunning that short-circuited a New York rally in the fifth. The *Times* noted that on his way to third, the Giants' pitcher "stopped short between the bases for a few minutes." Not surprisingly, Tom Rice wasn't buying claims of New York not trying, noting how the Giants rallied to tie the game in the fifth, "some quitting" in Rice's view. George Daley of the *World* felt the accusations were "unfair and absurd." He found it hard to believe a team that wasn't trying would get off to a 3–0 lead in the first inning, and attributed any fall off in New York's play to the end of the 26-game winning streak.[49]

Understandably, Wilbert Robinson and the Dodgers were furious at McGraw's attempt to stain their pennant. Calling the comments "unsportsmanlike," the Brooklyn manager said "he (McGraw) knows very well the Dodgers are superior to the Giants." That superiority was demonstrated by the Superbas' 1916 dominance of New York all year (12–6 before the series began and 15–7 for the season). According to Sam Crane, Jake Daubert said Fletcher told him that while the Giants loved Wilbert Robinson, they loved the bonuses promised by club ownership for a third-place finish even more. Jack Coombs added no team had played Brooklyn harder than the Giants that day, calling the Superbas "names that would make even the Braves blush," high or low praise indeed. Even more understandably, the New York players were furious at McGraw's comments, with both Fletcher and Perritt vehemently denying any lack of effort.[50]

After leaving his team in the middle of a game and setting off a firestorm, McGraw didn't return to the New York bench nor did he retract or expand on his statement. Although some attributed the outburst to the Giant manager's notorious temper, other speculation soon broke out. Given the way gambling permeated baseball in 1916, it's not surprising rumors about lost wagers entered the stage. According to Sid Mercer, this included anger on John's part that unnamed Giant fans had lost "a ton of dough" on bets New York would finish third. Considering McGraw's personal fondness for gambling, it wasn't a big step to imagine him also losing a large amount of money, perhaps as much as $15,000. Since the manager had no further comment, Giants management, in the person of team president Harry Hempstead, had no choice but to make a statement. He attributed the bizarre events and the manager's outburst to the up and down season, the end of the winning streak, and John's belief he would be blamed for any Giant loss to the Dodgers because of his relationship with Robinson. Probably seeking a way out of another controversy with McGraw, NL President Tener decided not to insert himself in this battle, stating it was a matter for team discipline and not for the league. Once again the leadership of Major League Baseball seemed unwilling to confront possible warning signs about how gambling was endangering the game's reputation. And there the matter, but not the debate, ended.[51]

Possible reasons for a lack of effort on New York's part centered on the alleged friendship between McGraw and Robinson. This is more than a little strange, considering the two supposedly didn't speak for 17 years after their 1913 feud. Also of note was the Giants' dislike for the Phillies because three late-season losses to Philadelphia helped cost New York the 1908 pennant. Interestingly, the only two current Giants who were on the 1908 team were Fletcher and Herzog, each of whom played "erratic ball" in both 1916 games. Darker possibilities, however, surfaced in an unsigned Philadelphia *Record* article several days later. The writer mentioned speculation there were deeper motives for McGraw's actions, suggesting that by leaving the team he "may have played a deep game in thus shifting the blame to his players in order to clear himself and his club." After acknowledging the manager's reputation was such there was no real justification for this speculation, the writer went on to disclose some strange behavior by Braves pitcher Ed Reulbach.

After defeating the Phils, 4–1, in the second game of the Monday, October 2 doubleheader, Reulbach was supposedly seen in the "Sub-Treasury," looking to change three $1,000 notes into smaller bills. The player apparently freely admitted the money belonged to a gambler who had won it betting on the Braves. He claimed, however, the players would receive only cigars as a

Hugh Doyle summarizes the controversial conclusion of the National League pennant race (Philadelphia *Press*, October 5, 1916).

reward for their good work, not money. The writer certainly believed Reulbach knew more than he was saying and went on to ask both rhetorically and
dangerously, "If it was worth $3,000 to stop the Phillies, how much do you
suppose it would be worth to stop the Giants in those two games that meant
so much?" Also interesting is the writer's inclusion of Monday's game as well
as Tuesday's ("those two games"). The Superbas' only run off Schupp on Monday was caused by Fletcher's near misplay and an error by Herzog, the two
1908 Giants remaining on the roster who might have wanted to hurt Philadelphia's chances for the pennant. Without that run, Schupp, who was pitching
lights out, would probably have stayed in the game, which might have led to
a different outcome.[52]

There is, of course, no way of proving any of this, but it does seem the
possibilities of a fix were higher for the lower scoring game on Monday. Considering Schupp's dominating September performances and Coombs' season-
long dominance of the Giants, the contest figured to be low scoring, and
therefore, easier to impact. Certainly Kauff could have struck out intentionally, and Fletcher, Herzog and even Burns could have intentionally contributed
to Brooklyn's fourth-inning run. The unsavory reputations of both Kauff and
Herzog certainly add fuel to the metaphorical fire. On the other hand, for all
that was written about Tuesday's game, there is far more speculation than
specifics. In the case of Fletcher, for example, why would he hit a home run
when he was intentionally going to play poorly in the field? If one is given to
looking for deeper conspiracies, like the unnamed Philadelphia writer, then
a possible explanation is McGraw created a controversy on Tuesday to cover
up something far more serious that occurred on Monday. In the final analysis, however, the absence of any real evidence, either then or since, suggests
there wasn't any real fire for all of the smoke. Even if the Giants did try to
aid the Superbas, that in the end didn't solely decide the 1916 pennant race
since just as much depended on what happened in Philadelphia. In addition,
unlike the much shorter World Series, the overall length of a pennant race,
be it 154 or 162 games, prevents it from being fixed or even influenced unduly.
Which bring us to the reason why and how the Brooklyn Superbas finally
won the 1916 National League flag.

Simply put, Brooklyn won because Ebbets and Robinson built the deepest pitching staff in the league, and the Brooklyn manager used that depth to
great advantage. The defending champion Phillies actually won one more
game than the did the prior year, but it wasn't enough because the Dodgers
added 14 wins to their 1915 total. Those additional victories were primarily
due to the 1915 acquisition of Larry Cheney and Rube Marquard. Unwanted
by the Cubs and Giants, they came to Brooklyn and contributed 31 wins in
1916. Since Pfeffer, Coombs and Smith added four more victories to their

combined 1915 total, it's not hard to see the key role pitching played in the Superbas' success. Brooklyn allowed 93 fewer runs in 1916 than in 1915, and this was due to better pitching, as 80 percent of the improvement was in earned runs. Pitching was the tangible reason Brooklyn won, but the intangible reason lies in the Superbas' refusal to quit in the face of adversity. Perhaps the best example is how, after losing seven straight and first place to the Phillies in early September, they came back to beat the best hurler in the National League (Alexander), as well as the hottest pitcher in baseball (Schupp) in consecutive must-win games.[53]

Unlike Brooklyn, but for understandable reasons, the Phils didn't make any major changes heading into 1916, and as a team, they matched their 1915 pennant-winning performance. The two factors that hurt Moran's club were the failure to develop a fourth starter and the dramatic drop-off in Gavy Cravath's offensive production. Philadelphia enjoyed a significant improvement in the pitching of Eppa Rixey in 1916, but this was offset by Erskine Mayers' decline. Cravath, after an incredible 24 home runs and 115 RBIs in 1915, saw those numbers fall to 11 and 70 in 1916. Still, the Phils also never quit, recovering from a four-game sweep to the Giants in early September to briefly take first place on September 30. Alexander and Demaree's doubleheader wins as well as George Whitted playing on one leg at season's end gave tangible witness to Nasium's image of defeated gladiators.[54]

Phils pitchers weren't the only ones carrying a heavy workload, as evidenced by the performance of the Braves' Tom Hughes. After leading the league in appearances with 50 in 1915, Hughes worked in 40 games in 1916 before suffering a season-ending injury on September 7. Both starting and relieving, Hughes was 16–3 at that point with an ERA of 2.35, and it is certainly reasonable to believe this greatly damaged Boston's pennant chances. At the same time, however, the Braves were three games out when Hughes went down and only dropped back another half game the rest of the way. Just staying in the race was a credit to Boston's never-say-die attitude, no matter how many times Nick Flatley gave up. And to their great credit, after being eliminated in the first contest to the Phils on October 2, the Braves never let up, beating Philadelphia three straight times to destroy the Phils' pennant hopes once and for all. If the integrity of the game was damaged during those first few days of October, it wasn't because of the Boston Braves.[55]

It is, in fact, sad such aspersions were cast upon the Giants because they, as much as any team, demonstrated true respect for the game late in the season. Rebuilt for the second time in one season, newly formed New York could have easily played out the string. Instead, the Giants went on the longest winning streak in baseball history, wreaking havoc with the pennant race in the process. John McGraw, who already had a World Series championship and four pennants to his credit, later said setting the record realized his fondest dream. Ironically, the Giants did contribute greatly to the Superbas winning the pennant, but not because of the two games in Brooklyn. In early September, the Giants beat the Phils four straight times while the Dodgers rallied to take three of four from Boston. Even a split of those four games would have put the Phillies in a very different position at the end. Similarly, at season's end, when the Braves closed to within one game of Brooklyn in the loss column, the Giants won the last three games of their streak at Boston's expense. Even though the Braves finally ended New York's winning streak, the three losses all but eliminated Boston from the race. In the final analysis, Brooklyn won the pennant because the Superbas had earned it and could with justifiable pride move on to Boston and the World Series.[56]

CHAPTER XI

"There was not much fight in them after that."

When the dust finally settled, the 1916 season produced a World Series between the Boston Red Sox and Brooklyn Dodgers. After dramatic pennant races between well-matched teams, a Brooklyn-Boston World Series didn't suggest the same level of competition. No doubt, part of this was because Boston had won two of the last four World Series, including 1915, while the Superbas were in the relatively young Fall Classic for the first time. Couple this with American League victories in five of the last six Series, and it wasn't surprising the outcome was seen by many as a foregone conclusion. However, this was still the World Series at a time when baseball was the preeminent national sport, meaning there wouldn't be a lack of interest in the proceedings.

Begun in 1903, the World Series was being played for only the 13th time in 1916. In fact, some still questioned the need for the event. Later in 1916, *Sporting Life* would take the position that the World Series should be abolished, saying among other things that there was little additional prestige for the winner beyond that of winning the pennant. The structure of the Fall Classic was also still being developed, so while there were similarities to today, there were also many differences. The first significant one was the venue, at least for the American League. Although the Boston Braves hadn't won the National League pennant, their new "home of big things" would host World Series play in 1916 as the home field of the Red Sox. With a capacity of 45,000, Braves Field could accommodate far more fans than Fenway's limit of roughly 35,000.[1] While that decision on the part of Red Sox ownership may seem surprising, it's much more understandable in the context of the game's finances in 1916. Unlike today, when television and even radio are the event's economic engines, as in the regular season, the primary source of World Series revenue were gate receipts.

As a result, the Red Sox would rent Braves Field for $1,000 a day, know-
ing they could more than make up that expense with the additional ticket
revenue. Like today, there was revenue sharing with the players in the World
Series, at least for the first four games. The first 10 percent of the gross receipts
went to the game's governing body, the National Commission, while the balance was split on a 30/60 basis between the competing owners and players.
The owners divided their 30 percent equally, and the players' share was split
60/40 between the winners and losers, providing a financial incentive to win.
As an example, in 1912, the victor received just over $4,000 compared to
$2,500 for the losers, a significant amount of money when the average player's
salary was $4,500 annually. Since Brooklyn's Ebbets Field could hold some-
where in the 25–30,000 range, there was even more incentive to maximize
ticket sales at the first two games. Ironically, although Charles Ebbets had the
reputation of being the ultimate bottom line owner, the Dodgers' home games
weren't shifted to the much-larger Polo Grounds.[2]

Typically, a coin toss determined where the series would begin. However, with the National League race undecided until the season's final days,
Ebbets didn't have enough time to prepare his ballpark, and the first two
games went to Boston. The first was set for Saturday, October 7. Sunday, the
eighth, was an off-day, with Game Two in the Hub City on Monday. Despite
the more arduous travel conditions of the time, there was no off-day for travel,
and the third and fourth contests would take place at Ebbets Field on Tuesday and Wednesday. If necessary, the fifth and sixth games would also alter-
nate between Boston and Brooklyn on Thursday and Friday, with the site for
a potential seventh and deciding game to be determined by a coin toss. It was
a grueling schedule to say the least.[3]

While many of the logistics were set, the Red Sox still had to deal with
ticket distribution. This would be no easy task for Joe Lannin, especially since
as Sam Crane claimed, had there been room, 75,000 would have turned out
for Game One. Successful ticket applicants received a card with a number
designating a place in line and a category of seats (i.e., grandstand, pavilion),
but not the specific location. This meant that the better the spot in line, the
better the seats one received in that category, leading to a disorganized if not
chaotic situation. When fans descended upon the Fenway Park ticket offices
on October 5, some were willing to use almost any means necessary to obtain
a better place in line. As a result, a police presence was required to keep everything moving smoothly.

All of this would have been complicated but manageable had the system
not included so many variables. Some fans received the cards at different
times, others never heard notification their application was successful or even
received, and some obtained tickets via mail. Additionally, there never seemed

to be a set date when the club began accepting applications or when fans were able to exchange their cards for tickets. All in all, some officials believed the system created more disappointed fans than in previous seasons. Symptomatic of a problem with broader implications was the individual who mailed in 18 applications and was successful three times. Clearly if this could happen, scalpers or speculators, as they were called then, could and would be a problem. Ticket prices in Boston were $5 for a box seat, $3 for the grandstand, $2 and $1 for the first and third base pavilions, respectively, and 50 cents for a spot in the bleachers. Of course, all tickets cost considerably more on the street.[4]

Although fans throughout the country had far more limited access to the Fall Classic than today, they could upon opening their morning and evening newspapers read articles covering literally dozens of storylines. One unusual feature was ghostwriting, where a player or manager sold his byline to a newspaper, allowing the publication to write a story under his name. This occurred during the regular season, but became extra-intense during the World Series, with the likes of Bill Carrigan, Ty Cobb and Grover Cleveland Alexander selling their bylines for the Fall Classic.

All other issues not withstanding, the one question in the forefront of most minds was the starting pitchers for Game One. In a secretiveness seldom displayed today, Brooklyn manager Wilbert Robinson and his counterpart Bill Carrigan gave few clues to their thinking, especially Rough. Brooklyn's best hitters were left-handed, so Boston southpaws Babe Ruth and Dutch Leonard seemed to be the two most logical candidates. But the story varied from source to source, and Ernie Shore and Carl Mays were getting equal press as possible starters. In typical "manager-speak" for the time, Carrigan wouldn't reveal a starter on the eve of Game One.[5]

On the Brooklyn side, there seemed to be clear consensus that Rube Marquard, a two-time reclamation project of Wilbert Robinson, would get the start. Marquard was 13–4 with an ERA of just 1.58, and had defeated the Red Sox twice in the 1912 World Series. Like Brooklyn, Boston also had a significant left-handed presence in its lineup, which argued for pitching the Dodger southpaw. Other Brooklyn pitchers that figured to see action were 20-game winner Jeff Pfeffer (25–11, 1.92) as well as Larry Cheney (18–12), 1.92), Jack Coombs (13–8, 2.66) and Sherry Smith (14–10, 2.34). Smith, Brooklyn's other left-handed starter, was receiving little to no press but would play a memorable part in the proceedings.[6]

Boston would be without the services of Rube Foster, but Carrigan still had plenty of pitching strength. At 22–11 with a 1.75 ERA, Ruth was the ace of the staff but had never pitched in a World Series. He and fellow southpaw Dutch Leonard (17–12, 2.36) figured to present problems to Brooklyn's best hitters, left-handed-batting Jake Daubert and Zack Wheat. The Red Sox also boasted Ernie Shore (14–10 2.63) and submariner Carl Mays (18–12, 2.39). Therefore, it was no surprise experts such as Grantland Rice and Hugh Fullerton gave the pitching advantage to Boston.[7]

As with pitching, most "dopesters" believed the Red Sox defense was far superior to that of Brooklyn. At first glance, that wasn't necessarily true since the Superbas' overall .968 fielding percentage was only slightly lower than Boston's .972. Further analysis, however, indicated Carrigan's team held an edge on defense, especially in the critical area of the middle infield. Brooklyn second baseman George Cutshaw (37) and shortstop Ivy Olson (45) had committed a whopping 82 errors between them. If this wasn't enough, Ollie O' Mara, who also played shortstop for the Dodgers, kicked in another 26 miscues. Although Red Sox second baseman Hal Janvrin, subbing for the injured Jack Barry, had a team-high 29 errors, shortstop Everett Scott had just 16 for a combined total of 45, or as many as Olson alone.[8]

Experts did give the offensive edge to Brooklyn, though it wasn't as if there was a real significant advantage. The Dodgers had a team batting average of .258 compared to Boston's .246, and Brooklyn scored 59 more runs over the course of the season. Further analysis, however, suggested the Dodgers had trouble hitting in the clutch, as they registered only four more runs than the runner-up Phillies, even though Brooklyn batters had 122 more hits. The Superbas' offense started with its two .300 hitters, Jake Daubert (.321) and Zack Wheat (.315), the latter being the Superbas' home run and RBI leader with nine and 72, respectively.[9]

Boston had no one who could match this production, especially in the power department. Any argument for the Red Sox offense was based on clutch hitting, particularly with the way Duffy Lewis and Harry Hooper had gotten hot late in the season. Carrigan's offense was led by Larry Gardner's .305 batting average, with no home runs but 56 RBIs. Additionally, Brooklyn had other batters who could drive in runs, with Cutshaw, Mowrey and Stengel each producing 50-plus RBIs. Besides Gardner, on the Boston side, only Duffy Lewis was that productive. The Red Sox would have to show they could win a World Series without the bats of Tris Speaker and Jack Barry and also overcome the weak hitting of Janvrin and Scott. The big question for the Dodgers on offense would be how they performed on a stage where they had precious little experience. Unlike Boston, all of Brooklyn's offensive stalwarts were playing in the World Series for the first time.[10]

In the dugout, the Red Sox clearly had an advantage in World Series managing experience. Bill Carrigan was matched against Wilbert Robinson, who was in his first Fall Classic as a manager. Robinson's team played extremely hard for him, but he was widely considered to be an easy-going, good-natured manager who wasn't necessarily a strong leader. Although Robby probably didn't receive his due for his managerial abilities, the key question for the Series was whether or not Robinson could maintain his regular-season success in picking spots for his pitchers. With regard to Carrigan, Hugh Fullerton believed he wasn't a "driving" manager, but more than capable as a leader who was "simply a hard working, earnest student of the game whose strong point is willingness to listen to advice." Something the Dodgers did have on their side was a lack of pressure. Jake Daubert noted this, saying, "We have the advantage inasmuch as we have everything to gain and nothing to lose. You will see the Superbas out there on the field as cool and collected as if just an ordinary game were to be played. On the other hand, I expect to find the world's champions nervous and fretful. They have everything to lose." Just who would feel pressure when the games actually began remained to be seen.[11]

Not surprisingly, most writers picked Boston to win. Of the 17 who submitted predictions to the Brooklyn *Eagle*, 13 chose the Red Sox. But as Game One approached, more and more experts were supporting the Dodgers, arguing this wouldn't be an easy series for Boston. Lester Rice's article in the Brooklyn *Citizen* the day before Game One pointed out the numerous times where the inexperienced team had pulled off the upset. The Dodgers were even drawing comparisons to the Miracle Braves of 1914. Hugh Fullerton, who had an uncanny knack for making predictions, projected Boston would win in five, dropping only the third game in "another series that will be decided largely by long hits."[12]

Increased support for the Dodgers was further illustrated in the gambling odds, which were a big part of the Fall Classic. The Washington *Post* reported on October 4 that odds had opened at 5 to 3 in favor of the Red Sox. With Game One drawing near, there had been little if any change to the odds, but there were varying reports on the amount of activity at the "betting windows." The Atlanta *Constitution* noted confidence in the Red Sox side had been reflected in the wagering, but the New York *Herald* argued bookmakers had never seen so little activity the night before the start. To stir things up, some even increased the odds to 2 to 1 in favor of Boston. One of the significant pastimes of the day was tracking large wagers, some of which were at the center of news stories. For example, in its October 5 edition, the Boston *American* featured a story around the odds, mentioning that horseman E.E. Smathers had placed $20,000 on Boston, while New York's John A. Drake had wagered $5,000.[13]

If the Superbas were concerned about predictions of their impending doom, it didn't show during an exuberant trip to the Hub City, starting with a royal sendoff from the "city of churches." A fleet of taxis carrying the Dodgers left Ebbets Field at 11:00 A.M. en route to Grand Central Terminal for a 1:00 P.M. train. According to William A. Rafter, "All along the line the party, which traveled in taxis, were recognized and cheered to the echo." The procession was headed by two motorcycled policemen and traveled through the Brooklyn business district, across Manhattan Bridge and up Fifth Avenue to the train station, where 1,000-plus joyous fans sent their heroes on their way.[14]

Two special cars carried the team as well as a number of traveling companions for the 6½ hour train ride. The weather was warm and most players removed coats, displaying silk shirts. Robinson wore a striped purple and white shirt (the mind boggles at the size), while Ebbets was dignified in a "black cut-away coat." The players passed the time with games like pinochle, poker and checkers, while Mike Mowrey, Hi Myers, John Meyers, Jack Coombs and eventually Casey Stengel enjoyed a sing-a-long. The Superbas had clearly taken to heart Robinson's order that he wanted no one thinking or talking about baseball during the trip. Finally, upon their arrival at 7:30 P.M., the Dodgers were greeted warmly by the Boston fans and checked into their headquarters, the Brunswick Hotel. Before retiring for the night there was a brief scouting meeting that featured insights and pep talks from Phillies manager Pat Moran, Grover Cleveland Alexander and National League president Governor John K. Tener.[15]

Little has changed in nearly a century. With first pitch now less than 24 hours away, the "Hub" was packed with fans and celebrities from the baseball world. Players such as the Braves' Johnny Evers and Sherwood Magee, the Yankees' Lee Magee, the aforementioned Phillies' Grover Cleveland Alexander and the Tigers' Ty Cobb were seen in hotel lobbies and around the city. Hotel accommodations were scarce, with reportedly somewhere in the range of 25,000–30,000 seeking a bed after the first game. On October 5, G. R. Hall of the Adams Hotel was preparing for the frenzied rush and said, "We are putting extra cots up all over the hotel, in preparation for the jam. Wherever it is possible, guests will be doubled up and in many cases three or four will be crowded into one room."[16]

Of course, Boston's famous fan club, the Royal Rooters, would be in attendance, seated in Section O of the grandstand. The Dodgers had also brought their own fan club, some coming with the team, but most, about 300 in total, arriving by boat early on the morning of Game One. The group would be seated in the 29th row of the grandstand, some seven rows deeper than the furthest row at Ebbets Field. Since the Dodgers' owner had promised Boston's fan club better accommodations in Brooklyn, he wasn't pleased and had words with Red Sox president Joe Lannin.[17]

All of this may have simply reflected the supposed limited ticket availability, which made Lannin's life very difficult. Remarkably, the Red Sox president reportedly was buying back tickets at a higher than face value price and selling them to friends. The two-dollar seats were doing the best business on the streets while going for up to $10, a markup of 500 percent. This wasn't without risk, however, and there had been a few arrests for "speculating." The last tickets would be sold on the day of the game on a general admission basis. According to the Boston *Daily Globe*, fans began lining up to obtain these seats at 2:00 P.M. on the sixth, a 24-hour wait until the gates opened the next morning at 9:00. David Cohen, a 17-year-old from East Boston, and Samuel Averett, also 17, of North Cambridge, were apparently the first two in line. They were alone for the first two hours until others arrived at 4:00 P.M., and there would be roughly two hundred by midnight setting up camp for the night. According to the Boston *American*, "by the time the first fans were admitted (the next morning) there were over a thousand outside. There was a wild whoop of joy as the turnstile clicked the first admission." During the wait, cranks were sustained by sandwich vendors and a tent that contained hot coffee and food.[18]

While elated fans were entering Braves Field, the National Commission was busy ironing out the final details for the World Series. Both managers and owners attended a meeting regarding the ground rules. One important issue was the infield fly rule; in the American League runners couldn't advance, while in the National League they could. The decision was that the American League version would be used at Braves Field and vice versa in Brooklyn.[19]

The weather at the "home of big things" was splendid, the Brooklyn *Eagle* reporting "a perfect day" since "an Indian summer sun turned the edge of what early threatened to be a brisk cool autumn day and noon found it warm and comfortable." On the field, pitcher Vean Gregg threw batting practice to the Red Sox, who wore white hats and uniforms on top of red and white socks. Part way through Boston's workout, Robinson led the Dodgers, decked out in gray uniforms with black and gray socks, onto the field to rousing cheers. Brooklyn took batting practice while Bill Carrigan held a team meeting with the Red Sox. Just before game time, the crowd appeared to be packing every nook and cranny of Braves Field, even spilling into a fenced-in area in right-center.[20]

Earlier, both managers continued to try to hide their pitching selections. While Wilbert Robinson selected Rube Marquard as his starter, he also had both Jack Coombs and Jeff Pfeffer warm up. Similarly, Bill Carrigan had Ernie Shore and southpaw Babe Ruth warming up in front of Boston's third-base dugout. The obvious selection was Ruth, but Rough, in a surprise, went with Shore. Both teams played their normal starting lineups, with the Dodgers starting Stengel against the right-handed Shore.[21]

The "dope" favoring the Red Sox was right on the money, or at least for the first eight innings. Once the pre-game ceremonies were complete, Shore threw the first pitch at 2:06 P.M. Hi Myers swung and fouled out, foreshadowing an easy inning for Ernie, who retired the over-aggressive Dodgers on just seven pitches. The Red Sox attacked Marquard early, but he was up to the challenge. Tilly Walker tripled with two out in the first and waved to the crowd upon his arrival at third, but Hoblitzell grounded out. Boston then loaded the bases in the second with one out on walks to Duffy Lewis and Hick Cady, sandwiched around an attempted sacrifice bunt Larry Gardner beat out for a hit. However, Marquard worked out of the bases-loaded, one-out jam with some big help from a great catch by Hi Myers. In the third, Rube struck out Janvrin and Walker to start the inning. Hoblitzell then tripled over Daubert's head on a 3–2 pitch, and Lewis hit the first offering he saw for an RBI double and a 1–0 lead. Any further scoring was short circuited when Duffy was picked off second.[22]

Boston's lead was short-lived, however, since Stengel singled over Gardner's head to open the fourth and scored the tying run on Wheat's triple to right field. Up next was George Cutshaw, who hit a low liner to right field. According to Charles A. Lovett, "Hooper raced in at top speed, lunged and caught the ball less than a foot above the turf." The Boston right fielder "somersaulted twice, but held the ball, and leaping up quickly, made a marvelous line throw to Cady." The toss was right on target, easily nailing Wheat at the plate and stopping a promising Brooklyn rally dead in its tracks. Boston had been helped by the first but certainly not the last Brooklyn mental lapse. Wheat had come 10–15 feet down the line before having to retreat back to the bag to tag up after the catch. Had Zack simply waited on the base, he would have had a much better chance to score. As the day wore on, the sun started to play havoc in the field. With one out in the fifth, Walker lost John Meyers' fly to deep center in the sun for a triple, but Shore got out of the inning without damage. Not so fortunate were the Dodgers in the bottom of the frame. Cutshaw and Hi Myers both lost Hooper's fly ball in the sun, which fell for a double, and Boston soon capitalized when Harry scored on Walker's single, making it 2–1.[23]

Marquard and Shore remained locked in a 2–1 pitchers duel in the bottom of the seventh when Brooklyn's defense came unglued. Janvrin, filling in admirably for Barry, doubled to lead off the inning, and an error by shortstop Olson put runners on the corners with no one out. Olson's problem was apparently contagious, as Cutshaw booted Hoblitzell's grounder, making it 3–1 Red Sox. After a Lewis' sacrifice put runners on second and third, Robinson played the infield in. Having caught fumblitis from Olson, Cutshaw seemed to catch brain lock from Wheat. Instead of taking the sure out at first on Gardner's grounder, the Brooklyn second baseman's throw home was wide and/or late, and everyone was safe. Another run scored on Scott's sacrifice fly, giving Boston a commanding 5–1 advantage. The questions about Brooklyn's middle infield had been answered in the negative, as the Red Sox scored three times on only one hit. The Dodger fans on hand were beginning to file out of Braves' Field.[24]

Another Brooklyn error in the eighth added what seemed to be a meaningless Red Sox run for a 6–1 lead. Suddenly, however, as Hugh Fullerton commented, "the game, the dope and everything blew up." The ninth didn't start well for Boston when, with a five-run lead, Shore walked Jake Daubert, who was 0-for-3 to that point. Stengel followed with a single to right, and although Shore got the first out on a force at third, he then hit Cutshaw with a pitch to load the bases. Submariner Carl Mays and Dutch Leonard were warming up, but Carrigan stuck with Shore, which did not prove to be a wise decision Mike Mowrey followed with a hard grounder off Janvrin's foot, scoring two runners to close the gap to 6–3. Next, Olson ripped one to third that Gardner stopped but was unable to field cleanly, loading the bases for John Meyers. Shore retired him on a pop foul but walked pinch-hitter Fred Merkle to bring home Cutshaw, making it 6–4. Finally, Rough went to Mays, and Pinch Thomas entered the game behind the plate for Cady. The drama had returned as the Dodgers were on the edge of the dugout, while Boston's Royal Rooters had been silenced.[25]

First up against Mays was Hi Myers, who beat out a slow roller to Janvrin to score Mowrey and keep the bases loaded. With Boston clinging to a one-run lead, Mays next faced Jake Daubert, one of Brooklyn's best hitters who could redeem his poor performance with just one swing of the bat. And Daubert nearly did, hitting a hard grounder to Scott's right. According to William A. Rafter, "Olson had crossed the plate with the run tying the score as Scott shot the ball on a line to Hoblitzell. He never made a better throw in his life, but at that the decision was about as close as ever made, Daubert diving head first for the initial sack." He was out by a whisker, and the Red Sox had hung on for a dramatic Game One victory. The inning had turned an otherwise dull game into one of the tensest moments in World Series history. For example, Paul Shannon said the rally would "go down in world series annals as the grittiest and most courageous spurt which baseball critics have ever chronicled." The obvious key to the game was fielding (Brooklyn had four errors, Boston one), particularly in the middle infield. Olson and Cutshaw had mangled what was an otherwise good performance by Marquard, while Boston's defense enabled Shore to survive even after allowing nine hits. The Dodgers' offensive totals of five runs on 10 hits received no help from Daubert's 0-for-4 performance.[26]

Although Boston prevailed as expected, the Red Sox's ninth inning blow-up raised some doubts heading into the off day between the first two games. Brooklyn's confidence remained high, since in spite of nerves and not getting the breaks, the Superbas still had a chance to win. Robinson said, "I know my boys are not a bit awed by the Red Sox since that first game." There was a report that the lone Dodger dwelling on Game One was Daubert, although he had reportedly and rhetorically asked a sportswriter, "Do you think that failure to quite come through in the ninth worried us or broke our hearts?" Answering his own question, Daubert said it "was just what we needed, I guess, for we feel a whole lot more confident than we did when we started the game." Brooklyn seemed to be doing the majority of the talking on Sunday, with the most important theme being the team's renewed confidence. Anger about being short-changed on tickets was also a concern, with both players and officials experiencing shabby treatment. John Meyers, for example, said he couldn't even obtain a "decent seat" for his wife through the box office.[27]

A much more important issue related to tickets was hanging over the heads of both teams — the attendance, or shocking lack thereof, at Game One.

In an era before television and radio, scenes like this one at the New York *Evening Telegram* in 1911 were the only way to obtain play-by-play coverage of a World Series contest (George Bain Collection, Library of Congress).

Just hours before the first pitch, there were no tickets available, with all 42,000 having apparently been sold, thus maxing out the players' share of the revenue. However, something was wrong since only 36,000-plus showed up at the ballpark, and officials were mandating that the shares of the gate receipts would be determined on that number. Players cried conspiracy and wondered how this could happen when it had already been ruled a sellout. There were, however, empty seats in Braves Field during that first game, and no matter the explanation, the Dodgers estimated they had lost $6,000.[28]

Regardless of how many fans were at Braves Field, beyond the ballpark, beyond even Boston itself, fans had gathered. Even though there were no television sets, radios or sports bars, they still gathered. Primarily, they gathered in front of the many real-time theater presentations of the contests produced by newspapers around the country. This happened in most major cities, and one of the biggest was a mammoth 12'x30" structure set up by the New York *Times* in Times Square. In the middle was a green baseball field, with white lines producing a diamond and nine electric light bulbs representing the fielders. Telegraph lines allowed fans to know what was going on almost as it happened. In fact, Game Two would set a record as information traveled 18,000 miles over telegraph lines. In spite of all the differences between 1916 and today, it's not hard, after the last-inning excitement of Game One, to envision the fans' anticipation and then reaction as they watched Game Two of the 1916 World Series at the "theater." A pair of southpaws, Red Sox ace Babe Ruth and the Dodgers' Sherrod Smith, would go head-to-head in a classic, still considered one of the greatest World Series games ever played.[29]

At Braves Field, the scene was intense as Ruth and Smith battled into the gathering darkness. By game time, clouds had moved over the "home of big things," and there was rain in the area. Coombs, the logical Brooklyn candidate, along with Cheney and Smith warmed up for Robinson, while Ruth and Carl Mays did the same. It was no surprise Rough sent Ruth to the hill, but Smith getting the call was unexpected. The move certainly threw Carrigan off, as he immediately replaced Chick Shorten with the right-handed Tilly Walker, but Boston still had to start the game with four lefties in the lineup. The Dodgers went to their right-handed platoon, with Jimmy Johnston leading off and Casey Stengel on the bench. Whether Ruth in his first World Series start was nervous or Brooklyn remained confident from Saturday's ninth inning, things started well for the Dodgers. With two out, Hi Myers drove Ruth's 1–0 delivery to the fence in right-center. Walker and Hooper both fell down retrieving the ball, and Myers scored easily for a 1–0 Brooklyn lead.[30]

Unfortunately for the Superbas, their weakness at middle infield was again on display when Boston tied the game in the third. After Everett Scott

These fans watched in the Braves Field bleachers during Game Two, as daylight waned with Babe Ruth and Sherrod Smith continuing to battle (George Bain Collection, Library of Congress).

led off with a triple to left, Cutshaw juggled a grounder by Ruth, and despite getting the batter at first, allowed Scott to score and tie the game. Coombs, although not pitching, was a big factor in the game through his coaching at third base. Just prior to Carrigan's team tying the contest, Smith had tried to stretch a double into a triple and was tagged out by Scott. There were varying reports, but someone — either Smith or Coombs — had made a big mistake. To make matters more frustrating for Brooklyn, Johnston followed with a single that probably would have scored Smith from second.

Coombs wasn't finished, however, and was involved in squandering another Brooklyn opportunity in the eighth. Mowrey was on second with one away when Miller singled to center field. With Smith up next, it certainly seemed the optimal time to test Walker's arm, but Coombs held Mowrey at third. There were again varying reports — would Mowrey have scored or was it the right decision — but regardless, once again Brooklyn was turned away. Walter Trumbull blamed the entire loss on Coombs' poor decisions. He even wrote Walker's throw in the eighth was 15 feet wide of the plate, while another report had it at 20 feet up the line. Despite the third-inning lapse, Smith and his defense kept pace with Boston, especially on Myers' spectacular diving catch to rob Hooper in the sixth. The Dodger defense weakened in the ninth, however, moving the winning run to third with one out, but Hi Myers again came through, nailing Janvrin at the plate as he tried to score on Hoblitzell's fly ball.[31]

Headed to extra innings, the game was really just starting. Ruth and Smith were both in command, and the defenses were solid behind them. The Red Sox answered Myers' play when Gardner caught Miller's liner to end the top of the 10th inning. In the bottom half of the inning, it was the Dodgers' turn, as Mowrey fielded Hooper's slow grounder, faked to first and then wheeled around to nail Scott, who had overrun third base. In the 13th, Brooklyn had another opportunity when Mowrey reached second on Gardner's error and a sacrifice, but Boston's defense made its final key play with a great catch by Lewis. On an already overcast day, darkness was approaching, and it seemed clear the 14th would be the last inning of play. If the game ended in a tie, the two teams would replay it the next day in Boston.[32]

The probability of a tie increased when Ruth shut down the Dodgers in the top of the 14th. As Henry P. Edwards noted, "There was not a chance for another inning to be played, and baseball celebrities who had surrendered their rooms at the Boston hotels were regretting their action." They could have relaxed, however, for "it was so ordained that on the Boston bench sat a man who was to turn the impending draw into a Red Sox victory." Things started poorly for Smith in the 14th — for the fourth time that afternoon, Hoblitzell drew a walk. Supposedly Smith struggled with the inside pitch, and Sherrod got burned trying to cut the corner too close. Lewis sacrificed, moving Hobby into scoring position with one out. Since this would clearly be the last inning, Rough took out Larry Gardner in favor of the right-handed Del Gainer. Gainer was on the team because he could hit lefties more effectively than Hoblitzell, but he was suffering from a slight foot injury that probably kept him out of that day's starting lineup. After Smith threw a ball, Carrigan went a step further, replacing Hoblitzell with a pinch-runner, speedster Mike McNally. Figuring Boston wouldn't play the field again, it was a no-lose decision, but when Gainer singled to left, the move seemed brilliant. The ball took a bad hop, as left fielder Zack Wheat made the pickup, and McNally, who had a big lead off second, scored the winning run after a wide and late throw.[33]

There was no shortage of controversy after the game, beginning with reports McNally never touched the plate. Some argued Wheat was playing too far back and should have gambled Gainer wouldn't hit the ball over his head. The other question was whether Smith should have walked Del to set up the double play, especially considering weak-hitting Everett Scott was the next batter. It was the longest game in World Series history to that point, and was unmatched until Game Three of the 2005 Series that also went 14 innings. The game broke the previous record of 13 innings, set in 1907. Once again, Brooklyn had played well but came up just short.[34]

The two teams had played 14 innings of dramatic baseball in just 2 hours and 32 minutes. Perhaps not surprisingly, such a close game had produced some remarkably similar statistics. Both hurlers threw nearly the same amount of pitches, somewhere in the neighborhood of 150. Both offenses were stymied, but the biggest offensive goat for the day, and thus far in the series, was Daubert. In 11 trips to the plate, the Brooklyn first baseman had hit the ball out of the infield just once. After two one-run losses, the Superbas were understandably down. According to one eyewitness, "They slunk from the field, silent and flabby. They blended into the descending darkness of the gloomy afternoon. It was their supreme effort, and it had failed." However, the train ride back to Brooklyn was supposedly upbeat. Upbeat or not, in the brief history of the World Series, no team had come back from a 2–0 deficit.[35]

Ebbets Field had never hosted a World Series game, ensuring a party-like atmosphere despite the two Dodger losses. An additional row of box seats and outfield bleachers had been added around the park, bringing the total capacity to 26,500. Brooklyn's home field was well decorated for the occasion, with multi-colored flags waving in a stiff wind. In a somewhat mean-spirited move, a temporary canvas screen, in places topped with pennants and flags, prevented those in and on outlying buildings to view the action for free. Reportedly, the obstruction wasn't totally effective, and many were still able to obtain a good view.[36]

As in Boston, thousands of fans gathered for an all-night wait to try for the last available seats. Although a sellout was expected, by the 2:00 P.M. first pitch, it was far from full. In fact, the total attendance was roughly 21,000, well short of capacity. Perhaps to some degree, this was due to complaints about the ticket prices, which ranged as high as $5. Many of the empty seats were located in those sections, while the less expensive ones were all taken. Furthermore, a temperature below 50 degrees and a northwest wind couldn't have helped attendance. It was so cold players wore thick flannels under their uniforms as well as mackinaw coats and heavy sweaters. Regardless of the reason for the low turnout, it didn't increase the players' pay, and it couldn't have been good for the Superbas' morale.[37]

With regard to the pitching match-ups, Bill Carrigan chose to put the right-handed Carl Mays on the hill instead of Dutch Leonard. Wilbert Robinson went with his Game One lineup, with Otto Miller catching. Miller would catch Jack Coombs, who despite aging had a 4–0 World Series record and figured to provide Brooklyn's best chance to win. Most likely, Carrigan went with Mays because his submarine-style delivery figured to bother the Dodgers. Brooklyn dodged a bullet in the first inning with its defense when Stengel threw out Chick Shorten at third base. The Dodgers were having little difficulty with Mays — even Daubert reached in the first — and Brooklyn loaded the bases with one out, only to see the submariner work out of the jam. Mays wasn't so fortunate in the third, and with one out, Daubert singled to right and moved to second on Stengel's single, as the home crowd came to life for Zack Wheat. Although Wheat was retired on a fly ball, Cutshaw followed with a single down the right-field line that scored Daubert for a 1–0 lead. The early Brooklyn advantage was observed with tin horns, cowbells and police whistles, filling the park with noise.[38]

Now it was Boston's turn to play poor defense, as Olson caught Gardner off-guard with a bunt to start the fourth inning and went to second on Larry's throwing error. When Otto Miller tried to sacrifice Olson to third, Mays, with a shot at the lead runner, chose the easy out at first. The combined poor defense and judgment cost Boston when Coombs lined a single past Janvrin for a 2–0 Brooklyn lead. Mays was battling, but surprisingly, the Dodgers were having little trouble with his style and delivery. The game appeared to break open in the fifth when Ivy "slashed the first ball far over Shorten's head in left center field to the left field bleachers for a three-bagger," driving in two more runs for a 4–0 lead.[39]

Boston wasn't going down without a fight, however, and started to get to a tiring but valiant Coombs in the sixth inning. Pinch-hitter Olaf Henriksen scored on Hooper's triple to right-center, and Harry scored on a Shorten single. Jeff Pfeffer and Rube Marquard were warming up, but Coombs got through the sixth without further damage. The Red Sox were now into their bullpen, as Foster, supposedly out with an injury, was in the game. For the most part he was in control but was saved by a lucky break in the sixth. With two down and no one on, Daubert smoked a ball to the left-field corner that Duffy Lewis played poorly. Daubert should have scored easily, but his slide was poor, and Pinch Thomas had the plate blocked. Hank O'Day ruled Jake safe at first, only to have Dick Hoblitzell point out Daubert never touched the plate.[40]

Brooklyn's missed opportunity looked costly in the seventh when Gardner hit a one-out home run over the King of Tablewaters sign on the right-field fence, his first of the year. Boston was within a run, and Coombs was clearly out of gas. Then, in a bizarre move, before Wilbert Robinson could even get to the mound, Coombs took himself out, waving in Pfeffer. The latter had allowed a run in one inning of relief in Game One, but he got out of the seventh with the help of Hi Myers' fielding. After that, Pfeffer was untouchable, as he retired the last eight in order while striking out three in the process.[41]

When Stengel clutched the final out in right field, it set off a celebration more characteristic of a football game. A band came onto the field, followed by jubilant fans singing a variety of songs. "Men and boys, with here and there a feminine companion, capered and danced about with joy," in "imitation of the college snake dance, while the more sedate of the spectators cheered and yelled," wrote the New York *Press*. The World Series was now a series. Boston's lead had been trimmed to 2–1, and with another victory on Wednesday, Brooklyn could send the two teams back to Boston dead even.[42]

The Superbas won by playing errorless defense, while Daubert, Cutshaw and Wheat went a combined 5-for-10 after a collective 0-for-15 in Game Two. Meanwhile, Coombs, utilizing an effective curve and fastball, (7 hits, 3 runs, 6⅓ innings) and Pfeffer (0 hits, 0 runs, 2⅔ innings) were outstanding. "Colby Jack Coombs proved himself the Moses born to Charles H. Ebbets' lost tribe," added W. J. Macbeth. Now he had a 5–0 World Series record. The only pitcher who had more wins was Charles Bender with six. Coombs' decision to remove himself was viewed as ingenious in many circles, and the Boston *Herald's* N. J. Flatley even went so far as to credit him for refusing to take all the glory by not finishing the game when he could have.[43]

Other than Gardner's error, Boston didn't perform poorly. It was Brooklyn's success against Mays (7 hits, 3 runs, 5 innings) that really hurt Boston. Bill Carrigan had taken chances with his starting pitchers in both the first and third games and got burned in the latter contest. He was justifiably criticized for his decision to start Mays over Dutch Leonard in Game Three, since it was hard to explain a team with significant World Series experience using two straight starters that had none. It was a mistake he certainly wouldn't repeat, but in the process, Brooklyn had regained its confidence.[44]

A Dodgers victory in Game Four would even the series at two, and no matter the ultimate outcome, would ensure no one could say Brooklyn was an easy victim. The Red Sox would have Tilly Walker back in center field, and Carrigan put himself behind the plate since he was basically Dutch Leonard's personal catcher. There had been scattered reports the southpaw was having some type of arm problems, and now everyone would finally find out for certain.[45]

Facing a lefty, manager Wilbert Robinson went back to his right-handed hitting lineup, this time to the extreme of platooning Daubert for the first time all year. With Marquard on the hill, Fred Merkle went to first and John Meyers was behind the plate, meaning the lineup had a New York Giant alumni like appearance. They all had World Series experience, but unfortunately it was all of the losing variety. Unlike the third contest, Game Four would be played in nearly ideal conditions on what was described as a "perfect Indian Summer day, with a clear sky" and slight wind. While the crowd was slightly bigger, with an announced attendance of 21,662, there were still numerous empty seats.[46]

The strange thing about the fourth game was how quickly things changed. At the start, Brooklyn's hopes were strong, and after a few minutes, the Dodgers felt even better, as the momentum from the third game seemed to have carried over. In the bottom of the first, Jimmy Johnston led off with a triple to deep center field and scored on Myers' single to right field for a 1–0 lead. Leonard clearly didn't seem right, and as Merkle worked a walk, Bill Carrigan already had Vean Gregg warming up. With one out, Hal Janvrin's error allowed Myers to tally for a 2–0 lead. A sound Boston defense seemed to be unglued, and the Dodgers had runners on the corners and still only one out. One of the game's critical plays then helped the Red Sox work out of the jam with no further damage. Robinson put a double steal on, but Janvrin took Carrigan's throw down and threw to third, where he caught Wheat, attempting to retreat to the bag. Mike Mowrey was easily retired to end the inning. The score was 2–0, but it very easily could have been three or four.[47]

Perhaps the narrow escape awakened Boston. In any event, in the Boston second, Dick Hoblitzell drew a walk and went to third on Duffy Lewis' double, bringing up Larry Gardner. Gardner drove a ball to the far reaches of center field for a three-run homer. The stunned silence from the Brooklyn faithful was offset in spirit, if not in volume, by the Royal Rooters singing "Tessie," while the Boston dugout was likened to "Dante's Inferno." It was Gardner's second home run of the World Series and, ironically, just his second of the season. He had even been pinch-hit for at the climatic moment of Game Two, due to his inability to hit lefties. Gardner had now equaled "Home Run" Baker's achievement of two World Series home runs in as many games, and Marquard had been victimized on each occasion. In fact, Larry had just three hits thus far in the World Series, and two were home runs. Just like that, Boston led, 3–2, quickly taking the wind out of Brooklyn's sails. When the inning ended, Paul Shannon said Marquard appeared "as though his last hope had departed" while heading to the bench. William B. Hanna went further, writing, "There was not much fight in them (Brooklyn) after that. They were less aggressive than in any previous game and the game itself was dull and the least interesting of the four."[48]

The devastating blow to the Dodgers' spirits, no doubt, helped Leonard, who despite working slowly, had settled down under the tutelage of Carrigan. Dutch worked so deliberately the game went "the inordinate length of two hours and thirty minutes," roughly the same time as the second game, which lasted 14 innings. Boston scored again in the fourth, knocking out Marquard, now the loser of Games One and Four. Robinson felt "Marquard was a victim of his over-anxiety," trying so hard "that he dug himself into hole after hole, and then to pull out, had to shoot the leather down the groove." Boston added two more runs for a decisive 6–2 victory and an even more decisive three games-to-one lead. Wilbert Robinson clearly threw up the white flag when, in a moment of admirable sentiment, he brought Nap Rucker in to pitch the final two innings. Rucker was in the last of his 10 seasons with Brooklyn, and this would be his one and only chance to pitch in a World Series. As Ebbets fled the scene quickly following the conclusion, Boston's Royal Rooters took advantage with a post-game parade of their own. After marching over to Joe Lannin's box, the group insisted the Red Sox owner head the march. Accompanied by a band playing songs like "Home, Sweet Home" and "Tessie," the Royal Rooters sang along vociferously.[49]

Along with Leonard, Gardner was clearly the star for Boston, but Hooper, Hoblitzell, Lewis, and Carrigan all played significant roles. The latter didn't figure to see any more action, and with his reported impending retirement, this was more than likely Rough's final game. Renowned sports writer T.H. Murnane noted, "The Boston players, to a man, displayed splendid staying powers this afternoon, and in the face of a hostile crowd tightened up after a poor start and went over the wire as strong as a pack of greyhounds." Brooklyn's offensive production was meager, with no multi-hit performances and the lone RBI from Hi Myers, who was one of the only Superbas consistently producing in the World Series. Decisions to double steal in the first and sacrifice with two on and no one out in the fourth, assuming the orders came from the bench, were also questionable, though the failure of the first move was more due to poor execution.[50]

Throughout the 1916 baseball season, there was non-stop excitement. From the Tris Speaker sale at its beginning, through dramatic pennant races and record-setting performances, to the Giants' controversy at the end, the suspense just kept building. Despite the 3–1 Boston advantage, the World Series had also been exciting with three one-run games, including a classic second contest. But when the end came, it was both quick and anticlimactic. Game Five seemed to the reporters and fans — and even possibly the players at some level — to be a formality. "There was a sharp contrast between the two teams as they took the field," wrote reporter H. Perry Lewis. "The Sox were bubbling over with confidence and pep," unlike Brooklyn, as "the Robins were downcast and sluggish in their warm-up. They were molting Robins and they looked like it."[51]

Some Red Sox fans didn't even wait for the conclusion of the series but started the party after the Game Four victory. The Boston team had been mobbed by fans upon its early-morning arrival back at Backbay Station. By 9:00 A.M., 3,000-plus "bugs" were in line to snap up the remaining seats in the left-field bleachers for Game Five. The contest was slated for the Columbus Day holiday, and finally an overflow crowd of 42,620 (one game late from the players' perspective) braved brisk conditions at Braves Field. According to some reports, the gathering broke the record for the largest-ever gathering to witness a baseball game by 300 spectators. During the contest, even the runways leading to the bleachers were jammed with fans trying to catch a glimpse of the action.[52]

Dodgers manager Wilbert Robinson gave the ball to Jeff Pfeffer, who after a weak relief outing in Game One, finished Jack Coombs' Game Three victory in dominating fashion. Meanwhile, with the 3–1 advantage in hand, Bill Carrigan had the luxury of giving Babe Ruth an extra day of rest for a possible Game Six and sent Ernie Shore to the hill. Against a right-hander, Robinson went back to his Game One lineup, with the exception that John Meyers would be behind the plate.

Shore struck Hi Myers out on three pitches, all of them looking, to start the game. It was a sign of things to come for Ernie, as there would be no lapse, as at the end of Game One. In fact, he would allow only three hits all day, and reportedly, not a solid one until the seventh. Brooklyn did, however, take the lead in the top of the second — albeit without a hit — when George Cutshaw walked and eventually scored on a passed ball. Boston quickly tied things up in the bottom half, and the culprit was once again poor defense by Brooklyn. Left fielder Zack Wheat misplayed a one-out drive by Duffy Lewis into a triple, and Larry Gardner's sacrifice fly evened things at one.[53]

Sensing the kill and a second straight World Series championship, Boston pushed harder in the third. Cady led off with a single, and Harry Hooper's one-out walk put two on. But Pfeffer then got Hal Janvrin to hit what should have been an easy inning-ending double play ball, but it bounded to short-stop Ivy Olson. He bobbled it and then threw wildly to first. Cady scored on the play, and Hooper went to third, while Olson was given two errors. With two down, Chick Shorten's single to center field brought Hooper home for a 3–1 Boston advantage.[54]

The Dodgers managed their first hit, a weak infield single, with two outs in the fifth. Nothing came of it, and Boston added another run in the bottom of the inning. After a seventh-inning rally proved fruitless, the Dodgers went quietly. Reporter W.J. Macbeth complained Brooklyn wasn't even running out balls toward the end. When Scott clutched the final out (that left both Everett and Ernie Shore fighting for the game ball), the Royal Rooters, along with other fans, paraded around Braves Field, headed by both Joe Lannin and Charles Ebbets, who were soon arm-in-arm. A band played songs, including "A Hot Old Time" and "Glory, Glory, Hallelujah!" and the group also stopped to hear a few words from Mayor Curley. The players headed for the locker rooms, but not before numerous fans had the opportunity to offer congratulatory handshakes to Carrigan and his team.[55]

Poor defense had again bitten Brooklyn, as Pfeffer had allowed only six hits and two earned runs in seven innings. "Wretched fielding by Zack Wheat and Ivan Olson, the latter establishing a world series record by absorbing two errors on one batted ball, tossed Big Jeff (Pfeffer) to the wolves before the combat was three innings old," wrote Grantland Rice. Offensively, the Dodgers did almost nothing against Ernie Shore, especially Daubert, who could only muster a walk in eight at-bats in two games. Shore was clearly the hero, allowing three singles and no earned runs while walking just one and striking out four.[56]

Writers, players and managers offered a variety of reasons for the World Series result. One of the most prevalent ones centered on the weakness of the National League versus the strength of the American League. Given how the Red Sox had dominated both the 1915 and 1916 World Series, the point was difficult to argue. At least one writer, however, took it a step further, suggesting the Dodgers weren't a worthy representative of the National League, claiming other teams, possibly the Phillies, would have fared better against Boston. This argument seems to be flawed. Brooklyn was a strong and talented team that survived a pennant race even closer than the one in the American League. The Dodgers simply didn't have the experience, and it showed. After all, it was Boston's third World Series title in the last five years. To that end, it seemed just about everything Bill Carrigan did — be it select pitchers, pinch hit or put on a sacrifice — worked while the opposite was true for Wilbert Robinson.[57]

Brooklyn even received good pitching, with the lone poor performance coming from Rube Marquard in Game Four. Boston's pitching was better, but not by much. It was the offense and fielding that was the real difference. The Dodgers had committed 13 errors to Boston's six, and the misplays were extremely costly, particularly in the first and last contests. The middle infield of Olson (4 errors) and Cutshaw (2 errors), which was a concern to start the World Series, proved exactly that. It was no different on the offensive end. As a team, Boston hit .238 to Brooklyn's .200. The Dodgers had gotten poor performances from some of their most important hitters, especially Jake Daubert (.176) and Zack Wheat (.211). Oddly, it was the platoon of Casey Stengel (.364) and Jim Johnston (.300), along with Ivy Olson (.250), that performed best at the plate.[58]

Boston's offense had been much more effective, especially Duffy Lewis (.353, 3 runs) and Harry Hooper (.333, 6 runs, 10-game World Series hitting streak), while Tilly Walker (.273) and Chick Shorten (.571) gave standout performances in their rotating roles. The timeliness of Boston's hitting is best demonstrated by Del Gainer and Larry Gardner. Gainer batted only once but delivered a game-winning hit, while Gardner batted only .176 but had two home runs and six RBIs. Of all the experts, it was Hugh Fullerton who doped it best. His pre–World Series prediction that the Red Sox would win in five, notching victories in Games One, Two, Four and Five, was right on the money. Speaking of money, the event set records, perhaps due as much to high ticket prices as anything else. Boston and Brooklyn split a record $162,927.45, with the winner's shares marked at $3,759.86 and the loser's shares at $2,833.52. Total attendance had been 162,359, leading to total financial returns of $385,590.50.[59]

Although the 1916 season was over, anyone who thought things would quiet down during the winter was in for a surprise. Almost at the moment the Red Sox were being crowned world champions, reports were surfacing that Ban Johnson would force Joe Lannin to sell his club. This was reportedly due to the latter's negative remarks regarding umpiring and a potential conspiracy against the Red Sox earlier in September. Charles A. Lovett of the St. Louis *Globe-Democrat* reported the sale had already been completed. Beginning to end, there were no dull moments during the 1916 baseball season.[60]

Epilogue

The final days of the 1916 season found newspapers filled with articles detailing the excitement and suspense of one of the greatest pennant races in baseball history. This should come as no surprise, since the races were fought among off-the-field distractions, controversy and record-setting performance. Ultimately, in the season's final days, two worthy winners overcame a plethora of other contenders who would have been just as worthy. In addition to this magical season, there have been many climatic, heart-pounding races that rival the 1916 one. Still, this DeadBall Era season warrants the claim of baseball at its best, even today. Like those who were fortunate enough to witness 1916 as it happened, we today can appreciate how this season gave tangible form to what we love about baseball.

At the heart of 1916 are the teams, players and managers who made it happen. To describe what happened to the participants afterward is beyond the scope of this book. The stories of some, such as Babe Ruth, Casey Stengel, John McGraw and Grover Cleveland Alexander, are well known. What follows is an attempt to briefly summarize what happened to the 1916 contenders and some of the lesser-known participants.

When Brooklyn, Philadelphia and Boston finished 1-2-3, with one exception it marked the last significant success for the three franchises for the next 25 years. Although Brooklyn fell to seventh place in 1917, the Dodgers were the only team to win a pennant in the next quarter-century, capturing the National League flag in 1920. Philadelphia and Boston weren't even serious competitors after 1916. The Braves won their second and last pennant in Boston in 1948, and it took the Phillies another two years before they won the 1950 pennant race, beating out Brooklyn on the last day of the season.

Perhaps somewhat ironically, it was the fourth-place Giants who enjoyed the most future success. John McGraw's club made Fred Lieb's 1916 prediction come true when New York won the 1917 pennant, and then, in remarkable fashion, went on to win four straight flags from 1921 to 1924. By that time, however, it was a very different New York team, as a number of McGraw's 1916 acquisitions had left not just the Giants, but baseball, under less than desirable circumstances. Benny Kauff, Buck Herzog and Heinie Zimmerman were all accused in one form or another of being involved in efforts to throw games. By 1921, all three were out of Major League Baseball, never to return. Ferdinand Schupp built on his 1916 success the following year when he posted a 21–7 record with a 1.75 ERA and one win in the World Series. Things went downhill for the left-hander after that, as he bounced around to the Cards, Dodgers and briefly the White Sox before leaving baseball. Reportedly bothered with arm trouble, Schupp had a career 61–39 record with a 3.30 ERA. His 0.90 ERA in 1916 remains the lowest ever in baseball, but there has been ongoing controversy as to whether he even led the league, much less set a record.[1]

Other pitchers who played a prominent role in 1916 saw their careers tail off relatively quickly. After a league-leading 50 appearances in 1915 and 40 in 1916 (before being injured), Tom Hughes managed only 11 in 1917 and was out of baseball after the 1918 season. Hughes had a career record of 56–39 with two no-hitters. Little is known about his life after he left baseball, and his *Sporting News* obituary mentions only the two no-hitters and nothing about his post-baseball years. Jack Coombs, more understandably, also suffered a downturn after his major contribution to Brooklyn's National League pennant. The right-hander had two subpar years as a spot starter and reliever before ending his playing career in 1918. After a brief and unhappy stint as manager of the Phillies, he found his niche as a college coach, especially in a 22-year career at Duke, where 21 of his players moved on to the major leagues.[2]

Like Coombs, Jake Daubert played two more seasons in Brooklyn and was then traded to Cincinnati after a salary dispute with Charles Ebbets. Daubert was named captain of the Reds team that won the 1919 World Series against the ill-fated White Sox. He continued to play for the Reds through 1924, hitting .336 in 1922 at the age of 38. Tragically, Daubert died after the 1924 season from a hereditary spleen disease that is easily treated today. In a major league career that spanned 15 seasons, he won two batting titles, racked up 2,300 hits and had a lifetime .303 batting average. Given that record, Daubert certainly seems to deserve at least consideration for the Baseball Hall of Fame. Dying earlier in 1924 was the 48-year-old Pat Moran, who after being fired by the Phillies in 1918 went on to manage Daubert and the Reds to the 1919 world championship.[3]

The Reds' opposition in 1919 was, of course, the infamous Chicago White Sox. The White Sox had followed their 1916 second-place finish by winning the 1917 American League pennant and defeating the New York Giants in six games in the World Series. Key to Chicago's success was the contribution of spitballer Red Faber. During the fateful 1919 campaign, Faber was sick with influenza and played little part in that season. Chicago catcher Ray Schalk always maintained that if Faber had been healthy, the conspirators couldn't have succeeded, as they wouldn't have controlled enough of the pitching staff. Faber played through 1933, when at 45, he was the oldest player in the majors. He earned a career 254–213 mark before going on to a career in automobiles and real estate. Faber was elected to the Baseball Hall of Fame in 1964. Another 1916 White Sox who played a major part in Chicago's 1917 World Series triumph was outfielder Hap Felsch. Sadly, Felsch became part of the 1919 World Series conspiracy, apparently due to an inability to say no. Although he was having his best season the following year, he was ultimately banished from baseball, along with the others. Like them, he played "outlaw" baseball for many years before becoming a tavern owner in Milwaukee.[4]

The Red Sox recaptured the American League pennant in 1918, going on to defeat the Cubs in the World Series. After that, the "Curse of the Bambino" was in full operation, and Boston wouldn't reach the World Series for almost 30 years, while taking 86 seasons to win another one. No longer part of the Red Sox was Larry Gardner, who was traded to the Athletics after a mediocre 1917 season. One can only imagine what it would be like leaving the dominant American League franchise for the lowly A's. Perhaps Connie Mack took mercy on Gardner, as he traded him to Cleveland for the 1919 season. Gardner was reunited there with former teammates Tris Speaker and Joe Wood and showed he had plenty of baseball left in him. Larry had three strong seasons in Cleveland, and helped the Indians defeat the Dodgers for the second time in the World Series in 1920. Retiring from baseball in 1926, Gardner returned to Vermont for business interests and many years of employment in the University of Vermont athletic department.[5]

Also leaving the Red Sox in the next few years after 1916 were Duffy Lewis and Dutch Leonard. After missing the 1918 season due to military service, Lewis was traded to the Yankees (along with Leonard and Ernie Shore) and went on to play for a number of minor league teams. Like many other Americans, he suffered a major financial setback in the 1920 stock market crash. He remained in the game, though, and was a coach with the Boston Braves during the 1930s. In 1975 (the 75th anniversary of the Red Sox), at the age of 87, he returned to throw out the first pitch, both on Opening Day and before the classic sixth game of the World Series. After moving to the Yankees with Lewis, Dutch Leonard became involved in numerous contract disputes with both New York and his next team, the Detroit Tigers. At one point, he broke the reserve clause and was suspended before being reinstated with Detroit. There, he was constantly at odds with his manager, Ty Cobb, who intentionally overworked him. Leonard left Major League Baseball after the 1925 season, but as a parting shot, made accusations against Cobb, Speaker and Wood for their involvement in the 1919 gambling conspiracy. The charges were never proved, and all three players were exonerated by commissioner Kenesaw Landis.[6]

Given Cobb's reputation as a teammate, it's hard to understand how he could be entrusted with an entire team. Leonard wasn't the only one to have trouble with the Detroit manager, as Bobby Veach was treated harshly by Cobb because he didn't like the outfielder's easygoing attitude. This included directing future Hall of Famer Harry Heilmann to heap verbal abuse on his teammate. Since Veach consistently hit over .300, the situation seems more than a little mean spirited. Finally and mercifully, Bobby was traded to Boston for his last major league season. Perhaps more fortunate than Veach in not having to put up with Cobb as manager was Harry Coveleski, who was kept on the bench by injuries for the next two seasons before ending his career in the minors. At least in retirement, Coveleski was able to build on his contribution to the legendary 1908 pennant race, opening a tavern in Shamokin, Pennsylvania, called "The Giant Killer." On those cold winter nights and hot summer days, as beer was poured and baseball stories told, one hopes the 1916 season was "in their flowing cups freshly remembered."[7]

Appendix A:
Team Rosters and
Final Statistics

1916 Boston Red Sox

Player	Position	Age	Bats	Throws	Height	Weight	AB	R	H	2B	3B	HR	RBI	BB	SO	SB	AVG
Sam Agnew	Catcher	29	Right	Right	5' 11"	185	67	4	14	2	1	0	7	6	4	0	0.209
Jack Barry	2nd Base	28	Right	Right	5' 9"	158	330	28	67	6	1	0	20	17	24	8	0.203
Hick Cady	Catcher	30	Right	Right	6' 2"	179	162	5	31	6	3	0	13	15	16	0	0.191
Bill Carrigan	Catcher	32	Right	Right	5' 9"	175	63	7	17	2	1	0	11	11	3	2	0.270
Rube Foster	Pitcher	28	Right	Right	5' 7½"	170	62	3	11	3	0	0	2	3	10	0	0.177
Del Gainer	1st Base	29	Right	Right	6'	180	142	14	36	6	0	3	18	10	24	5	0.254
Larry Gardner	3rd Base	29	Left	Right	5' 8"	165	493	47	152	19	7	2	62	48	27	12	0.308
Vean Gregg	Pitcher	30	Right	Left	6' 1"	185	18	0	2	1	0	0	0	0	3	0	0.111
Richard Haley	Catcher	25	Right	Right	5' 11"	180	1	0	0	0	0	0	0	0	1	0	0.000
Olaf Henricksen	Outfield	29	Left	Left	5' 7½"	158	99	13	20	2	2	0	11	19	15	2	0.202
Dick Hoblitzell	1st Base	27	Right	Right	6'	172	417	57	108	17	1	0	39	47	28	10	0.259
Harry Hooper	Right Field	28	Left	Right	5' 10"	168	575	75	156	20	11	1	37	80	35	27	0.271
Hal Janvrin	Infielder	23	Right	Right	5' 11½"	168	310	32	69	11	4	0	26	32	32	6	0.223
Sad Sam Jones	Pitcher	23	Right	Right	6'	170	6	0	2	0	0	0	0	0	2	0	0.333
Dutch Leonard	Pitcher	23	Left	Left	5' 10½"	185	85	2	17	3	0	0	10	6	16	0	0.200
Duffy Lewis	Left Field	27	Right	Right	5' 10½"	165	563	56	151	29	5	1	56	33	56	16	0.268
Carl Mays	Pitcher	24	Left	Right	5' 11½"	195	77	8	18	1	2	0	8	16	19	0	0.234
Marty McHale	Pitcher	29	Right	Right	5' 11½"	174	0	0	0	0	0	0	0	1	0	0	–
Mike McNally	Infielder	22	Right	Right	5' 11½"	150	135	28	23	0	0	0	9	10	19	9	0.170
Herb Pennock	Pitcher	22	Both	Left	6'	160	8	0	1	0	0	0	0	1	1	0	0.125
Babe Ruth	Pitcher	21	Left	Left	6' 2"	215	136	18	37	5	3	3	15	10	23	0	0.272
Everett Scott	Shortstop	23	Right	Right	5' 8"	148	366	37	85	19	2	0	27	23	24	8	0.232
Ernie Shore	Pitcher	25	Right	Right	6' 4"	220	77	3	7	2	0	0	3	3	31	0	0.091
Chick Shorten	Outfielder	23	Left	Left	6'	175	112	14	33	2	1	0	11	10	8	1	0.295
Pinch Thomas	Catcher	28	Left	Right	5' 9½"	173	216	21	57	10	1	1	21	33	13	4	0.264
Heinie Wagner	Infielder	35	Right	Right	5' 9"	183	8	2	4	1	0	0	0	3	0	2	0.500
Tilly Walker	Center Field	28	Right	Right	5' 11"	165	467	68	124	29	11	3	46	23	45	14	0.266

Player	Position	Age	Bats	Throws	Height	Weight	AB	R	H	2B	3B	HR	RBI	BB	SO	SB	AVG
Jimmy Walsh	Outfield, 3rd	30	Left	Right	5' 10½"	170	17	5	3	1	0	0	2	4	2	3	0.176
Weldon Wyckoff	Pitcher	25	Right	Right	6' 1"	175	6	1	1	0	0	0	0	0	1	0	0.167
Total							5018	548	1246	197	56	14	454	464	482	129	0.248

Pitcher	G	GS	CG	Shutout	IP	H	HR	ER	BB	SO	W-L	ERA
Rube Foster	33	19	9	3	182.1	173	0	62	86	53	14–7	3.06
Vean Gregg	21	7	3	0	77.2	71	0	26	30	41	2–p5	3.01
Sad Sam Jones	12	0	0	0	27	25	0	11	10	7	0–1	3.67
Dutch Leonard	48	34	17	6	274	244	6	72	66	144	18–12	2.36
Carl Mays	44	24	14	2	245	208	3	65	74	76	18–13	2.39
Marty McHale	2	1	0	0	6	7	0	2	4	1	0–1	3.00
Herb Pennock	9	2	0	0	26.2	23	0	9	8	12	0–2	3.04
Babe Ruth	44	41	23	9	323	230	0	63	118	170	23–12	1.75
Ernie Shore	38	28	10	3	225	221	1	66	49	62	16–10	2.63
Weldon Wyckoff	8	0	0	0	22.2	19	0	12	18	18	0–0	4.76
Total	259	156	76	23	1408.1	1221	10	388	463	584	91–63	2.48

1916 Chicago White Sox

Player	Postion	Age	Bats	Throws	Height	Weight	AB	R	H	2B	3B	HR	RBI	BB	SO	SB	AVG
Joe Benz	Pitcher	30	Right	Right	6' 1½"	196	46	3	3	1	0	0	2	2	19	0	0.065
Eddie Cicotte	Pitcher	31	Both	Right	5' 9"	175	57	6	12	2	0	0	4	4	16	0	0.211
Eddie Collins	2nd Base	28	Left	Right	5' 9"	175	545	87	168	14	17	0	52	86	36	40	0.308
Shano Collins	Right Field	30	Right	Right	6'	185	527	74	128	28	12	0	42	59	51	16	0.243
Dave Danforth	Pitcher	26	Left	Left	6'	167	23	3	2	2	0	0	0	4	12	0	0.087
Reb Faber	Pitcher	27	Right	Right	6' 2"	180	63	4	6	0	0	0	2	5	34	0	0.095
Joe Fautsch	Unknown	29	Right	Right	5' 10"	162	1	0	0	0	0	0	0	0	0	0	0.000
Happy Felsch	Center Field	24	Right	Right	5' 11"	175	546	73	164	24	12	7	70	31	67	13	0.300
Jack Fournier	1st Base	26	Left	Right	6'	195	313	36	75	13	9	3	44	36	40	19	0.240
Ziggy Hasbrook	1st Base	22	Right	Right	6' 1"	180	8	1	1	0	0	0	0	1	2	0	0.125
Joe Jackson	Left Field	26	Left	Right	6' 1"	200	592	91	202	40	21	3	78	46	25	24	0.341
Ted Jourdan	1st Base	20	Left	Left	6'	175	2	0	0	0	0	0	0	0	1	2	0.000
Jack Lapp	Catcher	31	Left	Right	5' 8"	160	101	6	21	0	1	0	7	8	10	1	0.208
Nemo Leibold	Outfield	24	Left	Right	5' 6½"	157	82	5	20	1	2	0	13	7	7	7	0.244
Byrd Lynn	Catcher	27	Right	Right	5' 11"	165	40	4	9	1	0	0	3	4	7	2	0.225
Fred McMullin	3rd Base	24	Right	Right	5' 11"	170	187	8	48	3	0	0	10	19	30	9	0.257
Geo. Moriarty	Infielder	30	Right	Right	6'	185	5	1	1	0	0	0	0	2	0	0	0.200
Eddie Murphy	Right Field	24	Left	Right	5' 9"	155	105	14	22	5	1	0	4	9	5	3	0.210
Jack Ness	1st Base	30	Right	Right	6' 2"	165	258	32	69	7	5	1	34	9	32	4	0.267
Reb Russell	Pitcher	27	Left	Left	5' 11"	185	91	9	13	2	0	0	6	0	18	1	0.143
Ray Schalk	Catcher	23	Right	Right	5' 9"	165	410	36	95	12	9	0	41	41	31	30	0.232
Jim Scott	Pitcher	27	Right	Right	6' 1"	235	52	2	6	0	0	0	3	0	13	0	0.115
Ray Shook	Unknown	26	Right	Right	5' 7½"	155	0	0	0	0	0	0	0	0	0	0	0.000
Zeb Terry	Shortstop	24	Right	Right	5' 8"	129	269	20	51	8	4	0	17	33	36	4	0.190
F. Von Kolnitz	Third Base	22	Right	Right	5' 10½"	175	44	1	10	3	0	0	7	2	6	0	0.227
Ed Walsh	Pitcher	34	Right	Right	6' 1"	193	0	0	0	0	0	0	0	0	0	0	0.000
Buck Weaver	SS/3B	25	Both	Right	5' 11"	170	582	78	132	27	6	3	38	30	48	22	0.227

Player	Postion	Age	Bats	Throws	Height	Weight	AB	R	H	2B	3B	HR	RBI	BB	SO	SB	AVG
Lefty Williams	Pitcher	23	Right	Left	5' 9"	160	74	5	10	2	1	0	4	7	30	0	0.135
Mel. Wolfgang	Pitcher	26	Right	Right	5' 9"	160	40	2	9	1	0	0	3	0	8	0	0.225
Cy Wright	Short Stop	22	Left	Right	5' 9"	150	18	0	0	0	0	0	0	1	7	0	0.000
Total							5018	601	1277	194	100	17	484	447	591	197	0.251

Pitcher	G	GS	CG	Shutout	IP	H	HR	ER	BB	SO	W-L	ERA
Joe Benz	28	16	6	4	142	108	0	32	32	57	9-5	2.03
Eddie Cicotte	44	19	11	2	187	138	1	37	70	91	15-7	1.78
Dave Danforth	28	8	1	0	93.2	87	1	34	37	49	6-5	3.27
Red Faber	35	25	15	3	205.1	167	1	46	61	87	17-9	2.02
Reb Russell	56	25	16	5	264.1	207	1	71	42	112	18-11	2.42
Jim Scott	32	21	8	1	165	155	3	50	53	71	7-4	2.72
Ed Walsh	2	1	0	0	3.1	4	0	1	3	3	0-1	2.70
Lefty Williams	43	26	10	2	224	220	5	72	65	138	13-7	2.89
Mel Wolfgang	27	14	6	1	127	103	2	28	42	36	4-6	1.98
Total	295	155	73	18	1411	1189	14	371	405	644	89-65	2.36

1916 Boston Braves

Player	Position	Age	Bats	Throws	Height	Weight	AB	R	H	2B	3B	HR	RBI	BB	SO	SB	AVG
Frank Allen	Pitcher	28	Right	Left	5' 9"	175	34	4	7	0	1	0	4	8	14	0	0.206
Fred Bailey	Outfield	21	Left	Left	5' 11"	150	10	0	1	0	0	0	1	0	3	0	0.100
Jesse Barnes	Pitcher	24	Left	Right	6'	170	48	1	9	1	0	0	2	2	4	0	0.188
Earl Blackburn	Catcher	24	Right	Right	5' 11"	180	110	12	30	4	4	0	7	9	21	2	0.273
Larry Chappell	Outfield	26	Right	Right	6'	186	53	4	12	1	1	0	9	2	8	1	0.226
Zip Collins	Outfield	24	Left	Left	5' 11"	152	268	39	56	1	6	1	18	18	42	4	0.209
Pete Compton	Outfield	27	Left	Left	5' 11"	170	98	13	20	2	0	0	8	7	7	5	0.204
Joe Connolly	Outfield	32	Left	Right	5' 7½"	165	110	11	25	5	2	0	12	14	13	5	0.227
Dick Egan	Infield	32	Right	Right	5' 11"	162	238	23	53	8	3	0	16	19	21	2	0.223
Johnny Evers	2nd Base	35	Left	Right	5' 9"	125	241	33	52	4	1	0	15	40	19	5	0.216
Ed Fitzpatrick	Infield	27	Right	Right	5' 8"	165	216	17	46	8	0	1	18	15	26	5	0.213
Hank Gowdy	Catcher	27	Right	Right	6' 2"	182	349	32	88	14	1	1	34	24	33	8	0.252
Tom Hughes	Pitcher	32	Right	Right	6' 2"	175	52	2	10	5	0	0	1	1	12	0	0.192
Elmer Knetzer	Pitcher	31	Right	Right	5' 10"	180	0	0	0	0	0	0	0	0	0	0	0.000
Ed Konetchy	1st Base	31	Right	Right	6' 2½"	195	566	76	147	29	13	3	70	43	46	13	0.260
Sherry Magee	Outfield	32	Right	Right	5' 11"	179	419	44	101	17	5	3	54	44	52	10	0.241
Rabbit Maranville	Shortstop	25	Right	Right	5' 5"	155	604	79	142	16	13	4	38	50	69	32	0.235
Joe Mathes	2nd Base	25	Both	Right	6' ½"	180	0	0	0	0	0	0	0	0	0	0	0.000
Art Nehf	Pitcher	24	Left	Left	5' 9½"	176	40	4	5	1	0	0	0	3	12	2	0.125
Pat Ragan	Pitcher	31	Right	Right	5' 10½"	185	60	2	13	2	1	0	4	2	25	0	0.217
Ed Reulbach	Pitcher	34	Right	Right	6' 1"	190	33	3	3	0	1	0	1	0	14	0	0.091
Art Rico	Catcher	21	Right	Right	5' 9½"	185	4	0	0	0	0	0	0	0	0	0	0.000
Dick Rudolph	Pitcher	29	Right	Right	5' 9½"	160	101	5	16	2	1	0	6	8	26	2	0.158
Red Smith	3rd Base	26	Right	Right	5' 11"	165	509	48	132	16	10	3	60	53	55	13	0.259
Fred Snodgrass	Outfield	29	Right	Right	5' 11½"	175	382	33	95	13	5	1	32	34	54	14	0.249
Walt Tragesser	Catcher	29	Right	Right	6'	175	54	3	11	1	0	0	4	5	10	0	0.204

Player	Position	Age	Bats	Throws	Height	Weight	AB	R	H	2B	3B	HR	RBI	BB	SO	SB	AVG
Lefty Tyler	Pitcher	27	Left	Left	6'	175	93	10	19	3	1	3	20	9	15	0	0.204
Joe Wilhoit	Outfield	31	Left	Right	6' 2"	175	383	44	88	13	4	2	38	27	45	18	0.230
Total							5075	542	1181	166	73	22	472	437	646	141	0.233

Pitcher	Games	Starts	CG	Shutouts	IP	Hits	HRs	ER	BB	SO	W-L	ERA
Frank Allen	19	14	7	2	113	102	1	26	31	63	8–2	2.07
Jesse Barnes	33	18	9	3	163	154	3	43	37	55	6–15	2.37
Tom Hughes	40	13	7	1	161	121	2	42	51	97	16–3	2.35
Elmer Knetzer	2	0	0	0	5	11	0	4	2	2	0–2	7.20
Art Nehf	22	13	6	1	121	110	1	27	20	36	7–5	2.01
Pat Ragan	28	23	14	3	182	143	3	42	47	94	9–9	2.08
Ed Reulbach	21	11	6	0	109	99	1	30	41	47	7–6	2.47
Dick Rudolph	41	38	27	5	312	266	7	75	38	133	19–12	2.16
Lefty Tyler	34	28	21	6	249	200	6	56	58	117	17–9	2.02
Total	240	158	97	21	1415	1206	24	345	325	644	89–63	2.19

1916 Detroit Tigers

Player	Position	Age	Bats	Throws	Height	Weight	AB	R	H	2B	3B	HR	RBI	BB	SO	SB	AVG
Del Baker	Catcher	23	Right	Right	5' 11½"	176	98	7	15	4	0	0	6	11	8	2	0.153
George Boehler	Pitcher	24	Right	Right	6' 2"	180	3	1	0	0	0	0	0	2	0	0	0.000
Bernie Boland	Pitcher	24	Right	Right	5' 8½"	168	32	4	8	0	0	0	2	5	12	0	0.250
George Burns	First Base	23	Right	Right	6' 1½"	180	479	60	137	22	6	4	73	22	30	12	0.286
Donie Bush	Shortstop	28	Both	Right	5' 6"	140	550	73	124	5	9	0	34	75	42	19	0.225
Ty Cobb	Center Field	29	Left	Right	6' 1"	175	542	113	201	31	10	5	68	78	39	68	0.371
Har. Coveleskie	Pitcher	29	Both	Left	6'	180	118	7	25	3	2	0	7	0	38	0	0.212
Sam Crawford	Right Field	35	Left	Left	6'	190	322	41	92	11	13	0	42	37	10	10	0.286
G. Cunningham	Pitcher	21	Right	Right	5' 11"	185	41	7	11	2	2	0	3	8	12	0	0.268
Jack Dalton	Outfield	30	Right	Right	5' 8"	145	11	1	2	0	0	0	0	0	5	0	0.182
Hooks Dauss	Pitcher	26	Right	Right	5' 10½"	168	72	8	16	3	2	1	5	15	30	0	0.222
Jean Dubuc	Pitcher	27	Right	Right	5' 10½"	185	78	3	20	2	2	0	7	7	12	0	0.256
Ben Dyer	Shortstop	23	Right	Right	5' 10"	170	14	4	4	1	0	0	1	1	1	0	0.286
Howard Ehmke	Pitcher	21	Right	Right	6' 3"	190	14	1	2	0	0	0	1	0	5	0	0.143
Babe Ellison	Third Base	19	Right	Right	5' 11"	170	7	0	1	0	0	0	1	0	1	0	0.143
Eric Erickson	Pitcher	21	Right	Right	6' 2"	190	4	0	0	0	0	0	0	0	2	0	0.000
Frank Fuller	Infielder	23	Both	Right	5' 7"	150	10	2	1	0	0	0	1	1	4	3	0.100
Earl Hamilton	Pitcher	24	Left	Left	5' 8"	160	13	0	1	0	0	0	2	1	6	0	0.077
George Harper	Outfield	23	Left	Right	5' 8"	167	56	4	9	1	0	0	3	5	8	0	0.161
Harry Heilmann	Right Field	21	Right	Right	6' 1"	195	451	57	127	30	11	2	73	42	40	9	0.282
Bill James	Pitcher	29	Both	Right	6' 4"	195	44	3	3	0	0	0	1	3	24	0	0.068
Deacon Jones	Pitcher	23	Right	Right	6'	174	2	0	0	0	0	0	0	0	0	0	0.000
Marty Kavanagh	Right Field	24	Right	Right	6'	187	78	6	11	4	0	0	5	9	15	0	0.141
George Maisel	Third Base	24	Right	Right	5' 10½"	180	5	2	0	0	0	0	0	0	2	0	0.000
Red McKee	Catcher	25	Left	Right	5' 11"	180	76	3	16	1	2	0	4	6	11	0	0.211
Bill McTigue	Pitcher	25	Left	Left	6' 1½"	175	1	0	0	0	0	0	0	0	0	0	0.000
Willie Mitchell	Pitcher	26	Right	Left	6'	176	36	3	9	0	0	0	3	5	6	0	0.250

Player	Position	Age	Bats	Throws	Height	Weight	AB	R	H	2B	3B	HR	RBI	BB	SO	SB	AVG
Tubby Spencer	Catcher	32	Right	Right	5' 10"	215	54	7	20	1	1	1	10	6	6	2	0.370
Oscar Stanage	Catcher	33	Right	Right	5' 11"	190	291	16	69	17	3	0	30	17	48	3	0.237
Billy Sullivan	Catcher	41	Right	Right	5' 9"	155	0	0	0	0	0	0	0	0	0	0	0.000
Bobby Veach	Left Field	27	Left	Right	5' 11"	160	566	92	173	33	15	3	91	52	41	24	0.306
Ossie Vitt	Third Base	26	Right	Right	5' 10"	150	597	88	135	17	12	0	42	75	28	18	0.226
Ralph Young	2nd Base	27	Both	Right	5' 5"	165	528	60	139	16	6	1	45	62	43	20	0.263
Totals							5193	673	1371	202	96	17	560	545	529	190	0.264

Pitcher	G	GS	CG	Shutout	IP	H	HR	ER	BB	SO	W-L	ERA
George Boehler	5	2	1	0	13.1	12	0	7	9	8	1–1	4.72
Bernie Boland	46	9	5	1	130.1	111	1	57	73	59	10–3	3.94
Harry Coveleskie	44	39	22	3	324.1	278	6	71	63	108	21–11	1.97
G. Cunningham	35	14	5	0	150.1	146	0	46	74	68	7–10	2.75
Hooks Dauss	39	29	18	1	238.2	220	2	85	90	95	19–12	3.21
Jean Dubuc	36	16	8	1	170	134	1	56	84	40	10–10	2.96
Howard Ehmke	5	4	4	0	37.1	34	0	13	15	15	3–1	3.13
Eric Erickson	8	0	0	0	16	13	0	5	8	7	0–0	2.81
Earl Hamilton	5	5	3	0	37	34	0	11	22	7	1–2	2.65
Bill James	30	20	8	0	151.2	141	1	62	79	61	8–12	3.68
Deacon Jones	1	0	0	0	7	7	0	2	5	2	0–0	2.57
Grover Lowdermilk	1	0	0	0	0	0	0	0	3	0	0–0	0
Bill McTigue	3	0	0	0	5	5	0	3	5	1	0–0	5.06
Willie Mitchell	23	17	7	2	127.2	119	1	47	48	60	7–5	3.31
Totals	281	155	81	8	1407	1254	12	465	578	531	87–67	2.97

1916 Brooklyn Dodgers

Player	Position	Age	Bats	Throws	Height	Weight	AB	R	H	2B	3B	HR	RBI	BB	SO	SB	BA
Ed Appleton	Pitcher	24	Right	Right	6' ½"	173	12	1	2	0	0	0	0	0	0	0	0.167
Leon Cadore	Pitcher	26	Right	Right	6' 1"	190	3	0	0	0	0	0	0	0	0	0	0
Larry Cheney	Pitcher	30	Right	Right	6' 1½"	185	79	4	9	2	0	0	2	5	29	2	0.114
Jack Coombs	Pitcher	34	Right	Right	6'	185	61	2	11	2	0	0	3	2	10	0	0.180
George Cutshaw	2nd Base	30	Right	Right	5' 9"	160	581	58	151	21	4	2	63	25	32	27	0.260
Jake Daubert	1st Base	32	Left	Left	5' 10½"	160	478	75	151	16	7	3	33	38	39	21	0.316
Artie Dede	Catcher	21	Right	Right	5' 9"	155	1	0	0	0	0	0	0	0	0	0	0
Wheezer Dell	Pitcher	30	Right	Right	6' 4"	210	44	1	4	0	0	0	3	1	14	0	0.091
Bunny Fabrique	Shortstop	29	Both	Right	5' 8½"	150	2	0	0	0	0	0	0	0	1	0	0
Gus Getz	3rd Base	27	Right	Right	5' 11"	165	96	9	21	1	2	0	8	0	5	9	0.219
Jim Hickman	Outfield	24	Right	Right	5' 7½"	170	5	3	1	0	0	0	0	2	0	1	0.200
Jimmy Johnston	Outfield	27	Right	Right	5' 10"	160	425	58	107	13	8	1	26	35	38	22	0.252
John Kelleher	Infield	23	Right	Right	5' 11"	150	3	0	0	0	0	0	0	0	0	0	0
Duster Mails	Pitcher	22	Left	Left	6'	195	4	1	1	0	0	0	0	0	2	0	0.250
Rube Marquard	Pitcher	30	Both	Left	6' 3"	180	63	3	9	0	1	0	5	4	17	1	0.143
Lew McCarty	Catcher	28	Right	Right	5' 11½"	192	150	17	47	6	1	0	13	14	16	4	0.313
Fred Merkle	1st Base	28	Right	Right	6' 1"	190	69	6	16	1	0	0	2	7	4	2	0.232
John Meyers	Catcher	36	Right	Right	5' 11"	194	239	21	59	10	3	0	21	26	15	2	0.247
Hack Miller	Outfield	22	Right	Right	5' 9"	195	3	0	1	0	1	0	1	1	1	0	0.333
Otto Miller	Catcher	27	Right	Right	6'	196	216	16	55	9	2	1	17	7	29	6	0.255
Mike Mowrey	3rd Base	32	Right	Right	5' 10"	180	495	57	121	22	6	0	60	50	60	16	0.244
Hi Myers	Outfield	27	Right	Right	5' 9½"	175	412	54	108	12	14	3	36	21	35	17	0.262
Al Nixon	Outfield	30	Right	Left	5' 7½"	164	2	0	2	0	0	0	0	0	0	0	1.000
Ivy Olson	Shortstop	31	Right	Right	5' 10½"	175	351	29	89	13	4	1	38	21	27	14	0.254
Ollie O'Mara	Shortstop	25	Right	Right	5' 9"	155	193	18	39	5	2	0	15	12	20	10	0.202
Jeff Pfeffer	Pitcher	28	Right	Right	6' 3"	210	122	5	34	2	2	0	12	4	32	2	0.279
Nap Rucker	Pitcher	32	Left	Left	5' 11"	190	11	1	1	0	0	0	2	0	2	0	0.091

Player	Position	Age	Bats	Throws	Height	Weight	AB	R	H	2B	3B	HR	RBI	BB	SO	SB	BA
Sherry Smith	Pitcher	25	Left	Left	6' 1"	170	77	4	21	1	2	0	7	4	18	1	0.273
Red Smyth	2nd Base	25	Left	Right	5' 9"	152	5	0	0	0	0	0	0	0	3	0	0
Casey Stengel	Outfield	26	Left	Left	5' 11"	175	462	66	129	27	8	8	53	33	51	11	0.279
Mack Wheat	Catcher	23	Right	Right	5' 11½"	167	2	0	0	0	0	0	0	0	1	0	0
Zack Wheat	Outfield	28	Left	Right	5' 10"	170	568	76	177	32	13	9	73	43	49	19	0.312
Total							**5234**	**585**	**1366**	**195**	**80**	**28**	**493**	**355**	**550**	**187**	**0.261**

Pitcher	G	GS	CG	Shutout	IP	H	HR	ER	BB	SO	W-L	ERA
Ed Appleton	14	3	1	0	47	49	1	16	18	14	1-2	3.06
Leon Cadore	1	0	0	0	6	10	0	3	0	2	0-0	4.50
Larry Cheney	41	32	15	5	253	178	5	54	105	166	18-12	1.92
Jack Coombs	27	19	10	3	159	136	3	47	44	47	13-8	2.66
Wheezer Dell	32	16	9	2	155	143	2	39	43	76	8-9	2.26
Duster Mails	11	0	0	0	17	15	1	7	9	13	0-1	3.63
Rube Marquard	36	21	15	2	205	169	2	36	38	107	13-6	1.58
Jeff Pfeffer	41	36	30	6	328	274	5	70	63	128	25-11	1.92
Nap Rucker	9	4	1	0	37	34	0	7	7	14	2-1	1.69
Sherry Smith	36	25	15	4	219	193	5	57	45	67	14-10	2.34
Total	**248**	**156**	**96**	**22**	**1426**	**1201**	**24**	**336**	**372**	**634**	**94-60**	**2.12**

1916 Philadelphia Phillies

Player	Position	Age	Bats	Throws	Height	Weight	AB	R	H	2B	3B	HR	RBI	BB	SO	SB	AVG
Bert Adams	Catcher	25	Both	Right	6' 1"	185	13	2	3	0	0	0	1	0	3	0	0.231
Grover Clv Alexander	Pitcher	29	Right	Right	6' 1"	185	138	10	33	7	4	0	9	5	15	1	0.239
Dave Bancroft	Shortstop	25	Right	Right	5' 9½"	165	477	53	101	10	0	3	33	74	57	15	0.212
Stan Baumgartner	Pitcher	22	Left	Left	6'	175	1	0	0	0	0	0	0	0	0	0	0.000
Charles Bender	Pitcher	32	Right	Right	6' 2"	185	43	2	12	4	0	0	5	3	9	0	0.279
Ed Burns	Catcher	29	Right	Right	5' 6"	165	219	14	51	8	1	0	14	16	18	3	0.233
Bobby Byrne	Infield	32	Right	Right	5' 7½"	145	141	22	33	10	1	0	9	14	7	6	0.234
George Chalmers	Pitcher	28	Right	Right	6' 1"	189	15	0	0	0	0	0	0	0	10	0	0.000
Claude Cooper	Outfield	24	Left	Left	5' 9"	158	104	9	20	2	0	0	11	7	15	1	0.192
Gavy Cravath	Outfield	35	Right	Right	5' 10½"	186	448	70	127	21	8	11	70	64	89	9	0.283
Al Demaree	Pitcher	32	Left	Right	6'	170	101	6	11	2	0	0	5	6	36	2	0.109
Oscar Dugey	Infield	29	Right	Right	5' 8"	160	50	9	11	3	0	0	1	9	8	3	0.220
Gary Fortune	Pitcher	22	Both	Right	5' 11½"	176	2	0	0	0	0	0	0	0	1	0	0.000
Bob Gandy	Outfield	23	Left	Right	6' 3"	180	2	0	0	0	0	0	0	0	1	0	0.000
Wilbur Good	Outfield	31	Left	Left	5' 11½"	180	136	25	34	4	3	1	15	8	13	7	0.250
Erv Kantlehner	Pitcher	24	Left	Left	6'	190	0	0	0	0	0	0	0	0	0	0	0.000
Bill Killifer	Catcher	29	Right	Right	5' 10½"	170	286	22	62	5	4	3	27	8	14	2	0.217
Fred Luderus	1st Base	31	Left	Right	5' 11½"	185	508	52	143	26	3	5	53	41	32	8	0.281
Billy Maharg	Outfield	35	Right	Right	5' 4½"	155	1	0	0	0	0	0	0	0	0	0	0.000
Erskine Mayer	Pitcher	28	Right	Right	6'	168	38	2	5	0	0	0	3	4	8	0	0.132
George McQuillan	Pitcher	31	Right	Right	5' 11½"	175	11	0	1	0	0	0	1	1	3	0	0.091
Bert Niehoff	2nd Base	32	Right	Right	5' 10½"	170	548	65	133	42	4	4	61	37	57	20	0.243
Joe Oescheger	Pitcher	24	Right	Right	6'	190	5	0	0	0	0	0	0	0	3	0	0.000
Dode Paskert	Outfield	35	Right	Right	5' 11"	165	555	82	155	30	7	8	46	54	76	22	0.279
Eppa Rixey	Pitcher	25	Left	Left	6' 5"	210	97	6	15	3	0	0	9	2	14	0	0.155
Milt Stock	3rd Base	23	Right	Right	5' 8"	154	509	61	143	25	6	1	43	27	33	21	0.281
Ben Tincup	Pitcher	23	Left	Right	6' 1"	180	1	0	0	0	0	0	0	0	0	0	0.000

Player	Position	Age	Bats	Throws	Height	Weight	AB	R	H	2B	3B	HR	RBI	BB	SO	SB	AVG
Bud Wiesner	Outfield	25	Right	Right	5' 11"	165	10	1	3	1	0	0	1	0	3	0	0.300
George Whitted	Outfield	26	Right	Right	5' 8½"	168	526	68	148	20	12	6	68	19	46	29	0.281
Total							4985	581	1244	223	53	42	486	399	571	149	0.250

Pitcher	G	GS	CG	Shutout	IP	H	HR	ER	BB	SO	W–L	ERA
Grover Cl. Alexander	48	45	38	16	389	323	6	67	50	167	33–12	1.55
Stan Baumgartner	1	0	0	0	4	5	0	1	1	0	0–0	2.25
Charles Bender	27	13	4	0	123	137	3	51	34	43	7–7	3.74
George Chalmers	12	8	2	0	53	49	2	19	19	21	1–4	3.19
Al Demaree	39	35	25	4	285	252	4	83	48	130	19–14	2.62
Gary Fortune	1	1	0	0	5	2	0	2	4	3	0–1	3.60
Erv Kantlehner	3	0	0	0	4	7	0	4	3	2	0–0	9.00
Erskine Mayer	28	16	7	2	140	148	7	49	33	62	7–7	3.15
George McQuillan	21	3	1	0	62	58	2	19	15	22	1–7	2.76
Joe Oescheger	14	0	0	0	30	18	2	8	14	17	1–0	2.37
Eppa Rixey	38	33	20	3	287	239	2	59	74	134	22–10	1.85
Total	232	154	97	25	1382	1238	28	362	295	601	91–62	2.36

1916 New York Giants

Player	Position	Age	Bats	Throws	Height	Weight	AB	R	H	2B	3B	HR	RBI	BB	SO	SB	AVG
Fred Anderson	Pitcher	31	Right	Right	6' 2"	180	58	6	8	2	1	0	3	1	18	0	0.138
Rube Benton	Pitcher	29	Left	Left	6' 1"	190	78	3	7	0	1	0	3	2	21	1	0.090
Fred Brainard	3rd Base	24	Right	Right	6'	176	7	0	0	0	0	0	0	0	0	0	0.000
George Burns	Outfield	27	Right	Right	5' 7"	160	623	105	174	24	8	5	41	63	47	37	0.279
Red Dooin	Catcher	37	Right	Right	5' 9½"	165	17	1	2	0	0	0	0	0	3	0	0.118
Mickey Doolan	Infield	36	Right	Right	5' 10½"	170	51	4	12	3	1	1	3	2	4	1	0.235
Larry Doyle	2nd Base	30	Left	Right	5' 10"	165	441	55	118	24	10	2	47	27	23	17	0.268
Art Fletcher	Shortstop	31	Right	Right	5' 10½"	170	500	53	143	23	8	3	66	13	36	15	0.286
Buck Herzog	2nd Base	31	Right	Right	5' 11"	160	280	40	73	10	4	0	25	22	24	19	0.261
Walter Holke	1st Base	24	Left	Left	6' 1½"	185	111	16	39	4	2	0	13	6	16	10	0.351
Herb Hunter	Infield	21	Left	Right	6' ½"	165	28	3	7	0	0	1	4	0	5	0	0.250
Benny Kauff	Outfield	26	Left	Left	5' 8"	157	552	71	146	22	15	9	74	68	65	40	0.264
Duke Kelleher	Catcher	23	Unknown	Right	5' 7"	180	0	0	0	0	0	0	0	0	0	0	0.000
George Kelly	Outfield	21	Right	Right	6' 4"	190	76	4	12	2	1	0	3	6	24	1	0.158
Red Killefer	Outfield	31	Right	Right	5' 9"	175	1	0	1	0	0	0	1	1	0	0	1.000
Brad Kocher	Catcher	28	Right	Right	5' 11"	188	65	1	7	2	0	0	1	2	10	0	0.108
Hans Lobert	Infield	35	Right	Right	5' 9"	170	76	6	17	3	2	0	11	5	8	2	0.224
Christy Mathewson	Pitcher	36	Right	Right	6' 1½"	195	17	1	0	0	0	0	1	4	4	0	0.000
Lew McCarty	Catcher	28	Right	Right	5' 11½"	192	68	6	27	3	4	0	9	7	9	0	0.397
Bill McKechnie	Infield	30	Both	Right	5' 10"	160	260	22	64	9	1	0	17	7	20	7	0.246
Fred Merkle	1st Base	28	Right	Right	6' 1"	190	401	45	95	19	3	7	44	33	46	17	0.237
Emilio Palmero	Pitcher	21	Left	Left	5' 11"	157	3	0	0	0	0	0	0	1	0	0	0.000
Pol Perritt	Pitcher	25	Right	Right	6' 2"	168	83	7	7	3	0	0	4	4	30	0	0.084
Bill Rariden	Catcher	28	Right	Right	5' 10"	168	351	23	78	9	3	1	29	55	32	4	0.222
Hank Ritter	Pitcher	23	Right	Right	6'	180	0	0	0	0	0	0	0	0	0	0	0.000
Dave Robertson	Outfield	27	Left	Left	6'	186	587	88	180	18	8	12	69	14	56	21	0.307
Jose Rodriguez	1st Base	22	Right	Right	5' 8"	150	0	0	0	0	0	0	0	0	0	0	0.000

Player	Position	Age	Bats	Throws	Height	Weight	AB	R	H	2B	3B	HR	RBI	BB	SO	SB	AVG
Edd Rousch	Outfield	23	Left	Left	5' 11"	170	69	4	13	0	1	0	5	1	4	4	0.188
Slim Sallee	Pitcher	31	Right	Left	6' 3"	180	35	1	9	1	0	0	1	2	4	0	0.257
Rube Schauer	Pitcher	25	Right	Right	6' 2"	192	9	1	2	1	0	0	2	0	0	0	0.222
Ferdie Schupp	Pitcher	25	Right	Left	5' 10"	150	41	1	4	0	0	0	0	1	17	0	0.098
George Smith	Pitcher	24	Right	Right	6' 2"	163	2	0	0	0	0	0	0	0	2	0	0.000
Heinie Stafford	Infield	25	Right	Right	5' 7"	160	1	0	0	0	0	0	0	0	0	0	0.000
Ralph Stroud	Pitcher	31	Right	Right	6'	160	14	0	1	0	0	0	1	1	0	0	0.071
Jeff Tesreau	Pitcher	27	Right	Right	6' 2"	218	94	8	18	2	1	1	4	1	4	1	0.191
Lew Wendell	Catcher	24	Right	Right	5' 11"	178	2	0	0	0	0	0	0	1	14	0	0.000
Heinie Zimmerman	3rd Base	29	Right	Right	5' 11½"	176	151	22	41	4	0	0	19	7	10	9	0.272
Total							5152	597	1305	188	74	42	500	356	558	206	0.253

Pitcher	G	GS	CG	Shutout	IP	H	HR	ER	BB	SO	W–L	ERA
Fred Anderson	38	27	13	2	188	206	7	71	38	98	9–13	3.40
Rube Benton	38	29	15	3	238.2	210	5	76	58	115	16–18	2.87
Christy Mathewson	12	6	4	1	65.2	59	3	17	7	16	3–4	2.33
Emilio Palmiero	4	2	0	0	15.2	17	2	14	8	8	0–3	8.04
Pol Perritt	40	29	17	5	251	243	11	73	56	115	18–11	2.62
Hank Ritter	3	0	0	0	5	3	0	0	0	3	1–0	0
Slim Sallee	15	11	7	2	111.2	96	2	17	10	35	9–4	1.37
Rube Schauer	19	3	1	0	45.2	44	0	15	16	24	1–4	2.96
Ferdie Schupp	30	11	8	4	140.1	79	1	14	37	86	9–3	0.9
George Smith	9	1	0	0	20.2	14	1	6	6	9	3–0	2.71
Sailor Stroud	10	4	0	0	46.2	47	1	14	9	16	3–2	2.7
Jeff Tesreau	40	32	23	5	268.1	249	9	87	65	113	14–14	2.29
Total	258	155	88	22	1394	1267	41	404	310	638	86–66	2.61

Appendix B:
Sportswriters

Edward Armistead Batchelor, Sr. (1883–1968) — After going to school at Brown University and Providence College, Batchelor took his first sports-writing position with the Providence *Journal*. He moved to Detroit, writing for the *Free Press* from 1906 through 1917, both as a sportswriter and editor. In 1916, he covered the Tigers. E.A. would leave to take a position as a war correspondent in France for the Detroit *News*. Upon his return home, Batchelor ended his working career in advertising.[1]

Sam Crane (1854–1925) — A nineteenth century player and manager who began a sports-writing career in New York City in 1890, Crane worked for 25 years for the New York *Evening Journal*, including the 1916 season when he wrote a regular column. Crane was a close personal friend of John McGraw and died after returning from a Giants' road trip during which he contracted pneumonia.[2]

Nicholas J. Flatley (1886–1930) — A 1907 graduate of Boston College, Flatley covered the Boston Braves during the 1916 pennant race. He subsequently became the sports editor of the Boston *American*, circa 1917–28, and was also a correspondent for the *Sporting News*. He died in 1930 at the age of 44 from heart disease.[3]

James Isaminger (1880–1946) — Isaminger began his newspaper career in Cincinnati, but moved to Philadelphia and joined the staff of the *North American* in 1905 and stayed there until the paper was sold in 1925. He then moved to the staff of the Philadelphia *Inquirer*. During 1916, Isaminger covered the Phillies and wrote baseball columns for the paper.[4]

Fred Lieb (1888–1980) — Lieb began his 70 plus-year sport-writing career at *Baseball Magazine* in 1909 but moved to the New York *Press* in 1911. During 1916, he covered the New York Giants for the *Press* and *The Sun* (the papers merged during the season), in addition to writing columns. He eventually left day-to-day sportswriting to write columns and articles for the *Sporting News*, as well as a number of baseball books, especially team histories. His book, *Baseball As I Have Known It*, gives a picture of sportswriting during the Deadball Era.[5]

Sid Mercer (1880–1945) — Mercer began his newspaper career as a printer's devil on the St. Louis *Republic*. He eventually became the traveling secretary for the St.

Louis Browns before moving to New York in 1906 to work for the *Globe and Commercial Advertiser,* where he remained until 1920. He later worked for the Hearst newspapers, covering boxing for many years. During 1916, he was a columnist for the *Globe and Commercial Advertiser.*[6]

Tim Murnane (1851–1917) — Considered one of the Deadball Era's most famed and recognized sportswriters, Tim Murnane started in Major League Baseball as a player and manager in the 1870s and 1880s. When J.D. Drohan retired, he was offered the position of baseball editor at the Boston *Daily Globe,* working at the publication from 1888 through 1917. In 1916, part of his responsibilities included covering the Red Sox.

Among other ventures, Murnane was president of the New England League and founded the National Association of Professional Baseball Leagues. With articles also appearing in the *Sporting Life* and *The Sporting News,* Murnane is credited with inventing the modern baseball column. At the age of 65, Tim died of heart disease when he dropped dead in the Shubert Theater, just 30 minutes after writing his daily article.[7]

Jim Nasium (1874–1958) — The pen name of Edgar Forrest Wolfe, a sportswriter and cartoonist, Nasium worked for a number of Pittsburgh and Philadelphia newspapers in both art and sportswriting. His longest tenure was with the Philadelphia *Inquirer* (1907–1922), where he covered the Phillies in 1916, typically contributing both game accounts and cartoons. After 1929, Nasium became a full-time free-lance cartoonist. Many of his cartoons appeared on the front page of *The Sporting News.*[8]

Thomas S. Rice (1878–1942) — A graduate of Baltimore City College and the University of Maryland Law School, Rice moved from the practice of law to writing sports for the Baltimore *Sun* and the Washington *Times.* In 1911, he moved to the Brooklyn *Daily Eagle* and covered the Brooklyn Dodgers until 1929. During that 18-year period, he reportedly saw every game Brooklyn played, including exhibition games. According to his New York *Times* obituary, he influenced Charles Ebbets to hire Wilbert Robinson as his manager in 1914, and then became one of Robinson's advisors during the 1916 and 1920 World Series.

A 1916 article in *The Sporting News* credited Rice with a number of achievements that made baseball games easier to follow for both fans and sportswriters. These include listing players by number on scoreboards, requiring managers to inform umpires of lineup changes, and the announcing of batting orders ten minutes prior to the game.

Rice left sportswriting in 1929 to focus on criminology and was named to the New York State Crime Commission, as well as the New York City Commission for Crime Prevention. Given the opening comments of many of his 1916 Dodger game accounts, it's no surprise that he took a hard line on crime, including the comment that the best response to crime was "hot lead or hemp rope."[9]

Damon Runyan (1884–1946) — From 1911 to 1920 he covered the New York Giants for the New York *American,* writing columns as well as game accounts. He left sportswriting to become a well-known columnist and feature writer focusing on Broadway. He also wrote a number of short stories, one of which — *Guys and Dolls* — was adapted into a hit Broadway musical. [10]

Henry Salsinger (1885–1958) — Salsinger took a position with the Detroit *News* at the age of 20, served as sports editor there for 24 years, and would work at the publication for more than 50. During the 1916 season, his articles appeared weekly in *The Sporting News*. Salsinger, who was at one time president of the Baseball Writers' Association of America, wrote about many sports, but baseball was his area of expertise. Reportedly, he was Ty Cobb's "biggest booster in print," and the two also got along well.[11]

I.E. Sanborn (1866–1934) — Born in Vermont, Sanborn attended Dartmouth College, intending to teach foreign languages. However, he accepted a job offer from the Springfield (Mass.) *Union* in 1889 and worked there for 11 years before moving on to the Chicago *Daily Tribune*, where he worked until 1920. In 1916, he provided most of the Chicago White Sox coverage. Tragically, he committed suicide at the age of 67, shooting himself through his head in the garden of his home, located in Canandaigua, New York. He had been in poor health and even spent time in a sanitarium.[12]

Paul Shannon (1876–1939) — Shannon obtained degrees at both Boston College and Harvard University, starting to work at the Boston *Post* while he was attending the latter institution. He would leave for the San Antonio *Gazette,* and then come back, covering murder trials and other news assignments. When baseball writer Fred O'Connell died, Shannon took over and would ultimately work as the sports editor of the publication for more than 30 years. Paul had the Red Sox beat in 1916. Shannon died tragically, drowning while vacationing in Florida, at the age of 65.[13]

Joe Vila (1886–1934) — Born in Boston, Vila had a background ranging from two years at Harvard to working as a baggage master on the railroad before going into journalism. He was the sporting editor of *The Sun* from 1915 until his death in 1934. During 1916, in addition to his sports editor duties, he wrote regular baseball columns.[14]

Melville Emerson Webb Jr. (1876–1961) — Webb joined the Boston *Daily Globe* sports staff after graduating high school, working there for more than 50 years. Working as an assistant to Murnane, he did much of the writing regarding the Red Sox in 1916. Webb was also a charter member of the Baseball Writers Association of America.[15]

Chapter Notes

Chapter I

1. Boston *Daily Globe*, October 14, 1915; *Washingtonian*, October 15, 1915.
2. Boston *Daily Globe*, October 14, 1915.
3. The *Reach Official American League Guide*, pp. 9–11.
4. Harold Seymour, *Baseball: The Golden Age* (New York: Oxford University Press, 1971), pp. 199–203; Marc Okkonen, *The Federal League of 1914–15* (Garrett Park, MD: The Society for American Baseball Research, 1989), p. 15; Timothy C. Gay, *Tris Speaker, The Rough and Tumble Life of a Baseball Legend* (Lincoln: University of Nebraska Press, 2005), pp. 144–45.
5. Seymour, *Baseball: The Golden Age*, pp. 212–13, 231–32; Okkonen, *The Federal League of 1914–15*, pp. 17, 21, 24.
6. Kevin Kerrane, *Dollar Sign on the Muscle: The World of Baseball Scouting* (New York: Beaufort Books, 1984), p. 5.
7. Mark L. Armour and Daniel R. Levitt, *Paths to Glory: How Great Baseball Teams Got That Way* (Washington, D.C.: Brassey's, 2003), pp. 26–7, 35.
8. Tom Simon, *Deadball Stars of the National League* (Dulles, VA: Brassey's, 2004), p. 308; Boston *Herald*, January 9, 1916; Boston *Daily Globe*, January 2, February 10, 1916; www.retrosheet.org.
9. Brooklyn *Daily Eagle*, January 17, 1916; *The Sporting News*, December 16, 1915. During Ned Hanlon's tenure as Brooklyn manager during the early twentieth century, there was a popular vaudeville troupe known as Hanlon's Superbas — a sportswriter apparently transferred the name to the Brooklyn team. Although Hanlon was long gone by 1916, Tom Rice in the Brooklyn *Daily Eagle* used Superbas all season, never once referring to the team as the Dodgers. Other papers referred to the team as the Robins (after Wilbert Robinson) more frequently than the Dodgers. This was typical of an era when sports writers used all kinds of variations of team names; for example, the Phillies were variously known as "Pat's Pals" and the "Moran Men." Frank Graham, *The Brooklyn Dodgers: An Informal History* (Carbondale and Edwardsville: Southern Illinois University Press, 1945), p. 11.
10. http://www.retrosheet.org; Okkonen, *The Federal League War of 1914–15*, p. 22; Charles Alexander, *John McGraw* (Lincoln: University of Nebraska Press, 1988), p. 189.
11. Armour and Levitt, *Paths to Glory*, pp. 47–8, 52, 58.
12. Jack Smiles, "*Ee-Yah*": *The Life and Times of Hughie Jennings, Baseball Hall of Famer* (Jefferson, NC: McFarland, 2006), pp. 121–22.
13. www.retrosheet.org. Throughout the text, the contemporary spelling of Coveleskie is used. In many instances today, it is spelled Coveleski.
14. Paul J. Zingg, *Harry Hooper: An American Baseball Life* (Champaign: University of Illinois Press, 2004), pp. 78–80, 121; www.retrosheet.org; David Jones, editor, *Deadball Stars of the American League* (Dulles, VA: Potomac Books, 2006), pp. 438–39.
15. Zingg, *Harry Hooper*, p. 122; www.retrosheet.org; Jones, *Deadball Stars of the American League*, p. 461.
16. Boston *Daily Globe*, January 1, 6, February 5, 1916; Zingg, *Harry Hooper*, p. 143.
17. Boston *Daily Globe*, February 27, 1916; Gay, *Tris Speaker*, pp. 3–4, 25, 35, 67; Fred Lieb, *Baseball As I Have Known It* (New York: Coward, McCann & Geoghegan, 1977), p. 57.
18. Gay, *Tris Speaker*, pp. 67, 77, 87–8, 93, 149; Jones, *Deadball Stars of the American League*, pp. 451–52.
19. Gay, *Tris Speaker*, pp. 144, 160–62.
20. *The Sporting News*, February 10, 1916; William A. Phelon, "On the Eve of the Baseball Season," *Baseball Magazine*, April 1916, pp. 69–75.
21. Gay, *Tris Speaker*, pp. 72–3.

22. Boston *Daily Globe*, February 22, March 1, 16, 1916; www.retrosheet.org; Jones, *Deadball Stars of the American League*, pp. 453–54; Society for American Baseball Research, *The SABR Baseball List and Record Book* (New York: Scribner, 2007), p, 241.

23. Boston *Daily Globe*, March 14, 23, 25, 1916.

24. Boston *Daily Globe*, March 26, 29, 30, 31, April 6, 1916; Boston *American*, April 6, 1916; Gay, *Tris Speaker*, p. 161.

25. Gay, *Tris Speaker*, pp. 161–63; Boston *Daily Globe*, April 8, 1916; Boston *Post*, April 7, 1916.

26. Gay, *Tris Speaker*, pp. 161–63; Boston *Daily Globe*, April 8, 1916; Boston *American*, April 9, 1916.

27. Gay, *Tris Speaker*, pp. 162–65; Boston *Daily Globe*, April 9, 10, 1916; George Sullivan, *The Picture History of the Boston Red Sox* (Indianapolis: Bobst-Merill Company, 1980), p. 50; Boston *Post*, April 5, 9, 1916.

28. www.retrosheet; www.baseballibrary.com; Jones, *Deadball Stars of the American League*, pp. 434–37.

29. Boston *Daily Globe*, April 10, 12, 1916; Gay, *Tris Speaker*, pp. 164–65; Peter Golenbock, *Fenway: An Unexpurgated History of the Boston Red Sox* (New York: G.P. Putnam & Son, 1992), p. 48; Boston *Herald*, April 11, 1916.

30. Boston *Daily Globe*, March 29, 1916; Chicago *Daily Tribune*, March 5, 12, 13, 1916.

31. Chicago *Daily Tribune*, March 13, 16, 1916; Jones, *Deadball Stars of the American League*, pp. 517–19.

32. www.baseballibrary.com; www.retrosheet.org; Chicago *Daily Tribune*, February 20, March 5, 28, 1916.

33. Chicago *Daily Tribune*, March 28, April 2, 1916.

34. www.retrosheet.org; www.baseballibrary.com.

35. www.retrosheet.org; *The Sporting News*, February 17, March 2, 16, 23, 30, 1916.

36. *The Sporting News*, March 23, 30, April 6, 1916; Detroit *News*, April 2, 4, 9, 1916, www.retrosheet.org.

37. Detroit *News*, April 6, 9, 10, 1916; Jones, *Deadball Stars of the American League*, pp. 573–74; www.retrosheet.org.

38. Alexander, *John McGraw*, pp. 129, 147–48.

39. Alexander, *John McGraw*, p. 147; New York *Times*, February 28, March 4, 10, 11, 25, 1916.

40. New York *Times*, March 17, April 6, 1916.

41. Boston *Daily Globe*, March 7, 8, 14, 1916.

42. Boston *Daily Globe*, March 24, 31, April 2, 3, 5, 6, 9, 1916.

43. Philadelphia *Inquirer*, March 5, 6, 7, 1916.

44. Philadelphia *Inquirer*, March 9, 10, 14, 16, 1916.

45. Philadelphia *Inquirer*, March 19, 27, 29, April 4, 5, 1916.

46. Philadelphia *Inquirer*, April 6, 7, 9, 11, 1916.

47. Brooklyn *Daily Eagle*, February 7, 8, 16, 17, 1916.

48. Brooklyn *Daily Eagle*, March 3, 4, 8, 1916; Lieb, *Baseball As I Known It*, p. 242; Robert S. Creamer, *Stengel: His Life and Times* (New York: Simon & Schuster, 1984), pp. 83–84.

49. Brooklyn *Daily Eagle*, March 11, 15, 25, 29, April 12, 1916.

50. Brooklyn *Daily Eagle*, March 31, April 1, 2, 3, 4, 12, 1916; Jones, *Deadball Stars of the American League*, pp. 615–16.

51. Philadelphia *Inquirer*, March 21, 27, April 4, 1916; Brooklyn *Daily Eagle*, April 11, 12, 1916; *The Sporting News*, April 13, 1916.

52. Boston *Daily Globe*, April 6, 1916.

53. www.retrosheet.org; www.baseballibrary.com.

54. www.retrosheet.org; www.baseballalmanac.com.

Chapter II

1. www.retrosheet.org.

2. Bob McGee, *The Greatest Ballpark Ever: Ebbets Field and the Story of the Brooklyn Dodgers* (Piscataway, NJ: Rutgers University Press, 2005), pp. 47–48, 62–63, 117; Michael Benson, *Ballparks of North America: A Comprehensive Historical Reference to Baseball Grounds, Yards, and Stadiums, 1845 to Present* (Jefferson, NC: McFarland, 1989), p. 64.

3. Benson, *Ballparks of North America*, p. 64; McGee, *Ebbets Field*, p, 48, 90–91.

4. Brooklyn *Daily Eagle*, April 13, 1916; New York *Times*, April 13, 1916; Boston *Herald*, April 13, 1916.

5. Brooklyn *Daily Eagle*, April 13, 1916, April, 1, 1889.

6. Boston *Herald*, April 13, 1916.

7. Lawrence S. Ritter, *Lost Ballparks: A Celebration of Baseball's Legendary Fields* (New York: Penguin Books, 1992), pp. 9–10; Philip J. Lowry, *Green Cathedrals: The Ultimate Celebration of Major League and Negro League Ballparks* (New York: Walker Publishing, 2006), pp. 173–74; *Phils Report*, August 11, 1990.

8. Philadelphia *Inquirer*, April 13, 1916; New York *Times*, April 13, 1916.

9. John C. Skipper, *Wicked Curve: The Life and Troubled Times of Grover Cleveland Alexander* (Jefferson, NC: McFarland, 2006), p. 15, 46.

10. Philadelphia *Inquirer*, April 13, 1916; New York *Times*, April 13, 1916.

11. Philadelphia *Inquirer*, April 14, 16, 1916.

12. Simon, *Deadball Stars of the National League*, pp. 39–40; Alexander, *John McGraw*, pp. 5–6, 108; Burt Solomon, *Where They Ain't* (New York: Doubleday, 1999), p. 71.

13. Pat Moran File, A. Bartlett Giamatti Research Center, National Baseball Hall of Fame and Museum, Cooperstown, NY.

14. Skipper, *Wicked Curve*, p. 17.

15. John J. Ward, "Manager Pat Moran," *Baseball Magazine*, November 1915, pp. 37–41; Pat Moran File, A. Bartlett Giamatti Research Center, National Baseball Hall of Fame and Museum, Cooperstown, NY.

16. Skipper, *Wicked Curve*, pp. 40, 43; Pat Moran biography, bioproj.sabr.org; Daniel Leavitt, *Sporting* Life, September 26, 1915.

17. Brooklyn *Daily Eagle*, April 16, 1916; Boston *Herald*, April 16, 1916; www.retrosheet.org.

18. Simon, *Deadball Stars of the National League*, pp. 323–24; Chicago *Daily Tribune* June 2, 1929; George Stallings File, A. Bartlett Giamatti Research Center, National Baseball Hall of Fame and Museum, Cooperstown, NY.

19. Thomas Meany, *Baseball's Greatest Teams* (New York: Bantam Books, 1950), pp. 165, 167; George Stallings File, A. Bartlett Giamatti Research Center, National Baseball Hall of Fame and Museum, Cooperstown, NY; Simon, *Deadball Stars of the National League*, p. 323.

20. Lawrence Ritter, *The Glory of Their Times: The Story of the Early Days of Baseball by the Men Who Played It* (New York: Macmillan, 1966), p. 171.

21. New York *Press*, November 11, 24, 1913; New York *Times*, August 11, 1934; Jack Kavanagh and Norman Macht, *Uncle Robbie* (Cleveland: Society for American Baseball Research, 1999), p. 82.

22. Charles Bevis, *Sunday Baseball: The Major Leagues Struggle to Play Baseball on the Lord's Day, 1876–1934* (Jefferson, NC: McFarland, 2003), pp. 11, 14–15, 214, 258.

23. Philadelphia *Inquirer*, April 19, 20, 1916; Boston *Herald*, April 19, 20, 1916.

24. Brooklyn *Daily Eagle*, April 20, 1916.

25. Ritter, *Lost Ballparks*, pp. 20–21; Lowry, *Green Cathedrals*, p. 32; Benson *Ballparks of North America*, p. 50.

26. Brooklyn *Daily Eagle*, April 21, 1916; Boston *Herald*, April 21, 1916.

27. Brooklyn *Daily Eagle*, April, 22, 1916; Boston *Herald*, April 22, 1916.

28. Ritter, *Lost Ballparks*, pp. 157, 160; Lowry, *Green Cathedrals*, p. 153; Benson, *Ballparks of North America*, p. 257; New York *Times*, April 9, 1916.

29. Philadelphia *Inquirer*, April 21, 22, 1916; New York *Herald*, April 21, 22, 1916.

30. Boston *Herald*, April 26, 1916; New York *Herald*, April 26, 1916; New York *Times*, April 26, 1916.

31. Boston *Herald*, April 28, 1916; New York *Herald*, April 28, 1916; New York *Times*, April 28, 1916.

32. Brooklyn *Daily Eagle*, April 28, April 29, 1916; Philadelphia *Inquirer*, April 29, 1916.

33. Brooklyn *Daily Eagle*, April 30, May 2, 3, 4, 1916; New York *Herald*, April 30, May 4, 1916; New York *Times*, April 30, May 2, 1916.

34. Philadelphia *Inquirer*, April 30, May 2, 3, 4, 1916; Boston *Herald*, April 30, May 2, 3, 4, 1916.

35. Boston *Herald*, May 5, 1916; New York *Herald*, May 5, 7, 1916.

36. Brooklyn *Daily Eagle*, May 6, 7, 1916; New York *Times*, May 7, 1916; Philadelphia *Inquirer*, May 6, 1916; www.retrosheet.org.

37. Brooklyn *Daily Eagle*, May 9, 1916; Philadelphia *Inquirer*, May 9, 1916.

38. John H. White, Jr., *The American Railroad Passenger Car* (Baltimore: John Hopkins Press, 1978), p. xi.

39. H. Roger Grant, editor, *We Took the Train* (DeKalb: Northern Illinois University Press, 1990), p. xi.

40. Christopher Morley, "A Ride in the Cab of the Twentieth Century," published in *We Took the Train*, Roger Grant, editor, p. 117.

41. John F. Stover, *History of the Baltimore and Ohio Railroad* (W. Lafayette, IN: Purdue University Press, 1987), pp. 224–26.

42. White, *The American Railroad Passenger Car*, pp. 203, 400.

43. Steve Goldman, *Forging Genius: The Making of Casey Stengel* (Dulles, VA: Potomac Books, 2005), p. 88; Peter Maiken, *Night Trains: The Pullman Systems in the Golden Years of American Rail Travel* (Baltimore: John Hopkins University Press, 1989), p. 9; White, *The American Passenger Car*, p. 268.

44. Benson, *Ballparks of North America*, p. 350.

45. Philadelphia *Inquirer*, May 11, 12, 13, 1916.

46. Philadelphia *Inquirer*, May 14, 15, 16, 17, 19, 20, 21, 22, 23, 24, 25, 1916.

47. Analysis of team and individual statistics taken primarily from Philadelphia *Inquirer* box scores.

48. Ritter, *Lost Ballparks*, pp. 41–42.

49. Brooklyn *Daily Eagle*, May 11, 12, 1916; Cincinnati *Enquirer*, May 12, 1916.

50. Brooklyn *Daily Eagle*, May 12, 13, 14, 15, 16, 17, 18, 19, 20, 21, 23, 24, 25, 26, 1916.

51. Boston *Herald*, May 12, 13, 1916; Chicago *Daily Tribune*, May 11, 1916.

52. Boston *Herald*, May 14, 16, 18, 19, 20, 22, 23, 24, 25, 1916.

53. Analysis of team and individual statistics

taken primarily from the Boston *Herald* box scores, May 24, 1916.

54. New York *Tribune*, May 10, 1916; New York *Times*, May 11, 12, 1916; New York *Herald*, May 13, 1916; Pittsburgh *Press*, May 12, 1916.

55. New York *Times*, May 15, 16, 18, 1916; New York *Tribune*, May 16, 1916; New York *American*, May 21, 1916; St. Louis *Globe-Democrat*, May 21, 1916.

56. New York *Times*, May 22, 24, 1916; New York *American*, May 22, 25, 1916; New York *Tribune*, May 24, 25, 1916.

57. New York *Times*, May 27, 28, 30, 1916; Boston *Herald*, May 27, 28, 30, 1916; New York *Tribune*, May 27, 30, 1916; New York *Herald*, May 28, 1916; New York, The *Sun*, May 30, 1916.

58. Brooklyn *Daily Eagle*, May 27, 1916; New York *Times*, May 27, 1916; Philadelphia *Inquirer*, May 27, 1916; The *Public Ledger*, May 27, 1916; The *North American*, May 27, 1916; Brooklyn *Citizen*, May 27, 1916.

59. Brooklyn *Daily Eagle*, May 28, 30, 1916; Philadelphia *Inquirer*, May 30, 1916.

60. Analysis of team and individual statistics taken primarily from the Brooklyn *Daily Eagle* and the Philadelphia *Inquirer* box scores, Brooklyn *Daily Eagle*, May 30, 1916.

61. New York *Times*, May 31, 1916; Philadelphia *Inquirer*, May 31, 1916.

62. Analysis of team and individual statistics from various newspaper box scores.

Chapter III

1. Boston *Daily Globe*, April 12, 13, 1916; Boston *Herald*, April 13, 1916; Chicago *Daily Tribune*, April 12, 1916.

2. Robert F. Bluthardt, "Fenway Park and the Golden Age of the Baseball Park, 1909–15," *Journal of Popular Culture*, Summer 1987, pp. 45–46, 48; Derek Gentile, *The Compete Boston Red Sox: The Total Encyclopedia of the Team* (New York: Black Dog & Leventhal Publishers, 2004) pp. 43–44; Boston *Daily Globe*, April 6, 1912.

3. Boston *Herald*, April 13, 1916; Boston *Daily Globe*, April 13, 1916; www.baseballlibrary.com.

4. Boston *Daily Globe*, April 13, 1916.

5. Chicago *Daily Tribune*, April 13, 1916.

6. Chicago *Daily Tribune*, April 13, 1916; Detroit *News*, April 13, 1916.

7. Chicago *Daily Tribune*, April 13, 1916.

8. Boston *Daily Globe*, April 17, 18, 1916; Boston *Herald*, April 18, 1916.

9. "The Manager of the Champions," *Baseball Magazine*, December 1915, p. 34; Boston *Daily Record*, January 11, 14, 18, 1943; *The Sporting News*, March 26, 1952, October 15, 1958.

10. Boston *Daily Record*, January 18, 1943,

"The Manager of the Champions," pp. 35–36; Ward Mason, "William Carrigan's Last Game," *Baseball Magazine*, December 1916, pp. 34–35.

11. Boston *Daily Record*, January 20, 21, 1943.

12. Boston *Post*, April 29, 1916; Boston *Daily Globe*, April 29, 1916.

13. Cleveland *Plain Dealer*, April 17, 18, 1916; Detroit *News*, April 18, 1916.

14. Chicago *Daily Tribune*, April 21, 1916.

15. Chicago *Daily Tribune*, April 22, 24, 25, 1916.

16. Detroit *Free Press*, April 25, 1916; Cleveland *Plain Dealer*, April 30, 1916.

17. Detroit *Free Press*, April 18, 1916; John Brown, "Hugh Jennings: The Live Wire of Modern Baseball," *Baseball Magazine*, December, 1911, pp. 35, 38.

18. Smiles, *Ee-Yah*, pp. 46–48, 111. Davy Jones File, A. Bartlett Giamatti Research Center, National Baseball Hall of Fame and Museum, Cooperstown, NY.

19. Smiles, *Ee-Yah*, pp. 121–22, 155.

20. *Chicago Tribune*, May 18, 1969; Warren N. Wilbert & William C. Hageman, *The 1917 White Sox: Their World Championship Season* (Jefferson, NC: McFarland, 2004), pp. 11, 16–17; Clarence Rowland, "How I Became the White Sox Leader," *Baseball Magazine*, August 1917.

21. F.C. Lane, "Pants Rowland, the Bush League Manager Who Made Good," *Baseball Magazine*, December, 1917, pp, 202, 246; Wilbert and Hageman, *The 1917 White Sox*, pp. 129–30; *The Sporting News*, December 29, 1954.

22. Chicago *Daily Tribune*, April 18, 19, 21, 1916.

23. Chicago *Daily Tribune*, April 21, 27, 1916.

24. Chicago *Daily Tribune*, April 28, 30, May 1, 1916.

25. Boston *Daily Globe*, May 4, 1916.

26. Cleveland *Plain Dealer*, May 2, 3, 1916; Chicago *Daily Tribune*, May 3, 1916.

27. Bludhardt, "Fenway Park and the Golden Age of the Baseball Park," *Journal of Popular Culture*, pp. 43–48; Ritter, *Lost Ballparks*, pp. 29–30; Lowry, *Green Cathedrals*, pp. 28–29.

28. Chicago *Daily Tribune*, May 6, 7, 1916; Cleveland *Plain Dealer*, May 8, 1916.

29. Cleveland *Plain Dealer*, May 8, 1916.

30. Boston *Daily Globe*, May 2, 3, 5, 1916.

31. New York *Times*, May 6, 7, 1916; Boston *Daily Globe*, May 7, 1916; *The Sporting News*, May 4, 1916; Boston *Sunday Advertiser*, January 24, 1943.

32. Boston *Daily Globe*, May 9, 1916 (Evening Edition); Cleveland *Plain Dealer*, May 10, 1916; www.alepposhriners.com.

33. Chicago *Daily Tribune*, May 10, 1916; Detroit *Free-Press*, May 5, 6, 8, 1916.

34. Detroit *Free Press*, May 10, 11, 1916; De-

troit *News*, May 10, 1916; www.baseballlibrary.com.

35. Chicago *Daily Tribune*, May 11, 17, 1916; Boston *Daily Globe*, May 14, 1916.

36. Chicago *Daily Tribune*, May 18, 1916; *The Sporting News*, May 25, 1916.

37. Chicago *Daily Tribune*, May 23, 1916.

38. Chicago *Daily Tribune*, May 24, 25, 27, 1916; Cleveland *Plain Dealer*, May 29, 1916.

39. *The Sporting News*, May 25, 1916.

40. William A. Harper, *How You Played the Game: The Life of Grantland Rice* (Columbia: University of Missouri Press, 1999), p. 476; James T. Farrell, *My Baseball Diary* (Carbondale; Southern Illinois University Press, 1998), p. xxii.

41. Harper, *Grantland Rice*, pp. 11–12, 51, 224.

42. Harper, *Grantland Rice*, pp. 16, 117, 186.

43. Lieb, *Baseball As I Have Known It*, pp. 214–215, 218; Harper, *Grantland Rice*, p. 122.

44. Lieb, *Baseball As I Have Known It*, p. 215; Detroit *News*, June 22, 1916.

45. Lieb, *Baseball As I Have Known It*, pp. 26–28, 215–216.

46. Lieb, *Baseball As I Have Known It*, p. 21; Harper, *Grantland Rice*, p. 397.

47. Lieb, *Baseball As I Have Known It*, pp. 36–37.

48. Detroit *Free Press*, May 14, 1916.

49. www.baseballlibrary.com; Detroit *News*, May 16, 1916.

50. Washington *Post*, May 16, 1916.

51. Detroit *Free Press*, May 21, 1916.

52. Boston *Daily Globe*, May 21, 1916.

53. Detroit *Free Press*, May 22, 1916; *The Sporting News*, June 1, 1916; www.baseballlibrary.com.

54. Boston *Daily Globe*, May 23, 25, 26, 1916; Detroit *Free Press*, May 8, 25, 1916; Detroit *News*, May 23, 1916; *The Sporting News*, May 18, 1916.

55. Detroit *Free Press*, May 28, 30, 31, 1916; Chicago *Daily Herald*, May 31, 1916.

56. Chicago *Daily Tribune*, May 31, June 1, 1916.

57. Boston *Daily Globe*, May 30, 31, June 1 (Morning & Evening Edition), 1916.

Chapter IV

1. Daniel E. Ginsburg, *The Fix Is In: A History of Baseball Gambling and Game Fixing Scandals* (Jefferson, NC: McFarland, 1995), pp. 2, 17.

2. Ginsburg, *The Fix Is In*, pp. 52, 69; Seymour, *Baseball: The Golden Age*, pp. 283–84.

3. Seymour, *Baseball: The Golden Age*, pp. 281, 293–94; Ginsburg, *Fix*, pp. 84–85.

4. Boston *Daily Globe*, June 2, 1916; Boston *Post*, June 2, 1916.

5. *The Sporting News*, June 15, 1916; Chicago *Daily Tribune*, June 2, 1916.

6. Detroit *Free Press*, June 3, 4, 5, 6, 1916.

7. Boston *Daily Globe*, June 1, 4, 5, 6, 1916; Cleveland *Plain Dealer*, June 5, 1916; Boston *Herald*, June 6, 1916.

8. Boston *Daily Globe*, June 7, 10, 1916.

9. Detroit *Free Press*, June 11, 12, 15, 1916.

10. Detroit *Free Press*, June 15, 1916.

11. Boston *Daily Globe*, June 26, 1916; Detroit *Free Press*, June 16, 17, 18, 19, 1916.

12. Lowry, *Green Cathedrals*, pp. 82–84; Bluthardt, "Fenway Park and the Golden Age of the American Ballpark," *Journal of American Culture*, pp. 43–46.

13. Detroit *Free Press*, June 21, 22, 23, 1916; Detroit *News*, June 22, 1916; Cleveland *Plain Dealer*, June 20, 1916; Boston *Daily Globe* (Evening Edition), June 22, 1916.

14. *The Sporting News*, June 29, 1916; www.retrosheet.org.

15. Detroit *Free Press*, June 25, 1916.

16. Detroit *Free Press*, June 26, 27, 28, 1916; St. Louis *Post-Dispatch*, June 28, 1916.

17. Chicago *Daily Tribune*, June 4, 5, 6, 1916.

18. Chicago *Daily Tribune*, June 13, 14, 1916.

19. Chicago *Daily Tribune*, June 13, 14, 1916; *The Sporting News*, June 22, 1916.

20. Chicago *Daily Tribune*, June 15, 1916; Boston *Daily Globe*, June 11, 12, 13, 14, 15, 1916.

21. Boston *Daily Globe*, June 7, 16, 17, 1916.

22. Chicago *Daily Tribune*, June 18, 19, 1916; *The Sporting News*, June 8, 1916.

23. Chicago *Daily Tribune*, June 23, 25, June 29, 1916.

24. Chicago *Daily Tribune*, June 26, 28, June 29, 1916; Cleveland *Plain Dealer*, June 27, 1916; www.baseballlibrary.com.

25. Chicago *Daily Tribune*, June 30, 1916.

26. Detroit *Free Press*, June 30, 1916.

27. Boston *Daily Globe*, June 20, 1916.

28. Boston *Daily Globe*, June 22, 1916; New York *Times*, June 23, 1916; www.baseballlibrary.com.

29. Boston *Daily Globe*, June 23, 27, 28, 29, 30, July 1, 1916.

30. Washington *Post*, July 1, 1916; Boston *Daily Globe*, July 1, 1916.

31. *The Sporting News*, July 6, 1916.

32. Chicago *Daily Tribune*, July 2, 3, 1916; Detroit *Free Press*, July 2, 3, 1916; Chicago *Daily Herald*, July 3, 1916.

33. Boston *Daily Globe*, July 3, 1916.

34. *The Sporting News*, July 13, 1916; Cleveland *Plain Dealer*, July 5, 1916; Detroit *Free Press*, July 4, 1916.

35. Detroit *Free Press*, July 4, 1916.

36. *The Sporting News*, July 6, 1916; Chicago *Daily Tribune*, July 5, 1916.

37. Chicago *Daily Tribune*, July 8, 9, 1916; Detroit *Free Press*, July 6, 7, 1916.

38. Cleveland *Plain Dealer*, July 7, 1916;

Boston *Daily Globe*, July 7, 8, 9, 1916; www.retro sheet.org.

39. Boston *Herald*, July 11, 1916; Chicago *Daily Tribune*, July 11, 1916.

40. Boston *Daily Globe*, July 12, 13, 1916; Chicago *Daily Tribune*, July 12, 14, 1916.

41. Boston *Herald*, July 13, 1916; Fred Stein, *A History of the Baseball Fan* (Jefferson, NC: McFarland, 2005), p. 38.

42, Stein, *Baseball Fan*, pp. 30, 33, 35, 38; Farrell, *Baseball Diary*, pp. XIX, XX, XXI; Chicago *Daily Tribune*, May 4, 1916.

43. Detroit *Free Press*, July 10, 11, 12, 13, 14, 1916; Detroit *News*, July 11, 1916.

44. New York *Times*, July 15, 19, 1916; Detroit *Free Press*, July 15, 16, 1916.

45. Boston *Daily Globe*, July 15, 19, 1916.

46. Chicago *Daily Tribune*, July 16, 17, 1916.

47. *The Sporting News*, July 20, 1916.

48. *The Sporting News*, July 20, 1916.

49. Detroit *Free Press*, July 20, 1916.

50. Detroit *Free Press*, July 20, 1916; Boston *Daily Globe*, July 31, 1916.

51. Boston *Daily Globe*, July 21, 1916.

52. Detroit *Free Press*, July 22, 23, 1916.

53. Boston *Daily Globe*, July 24, 1916.

54. Chicago *Daily Tribune*, July 20, 21, 23, 1916.

55. Detroit *News*, July 24, 1916; Detroit *Free Press*, July 24, 1916.

56. Detroit *News*, July 25, 1916; Chicago *Daily Herald*, July 25, 1916.

57. Philadelphia *Inquirer*, March 14, 1916.

58. Charles F. Faber and Richard B. Faber, *Spitballers: The Last Legal Hurlers of the Wet One* (Jefferson, NC: McFarland, 2006), pp. 3–4; Clark Griffith, "Why the Spit Ball Should Be Abolished," *Baseball Magazine*, July, 1917, p. 371.

59. Faber and Faber, *Spitballers: Last Legal Hurlers*, pp. 1, 9; Washington *Post*, March 28, 1911; Griffith, "Why the Spit Ball Should Be Abolished," pp. 371, 390, Stanley Coveleskie, "A Good Word for the Spit Ball," *Baseball Magazine*, March 1920, pp. 571–572.

60. Boston *Daily Globe*, July 24, 1916; *The Sporting News*, August 3, 1916; Cleveland *Plain Dealer*, July 27, 1916; Boston *Post*, July 29, 1916.

61. Detroit *News*, July 26, 1916; Detroit Free Press, July 28, 29, 1916.

62. Boston *Post*, July 30, 1916; Detroit *Free Press*, July 30, 1916.

63. Boston *Herald*, July 31, August 1, 1916; Boston *Sunday Advertiser*, January 24, 1943.

64. Chicago *Daily Tribune*, July 26, 27, 28, 30, 1916; *The Sporting News*, August 3, 1916.

Chapter V

1. Retrosheet.org; Brooklyn *Daily Eagle*, May 31, 1916; Brooklyn *Citizen*, May 31, 1916;

The *World*, May 16, 1916; New York *Times*, May 31, 1916; New York *Herald*, May 31, 1916.

2. Brooklyn *Daily Eagle*, June 1, 2, 1916; The *Standard Union*, June 2, 1916; The *World*, June 2, 1916.

3. New York *Press*, May 31, 1916; Seymour, *Baseball: The Golden Age*, p. 40.

4. Robert T. Burk, *Never Just a Game: Players, Owners and American Baseball to 1920* (Chapel Hill: University of North Carolina Press, 1994), p. 243; Seymour, *Baseball: The Golden Age*, p. 71; Edward Moss, "The Dollar Sign Behind the Diamond," *Harpers' Weekly*, August 31, 1912.

5. New York *Times*, June 3, 4, 6, 1916.

6. Brooklyn *Daily Eagle*, June 3, 1916.

7. Boston *Herald*, June 6, 1916.

8. Philadelphia *Inquirer*, June 3, 6, 1916; St. Louis *Globe-Democrat*, June 3, 4, 1916.

9. Boston *Herald*, June 7, 8, 14, 15, 1916; St. Louis *Globe-Democrat*, June 7, 1916.

10. Brooklyn *Daily Eagle*, June 7, 13, 14, 15, 1916.

11. New York *Times*, June 7, 11, 13, 14, 15, 16; Chicago *Daily Tribune*, June 11, 15, 1916.

12. Philadelphia *Inquirer*, June 7, 13, 15, 1916; Chicago *Daily Tribune*, June 7, 1916; Pittsburgh *Press*, June 15, 1916; The *North American*, June 15, 1916.

13. Philadelphia *Inquirer*, June 16, 18, 1916.

14. Brooklyn *Daily Eagle*, June 16, 18, 1916; New York *Times*, June 18, 1916.

15. Boston *Herald*, June 16, 17, 1916; Boston Daily *Globe*, June 17, 1916; Pittsburgh *Press*, June 17, 1916,

16. Philadelphia *Inquirer*, June 20, 1916; The *Globe and Commercial Advertiser*, June 20, 1916; Brooklyn *Daily Eagle*, June 20, 1916; The *Standard Union*, June 20, 1916; New York *Times*, June 20, 1916.

17. Brooklyn *Daily Eagle*, June 21, 23, 1916; Philadelphia *Inquirer*, June 21, 23, 1916.

18. New York *Herald*, June 22, 1916; New York *Times*, June 22, 1916; Boston *Herald*, June 22, 1916.

19. Boston *Herald*, June 23, 1916; New York *Herald*, June 23, 1916.

20. Philadelphia *Inquirer*, June 24, 25, 1916; Boston *Herald*, June 25, 1916.

21. Philadelphia *Inquirer*, June 27, 28, 1916; Boston *Herald*, June 27, 28, 1916.

22. Brooklyn *Daily Eagle*, June 22, 24, 25, 1916; New York *Herald*, June 25, 1916; Simon, *Deadball Stars*, pp. 283–86.

23. The *World*, June 27, 1916; Brooklyn *Daily Eagle*, June 27, 1916.

24. Brooklyn *Citizen*, June 27, 1916; The *World*, June 27, 1916; *The Sun*, June 27, 1916.

25. Brooklyn *Daily Eagle*, June 29, 30, July 1, 1916; Boston *Herald*, June 30, 1916; New York *Times*, June 30, July 1, 1916.

26. Brooklyn *Daily Eagle,* July 2, 1916; Boston *Herald,* July 2, 1916; New York *Times,* July 2, 1916.
27. Philadelphia *Inquirer,* June 29, 30, July 1, 2, 1916; New York *Herald,* June 29, 30, July 1, 2, 1916.
28. Philadelphia *Inquirer,* July 4, 1916; Boston *Herald,* July 6, 1916; Pittsburgh *Press,* July 12, 1916.
29. Brooklyn *Daily Eagle,* July 3, 5, 1916; New York *Herald,* July 4, 5, 1916; New York *Times,* July 4, 1916; New York *Tribune,* July 5, 1916.
30. Brooklyn *Daily Eagle,* July 9, 10, 11, 1916.
31. Brooklyn *Daily Eagle,* July 12, 14, 1916; various newspaper articles provided by Paul Sallee.
32. Brooklyn *Daily Eagle,* July 16, 17, 18, 19, 1916; Chicago *Daily Tribune,* July 16, 17, 1916; New York *Times,* July 17, 1916; The *Evening Sun,* July 17, 1916; The *Standard Union,* July 19, 1916.
33. Brooklyn *Daily Eagle,* July 20, 23, 1916; The *Standard Union,* July 23, 1916; The *Sun,* July 23, 1916; Pittsburgh *Press,* July 23, 1916.
34. Brooklyn *Daily Eagle,* July 21, 1916.
35. Alexander, *John McGraw,* p. 191.
36. New York *Times,* July 21, July 22, 23, 24, 1916; Chicago *Daily Tribune,* July 24, 1916.
37. Philadelphia *Inquirer,* July 8, 12, 14, 15, 1916; Chicago *Daily Tribune,* July 14, 1916.
38. Philadelphia *Inquirer,* July 16, 1916; Pittsburgh *Press,* July 16, 1916.
39. Philadelphia *Inquirer,* July 21, 22, 23, 24, 1916.
40. Boston *Herald,* July 8, 9, 10, 11, 1916; Chicago *Daily Tribune,* July 9, 11, 1916.
41. Boston *Herald,* July 12, 13, 15, 1916; Pittsburgh *Press,* July 12, 1916.
42. Boston *Herald,* July 16, 17, 18, 19, 1916.
43. Boston *Herald,* July 20, 21, 22, 23, 24, 1916; St. Louis *Globe-Democrat,* July 24, 1916.
44. Analysis of Brooklyn Dodgers hitting and pitching statistics primarily from the Brooklyn *Daily Eagle.*
45. Analysis of Philadelphia Phillies hitting and pitching statistics primarily from the Philadelphia *Inquirer,* Pittsburgh *Press,* July 16, 1916.
46. Analysis of Boston Braves hitting and pitching statistics primarily from the Boston *Herald.*
47. Analysis of New York Giants hitting and pitching statistics primarily from the New York *Times.*

Chapter VI

1. Boston *Herald,* July 26, 1916.
2. Boston *Herald,* July 27, 28, 29, 1916.
3. New York *Times,* July 27, 28, 29, 1916.

4. Brooklyn *Daily Eagle,* July 27, 28, 29, 1916.
5. Philadelphia *Inquirer,* July 27, 28, 19, 1916; Pittsburgh *Press,* July 27, 29, 1916.
6. New York *Times,* July 30, 1916; Pittsburgh *Press,* August 1, 2, 3, 1916.
7. Philadelphia *Inquirer,* July 30, August 1, 2, 3, 1916; Chicago *Daily Tribune,* July 30, August 1, 3, 1916.
8. Boston *Herald,* July 30, August 1, 2, 3, 1916.
9. New York *Times,* July 30, 1916; Brooklyn *Daily Eagle,* July 31, August 2, 1916; The *Sun,* July 30, 1916.
10. New York *Tribune,* July 30, 1916; The *World,* July 30, 1916; Brooklyn *Daily Eagle,* August 1, 1916; Cincinnati *Enquirer,* August 1, 1916.
11. Brooklyn *Daily Eagle,* August 2, 3, 1916.
12. Brooklyn *Daily Eagle,* August 4, 5, 6, 1916; Pittsburgh *Press,* August 6, 1916.
13. Brooklyn *Daily Eagle,* August 9, 10, 12, 1916; Chicago *Daily Tribune,* August 10, August 12, 1916.
14. New York *Times,* August 4, 6, 1916; Chicago *Daily Tribune,* August 6, 8, 1916.
15. New York *Times,* August 10, 1916; St. Louis *Globe-Democrat,* August 10, 1916.
16. Philadelphia *Inquirer,* August 4, 5, 6, 8, 1916; St. Louis *Globe-Democrat,* August 8, 1916.
17. Philadelphia *Inquirer,* August 10, 11, 1916.
18. Philadelphia *Inquirer,* August 12, 1916.
19. Boston *Herald,* August 4, 1916.
20. Boston *Herald,* August 5, 6, 8, 1916.
21. Boston *Herald,* August 5, 8, 12, 1916; Pittsburgh *Press,* August 12, 1916.
22. Brooklyn *Daily Eagle,* August 11, 13, 1916; Boston *Post,* August 13, 1916; New York *American,* August 13, 1916.
23. Brooklyn *Daily Eagle,* August 13, 1916,
24. Brooklyn *Daily Eagle,* August 13, 1916; Boston *Herald,* August 13, 1916.
25. New York *Times,* August 13, 1916; Philadelphia *Inquirer,* August 13, 1916.
26. Philadelphia *Press,* August 15, 1916; Philadelphia *Record,* August 15, 1916; Philadelphia *Inquirer,* August 15, 1916; New York *Times,* August 15, 1916; The *Globe and Commercial Advertiser,* August 15, 1916.
27. Brooklyn *Daily Eagle,* August 15, 1916; New York *Times,* August 15, 1916; Boston *Herald,* August 15, 1916; The *World,* August 15, 1916; Brooklyn *Citizen,* August 15, 1916.
28. Brooklyn *Daily Eagle,* August 16, 1916; Boston *Herald,* August 16, 1916.
29. Philadelphia *Inquirer,* August 16, 1916; New York *Times,* August 16, 1916.
30. Brooklyn *Daily Eagle,* August 17, 1916; The *Evening Mail,* August 16, 1916; Simon, *Deadball Stars of the National League,* pp. 125–128.

31. The *Evening Mail*, August, 16, 1916; Brooklyn *Daily Eagle*, August 18, 1916.

32. Brooklyn *Daily Eagle*, August 19, 1916; Philadelphia *Inquirer*, August 19, 1916; Boston *Herald*, August 19, 1916.

33. Brooklyn *Daily Eagle*, August 20, 1916; Boston *Herald*, August 20, 1916.

34. Brooklyn *Daily Eagle*, August 21, 1916; Chicago *Daily Tribune*, August 21, 1916; Philadelphia *Inquirer*, August 21, 1916; Boston *Herald*, August 21, 1916.

35. Philadelphia *Inquirer*, August 22, 1916; Philadelphia *Record*, August 22, 1916; Pittsburgh *Press*, August 22, 1916; Brooklyn *Daily Eagle*, August 22, 1916; www.retrosheet.org.

36. Boston *Herald*, August 22, 1916.

37. Brooklyn *Daily Eagle*, August 23, 1916; Boston *Herald*, August 23, 1916.

38. Philadelphia *Inquirer*, August 23, 1916; Pittsburgh *Press*, August 23, 1916.

39. Philadelphia *Inquirer*, August 24, 1916; Philadelphia *Record*, August 24, 1916; *Public Ledger*, August 24, 1916.

40. Brooklyn *Daily Eagle*, August 24, 1916; Chicago *Daily Tribune*, August 24, 1916.

41. Philadelphia *Inquirer*, August 25, 1916; Brooklyn *Daily Eagle*, August 25, 1916; Boston *Herald*, August 25, 1916; Pittsburgh *Press*, August 25, 1916; Chicago *Daily Tribune*, August 25, 1916.

42. Boston *Herald*, August 26, 1916; Chicago *Daily Tribune*, August 26, 1916; Brooklyn *Daily Eagle*, August 26, 1916; Philadelphia *Inquirer*, August 26, 1916.

43. Boston *Herald*, August 27, 1916; Brooklyn *Daily Eagle*, August 27, 1916; Philadelphia *Inquirer*, August 27, 1916.

44. Boston *Herald*, August 28, 1916; Brooklyn *Daily Eagle*, August 28, 1916; New York *Times*, August 28, 1916; Philadelphia *Inquirer*, August 28, 1916; St. *Louis Globe-Democrat*, August 28, 1916.

45. Boston *Herald*, August 29, 1916; Brooklyn *Daily Eagle*, August 29, 1916; Philadelphia *Inquirer*, August 29, 1916; Chicago *Daily Tribune*, August 29, 1916; The *Globe and Commercial Advertiser*, August 15, 1916; Analysis of Larry Doyle's offensive statistics as found on www.retrosheet.org.

46. New York *Times*, August 18, 21, 31, 1916.

47. Boston *Herald*, August 30, 1916; Pittsburgh *Press*, August 30, 1916.

48. Brooklyn *Daily Eagle*, August 30, 1916; St. Louis *Globe-Democrat*, August 30, 1916.

49. Brooklyn *Daily Eagle*, August 31, 1916; St. Louis *Globe-Democrat*, August 31, 1916; Philadelphia *Inquirer*, August 31, 1916; Analysis of Brooklyn offensive and pitching statistics.

50. Boston *Herald*, August 31, 1916; Pittsburgh *Press*, August 31, 1916; www.retrosheet.org.

51. Boston *Herald*, September 1, 1916; Pittsburgh *Press*, September 1, 1916.

52. Philadelphia *Inquirer*, August 28, 1916.

Chapter VII

1. Boston *Daily Globe*, August 2, 1916; Boston *Herald*, August 2, 1916; Detroit *Free Press*, August 2, 1916.

2. Detroit *Free Press*, August 3, 1916.

3. Boston *Herald*, August 3, 1916.

4. Boston *Daily Globe*, August 4, 1916; St. Louis *Post-Dispatch*, August 6, 1916; www.baseballlibrary.com.

5. Boston *Herald*, August 6, 1916; Boston *Daily Globe*, August 6, 7, 1916; Boston *Post*, August 7, 1916; St. Louis *Post-Dispatch*, August 7, 1916.

6. Chicago *Daily Tribune*, August 5, 1916.

7. Chicago *Daily Tribune*, August 5, August 6, August 7, 1916.

8. Detroit *Free Press*, August 4, 6, 1916; Detroit *News*, August 6, 1916.

9. Detroit *Free Press*, August 7, 9, 1916.

10. *The Sporting News*, August 10, 1916; Detroit *Free Press*, August 10, 11, 1916; www.baseball library.com.

11. Boston *Daily Globe*, August 8, 9, 1916; Chicago *Daily Tribune*, August 8, 9, 1916.

12. Boston *Daily Globe*, August 10, 1916; Chicago *Daily Tribune*, August 10, 1916.

13. Boston Daily Globe, August 11, 1916; Chicago *Daily Tribune*, August 11, 1916.

14. Boston *Daily Globe*, August 12, 1916.

15. Chicago *Daily Tribune*, August 12, 1916; Detroit *Free Press*, August 12, 1916; Detroit *News*, August 12, 1916.

16. Chicago *Daily Tribune*, August 13, 1916; Detroit *Free Press*, August 13, 1916; Detroit *News*, August 13, 1916.

17. Chicago *Daily Tribune*, August 14, 15, 1916; Chicago *Daily Herald*, August 14, 1916; Detroit *Free Press*, August 14, 1916; Detroit *News*, August 14, 1916.

18. Boston *Daily Globe*, August 13, 16, 1916; Washington *Post*, August 13, 1916.

19. Washington *Post*, August 16, 1916; Boston *Daily Globe*, August 16, 1916.

20. Boston *Herald*, August 17, 1916; Boston *Daily Globe*, August 17, 1916.

21. Boston *Herald*, August 17, 1916.

22. Boston *Daily Globe*, August 17, 1916; Boston *Herald*, August 17, 1916; Boston *Post*, August 17, 1916.

23. Boston *Daily Globe*, August 17, 18 (Evening Edition), 1916; Boston *Post*, August 17, 1916; Chicago *Daily Tribune*, August 17, 18, 1916.

24. Chicago *Daily Tribune*, August 19, 1916; Chicago *Daily Herald*, August 19, 1916.

25. Boston *Daily Globe*, August 19, 1916.

26. Detroit *Free Press*, August 15, 16, 1916; Cleveland *Plain Dealer*, August 15, 1916; Boston *Daily Globe*, August 19, 1916.

27. Detroit *Free Press*, August 17, 1916.

28. *The Sporting News*, August 17, 1916.

29. Cleveland *Plain Dealer*, August 19, 21, 1916; Boston *Daily Globe*, August 20, 1916; Boston *Herald*, August 20, 1916; Boston *Post*, August 20, 1916.

30. Boston *Herald*, August 20, 1916; Boston *Daily Globe*, August 22, 24, 1916; Cleveland *Plain Dealer*, August 24, 1916.

31. Chicago *Daily Tribune*, August 20, 22, 24, 1916; New York *Times*, August 23, 1916; *The Sporting News*, August 17, 24, 1916.

32. Detroit *Free Press*, August 20, 22, 23, 24, 1916; Detroit *News*, August 24, 1916.

33. Detroit *Free Press*, August 21, 24, 25, 1916; Detroit *News*, August 26, 1916; Boston *Herald*, August 25, 1916; Boston *Daily Globe*, August 25, 1916; www.baseballlibrary.com.

34. Boston *Herald*, August 25, 1916; Detroit *News*, August 25, 1916; *The Sporting News*, August 31, 1916.

35. Detroit *Free Press*, August 26, 1916; Boston *Herald*, August 26, 1916; Boston *Daily Globe*, August 26, 1916.

36. Boston *Daily Globe*, August 27, 1916; Boston *Herald*, August 27, 1916; Detroit *Free Press*, August 27, 1916; Detroit *News*, August 27, 1916.

37. Detroit *Free Press*, August 29, 1916; New York *Times*, August 30, 1916; *The Sporting News*, September 7, 1916.

38. Boston *Daily Globe*, August 30, 1916; St. Louis *Post-Dispatch*, August 30, 1916.

39. Boston *Daily Globe*, August 31, 1916; Boston *Herald*, August 31, 1916; St. Louis *Post-Dispatch*, August 31, 1916.

40. New York *Times*, August 31, 1916; Detroit *Free Press*, September 1, 1916; Boston *Daily Globe*, September 1, 1916; St. Louis *Post-Dispatch*, September 1, 1916.

41. Chicago *Daily Tribune*, August 24, 25, 26, 1916.

42. Detroit *News*, August 26, 1916; Boston *Daily Globe*, August 31, 1916 (Evening Edition).

43. St. Louis *Post-Dispatch*, September 1, 1916.

44. New York *Times*, August 31, 1916.

Chapter VIII

1. T.S. Eliot, *The Waste Land*.

2. Brooklyn *Daily Eagle*, September 1, 1916; *Sport Magazine*, August 1962.

3. *The Globe and Commercial Advertiser*, September 1, 1916; Philadelphia *Inquirer*, March 14, September 2, 1916; New York *Evening Journal*, September 2, 1916; Philadelphia *Press*, September 2, 1916.

4. Brooklyn *Daily Eagle*, September 2, 1916; The *North American*, September 2, 1916; Philadelphia *Inquirer*, September 2, 1916.

5. Brooklyn *Daily Eagle*, September 2, 1916; Philadelphia *Inquirer*, September 2, 1916; The *Public Ledger*, September 2, 1916.

6. Boston *Herald*, September 2, 1916; New York *Times*, September 2, 1916.

7. New York *American*, September 3, 1916; Boston *Herald*, September 3, 1916.

8. *The North American*, September 3, 1916; Brooklyn *Daily Eagle*, September 3, 1916; Philadelphia *Inquirer*, September 3, 1916.

9. Brooklyn *Daily Eagle*, September 5, 1916; Philadelphia *Inquirer*, September 5, 1916; The *Public Ledger*, September 5, 1916; Philadelphia *Press*, September 5, 1916; Philadelphia *Record*, September 5, 1916; The *North American*, September 5, 1916; New York *Times*, September 5, 1916.

10. New York *Tribune*, September 3, 5, 1916; Philadelphia *Inquirer*, September 5, 1916; Brooklyn *Daily Eagle*, September 5, 1916.

11. Brooklyn *Daily Eagle*, September 5, 1916; Philadelphia *Inquirer*, September 5, 1916; New York *Times*, September 5, 1916; Analysis of Brooklyn and Philadelphia offensive statistics taken primarily from the Brooklyn *Daily Eagle* and the Philadelphia *Inquirer*.

12. Boston *Herald*, September 5, 1916.

13. Philadelphia *Record*, September 4, 1916; The *Evening Mail*, September 4, 1916.

14. Chicago *Daily Tribune*, September 5, 1916.

15. Philadelphia *Inquirer*, September 6, 1916; Boston *Herald*, September 6, 1916.

16. Philadelphia *Inquirer*, September 6, 1916.

17. Philadelphia *Inquirer*, September 6, 1916; Boston *Herald*, September 6, 1916; The *Public Ledger*, September 6, 1916; Philadelphia *Record*, September 6, 1916.

18. New York *Herald*, September 6, 1916; The *Globe and Commercial Advertiser*, September 6, 1916; Brooklyn *Daily Eagle*, September 6, 1916.

19. Brooklyn *Daily Eagle*, September 7, 1916; The *World*, September 7, 1916.

20. Brooklyn *Daily Eagle*, September 7, 1916.

21. Philadelphia *Inquirer*, September 7, 1916.

22. New York *American*, September 8, 1916; New York *Times*, September 8, 1916; The *World*, September 8, 1916; New York *Herald*, September 8, 1916; Brooklyn *Daily* Eagle, September 8, 1916; Analysis of Brooklyn Dodger offensive statistics taken from the Brooklyn *Daily Eagle*.

23. Boston *Herald*, September 7, 1916; Philadelphia *Inquirer*, September 8, 1916; The *North American*, September 8, 1916.

24. The *Globe and Commercial Advertiser*, September 9, 1916; New York *Tribune*, September 9, 1916; The *Evening Sun*, September 9, 1916; The *World*, September 9, 1916.

25. New York *Evening Journal*, September 9, 1916; Boston *Daily Globe*, September 9, 1916; Brooklyn *Daily Eagle*, September 9, 1916.

26. Brooklyn *Daily Eagle*, September 9, 1916; The *Standard Union*, September 9, 1916.

27. Boston *Herald*, September 9, 1916; Brooklyn *Daily Eagle*, September 9, 1916.

28. Philadelphia *Record*, September 9, 1916; Philadelphia *Inquirer*, September 9, 1916.

29. The *Sun*, September 10, 1916; Philadelphia *Inquirer*, September 10, 1916; New York *Tribune*, September 10, 1916.

30. www.retrosheet.org; Philadelphia *Press,* September 10, 1916; Philadelphia *Inquirer*, September 10, 1916.

31. New York *American*, September 10, 1916; Philadelphia *Inquirer*, September 10, 1916.

32. Brooklyn *Daily Eagle*, September 10, 1916; Boston *Herald*, September 10, 1916; New York *Tribune*, September 10, 1916; Boston *Sunday Post*, September 10, 1916.

33. The *Evening Sun*, September 11, 1916; Philadelphia *Inquirer*, September 11, 1916; Brooklyn *Daily Times*, September 11, 1916; Brooklyn *Daily Eagle*, September 11, 1916; Brooklyn *Citizen*, September 11, 1916.

34. Philadelphia *Inquirer*, September 12, 1916.

35. The *Globe and Commercial Advertiser*, September 12, 1916; New York *Times*, September 12, 1916; Philadelphia *Inquirer*, September 12, 1916; New York *Herald*, September 11, 1916.

36. Brooklyn *Daily Eagle*, September 12, 1916; Boston *Herald*, September 12, 1916; Brooklyn *Daily Times*; www.retrosheet.org.

Chapter IX

1. Boston *Daily Globe*, September 2, 3, 1916; www.retrosheet.org.

2. Detroit *Free Press*, September 2, 3, 1916; Chicago *Daily Tribune*, September 3, 1916.

3. Boston *Daily Globe*, September 5, 1916.

4. Detroit *Free Press*, September 2, 3, 4, 5, 1916; Detroit *News*, September 5, 1916; Cleveland *Plain Dealer*, September 4, 1916.

5. St. Louis *Globe-Democrat*, September 4, 5, 1916; Chicago *Daily Herald*, September 5, 1916.

6. The *Sporting News*, September 7, 1916.

7. Boston *Daily Globe*, September 6, 1916.

8. Boston *Daily Globe*, September 7, 8, 1916.

9. Boston *Daily Globe*, September 7, 8, 1916; Boston *American*, September 7, 1916.

10. Detroit *News*, September 6, 1916; Detroit *Free Press*, September 7, 8, 1916.

11. Chicago *Daily Tribune*, September 7, 1916; Chicago *Daily Herald*, September 7, 1916, The *Sporting News*, August 31, 1916.

12. Chicago *Daily Tribune*, September 8, 1916; Cleveland *Plain Dealer*, September 8, 1916.

13. Chicago *Daily Tribune*, September 9, 10, 1916; Cleveland *Plain Dealer*, September 9, 10, 1916.

14. St. Louis *Globe-Democrat*, September 10, 1916.

15. Washington *Post*, September 9, 1916.

16. Boston *Daily Globe*, September 10, 1916; www.retrosheet.org.

17. Boston *Daily Globe*, September 11, 1916.

18. Detroit *Free Press*, September 11, 1916; Chicago *Daily Tribune*, September 11, 1916.

19. Detroit *Free Press*, September 11, 12, 13, 1916; Boston *Daily Globe*, September 11, 1916.

20. Detroit *News*, September 13, 1916; Cleveland *Plain Dealer*, September 13, 1916.

21. Chicago *Daily Tribune*, September 12, 13, 1916; St. Louis *Globe-Democrat*, September 12, 1916.

22. Boston *Daily Globe*, September 12, 1916.

23. Boston *Post*, September 13, 1916.

24. Boston *Herald*, September 13, 1916; Boston *Daily Globe*, September 13, 1916; Boston *Post*, September 13, 1916.

25. Boston *Daily Globe*, September 13, 1916.

26. Boston *Daily Globe*, September 13, 1916; Washington *Post*, September 13, 1916.

27. Chicago *Daily Tribune*, September 13, 1916.

28. Washington *Post*, September 14, 1916; www.en.wikipedia.org/wiki/Wiki.

29. Chicago *Daily Tribune*, September 15, 16, 1916; Washington *Post*, September 15, 1916.

30. Detroit *Free Press*, September 14, 1916; New York *Times*, September 14, 1916.

31. The *Sporting News*, September 14, 1916.

32. Detroit *Free Press*, September 15, 1916.

33. Boston *Daily Globe*, September 14, 15, 1916.

34. Detroit *Free Press*, September 16, 1916.

35. Boston *Daily Record*, January 23, 1943.

36. Boston *Daily Record*, January 23, 1943.

37. Boston *Daily Globe*, September 16, 1916.

38. Boston *Daily Record*, January 23, 1943.

39. Boston *Daily Globe*, September 16, 1916; Chicago *Daily Herald*, September 16, 1916.

40. The *Sporting News*, September 14, 1916; Boston *Post*, September 17, 1916; Chicago *Daily Tribune*, September 17, 1916; Chicago *Daily Herald*, September 17, 1916.

41. Chicago *Daily Herald*, September 17, 1916; Boston *Herald*, September 17, 1916.

42. Chicago *Daily Herald*, September 17, 1916; Chicago *Daily Tribune*, September 17, 20, 1916; Boston *Herald*, September 17, 1916; Boston *Daily Globe*, September 17, 1916.

43. Detroit *Free Press*, September 17, 1916; Detroit *News*, September 17, 1916; Philadelphia *Record*, September 17, 1916.

44. Detroit *Free Press*, September 17, 1916.

45. Detroit *Free Press*, September 17, 18, 1916.

46. Detroit *Free Press*, September 18, 1916.

47. Chicago *Daily Tribune*, September 18, 1916; Chicago *Daily Herald*, September 18, 1916.

48. Chicago *Daily Tribune*, September 18, 1916.

49. Chicago *Daily Tribune*, September 18, 1916; Chicago *Daily Herald*, September 18, 1916.

50. Boston *Daily Globe*, September 18, 1916; Boston *Post*, September 18, 1916; Boston *American*, September 18, 1916; Boston *Herald*, September 18, 1916.

51. Chicago *Daily Tribune*, September 19, 1916.

52. The Boston *Post*, September 19, 1916; Chicago *Daily Tribune*, September 19, 1916; Chicago *Daily Herald*, September 19, 1916; Boston *Daily Globe*, September 20, 1916.

53. Chicago *Daily Tribune*, September 19, 1916.

54. Boston *Post*, September 19, 1916; Boston *Daily Globe*, September 19, 1916.

55. Boston *Daily Globe*, September 19, 1916; Chicago *Daily Herald*, September 19, 1916; Boston *Daily Globe*, September 19, 1916.

56. Chicago *Daily Tribune*, September 19, 1916; Boston *Daily Globe*, September 19, 1916.

57. Detroit *Free Press*, September 19, 1916; Philadelphia *Record*, September 19, 1916; www.baseballlibrary.com; www.retrosheet.org.

58. Detroit *Free Press*, September 19, 1916; Chicago *Daily Tribune*, September 19, 1916.

59. Detroit *Free Press*, September 19, 1916.

60. Detroit *Free Press*, September 20, 1916; Boston *Herald*, September 20, 1916; Boston *Daily Record*, January 23, 1943.

61. Detroit *Free Press*, September 20, 1916; Boston *Post*, September 20, 1916; Boston *Herald*, September 20, 1916.

62. Boston *Daily Globe*, September 20, 1916; Boston *Post*, September 20, 1916; Detroit *Free Press*, September 20, 1916.

63. Detroit *Free Press*, September 20, 1916.

64. Chicago *Daily Tribune*, September 20, 1916; Detroit *News*, September 20, 1916.

65. Chicago *Daily Tribune*, September 21, 1916; Chicago *Daily Herald*, September 21, 1916.

66. Boston *Post*, September 21, 1916; Detroit *Free Press*, September 21, 1916, Chicago *Daily Herald*, September 21, 1916.

67. Boston *Herald*, September 21, 1916; Detroit *Free Press*, September 21, 1916; Detroit *News*, September 21, 1916.

68. Boston *Post*, September 21, 1916; Boston *American*, September 21, 1916.

69. Chicago *Daily Tribune*, September 22, 1916.

70. Boston *Daily Globe*, September 22, 1916.

71. Boston *Post*, September 22, 1916.

72. Boston *Post*, September 22, 1916; Boston *Herald*, September 22, 1916.

73. Boston *Post*, September 22, 1916; Boston *Daily Globe*, September 22, 1916.

74. Boston *Herald*, September 25, 1916.

75. Boston *Daily Globe*, September 23, 24, 1916.

76. Chicago *Daily Tribune*, September 24, 1916; Detroit *Free Press*, September 24, 26, 1916; Boston *Daily Globe*, September 24, 25, 26, 1916.

77. Chicago *Daily Tribune*, September 25, 1916.

78. Boston *Daily Globe*, September 26 (Evening Edition), 27, 1916; Detroit *Free Press*, September 27, 1916.

79. Boston *Daily Globe*, September 27 (Evening Edition), 28, 29, 1916; Chicago *Daily Tribune*, September 29, 1916.

80. Boston *Daily Globe*, September 30 (Morning & Evening), 1916; Detroit *Free Press*, September 30, 1916; www.baseballlibrary.com; www.retrosheet.org.

81. Boston *Daily Globe*, October 1, 1916; Chicago *Daily Tribune*, October 1, 1916; Cleveland *Plain Dealer*, October 1, 1916.

82. Chicago *Daily Tribune*, October 2, 1916.

83. Chicago *Daily Tribune*, October 2, 1916; Boston *Post*, October 2, 1916.

84. www.baseballlibrary.com; www.retrosheet.org; Clarence Rowland, "How I Became the White Sox Leader," *Baseball Magazine*, p. 413.

85. www.baseballlibrary.com; *The Sporting News*, October 5, 1916; retrosheet.org.

86. Boston *Daily Globe*, October 2, 1916.

Chapter X

1. Brooklyn *Daily Eagle*, September 13, 1916; New York *Times*, September 13, 1916; Pittsburgh *Press*, September 13, 1916.

2. Philadelphia *Inquirer*, September 13, 1916.

3. Boston *Herald*, September 13, 1916; Chicago *Daily Tribune*, September 13, 1916.

4. New York *Times*, September 13, 1916; Cincinnati *Enquirer*, September 13, 1916.

5. Brooklyn *Daily Eagle*, September 14, 1916; New York *Times*, September 14, 1916; The *Evening Sun*, September 14, 1916; Philadelphia *Inquirer*, September 14, 1916.

6. Boston *Herald*, September 14, 1916; Chicago *Daily Tribune*, September 14, 1916; New York *Times*, September 14, 1916.

7. New York *American*, September 15, 1916; Philadelphia *Inquirer*, September 15, 1916; Philadelphia *Press*, September 15, 1916; The *North American*, September 15, 1916.

8. Boston *Herald*, September 15, 1916; Chicago *Daily Tribune*, September 15, 1916; Brooklyn *Daily Eagle*, September 15, 16, 1916; The *World*, September 15, 1916; New York *Tribune*, September 16, 1916.

9. Brooklyn *Daily Eagle*, September 17, 1916;

Cincinnati *Enquirer*, September 17, 1916; New York *Times*, September 17, 1916; Pittsburgh *Press*, September 17, 1916.

10. The *Sun*, September 18, 1916; *North American*, September 17, 1916.

11. Brooklyn *Daily Eagle*, September 19, 1916; Philadelphia *Inquirer*, September 19, 1916; Boston *Herald*, September 19, 1916; New York *Times*, September 19, 1916.

12. New York *Times*, September 20, 1916; Brooklyn *Daily Eagle*, September 20, 1916; Boston *Herald*, September 20, 1916; Philadelphia *Inquirer*, September 20, 1916.

13. Boston *Herald*, September 21, 1916; Brooklyn *Daily Eagle*, September 21, 1916; New York *Times*, September 21, 1916; New York *Tribune*, September 21, 1916.

14. Philadelphia *Inquirer*, September 21, 1916; Philadelphia *Press*, September 21, 1916; The *Public Ledger*, September 21, 1916; Philadelphia *Record*, September 21, 1916; Pittsburgh *Press*, September 21, 1916.

15. Brooklyn *Daily Eagle*, September 22, 1916; Boston *Herald*, September 22, 1916.

16. Philadelphia *Inquirer*, September 22, 1916; New York *American*, September 22, 1916; New York *Times*, September 22, 1916.

17. Brooklyn *Daily Eagle*, September 23, 1916; Philadelphia *Inquirer*, September 23, 1916; Philadelphia *Press*, September 23, 1916; Boston *Herald*, September 23, 1916; New York *Times*, September 23, 1916; Chicago *Daily Tribune*, September 23, 1916; New York *Tribune*, September 23, 1916.

18. Philadelphia *Inquirer*, September 24, 1916; Cincinnati *Enquirer*, September 24, 1916; The *Public Ledger*, September 24, 1916; Philadelphia *Press*, September 24, 1916; Philadelphia *Record*, September 24, 1916; The *North American*, September 24, 1916.

19. The *Public Ledger*, September 24, 1916; Cincinnati *Enquirer*, September 24, 1916; Brooklyn *Daily Eagle*, September 24, 1916; New York *Times*, September 24, 1916; Chicago *Daily Tribune*, September 24, 1916.

20. New York *Times*, September 24, 1916; New York *Herald*, September 24, 1916; Boston *Herald*, September 24, 1916; Pittsburgh *Press*, September 24, 1916.

21. The *Evening Sun*, September 25, 1916; *Globe and Commercial Advertiser*, September 25, 1916; New York *American*, September 24, 1916; Brooklyn *Daily Eagle*, September 25, 1916; www.retrosheet.org.

22. Brooklyn *Daily Eagle*, September 26, 1916; New York *Times*, September 26, 1916; Chicago *Daily Tribune*, September 26, 1916.

23. Philadelphia *Inquirer*, September 26, 1916; Cincinnati *Enquirer*, September 26, 1916; Boston *Herald*, September 26, 1916.

24. New York *Times*, September 26, 1916; New York *Herald*, September 26, 1916; New York *Tribune*, September 26, 1916.

25. Boston *Herald*, September 27, 1916; Pittsburgh *Press*, September 27, 1916; New York *Times*, September 27, 1916; Philadelphia *Inquirer*, September 27, 1916; Brooklyn *Daily Eagle*, September 27, 1916.

26. Boston *Herald*, September 28, 1916; www.retrosheet.org.

27. New York *Times*, September 28, 1916; St. Louis *Globe-Democrat*, September 28, 1916.

28. The *North American*, September 28, 1916; Philadelphia *Press*, September 28, 1916; The *Evening Sun*, September 27, 1916.

29. The *Evening Sun*, September 27, 1916; Philadelphia *Inquirer*, September 29, 1916; Philadelphia *Record*, September 29, 1916; Brooklyn *Daily Eagle*, September 29, 1916; The *Public Ledger*, September 29, 1916.

30. Boston *Daily Globe*, September 29, 1916; New York *Herald*, September 29, 1916; New York *Evening Journal*, September 29, 1916; New York *Tribune*, September 29, 1916; New York *Times*, September 29, 1916; The *World*, September 29, 1916.

31. New York *Evening Journal*, September 29, 1916; Brooklyn *Daily Eagle*, September 30, 1916; Philadelphia *Inquirer*, September 30, 1916.

32. The *Evening Mail*, September 30, 1916; New York *Times*, September 30, 1916.

33. Philadelphia *Record*, October 1, 1916; New York *Tribune*, October 1, 1916; New York *Times*, October 1, 1916; The *World*, October 1, 1916; The *Sun*, October 1, 1916.

34. Philadelphia *Record*, October 1, 1916; New York *Times*, October 1, 1916; Philadelphia *Inquirer*, October 1, 1916; The *Sun*, October 1, 1916; New York *Herald*, October 1, 1916; The *North American*, October 1, 1916.

35. The *North American*, October 1, 1916; New York *Tribune*, October 1, 1916; Brooklyn *Daily Eagle*, October 1, 1916.

36. Brooklyn *Daily Eagle*, October 1, 1916; The *North American*, October 1, 1916; New York *Times*, October 1, 1916; The *World*, October 1, 1916; New York *American*, October 1, 1916.

37. Philadelphia *Inquirer*, October 2, 1916; The *Evening Sun*, October 2, 1916; *The North American*, October 1, 1916; New York *Evening Journal*, October 2, 1916; New York *Tribune*, October 2, 1916.

38. Brooklyn *Daily Eagle*, October 2, 1916; New York *Tribune*, October 2, 1916; Philadelphia *Record*, October 2, 1916.

39. Paterson *Morning Call*, May 15, August 13, October 2, 1916; *Washington Post*, August, 11, 1922.

40. Brooklyn *Daily Times*, October 3, 1916; The *World*, October 3, 1916; New York *Times*,

October 3, 1916; New York *Herald*, October 3, 1916.

41. The *World*, October 3, 1916; The *Evening Sun*, October 3, 1916; The *Evening Mail*, October 3, 1916; New York *Herald*, October 3, 1916; *Morning Telegraph*, October 3, 1916; New York *Tribune*, October 3, 1916.

42. The *Evening Mail*, October 3, 1916; Boston *Herald*, October 3, 1916; Philadelphia *Record*, October 3, 1916; The *Public Ledger*, October 3, 1916; Philadelphia *Press*, October 3, 1916; New York *Tribune*, October 3, 1916.

43. Philadelphia *Record*, October 4, 1916; *North American*, October 4, 1916; Philadelphia *Inquirer*, October 4, 1916.

44. Philadelphia *Inquirer*, October 4, 1916; Brooklyn *Daily Eagle*, October 4, 1916; New York *Times*, October 4, 1916; The *World*, October 4, 1916.

45. New York *Times*, October 4, 1916; The *Standard Union*, October 4, 1916; Brooklyn *Daily Times*, October 4, 1916.

46. Brooklyn *Daily Eagle*, October 4, 1916; The *Standard Union*, October 4, 1916; Brooklyn *Daily Times*, October 4, 1916.

47. The *North American*, October 4, 1916; New York *Times*, October 4, 1916; Philadelphia *Inquirer*, October 4, 1916.

48. New York *Times*, October 4, 1916; The *Evening Mail*, October 3, October 4, 1916; The *World*, October 5, 1916; New York *Evening Journal*, October 5, 1916; The *Evening Sun*, October 4, 1916. Nine box scores have errors for Fletcher, eight have an error for George Smith, who mopped up after Perritt. One box score (*Morning Telegraph*) has an error for Herzog while the New York *Herald* lists one for Benton.

49. New York *Times*, October 4, 1916; *Evening Mail*, October 3, 1916; New York *Tribune*, October 4, 1916; The *Globe and Commercial Advertiser*, October 4, 1916; *The Sporting News*, October 12, 1916; Brooklyn *Daily Eagle*, October 4, 1916; The *World*, October 4, 1916.

50. New York *Herald*, October 4, 1916; Brooklyn *Daily Times*, October 4, 1916; New York *Evening Journal*, October 4, 1916; New York *Tribune*, October 4, 1916.

51. New York *Tribune*, October 4, 1916; The *Globe and Commercial Advertiser*, October 5, 1916; Alexander, *John McGraw*, p. 194; The *World*, October 5, 1916.

52. Alexander, *John McGraw*, p. 171; *Morning Telegraph*, October 4, 1916; Philadelphia *Record*, October 9, 1916.

53. www.retrosheet.org.

54. www.retrosheet.org.

55. www.retrosheet.org.

56. John J. McGraw, "My Pet Ambition: How the Season of 1916 Brought the Realization of a Twelve Years' Hope," *Baseball Magazine*, January 1917, pp. 28–30.

Chapter XI

1. New York *Times*, October 7, 1916; *Sporting Life*, October 21, 1916.

2. Boston *Herald*, October 4, 1916; Brooklyn *Citizen*, October 6, 1916; New York *Times*, October 7, 1916; Chicago *Daily Tribune*, October 7, 1916; Burk, *Never Just a Game*, p. 243.

3. New York *Times*, October 7, 1916; Boston *Herald*, October 7, 1916.

4. New York *Evening Journal*, October 7, 1916; Boston *Herald*, October 4, 6, 1916; Boston *American*, October 6, 1916; Cleveland *Plain Dealer*, October 6, 1916.

5. Boston *Daily Globe*, October 7, 1916; Boston *Herald*, October 7, 1916; New York *Tribune*, October 7, 1916.

6. www.retrosheet.org; The *Sun*, October 6, 1916.

7. The *World*, October 6, 1916; Chicago *Daily Tribune*, October 7, 1916; Washington *Post*, October 7, 1916; New York *Times*, October 7, 1916; New York *Tribune*, October 7, 1916; www.retrosheet.org.

8. Washington *Post*, October 7, 1916.

9. Washington *Post*, October 7, 1916; www.retrosheet.org.

10. Brooklyn *Daily Eagle*, October 6, 1916; Washington *Post*, October 7, 1916; www.retrosheet.org.

11. The *Standard Union*, October 6, 1916; Boston *American*, October 7, 1916.

12. Brooklyn *Daily Eagle*, October 6, 1916; Brooklyn *Citizen*, October 6, 1916; New York *Times*, October 7, 1916; *Morning Telegraph*, October 7, 1916.

13. Washington *Post*, October 4, 1916; Boston *American* October 5, 1916; New York *Herald*, October 7, 1916; Atlanta *Constitution*, October 7, 1916.

14. The *Standard Union*, October 6, 7, 1916; The *Evening Sun*, October 7, 1916.

15. The *Sun*, October 7, 1916; The *Standard Union*, October 7, 1916; Brooklyn *Daily Eagle*, October 7, 1916.

16. Cleveland *Plain Dealer*, October 7, 1916; Boston *American*, October 7, 1916.

17. The *Globe & Commercial Advertiser*, October 7, 1916; The *Standard Union*, October 7, 1916.

18. Los Angeles *Times*, October 7, 1916; Boston *American*, October 7, 1916; New York *Evening Journal*, October 7, 1916; Chicago *Daily Tribune*, October 7, 1916; Boston *Daily Globe*, October 7, 1916.

19. Detroit *News*, October 5, 1916; The *Stan-*

dard Union, October 7, 1916; Los Angeles *Times,* October 7, 1916.

20. Brooklyn *Daily Eagle,* October 8, 1916.

21. Boston *American,* October 8, 1916; Boston *Herald,* October 8, 1916.

22. Philadelphia *Press,* October 8, 1916; St. Louis *Globe-Democrat,* October 8, 1916, Brooklyn *Daily Eagle,* October 8, 1916; Boston *American,* October 8, 1916.

23. The *Evening Sun,* October 7, 1916; St. Louis *Globe-Democrat,* October 8, 1916; Brooklyn *Daily Eagle,* October 8, 1916; Cleveland *Plain Dealer,* October 9, 1916.

24. Brooklyn *Daily Eagle,* October 8, 1916; Boston *Herald,* October 8, 1916; Boston *American,* October 8, 1916; Cleveland *Plain Dealer,* October 8, 1916.

25. Cleveland *Plain Dealer,* October 8, 1916; Boston *American,* October 8, 1916; Brooklyn *Daily Eagle,* October 8, 1916; Washington *Post,* October 8, 1916.

26. The *Standard Union,* October 8, 1916; Boston *Herald,* October 8, 1916; Boston *Post,* October 8, 1916.

27. Brooklyn *Daily Eagle,* October 8, 1916; The *Globe and Commercial Advertiser,* October 9, 1916; Brooklyn *Citizen,* October 9, 1916; New York *Tribune,* October 9, 1916.

28. New York *Tribune,* October 9, 1916.

29. New York *Times,* October 7, 1916; The *Sun,* October 10 1916.

30. Washington *Post,* October 9, 1916; St. Louis *Globe-Democrat,* October 10, 1916; The *Standard Union,* Oct. 10, 1916; Chicago *Daily Tribune,* October 10, 1916; Detroit *News,* October 10, 1916; Boston *Herald,* October 10, 1916.

31. The *World,* October 10, 1916; Boston *Herald,* October 10, 1916; Brooklyn *Daily Eagle,* October 10, 1916; The *Globe and Commercial Advertiser,* October 10, 1916.

32. New York *Times,* October 7, 1916; Chicago *Daily Tribune,* October 10, 1916; Boston *Herald,* October 10, 1916; Pittsburgh *Gazette Times,* October 10, 1916.

33. Cleveland *Plain Dealer,* October 10, 1916; Brooklyn *Daily Eagle,* October 10, 1916; Detroit *News,* October 10, 1916; Boston *Herald,* October 10, 1916; Atlanta *Constitution,* October 10, 1916; Brooklyn *Daily Times,* October 10, 1916.

34. Philadelphia *Inquirer,* October 10, 1916; The *Globe and Commercial Advertiser,* October 10, 1916; Atlanta *Constitution,* October 10, 1916; Washington *Post,* October 10, 1916; www.mlb.com.

35. The *Public Ledger,* October 10, 1916; The *Sun,* October 10, 1916; New *York Tribune,* October 10, 1916; Detroit *News* October 10, 1916; Boston *Herald,* October 10, 1916.

36. Detroit *News,* October 6, 1916; The *Evening Sun,* October 10, 1916; Boston *Herald,*

October 11, 1916; New York *Times,* October 11, 1916.

37. Detroit *News,* October 4, 1916; The *Standard Union,* October 10, 1916; The *Evening Sun,* October 10, October 11, 1916; New York *Times,* October 11, 1916; The *Public Ledger,* October 11, 1916; *The Sun,* October 11, 1916.

38. Brooklyn *Daily Eagle,* October 7, 1916; The *Evening Sun,* October 10, 1916; Boston *Herald,* October 11, 1916; New York *Times,* October 11, 1916; Pittsburgh *Gazette Times,* October 11, 1916.

39. Boston *Herald,* October 11, 1916.

40. Boston *Herald,* October 11, 1916; Pittsburgh *Gazette Times,* October 11, 1916; The *Sun,* October 11, 1916.

41. Boston *Herald,* October 11, 1916; Cleveland *Plain Dealer,* October 11, 1916; Philadelphia *Inquirer,* October 11, 1916.

42. The *Evening Sun,* October 11, 1916; New York *Press,* October 11, 1916.

43. Cleveland *Plain Dealer,* October 10, 1916; Boston *Herald,* October 11, 1916; Brooklyn *Citizen,* October 11, 1916; New York *Tribune,* October 11, 1916; Los Angeles *Times,* October 11, 1916.

44. Philadelphia *Inquirer,* October 11, 1916; Pittsburgh *Gazette Times,* October 11, 1916; Washington *Post,* October 11, 1916.

45. New York *Evening Journal,* October 11, 1916; Boston *Post,* October 12, 1916.

46. Pittsburgh *Gazette Times,* October 12, 1916; *The Sun,* October 12, 1916; Pittsburgh *Press,* October 12, 1916.

47. Boston *Post,* October 12, 1916; New York *Tribune,* October 12, 1916; New York *Times,* October 12, 1916.

48. Boston *Post,* October 12, 1916; New York *Tribune,* October 12, 1916; Chicago *Daily Tribune,* October 12, 1916; Washington Post, October 12, 1916; St. Louis *Globe-Democrat* October 12, 1916; Pittsburgh *Press,* October 12, 1916.

49. New York *Tribune,* October 12, 1916; St. Louis *Globe-Democrat,* October 12, 1916; Boston *Post,* October 12, 1916; Boston *Daily Globe,* October 12, 1916; The *Sun,* October 12, 1916; The *Public Ledger,* October 12, 1916; www.retrosheet.org.

50. Boston *Post,* October 12, 1916; Boston *Daily Globe,* October 12, 1916; The *Standard Union,* October 12, 1916.

51. The *Public Ledger,* October 13, 1916.

52. New York *Evening Journal* October 12, October 13, 1916; Pittsburgh *Gazette Times,* October 13, 1916; The *Evening Sun,* October 13, 1916; The *Public Ledger,* October 13, 1916.

53. Boston *Herald,* October 13, 1916; The *World,* October 13, 1916.

54. Boston *Herald,* October 13, 1916; The *World,* October 13, 1916.

55. Boston *Herald*, October 13, 1916; Philadelphia *Press*, October 13, 1916; Boston *Post*, October 13, 1916; New York *Times*, October 13, 1916; Cleveland *Plain Dealer*, October 13, 1916; The *Public Ledger*, October 13, 1916; New York *Tribune*, October 13, 1916.

56. Boston *Post*, October 13, 1916; New York *Tribune*, October 13, 1916.

57. Philadelphia *Inquirer*, October 13, 1916.

58. Boston *American*, October 13, 1916.

59. Boston *American*, October 13, 1916; Chicago *Daily Tribune*, October 13, 1916; Detroit *News*, October 13, 1916.

60. Philadelphia *Record*, October 13, 1916; St. Louis *Globe-Democrat*, October 13, 1916.

Epilogue

1. Simon, *Deadball Stars of the National League*, pp. 70, 86, 128; *The Sporting News,* January 1, 1972; www.retrosheet.org.

2. *The Sporting News*, November 8, 1916; www.retrosheet.org; Jones, *Deadball Stars of the American League*, p. 616.

3. Simon, *Deadball Stars of the National League*, pp, 208, 295; www.retrosheet.org.

4. Jones, *Deadball Stars of the American League*, pp. 517–22.

5. Jones, *Deadball Stars of the American League*, pp. 438–40.

6. Jones, *Deadball Stars of the American League*, pp. 451–56.

7. Jones, *Deadball Stars of the American League*, pp. 570–74; William Shakespeare, *Henry V*, 4.3.55.

Appendix B

1. www.baseball-fever.com.

2. New York *Times*, June 27, 1925; New York *Herald Tribune*, June 27, 1925.

3. www.baseball-fever.com.

4. www.baseball-fever.com.

5. *The Sporting News*, June 21, 1980; www.baseball-fever.com

6. www.baseball-fever.com.

7. www.baseball-fever.com; Homer Croy, "The Boston Dope Artists," *Baseball Magazine*, April 1909.

8. www.baseballreference.com.

9. New York *Times*, February 15, 1942; *The Sporting News*, July 7, 1916; New York *Herald Tribune*, February 15, 1942.

10. www.baseball-fever.com.

11. www.baseball-fever.com.

12. www.baseball-fever.com, Peter Vroom, "Chicago's Baseball Writers," *Baseball Magazine*, September 1908.

13. http://www.baseball-fever.com, Homer Croy, "The Boston Dope Artists," *Baseball Magazine*, September 1908.

14. New York *Times*, April 28, 1934, www.baseball-fever.com.

15. www.baseball-fever.com.

Bibliography

Books

Alexander, Charles. *John McGraw*. Lincoln: University of Nebraska Press, 1988.

Armour, Mark L., and Daniel R. Levitt. *Paths to Glory: How Great Baseball Teams Got That Way*. Washington, D.C.: Brassey's Inc., 2003.

Benson, Michael. *Ballparks of North America: A Comprehensive Historical Reference to Baseball Grounds, Yards and Stadiums, 1845 to Present*. Jefferson, North Carolina: McFarland, 1989.

Bevis, Charles. *Sunday Baseball: The Major Leagues Struggle to Play Baseball on the Lord's Day, 1876–1934*. Jefferson, North Carolina: McFarland, 2003.

Burk, Robert T. *Never Just a Game: Players, Owners and American Baseball to 1920*. Chapel Hill: University of North Carolina Press, 1994.

Creamer, Robert S. *Stengel: His Life and Times*. New York: Simon and Schuster, 1984.

Faber, Charles F., and Richard B. Faber. *Spitballers: The Last Legal Hurlers of the Wet One*. Jefferson, North Carolina: McFarland, 2006.

Farrell, James T. *My Baseball Diary*. Carbondale: Southern Illinois University Press, 1998.

Gay, Timothy C. *Tris Speaker: The Rough-and-Tumble Life of a Baseball Legend*. Lincoln: University of Nebraska Press, 2005.

Gentile, Derek. *The Complete Boston Red Sox: The Total Encyclopedia of the Team*. New York: Black Dog & Leventhal, 2004.

Ginsburg, Daniel. *The Fix Is In: A History of Baseball Gambling and Game Fixing Scandals*. Jefferson, North Carolina: McFarland, 1995.

Goldman, Steve. *Forging Genius: The Making of Casey Stengel*. Dulles, Virginia: Potomac Books, 2005.

Golenbock, Peter. *Fenway: An Unexpurgated History of the Boston Red Sox*. New York: G. P. Putnam's Sons, 1992.

Graham, Frank. *The Brooklyn Dodgers: An Informal History*. Carbondale: Southern Illinois University Press, 1945.

Grant, H. Roger, ed. *We Took the Train*. DeKalb: Northern Illinois University Press, 1990.

Harper, William A. *How You Played the Game: The Life of Grantland Rice*. Columbia: University of Missouri Press, 1999.

Jones, David, ed. *Deadball Stars of the American League*. Dulles, Virginia: Potomac Books, 2006.

Kavanagh, Jack, and Norman Macht. *Uncle Robbie*. Cleveland: Society for American Baseball Research, 1999.

Kerrane, Kevin. *Dollar Sign on the Muscle: The World of Baseball Scouting.* New York: Beaufort Books, 1984.

Lieb, Fred. *Baseball As I Have Known It.* New York: Coward, McCann & Geoghegan, 1977.

Lowry, Philip J. *Green Cathedrals: The Ultimate Celebration of Major League and Negro League Ballparks.* New York: Walker, 2006.

Maiken, Peter. *Night Trains: The Pullman Systems in the Golden Years of American Rail Travel.* Baltimore: Johns Hopkins University Press, 1989.

McGee, Bob. *The Greatest Ballpark Ever: Ebbets Field and the Story of the Brooklyn Dodgers.* New Brunswick, New Jersey: Rutgers University Press, 2005.

Meany, Thomas. *Baseball's Greatest Teams.* New York: Bantam Books, 1950.

Okkonen, Marc. *The Federal League of 1914–15.* Garrett Park, Maryland: Society for American Baseball Research, 1989.

Ries, Stephen A. *Touching Base: Baseball in the Progressive Era.* Westport, Connecticut: Greenwood Press, 1980.

Ritter, Lawrence. *The Glory of Their Times: The Story of the Early Days of Baseball by the Men Who Played It.* New York: Macmillan, 1966.

_____. *Lost Ballparks: A Celebration of Baseball's Legendary Fields.* New York: Penguin Books, 1992.

Seymour, Harold. *Baseball: The Golden Age.* New York: Oxford University Press, 1971.

Simon, Tom, ed. *Deadball Stars of the National League.* Dulles, Virginia: Brassey's, 2004.

Skipper, John C. *Wicked Curve: The Life and Troubled Times of Grover Cleveland Alexander.* Jefferson, North Carolina: McFarland, 2006.

Smiles, Jack. *"Ee-Yah": The Life and Times of Hughie Jennings, Baseball Hall of Famer.* Jefferson, North Carolina: McFarland, 2006.

Solomon, Burt. *Where They Ain't.* New York: Doubleday, 1999.

Spatz, Lyle, ed. *The SABR Baseball List & Record Book.* New York: Scribner, 2007.

Stein, Fred, *A History of the Baseball Fan.* Jefferson, North Carolina: McFarland, 2005.

Stover, John F. *History of the Baltimore and Ohio Railroad.* Western Lafayette, Indiana: Purdue University Press, 1987.

Sullivan, George. *The Picture History of the Boston Red Sox.* Indianapolis: Bobbs-Merrill, 1980.

White, John H., Jr. *The American Railroad Passenger Car.* Baltimore: Johns Hopkins University Press, 1978.

Wilbert, Warren N., and Wilbert C. Hageman. *The 1917 White Sox: Their World Championship Season.* Jefferson, North Carolina: McFarland, 2004.

Zingg, Paul. *Harry Hooper: An American Baseball Life.* Champaign: University of Illinois Press, 2004.

Newspapers

Atlanta *Constitution*

Boston *American*

Boston *Daily Globe*

Boston *Daily Record*

Boston *Herald*

Boston *Post*

Boston *Sunday Advertiser*

Boston *Sunday Post*

Brooklyn *Citizen*

Brooklyn *Daily Eagle*

Brooklyn *Daily Times*

Chicago *Daily Herald*

Chicago *Daily Tribune*

Cincinnati *Enquirer*

Cleveland *Plain Dealer*

Detroit *Free Press*

Detroit *News*

Evening Mail

Evening Sun

Globe and Commercial Advertiser

Los Angeles *Times*

Morning Telegraph

New York *American*

New York *Evening Journal*

New York *Herald*
New York *Times*
New York *Press*
New York *Tribune*
North American
Paterson *Morning Call*
Philadelphia *Inquirer*
Philadelphia *Press*
Philadelphia *Record*
Pittsburgh *Press*

Public Ledger
St. Louis *Globe-Democrat*
St. Louis *Post-Dispatch*
Sporting Life
The Sporting News
Standard Union
The Sun
Washington *Post*
Washingtonian
The World

Periodicals

Bluthardt, Robert, F. "Fenway Park and the Golden Age of the Baseball Park, 1909–15." *Journal of Popular Culture*, Summer 1997.

Brown, John. "Hugh Jennings: The Live Wire of Modern Baseball." *Baseball Magazine*, December 1911.

Coveleskie, Stanley. "A Good Word for the Spitball." *Baseball Magazine*, March 1920.

Croy, Homer. "The Boston Dope Artists." *Baseball Magazine*, April 1909.

Griffin, Clark. "Why the Spitball Should be Abolished." *Baseball Magazine*, March 1920.

Lane, F.C. "Pants Rowland, the Bush League Manager Who Made Good." *Baseball Magazine*, December 1917.

Mason, William. "William Carrigan's Last Game." *Baseball Magazine*, December 1916.

McGraw, John J. "My Pet Ambition: How the Season of 1916 Brought the Realization of a Twelve Years' Hope." *Baseball Magazine*, January 1917.

Moss, Edward, "The Dollar Sign Behind the Diamond." *Harper's Weekly*, August 31, 1912.

Phelon, William, A. "On the Eve of the Baseball Season." *Baseball Magazine*, April 1916.

Rowland, Clarence. "How I Became the White Sox Leader." *Baseball Magazine*, August 1917.

Vroom, Peter. "Chicago's Baseball Writers." *Baseball Magazine*, September 1908.

Ward, John J. "Manager Pat Moran." *Baseball Magazine*, November 1915.

"The Manager of the Champions." *Baseball Magazine*, December 1915.

Other Sources

Reach American League Guide
Phils Report
A. Bartlett Giamatti Research Center, National Baseball Hall of Fame and Museum, Cooperstown, New York
Davy Jones File, A. Bartlett Giamatti Research Center.
Pat Moran File, A. Bartlett Giamatti Research Center.
George Stallings File, A. Bartlett Giamatti Research Center.

Websites

http://www.alepposhriners.com.
http://baseballalmanac.com.
http://www.baseballlibrary.com.
http://bioproj.sabr.org.

http://www.mlb.com.
http://www.retrosheet.org.
http://en.wikipedia.org.

Index

Numbers in **_bold italics_** indicate pages with photographs